AF564937

INDIA–KAZAKHSTAN
Partnership in a Changing Geopolitical Order

INDIA–KAZAKHSTAN
Partnership in a Changing Geopolitical Order

Editors

Ramakant Dwivedi

Lalit Aggarwal

Kuralay Baizakova

PENTAGON PRESS LLP

First published in 2025 by
PENTAGON PRESS LLP
206, Peacock Lane, Shahpur Jat
New Delhi-110049, India
Contact: 011-26490600

Typeset in Times Roman, 11 Point
Printed at
PRINTS 24X7, Quiinkit Infotech Pvt. Ltd., Gurugram

ISBN 978-81-997728-4-7

www.pentagonpress.in

Contents

V. CIVILISATIONAL LINKAGES, SOCIETAL INTERFACES AND FUTURE OUTLOOK

Foreword

The MERI Group of Institutions, with its nearly four decades of commitment to academic excellence, research and policy-oriented dialogue, has consistently endeavoured to promote informed discussions on issues of global significance. The MERI Centre for International Studies (CIS), functioning under the MERI Group, has been instrumental in advancing scholarly engagement between India and the wider international community. Through sustained academic collaborations, conferences and dialogues, CIS has emerged as an important platform for fostering intellectual exchange among scholars, policymakers and practitioners.

In an era marked by profound geopolitical transformations, shifting power equations and the emergence of new regional and global alignments, scholarly engagement with international partnerships has become both timely and necessary. The present volume, *India–Kazakhstan Partnership in a Changing Geopolitical Order*, is a thoughtful and comprehensive academic endeavour that seeks to examine one such vital partnership through multidisciplinary and policy-relevant perspectives.

The book is a outcome of such sustained academic engagement. It brings together distinguished scholars and experts from India and Kazakhstan, offering nuanced insights into the evolving contours of bilateral relations against the backdrop of a rapidly changing geopolitical order. The India–Kazakhstan partnership holds a special place in India's engagement with Central Asia. Kazakhstan, as the largest economy in Central Asia and a key regional player, plays a significant role in shaping the region's interactions with major global powers and multilateral institutions.

The book examines issues related to geopolitics, diplomacy, economic cooperation, energy security, multilateralism, cultural and educational exchanges, security challenges and future trajectories of cooperation. A holistic approach allows readers to appreciate not only the depth of India–Kazakhstan relations but also their broader implications for regional stability, connectivity and global governance. The volume succeeds in situating bilateral cooperation within the larger framework of emerging multipolarity and strategic autonomy.

Of particular significance is the book's emphasis on people-centric engagement, institutional cooperation and long-term strategic thinking. In a world increasingly affected by geopolitical fragmentation and uncertainty, partnerships such as that between India and Kazakhstan offer valuable lessons in dialogue, mutual respect and pragmatic cooperation. The contributors to this volume have effectively combined academic rigour with policy relevance, making the book useful not only for scholars and students of international relations but also for diplomats, policymakers and practitioners.

The editors have undertaken a meticulous and commendable effort in conceptualising and curating this volume. Their academic leadership and commitment to fostering India–Central Asia engagement are evident throughout the book. The collaboration reflected in this publication also underscores the importance of institutional linkages and academic diplomacy in strengthening international understanding.

The book will serve as a valuable reference for those interested in Central Asian studies, India's foreign policy and contemporary geopolitics. It is hoped that this work will stimulate further research, dialogue and cooperation between India and Kazakhstan and contribute meaningfully to the broader discourse on regional and global partnerships.

I congratulate the editors, contributors, MERI Group of Institutions, India Central Asia Foundation and Institute for Security & Cooperation Studies, Al-Farabi Kazakh National University for this commendable academic contribution and wish the book a wide readership and enduring relevance.

I P Aggarwal
President
Triveni Educational & Social Welfare Society,
New Delhi

Preface

General

The evolving geopolitical landscape of the twenty-first century has brought renewed attention to partnerships that combine strategic depth, economic complementarities and civilisational linkages. Within this broader context, the relationship between India and Kazakhstan has acquired growing significance, shaped by shared interests in regional stability, energy security, connectivity and multilateral cooperation. As global power structures undergo transformation and new centres of influence emerge, India–Kazakhstan relations offer an instructive example of constructive engagement between two responsible regional actors committed to dialogue, sovereignty and development.

This edited volume, *India–Kazakhstan Partnership in a Changing Geopolitical Order*, seeks to provide a comprehensive and interdisciplinary assessment of this relationship. Bringing together scholars, practitioners and policy experts from India and Kazakhstan, the book examines the bilateral partnership through the lenses of geopolitics, political economy, security, energy, cultural exchange and future-oriented cooperation. The volume aims not only to document existing dimensions of engagement but also to offer analytical insights into emerging opportunities and challenges in a rapidly changing international environment.

By combining strategic analysis with historical depth and policy relevance, the book aspires to contribute meaningfully to the literature on Central Asia, India's extended neighbourhood and contemporary international relations. It is intended to serve as a useful reference for scholars, students, diplomats, policymakers, technocrats and all those interested in understanding the present and future trajectory of India–Kazakhstan relations.

Coverage of Topics

The volume opens with a strong focus on geopolitics, strategic environment and power dynamics, setting the analytical foundation for understanding India–Kazakhstan relations. Prof. (Dr.) Ramakant Dwivedi in *An Indian Perspective on Changing Geopolitics in Central Asia*, situates Central Asia within the broader shifts of global power, examining India's strategic interests, regional connectivity aspirations and engagement with Eurasia amidst emerging multipolarity. He provides an Indian strategic lens through which evolving regional and global dynamics are assessed.

Prof. Fatima Kukeyeva contributes two analytically interlinked chapters. In *Analysis of Kazakhstan's Geopolitical Position*, she examines Kazakhstan's unique geostrategic location at the crossroads of Europe and Asia, highlighting how geography, history and diplomacy shape its foreign policy behaviour. In her second chapter, *Kazakhstan's Relations with Global Powers and Regional Actors*, she offers a nuanced assessment of Kazakhstan's engagement with major powers and neighbouring regions, providing valuable insight into the country's balancing strategy in a complex international environment.

Ambassador Ashok Sajjanhar, in his chapter *India's Geopolitical Strategy Amidst Global Turbulence*, analyses India's evolving foreign policy in an era marked by geopolitical fragmentation, intensifying strategic competition and shifting global alliances. Drawing upon his extensive diplomatic experience, he offers practitioner-level insights into India's pursuit of strategic autonomy, its diplomatic engagement with major powers and its growing interaction with regions such as Central Asia within the changing international order.

In a complementary yet distinct analysis, Dr. Anita Sengupta, in her chapter *Multilateral Engagement in Indo-Kazakh Relations*, examines the importance of multilateral platforms and regional organisations in strengthening bilateral cooperation between India and Kazakhstan. She highlights the role of multilateral diplomacy in advancing shared interests, enhancing institutional engagement and reinforcing bilateral ties beyond traditional state-to-state frameworks.

The second thematic section focuses on state-building and political-economic development. Dr. Pramod Kumar's chapter, *State and Nation Building in Kazakhstan: Issues and Challenges*, examines the historical and contemporary processes of nation-building in post-Soviet Kazakhstan. It analyses governance structures, identity formation and institutional consolidation, highlighting the political and social complexities involved in shaping a cohesive national framework since independence.

Dr. Zhapar Zhuman's chapter, *Economic and Political Development of Kazakhstan*, explores the interlinkages between political evolution and economic reform in Kazakhstan. The chapter provides a detailed assessment of the country's transition from a centrally planned system to a market-oriented economy, examining state-led reforms, institutional restructuring and development strategies. By situating economic transformation within its political context, the chapter offers valuable insights into the domestic foundations of Kazakhstan's stability and long-term growth.

Dr. Beena's chapter, *Economic and Political Development between India and Kazakhstan*, bridges domestic developments with bilateral engagement by examining how political and economic trajectories in both countries intersect to shape cooperation. The chapter analyses policy frameworks, institutional linkages and evolving priorities that have influenced bilateral relations, offering a nuanced understanding of how internal developments translate into external engagement.

Dr. Saniya Nurdavletova's chapter, *History of Diplomatic Relations and Political Cooperation between Kazakhstan and India*, presents a comprehensive historical account of bilateral relations since Kazakhstan's independence. It traces the evolution of diplomatic engagement, high-level political dialogue and institutional cooperation across different phases. By highlighting key milestones and agreements, the chapter provides essential context for understanding the contemporary foundations and continuity of India–Kazakhstan relations.

The third section addresses economic cooperation, trade, connectivity and business engagement, highlighting the material foundations of the India–Kazakhstan partnership. Dr. Zhapar Zhuman's chapter, *Economic Cooperation and Trade*, examines bilateral trade patterns, key sectors of cooperation, and existing structural constraints, offering an analytical overview of trade dynamics and their implications for long-term economic engagement.

Dr. Malik Augan's chapter, *Opportunities for Transport and Logistics Cooperation between Kazakhstan and India*, underscores the strategic importance of connectivity in strengthening bilateral economic ties. The chapter analyses transport corridors, multimodal logistics networks, and infrastructure development, situating Kazakhstan's role as a transit hub within broader regional connectivity initiatives. It highlights how improved logistics cooperation can facilitate trade, reduce costs and enhance regional integration.

Dr. Anil Sharma, in *Indo-Kazakhstan Business Prospects*, brings an industry-oriented and practitioner-driven perspective to the discussion. He focuses on the investment climate, regulatory frameworks and emerging opportunities for private sector participation. By examining business-friendly reforms, financial mechanisms and sector-specific potential, the chapter highlights the role of entrepreneurship and corporate engagement in deepening economic relations between India and Kazakhstan.

The fourth section examines energy, nuclear issues and strategic security cooperation, highlighting areas of growing strategic convergence between India and Kazakhstan. Dr. Cauvery Ganapathy's chapter, *Investing in Future Trajectories: Indo-Kazakh Cooperation in Civil Nuclear Energy and Critical Minerals*, explores cooperation in emerging and high-priority sectors that are central to global energy transition and technological advancement. The chapter analyses opportunities for collaboration in civil nuclear energy, supply chains of critical minerals and long-term strategic planning, underscoring their significance for sustainable development and strategic resilience.

Dr. Zhulduz Baizakova, in *India's and Kazakhstan's Approaches to Energy Security*, examines the national energy strategies of both countries, focusing on diversification, resource management, and energy diplomacy. The chapter assesses complementarities in energy policies and highlights areas where bilateral cooperation can contribute to stability, efficiency and resilience in energy markets.

Prof. Kuralay Baizakova contributes two interrelated chapters addressing core security concerns. In *India and Kazakhstan's Approaches to Nuclear Non-Proliferation Issues*, the focus is on shared commitments to global non-proliferation norms, arms control and responsible nuclear governance. Her second chapter, *Opportunities for Cooperation between India and Kazakhstan in Combating International Terrorism*, analyses avenues for collaboration in counter-terrorism, intelligence sharing and regional security frameworks, emphasising the importance of coordinated responses to transnational threats.

The final section focuses on civilisational linkages, societal interfaces and future outlook, emphasising the softer yet enduring foundations of the India–Kazakhstan partnership. Yashvi Bhat's chapter, *Tracing Civilisational Ties between India–Kazakhstan and Future Prospects*, explores historical interactions, cultural exchanges and people-to-people connections that have shaped mutual perceptions over centuries. The chapter highlights how shared civilisational narratives and cultural memory continue to influence contemporary engagement and provide a durable basis for future cooperation.

Dr. Laura Nurdavletova, in *Kazakhstan–India Cooperation in the Fields of Education, Culture and Tourism*, examines the role of educational exchanges, cultural diplomacy and tourism in strengthening bilateral ties. The chapter analyses institutional initiatives, academic collaboration, and cultural outreach as key instruments of soft power and mutual understanding.

Prof. Tabasum Firdous and Muhtashim Ishaq, in their joint chapter on the *Role of Civil Society and Scientific Institutions*, assess how non-state actors, academic institutions and research networks contribute to deepening cooperation. Their analysis underscores the importance of grassroots engagement, knowledge exchange and scientific collaboration in sustaining long-term partnerships.

Ramanshi Dwivedi's chapter, *Analysis of Contemporary Challenges and Threats for India*, situates India–Kazakhstan engagement within broader regional and global security concerns, examining emerging risks and strategic uncertainties.

The volume concludes with Dr. Syrym Parpiyev's *Forecasting the Development of Relations in the Long-Term Perspective*, which offers a forward-looking assessment of bilateral relations by identifying future trajectories, opportunities and strategic priorities in a changing geopolitical environment.

Ramakant Dwivedi
New Delhi, India

Lalit Aggarwal
New Delhi, India

Kuralay Baizakova
Almaty, Kazakhstan

Acknowledgements

We would like to thank all the authors of papers published in the book. Without their dedication and persistent hard work, this book may not have seen the light of day. Gratitude to Shri IP Aggarwal, Hon'ble President, Triveni Educational and Social Welfare Society, New Delhi, for his support and inspiration. We are also pleased to extend a special word of thanks to the India-Central Asia Foundation (ICAF) team in New Delhi, India and Institute for Security and Cooperation Studies, Al-Farabi Kazakh National University, Almaty, Kazakhstan. We remain grateful to all who directly or indirectly supported the successful conduct of this book.

We would like to thank Pentagon Press LLP for copy-editing and publishing the book in record time.

Ramakant Dwivedi
New Delhi, India

Lalit Aggarwal
New Delhi, India

Kuralay Baizakova
Almaty, Kazakhstan

About the Contributors

Prof. (Dr.) Ramakant Dwivedi is currently (since 4 November 2024), Head, Centre for International Studies, Management Education & Research Institute (MERI), New Delhi. He is also Director of the India Central Asia Foundation (ICAF), New Delhi. He graduated from the University of Allahabad in 1986 in the Commerce stream. He completed his post-graduation (1992), M.Phil (1997) and Ph.D. (2002) from Jawaharlal Nehru University, New Delhi. His doctorate is from the School of International Studies, Jawaharlal Nehru University, New Delhi.

Dr. Dwivedi was a Visiting Research Fellow at the Al-Beruni Institute of Oriental Studies, Tashkent (1998-2001). He was Associate Fellow at the Manohar Parrikar Institute for Defence Studies and Analyses (MP-IDSA), New Delhi (2003–2007). He worked as Officer on Special Duty (OSD) with the National Security Advisor's Office, Prime Minister's Office, Government of India (2007–2024). He has looked after a variety of domains assigned to him during his service. He has represented India in 14 countries as domain expert and part of official delegations for scholarly presentations. His published works include 50 research papers in national/international journals, and edited books. He has authored/edited eleven books on international relations.

Prof. Dwivedi was awarded the Nehru Memorial Scholarship for Doctoral Studies by Prime Minister Museum and Library (earlier Nehru Memorial Museum and Library & Jawaharlal Nehru Memorial Fund), Teen Murti House, New Delhi (1998–2000). He received a Commendation Certificate and Letter of Appreciation from the Director of IDSA (2004). He was conferred a 'Diploma of Honorary Professor' by the University of Innovation and Digital Technologies (UIDT) of Tajikistan, Agency of Innovation and Digital Technologies, under the President of the Republic of Tajikistan in Kulov city of Tajikistan on 16 October 2025.He was awarded a Certificate of Appreciation by the National Academy of Manas (NAM)of the Kyrgyz Republic for his contribution in the translation of the Kyrgyz epic 'Manas' into Hindi in December 2025.He appears widely on TV panel discussions.

Prof. (Dr.) Dwivedi is Founding & Life Member of the India-Central Asia Foundation (ICAF), New Delhi; Life Member, United Services Institution of India (USI), New Delhi, Life Member, India Islamic Cultural Centre (IICC), New Delhi and Associate Member, Manohar Parrikar Institute for Defence Studies and Analyses (MP-IDSA), India International Centre (IIC), and Press Club of India (PCI), New Delhi. He is married to Mrs. Renu Dwivedi and they have two daughters.

e-mail: rkdwivedi@meri.edu.in

Prof. Lalit Aggarwal, a visionary in the field of education is an approved Prof. from GGSIP University Delhi. He is M.Tech in Computer Science and Post Graduate Diploma in Personnel Management. After completing his engineering degree, he chalked out a career as an entrepreneur by taking active interest in the development of educational institutions.

Prof. Aggarwal is a life member of several academic bodies such as AIMA, AIMS, EPSI, Association of Self Financing Institutions Haryana at national levels and Association of Advanced Collegiate Schools of Business (AACSB, USA) etc. at international level. Prof. Aggarwal has published a number of research papers in national and international journals. He has attended various International conferences & seminars. MERI Group of Institutions continuously diversify, expand and had been able to secure its place among A+ category institutions under his guidance.

e-mail: vp@meri.edu.in

Prof. Fatima Kukeyeva is a Professor of International Relations and the World Economy Department at al-Farabi Kazakh National University specializing in foreign and security policy, American studies, and issues of globalization and security. She is the author of three monographs and numerous articles on Central Asian issues, US foreign policy, international organizations, and international engagement more broadly.

Prof. Kukeyeva is a Director of the Resource Centre for American and Democratic Studies. She is the organizer and Director of the annual Summer School on different issues of Central Asian countries. She was co-director of the 'al-Farabi Carnegie Program on Central Asia', established by al-Farabi University and the Carnegie Endowment for International Peace (2011-2014). She is an alumni of Fulbright and other US research programs and recipient of

the presidential 'Best Lecturer of the Year' fellowship (2007, 2015), and 'Outstanding Scholar' fellowship (2008).
e-mail: icafindia@gmail.com

Ambassador Ashok Sajjanhar has worked for the Indian Foreign Service for over three decades. He was the ambassador of India to Kazakhstan, Sweden and Latvia and has worked in diplomatic positions in Washington DC, Brussels, Moscow, Geneva, Tehran, Dhaka and Bangkok. He is a Distinguished Fellow, Ananta Centre. He negotiated for India in the Uruguay Round of Multilateral Trade Negotiations and in negotiations for India-EU, India-ASEAN and India-Thailand Free Trade Agreements. He contributed significantly to strengthening strategic ties and promoting cultural cooperation between India and the USA, EU, Russia and other countries. Ambassador Sajjanhar has been decorated by the Governments of Kazakhstan and Latvia with their National Awards and by the Universal Peace Federation with the title of "Ambassador of Peace." Currently, Ambassador Sajjanhar is the President of Institute of Global Studies, New Delhi. He writes, travels and speaks extensively on issues relating to international relations, foreign policy and themes of contemporary relevance and significance. He appears widely on TV panel discussions. His wife, Madhu, is an economist and an educationist. They have a son and a daughter.
e-mail: icafindia@gmail.com

Dr. Anita Sengupta is an area studies specialist engaged in the study of the Eurasian region. Her areas of interest include issues of identity politics, migration, gender, borders, critical geopolitics and logistics. She is a regular commentator on debates on Asian Affairs. She has been a Fellow, Maulana Abdul Kalam Azad Institute of Asian Studies, Kolkata; Senior Fellow, Indian Council of Social Science Research, New Delhi; and Director, Calcutta Research Group, Kolkata. She is currently Director, Asia in Global Affairs, Kolkata.
e-mail: anitasengupta@hotmail.com

Dr. Pramod Kumar is serving as an Associate Professor in the Centre for Russian and Central Asian Studies, School of International Studies, Jawaharlal Nehru University, New Delhi, India. He earned his M.Phil. and Ph.D. from the Centre for Russian and Central Asian Studies, School of International Studies, Jawaharlal Nehru University, New Delhi, India, in 2005 and 2010, respectively. Dr. Pramod Kumar served in Pondicherry University (A Central University) from March 2012 to April 2023. He is a Life Member of the India Central Asia

Foundation, Society for South Asian Studies, Indian Academy of Social Sciences, Indian Political Science Association and Indian Sociological Society. He is a Member of the Board of Studies in the Department of Politics and International Studies, Pondicherry University and Pondicherry Engineering College (now Pondicherry Technical University), Pondicherry, India.
e-mail: icafindia@gmail.com

Dr. Zhapar Zhuman serves as a senior researcher at the Institute for Security and Cooperation Studies and lectures in the Department of International Relations at Al-Farabi Kazakh National University. Her academic work examines politico and economic conditions in Kazakhstan. She actively contributes to national and international research projects and produces analytical briefings for policy institutions.
e-mail: icafindia@gmail.com

Dr. Beena is an Assistant Professor at the MERI Centre for International Studies, New Delhi. She previously taught Political Science at Amity Law School, and the University of Delhi. She has completed two Post-Doctoral fellowships—one as a Maharishi Kanad Post-Doctoral Fellow at the Delhi School of Transnational Affairs (Institution of Eminence), University of Delhi, and another under Rashtriya Uchchatar Shiksha Abhiyan (RUSA) at Utkal University, Odisha.

She holds a Ph.D. from the School of International Studies, Jawaharlal Nehru University, New Delhi. Her work has been published in Scopus-indexed journals, UGC Care-listed journals, and peer-reviewed academic platforms. Her research interests include Central Asian studies, South Asian studies, particularly migration and refugee movements in the region.
e-mail: drbeena@meri.edu.in

Dr. Saniya Nurdavletova is an Associate Professor of International Relations at L.N. Gumilyov Eurasian National University, Candidate of Historical Sciences (Ph.D.), Director of the Centre for International Studies. Scientific interests are international relations, foreign policy of the Republic of Kazakhstan, security issues, Central Asia, and integration process.
e-mail: icafindia@gmail.com

Dr. Malik Augan is a Doctor of Sciences in Historical Sciences, Professor of the Department of International Relations and World Economy, International Relations Faculty, Al-Farabi Kazakh National University. He is the author of monographs and numerous articles. He has also been the recipient of the

Kazakh presidential 'Best Lecturer of the Year' fellowship in 2016. Professor Augan has been honoured with scholarship of the German scholarship funds DAAD, DFG, Marion Donhoff (2000-2001), Japanese Sasakawa Foundation (2003, 2007), Soros Fund (2005, 2006), Korea Foundation for Advanced Studies (2012), NATO's PfPC Project (2013), G. Marshall Centre Scholar (2015). His academic focus spans foreign and security policy of the Central Asian region.
e-mail: icafindia@gmail.com

Dr. Anil Sharma is a Chartered Accountant by profession. He is a Member of the National Financial Reporting Authority, Ministry of Corporate Affairs, Government of India, and an Adjunct Faculty with the Indian Institute of Corporate Affairs. He was an Independent Director with UCO Bank from 2016-19. He is actively associated with various NGOs working in the social sector.
e-mail: anil54@gmail.com

Dr. Cauvery Ganapathy is a Strategic Risk Management Consultant with subject expertise in energy security. She is a Non-Resident Fellow with the Observer Research Foundation (Middle East) and has been a Research Associate with the Office of Net Assessment under the US Department of Defence. Cauvery has been a recipient of the Wrangler Pavate Fellowship to POLIS and Sidney Sussex College, University of Cambridge and a Fulbright Doctoral Fellow with the Energy and Resources Group, University of California, Berkeley. As a Fellow of Global India Foundation, she has presented and published at various national and international forums, and earned her B.A. in Political Science from St. Xavier's College and Ph.D. from Jadavpur University, Calcutta.
e-mail: icafindia@gmail.com

Dr. Zhulduz Baizakova serves as a senior researcher at the Institute for Security and Cooperation Studies and lectures in the Department of International Relations at Al-Farabi Kazakh National University. Her academic work examines security challenges in Central Asia, the strategic behaviour of middle powers, and the impact of geopolitical transformations on regional stability. She actively contributes to national and international research projects and produces analytical briefings for policy institutions.
e-mail: icafindia@gmail.com

Prof. Kuralay Baizakova is a Professor at the Department of International Relations and World Economy and the Director of the Institute for Security and Cooperation Studies, Al-Farabi Kazakh National University. She has been the Dean of the Faculty of International Relations of Al-Farabi KazNU in 2005-2009 and Head of the Department of International Relations and Foreign Policy in Al-Farabi KazNU in 2000-2005. Her research interests include international and regional security issues, role of Central Asia in international relations, foreign policy of France, EU, NATO activity in Central Asia, regional integration, bilateral relations of the Republic of Kazakhstan. She has more than 300 scientific publications published in Kazakhstan, France, Belgium, Korea, Russia, India, China, Kyrgyzstan, Armenia, etc.

She is the head of a number of projects of the Ministry of Science and Higher Education of the RK and international projects. She had been a visiting professor to the University of Le Havre, Strasbourg University (France) and to the Hanyang University (Seoul), etc. She has been awarded by the President of Kazakhstan, the Ministry of Foreign Affairs and the Ministry of Science and Education of Kazakhstan for her distinguished contributions in the field of International Relations.

e-mail: kbaizakova@mail.ru

Yashvi Bhat is currently pursuing an advanced programme on Parliamentary Institutions and Procedures at the Institute of Constitutional and Parliamentary Studies (ICPS), New Delhi. She holds an Honours degree in Political Science from Miranda House, University of Delhi.

She has also completed a specialised training programme under the iLead Global Foundation and Konrad-Adenauer-Stiftung (KAS), strengthening her analytical grounding in international relations, policy processes, and leadership in democratic governance.

Her academic interests span international relations, global politics, diplomacy, and India's evolving role in the contemporary world order. Driven by a strong orientation towards public service and informed policy engagement, she endeavours to channel her knowledge and aspirations into constructive contributions to India's democratic and strategic landscape.

e-mail: yashvibhat1607@gmail.com

Dr. Laura Nurdavletova, doctoral student in International Relations, Al-Farabi Kazakh National University. Research areas are South East Asia, India in the foreign policy of Kazakhstan, Kazakh-Indian Relations, energy and economic relations.

e-mail: icafindia@gmail.com

Prof. Tabasum Firdous is the former Director, Centre of Central Asian Studies (CCAS), University of Kashmir. She has over 70 research papers, monographs, and chapters in edited volumes published in India, Korea, Iran, Iraq, Russia, Kyrgyzstan, and Turkmenistan. Her research interests include Gender, the Middle East, and Central Asian Politics. She has guided more 30 M.Phil. and Ph.D. research scholars, and also evaluated 20 theses till date. She has authored *Women's Arduous Journey: from Estrangement to Engagement* (2024), *India-Afghanistan Relations* (2024), *Central Asia: Geopolitical Dynamics and Shifting Political Patterns* (2023), *Gendering Women in the 21st Century: Critical Perspectives* (2021), *Political Reforms in Uzbekistan* (2015), *Peace Strategies in Central Asia* (2009), *Central Asia: Security and Strategic Imperatives* (2002), and *Defence Strategies in Central Asia* (2001).

She is a Visiting Fellow at the Centre of International Studies, Cambridge University, UK, a Visiting Fellow at the Institute of History, Uzbekistan, and an Honorary Member of IRSEA, Bucharest, Romania. Besides academic accomplishments, she has extensively worked for empowering marginalised communities and has passionately worked for integrating research, policy advocacy, and grassroots initiatives to create inclusive educational opportunities. This commitment has materialised in various field surveys and projects sponsored by UGC, ICSSR, etc.
e-mail:icafindia@gmail.com

Muhtashim Ishaq is a Ph.D. (Political Science) Scholar in the Centre of Central Asian Studies, University of Kashmir.
e-mail:icafindia@gmail.com

Ramanshi Dwivedi is a Research Fellow at the IC Centre for Governance, New Delhi, India and India-Central Foundation, New Delhi, India. She holds an Honours degree in Political Science from the University of Delhi. Her academic and professional pursuits are driven by an intellectual fervour for the complexities of international relations, diplomacy, and global security. Her research has been featured in both national and international publications. Anchored in a profound respect for her homeland, India, she is committed to contributing meaningfully to society through her work.
e-mail:ramanshidwivedi200308@gmail.com

Dr. Syrym Parpiyev, Ph.D., is a Senior Lecturer in the Department of International Relations and a member of the Questioning Regional Affairs Research Centre at Al-Farabi Kazakh National University. He received his

Ph.D. in International Studies from Chonnam National University in the Republic of Korea. His primary research interests include nationalism, national identity, nation-building, separatism, ethnic conflict, and state sovereignty.

From 2012 to 2019, he took part in several research projects, including 'Diaspora as an Ethnic Dispersion and an Actor of Global Communication,' 'Jangbogo Colossus'—Cultivating Global Korean Businessmen,' etc. In 2023, under the Bolashaq program, he undertook a research internship at IERES, Elliott School of International Affairs, George Washington University, USA As an emerging scholar, he has authored more than 15 social science articles.
e-mail:icafindia@gmail.com

List of Abbreviations

APEDA	Agricultural and Processed Food Products Export Development Authority
ASSR	Autonomous Soviet Socialist Republic
CCSD	Committee for Civil Society Development
CICA	Conference on Interaction and Confidence-Building Measures in Asia
CIS	Community of Independent States
CSOs	Civil Society Organisations
CSR	Corporate Social Responsibility
CSTO	Collective Security Treaty Organisation
DRDO	Defence Research and Development Organisation
EAM	External Affairs Minister
EPCA	Enhanced Partnership and Cooperation Agreement
EU	European Union
FCRA	Foreign Contributions Regulation Act
FDI	Foreign Direct Investment
FICCI	Federation of Indian Chambers of Commerce and Industry
FM	Foreign Minister
FOC	Foreign Office Consultations
GDP	Gross Domestic Product
GNH	Greenhouse Gas
ICABC	India-Central Asia Business Council
ICCR	Indian Council for Cultural Relations
IGC	Inter-Governmental Commission
INSTC	International North-South Transport Corridor

IPKF	Indian Peace Keeping Force
ISA	International Solar Alliance
ISRO	Indian Space Research Organisation
ITEC	Indian Technical and Economic Cooperation
JBC	Joint Business Council
JWGs	Joint Working Groups
Kazakh SSR	Kazakh Soviet Socialist Republic
KazISS	Kazakhstan Institute for Strategic Studies
LAC	Line of Actual Control
LTTE	Liberation Tigers of Tamil Eelam
MOSPI	Ministry of Statistics and Programme Implementation
NGOs	Non-Governmental Organisations
NITI	National Institution for Transforming India Aayog
NPIs	Non-Profit Institutions
NPOs	Non-Profit Organisations
NSG	Nuclear Suppliers Group
OECD	Organisation for Economic Co-operation and Development
OVL	ONGC Videsh Limited
PRIA	Participatory Research in Asia
SCO	Shanghai Cooperation Organisation
SEZs	Special Economic Zones
UNCCD	UN Convention to Combat Desertification
UPI	Unified Payments Interface
USSR	Union of Soviet Socialist Republics
VANI	Voluntary Action Network India
WTO	World Trade Organisation

SECTION I

Geopolitics, Strategic Environment and Power Dynamics

1

An Indian Perspective on Changing Geopolitics in Central Asia

Prof. (Dr.) Ramakant Dwivedi

India's aspiration to play a more influential role in world affairs naturally extends to regions with which it shares deep civilisational, economic, and strategic linkages. Central Asia, long embedded in the historical consciousness of the subcontinent, forms an essential component of this outward vision. The region was not only a cradle of major civilisations but also a geographic hinge of Eurasian connectivity, situated at the intersection of ancient trade routes, imperial exchanges, religious movements, and cultural interactions. Its location at the crossroads of Eurasia places it at the heart of continental geopolitics, rendering it a structurally indispensable space in the wider international system.

Across centuries, movements of people, ideas, goods, and administrative traditions flowed between the Indian subcontinent and Central Asia. Empires on the subcontinent were repeatedly influenced by political transformations in Inner Asia, and many ruling houses and cultural influences in India bore direct or indirect Central Asian roots. This long history has fostered a certain familiarity and ease in India's modern engagement with the region. Even today, the imprint of these historical interactions shapes India's political imagination of Eurasia while reinforcing the sense that Central Asia is not a distant periphery but an area with which India shares accumulated cultural memory and strategic sensitivity.

In the contemporary era, India's engagement with Central Asia has taken on renewed significance. New Delhi's policies in the region evolve within a broader geopolitical environment characterised by the presence of major external actors, principally Russia and China, but also the USA, Turkey, Japan, the Gulf states, and the European Union. These actors bring their own agendas, institutional frameworks, and connectivity projects into the region, inevitably shaping how India manoeuvres and positions itself. Rather than treating Central Asia as an arena for rivalry, India has chosen a constructive, partnership-oriented approach rooted in capacity building, economic cooperation, and support for regional autonomy. New Delhi's policies avoid coercive tactics and emphasise sovereignty, stability, and multi-vectorism, values that Central Asian states, including Kazakhstan, themselves articulate.

India's Strategic Approach to Central Asia

India's strategic outlook towards Central Asia is distinctive because it unfolds alongside its maritime ambitions in the Indo-Pacific. While India continues to strengthen its naval presence and regional partnerships across the Indian Ocean and Pacific littorals, it simultaneously recognises the strategic weight of continental Asia. Central Asia forms the northern vector of India's broader foreign policy orientation, extending the logic of the 'Look West' and 'Look North' policies while complementing its 'Act East' strategy.

New Delhi's central challenge has been how to balance its maritime and continental imperatives without overstretch. In practical terms, India seeks to deepen its influence in Central Asia for several reasons: to ensure that the region does not fall exclusively under Chinese influence; to counter Pakistan's strategic alignment with certain regional actors; to secure access to energy and mineral resources; and to enhance its role in shaping Eurasian security discourses. India's engagement is, therefore, not reactive but anchored in long-term strategic thinking.

In the 1990s, after the dissolution of the Soviet Union, India was among the earliest states to articulate a forward presence in Central Asia. This culminated in the establishment of the Ayni air base in Tajikistan, India's only overseas military facility. Although its operationalisation has been shaped by Tajik domestic considerations and regional sensitivities, the base symbolises India's early recognition that continental security is integral to its national interests. India's long-standing partnership with Russia further facilitated this presence, reflecting a shared understanding of Eurasian stability.

However, New Delhi's engagement extends far beyond Tajikistan. Uzbekistan, often regarded as the geopolitical core of Central Asia due to its demography and centrality, occupies an important place in India's regional thinking. The two countries share historic cultural linkages and have cultivated modern partnerships in education, medicine, IT, defence training, and trade. Kazakhstan, though not singled out excessively, naturally occupies a relevant position in this broader matrix due to its economic weight, multivector diplomacy, and stable foreign policy orientation. Similarly, Turkmenistan's significance stems from its gas reserves and transit potential, while Kyrgyzstan's hydropower capabilities, mining sector, and educational linkages with India add further layers to cooperation.

Connectivity and the Geography Dilemma

India's most persistent obstacle in Central Asia remains geography. Without a direct land border with any of the Central Asian republics, India lacks natural access to the region. For two decades, New Delhi attempted to secure access through the Persian Gulf and Iran, an approach that, for reasons ranging from geopolitical shifts to sanctions, did not fully realise its potential. Even today, many of India's connectivity initiatives face structural constraints, despite their conceptual attractiveness.

The International North-South Transport Corridor (INSTC), which seeks to link India to Russia and Central Asia through Iran and the Caspian Sea, remains the most promising long-term route. Yet even well-conceived projects such as the Iran-Pakistan-India (IPI) pipeline or the Turkmenistan-Afghanistan-Pakistan-India (TAPI) gas pipeline have not materialised due to political, logistical, and security-related impediments. India continues to support these initiatives because they embody the logic of a more integrated Eurasian space, even if their timelines remain uncertain.

Despite these obstacles, India has not allowed geography to limit ambition. Instead, New Delhi has pivoted towards a multi-layered connectivity strategy combining maritime routes, regional partnerships, digital connectivity, energy cooperation, and collaborative infrastructure development. Increased diplomatic and strategic cooperation with the Central Asian republics ensures that India remains a relevant actor in shaping future connectivity frameworks, even if the physical routes remain complicated.

Shared Security Concerns

Security cooperation forms a core pillar of India-Central Asia engagement. The region has faced rising challenges related to extremism, radicalisation, narcotics trafficking, and instability emanating from Afghanistan. The re-emergence of the Taliban-Haqqani networks and the persistent volatility of the

Af-Pak region have intensified regional apprehensions. Central Asian states have long viewed India as a stable partner in counter-terrorism, intelligence sharing, and capacity building. India's own experiences with terrorism and its credible track record in multilateral counter-terrorism forums enhance its relevance.

The 'Connect Central Asia' policy, formally articulated in the early 2010s, places security collaboration at the centre of regional engagement. India's cooperation with Tajikistan is especially important in this respect. Tajikistan's proximity to Afghanistan and Pakistan-occupied Kashmir, combined with its strategic location bordering China and Central Asian neighbours, makes it a significant partner. India has contributed to capacity building in Tajik defence establishments, trained military cadets and officers, and maintained close institutional exchanges.

Country-Specific Relevance within a Regional Logic

While India maintains a collective regional approach, each of the five Central Asian republics holds particular relevance:

Kazakhstan

- The region's largest economy and a key supplier of hydrocarbons
- Increasingly prominent regional role and stable, predictable diplomacy
- Areas of cooperation include civil nuclear energy, IT, space, pharmaceuticals, agriculture, and cultural exchange
- Kazakhstan's multi-vector foreign policy aligns harmoniously with India's preference for balanced, non-exclusive partnerships

Uzbekistan

- Geopolitical and demographic centre of Central Asia
- Strong cultural linkages with India
- Expanding cooperation in pharmaceuticals, education, health, IT, and defence

Kyrgyzstan

- Hydropower, mining, and strong educational ties
- Participates actively in India-led human resource development initiatives

Turkmenistan

- Holds among the world's largest natural gas reserves

- Central to the TAPI pipeline vision
- Critical for energy diversification as India's oil imports are projected to rise
- Offers transit access to wider Central Asia via Iran

Tajikistan

- Strategic location near the Af-Pak theatre
- Rich hydropower potential and mineral resources
- Host to India's only overseas military foothold
- Broad India-Tajik cooperation ranging from health to defence training

This country-specific diversification strengthens India's regional footprint without reducing Central Asia to bilateral axes.

The Heartland and India's Vision of Eurasia

Central Asia's significance can also be framed through classic geopolitics. Mackinder's 'Heartland Theory', although historically contextual, remains analytically useful in capturing the structural importance of continental Eurasia. Central Asia, bounded by the Volga to the west, the Yangtze to the east, the Himalayas to the south, and the Arctic to the north, sits at the geographic core of this heartland. Whether or not one subscribes entirely to determinist interpretations, Central Asia's position undeniably shapes both continental and global dynamics.

India's engagement, therefore, is not merely sentimental or historical, but grounded in strategic logic. The region offers energy security opportunities, mineral resources, transit corridors, and a platform for continental diplomacy. India's intention is not to dominate the region, but to participate constructively in shaping a stable Eurasian order that accommodates multipolarity, respects sovereignty, and fosters economic cooperation.

One of the principal incentives extended to India in recent years has been the evolving architecture of the Northern Distribution Network (NDN), a logistical corridor originally established by the USA to transport non-lethal supplies and weaponry to its forces in Afghanistan while deliberately circumventing Pakistan. Within this broader framework, the initial blueprint of the Northern Distribution System (NDS) sought to integrate the Zaranj–Delaram road with Afghanistan's internal 'garland highway,' ultimately linking these routes to Iran's strategically vital Chabahar Port. Should Tehran grant final approval for this alignment, India would be positioned to participate as a central stakeholder, working in concert with Moscow. Yet, such an arrangement may also require Washington's acquiescence, given the United States' parallel interest in repurposing sections of the existing logistical chain into what it envisions as a new Silk Route.

It is precisely at this juncture that India's diplomatic dexterity becomes critical. If New Delhi is able to leverage its constructive relations with Russia, Iran, and the USA simultaneously, it could significantly raise its diplomatic and economic profile in Central Asia. This strengthened engagement, especially through trade corridors acceptable to all three capitals, would carry strategic value: Moscow, Tehran, and Washington stand to benefit economically and politically from more diversified regional connectivity, while India secures deeper access into a region of long-standing cultural and geopolitical significance. Furthermore, such heightened diplomatic capital could encourage Moscow to back India's full and uncontested membership within the Shanghai Cooperation Organisation (SCO), particularly in circumstances where Beijing's advocacy for Pakistan's admission has created strategic dilemmas for New Delhi.

India's contemporary outreach to Central Asia is increasingly mediated through the institutional framework of the SCO, which has acquired renewed salience for both Russia and China amid their steadily deteriorating relations with Western powers. Analysts have noted that the organisation's strategic potential is substantial despite the presence of other prominent multilateral groupings such as BRICS, the G20, and the G7. The SCO today encompasses roughly 40 per cent of the world's population and more than one-fifth of global GDP; with Iran's recent accession, the grouping collectively commands access to nearly 20 per cent of the world's proven oil reserves. Iran's membership further strengthens the SCO's energy credentials, though it simultaneously generates anxiety in Western capitals. As the organisation becomes increasingly juxtaposed against Western-aligned institutions, India's ability to maintain balanced relationships across competing geopolitical blocs will likely experience greater strain.

The SCO originated in 2001 as a joint initiative of China, Russia, and four Central Asian republics, conceived primarily as a mechanism to limit Western influence in the Eurasian heartland and promote regional security cooperation. India and Pakistan's accession in 2017 represented the first major expansion of the grouping. Since then, the organisation's relevance for Moscow and Beijing has only intensified as both states seek alternative platforms for political coordination and economic engagement beyond the Western orbit.

For India, the SCO presents both opportunities and challenges. New Delhi must navigate a complex diplomatic landscape defined by its strategic divergences with China, its adversarial relationship with Pakistan, and its otherwise warm historic partnership with Russia. How India manages these competing relationships will have a significant impact on the SCO's internal equilibrium and its long-term evolution. Russia, in particular, has been receptive to India's ambition to integrate South and Central Asia through logistical routes that bypass Pakistan. India's cooperation with Iran in developing Chabahar Port serves precisely this purpose, facilitating an emerging connectivity geometry that links India with the Central Asian republics while simultaneously deepening India-Iran-Russia cooperation within the INSTC framework.

Yet the actions of certain SCO member-states have compelled India to reassess aspects of its strategic posture. Persistent disagreements on issues of terrorism, regional security, and China's expanding political and economic footprint have made the SCO an increasingly intricate arena for Indian diplomacy. In response, New Delhi has adopted a calibrated dual-track approach: it continues to value participation in the SCO while simultaneously reinforcing bilateral partnerships with key Central Asian economies. Notably, all SCO members other than China and Pakistan have shown enthusiasm for expanded collaboration on connectivity initiatives. The Chabahar trilateral partnership between Uzbekistan, India, and Iran, aimed at linking the eastern route of the International North–South Transport Corridor (INSTC) with Chabahar, exemplifies this trend. The eastern branch of the INSTC, also known as the 928-km Kazakhstan-Turkmenistan-Iran (KTI) line, runs along the eastern flank of the Caspian Sea. Once this corridor is physically integrated with the 628-km Chabahar–Zahedan railway line, it is expected to significantly enhance trade flows between India and the wider Eurasian region. During the inaugural India--Central Asia Summit in 2022, all five Central Asian republics endorsed the proposal to formally incorporate Chabahar into the INSTC, signalling their recognition of India's constructive role in regional connectivity.

China has sought to assert an increasingly dominant role within the SCO, a trend accelerated by the fragile global geopolitical environment and compounded by the ongoing Russia-Ukraine conflict. Beijing aims to reshape the SCO into a platform aligned more closely with Chinese geo-economic ambitions, particularly those linked to the Belt and Road Initiative (BRI). The BRI has offered attractive financing options for large-scale infrastructure and connectivity projects; however, in several cases, it has also created structural dependencies, leaving participating countries vulnerable to debt distress. Many analysts argue that the initiative has been deployed not to promote genuine regional development but to advance China's broader strategic interests.

Despite these efforts, the Central Asian republics remain among the world's least connected economies, leaving space for India to expand its presence through more sustainable and mutually respectful partnerships. Historically, China has attempted to utilise the SCO to bolster its bilateral ties, especially in economic terms, through initiatives such as the China-Kyrgyzstan-Uzbekistan railway project, the proposed SCO Development Bank, and the SCO road transportation framework. However, Russia's traditionally cautious stance has served as a constraint on unchecked Chinese expansion. With Russia's relative influence waning due to its military entanglement in Ukraine and the resulting geopolitical recalibrations, Beijing has encountered fewer obstacles in deepening its engagement with the Central Asian states.

The SCO has evolved substantially since its inception, maturing into a significant international organisation with widening global attention. Its openness to expanding membership, illustrated by the earlier admission of India, Iran, Pakistan, and Mongolia as observers before their progression towards greater participation, reflects a broader attempt to reconfigure regional alliances and reduce the unipolar orientation of the post-Cold War order. The organisation's strategic objective has gradually shifted towards transforming the broader Eurasian region into an energy and economic hub capable of shaping global power dynamics.

India's relationship with the SCO member-states is grounded in long-standing political goodwill, shared cultural linkages, and mutual trust, elements that form the foundation of India's multi-dimensional foreign policy. These favourable conditions facilitated India's smooth entry into the SCO: after being granted Observer Status in 2005, India advanced to full membership in 2017. This more than decade-long period of association underscored India's commitment to playing a constructive and proactive role within the organisation.

Since joining the SCO, India has consistently provided meaningful support to the organisation's mechanisms and has actively participated in its various working groups, ministerial dialogues, and summits. India has placed emphasis on proposing initiatives that generate shared benefits for all member-states, observers, and dialogue partners. New Delhi's sustained engagement has contributed to strengthening the SCO's institutional relevance and enhancing its visibility in the international system.

India ensures high-level representation at key SCO meetings. The Prime Minister attends the Council of Heads of State (CHS), while the Council of Heads of Government (CHG) is usually led by the External Affairs Minister. India has also maintained active participation in other ministerial and specialised dialogues, advancing the SCO agenda across different domains. To further institutionalise its role, India has deputed two officials each to the SCO Secretariat in Beijing and the SCO Regional Anti-Terrorist Structure (RATS) in Tashkent. These postings facilitate deeper engagement with the organisation's day-to-day operations, particularly in the areas of counter-terrorism, capacitybuilding, and regional security cooperation.

India's Active Participation in Regional Diplomacy

To consolidate its commitment to multilateral engagement within the Shanghai Cooperation Organisation (SCO), the Indian Prime Minister, Narendra Modi, has maintained a consistent presence at the organisation's summits over the past several years. His attendance spans the SCO gatherings held in 2018 in Qingdao, 2019 in Bishkek, 2020 in Moscow (conducted in virtual format due to the global COVID-19 pandemic), 2021 in Dushanbe (also in virtual format), and 2022 in Tashkent. At each of these high-level meetings, Prime Minister Modi articulated a series of proposals designed to deepen cooperation across multiple domains: regional security, economic interconnectivity, and cultural and humanitarian exchanges. These initiatives reflect India's strategic approach to ensuring that the SCO serves not merely as a symbolic multilateral forum, but as a platform capable of translating dialogue into tangible regional benefits.

China's Strategic Expansion in Central Asia and India's Geopolitical Stakes

While India seeks to expand its influence within Central Asia, it faces a complex geopolitical environment shaped by China's concurrent strategic ambitions. Beijing, as part of its overarching Eurasian strategy, has intensified outreach to the Central Asian republics, blending diplomatic engagement with infrastructural investment. The recent physical gathering of Chinese and Central Asian leaders in Xi'an in May 2023 exemplifies this effort. Although it was only the third summit in the China-Central Asia format since its inception in 2020, the meeting marked the first in-person encounter of the leaders, including Kazakh President Kassym-Jomart Tokayev, Kyrgyz President Sadyr Japarov, Tajik President Emomali Rahmon, Turkmen President Serdar

Berdymuhamedov, and Uzbek President Shavkat Mirziyoyev. Xi'an, historically known as Chang'an, carries significant symbolic weight in China's civilisational narrative, reinforcing the emphasis on historical continuity and strategic depth in Beijing's engagement with the region.

The China-Central Asia Summit of 2022, commemorating thirty years of bilateral relations between China and the Central Asian states, witnessed the announcement of a 'China-Central Asian community with a shared future,' echoing the broader Chinese diplomatic philosophy of building a 'community with a shared future for mankind.' During this summit, President Xi articulated four core principles aimed at enhancing mutual economic, political, and security cooperation, signalling Beijing's determination to integrate Central Asia into its broader regional strategy. Beyond the summit, numerous bilateral visits and negotiations on the sidelines further reinforced the multi-layered nature of China's influence, encompassing trade, energy, and strategic collaboration.

China's strategic footprint in the region is not limited to diplomacy and trade. The Pamir Mountain base, operational for the past two years, is slated for permanent upgrading. Situated near the Wakhjir Pass, the base connects via road networks to China's TaxkorganTajik Autonomous County in Xinjiang. Access to the immediate area is restricted exclusively to military personnel, reflecting its strategic sensitivity. An access road on the Chinese side links to the Karakoram Highway, approximately 80 kilometres east, facilitating logistical movements for border security operations. Analysts have posited that a new '5+2' axis is emerging in Eurasia, comprising the Central Asian republics alongside China and Russia, highlighting the evolving geo-strategic architecture in the region. Even though Russian President Vladimir Putin was not physically present at the Xi'an summit, Moscow's interests were carefully considered, indicating tacit coordination between the two major powers in Central Asia.

China's decision to assume a leadership role in regional security, particularly in the context of the Ukraine crisis, represents a paradigm shift that challenges conventional interpretations of the United States' Indo-Pacific strategy. The strategic geography of Inner Asia renders the region relatively impervious to Western influence, thereby negating attempts at encirclement of Russia and China. Central Asia's positioning as a buffer and strategic periphery enhances its significance for both Moscow and Beijing, especially in scenarios involving instability in neighbouring Afghanistan and Pakistan.

From an economic and infrastructural perspective, Beijing has meticulously developed oil and gas pipelines across Central Asia, including those linking to Kazakhstan and the Turkmenistan-Uzbekistan-Kazakhstan-China gas pipeline. These corridors not only secure energy supplies for China's growing domestic demand but also reinforce Beijing's long-term strategic leverage over the resource-rich Central Asian republics. Moscow remains cognisant of China's expanding presence, particularly via SCO mechanisms and bilateral energy agreements, signalling a recalibration of traditional Russian influence in the region. Afghanistan and Pakistan, both contiguous to China and maintaining robust political relations with Beijing, increasingly rely on China's diplomatic capacity to mediate regional conflicts, exemplified in interventions between Saudi Arabia and Iran, as well as in broader global crises such as Ukraine. Trilateral meetings in Islamabad have reflected the growing confidence of these countries in China's role as a stabilising actor and regional security provider.

Security Cooperation and Counter-terrorism Alignment

A significant point of convergence among Russia, China, and the Central Asian republics is the shared perception of terrorism and religious extremism as existential threats. This long-standing security concern, historically emphasised by the USA, has fostered trilateral cooperation aimed at preventing the establishment of Western military basing or the use of Central Asia as a sanctuary by armed groups such as the Afghan Resistance in Panjshir. Such alignment underscores the strategic importance of Central Asia as a geopolitical buffer zone and illustrates India's opportunity to engage with regional partners within a relatively insulated environment.

Historical and Civilisational Context

Central Asia's historic role as a nexus of Eurasian trade and cultural exchange continues to inform contemporary strategic calculations. The ancient Silk Routes facilitated the movement of people, goods, and ideas between Europe and the Far East, leaving an indelible imprint on the region's cultural, economic, and political landscape. Following the dissolution of the Soviet Union in 1991, the five Central Asian republics – Kazakhstan, Kyrgyzstan, Tajikistan, Turkmenistan, and Uzbekistan – attained independence, embarking on processes of political transformation, modernisation, and economic development. Their emergence as independent actors has intensified global and regional attention, particularly in the light of ongoing crises such as the Russia-

Ukraine war, which has amplified the geopolitical and economic salience of Central Asia.

The Russia-Ukraine conflict, which escalated in 2022, has profoundly affected the economic and political landscape of Central Asia. Energy supply chains have experienced significant disruptions, particularly given the region's historical reliance on Russian infrastructure and markets. Economic sanctions imposed on Russia by Western states have had spillover effects, creating pressures on Central Asian economies closely linked to Moscow. Conversely, the conflict has rekindled Western interest in the region, epitomised by the summit in September 2023, during which all five Central Asian heads of state convened with US President Joe Biden. This first summit-level engagement symbolises a renewed Western strategic focus, underscoring Central Asia's increasing importance in global geopolitics.

India's Strategic Stake in Chabahar Port and Connectivity

India's efforts to strengthen its influence in Central Asia are closely tied to its investment in Iran's Chabahar Port. This strategic initiative is central to India's connectivity and trade ambitions in the region. The Trump Administration's decision to modify or rescind India's sanctions waiver for the port represented a deliberate attempt to exert 'maximum pressure' on Tehran. This development threatened India's long-term investments, valued at approximately $24 million in equipment and infrastructure, and cast uncertainty over the operational viability of the International North-South Transport Corridor (INSTC). The corridor is envisioned as an alternative trade route linking India, Iran, Russia, and Europe, bypassing conventional maritime pathways.

The imposition or intensification of sanctions by the USA aligns with its broader strategic objective of constraining Iran's nuclear ambitions and regional influence. These measures also reinforce the US-Israel strategic partnership, given Israel's perception of Iran as a principal adversary. For India, such developments create a complex diplomatic scenario: maintaining strong ties with Washington while simultaneously preserving historic and strategic cooperation with Tehran requires careful navigation. The potential disruption of the Chabahar investment could compel India to explore alternative trade pathways, including routing goods via Israel or the UAE, although such alternatives may not replicate the strategic and economic advantages offered by the Chabahar corridor.

Despite these challenges, Chabahar Port has demonstrated tangible economic growth. Between 2023 and 2024, vessel traffic increased by 43 per cent, and container traffic rose by 34 per cent, reflecting the port's growing capacity as a regional trade hub. In support of this trajectory, Indian Minister of Ports, Shipping, and Waterways Sarbananda Sonowal, and Iranian Minister of Roads and Urban Development Mehrdad Bazrpash, signed a 10-year operational agreement for the port. Under this accord, India committed $120 million for infrastructure development at the Shahid Beheshti terminal and extended a $250 million line of credit to Iran. These investments are intended to facilitate trade with landlocked Afghanistan and Central Asian states, while simultaneously bypassing competing regional ports, such as China-backed Gwadar, and increasing India's geopolitical leverage.

Nonetheless, a range of obstacles persists. US-backed sanctions against Iran, including blacklisting by the Financial Action Task Force (FATF) and exclusion from the SWIFT financial system, constrain Tehran's ability to participate fully in international financial networks. Logistical delays in constructing the Chabahar-Zahedan and Rasht-Astara railway lines further challenge the realisation of India's broader connectivity objectives. Complicating the environment is China's 25-year, $400 billion partnership with Iran, raising speculation over potential Chinese investments in both Chabahar and Gwadar. At present, India's tangible investment is concentrated in the Shahid Beheshti and Shahid Kalantari terminals, highlighting both the strategic potential and the competitive pressures inherent in this critical regional infrastructure.

Tehran, despite its expectations of substantial Chinese support, has not received the level of investment or diplomatic backing it anticipated. Between 2018 and 2022, China invested only $618 million in Iranian projects, with the bulk of these funds directed towards the construction sector. By contrast, during the same period, China allocated significantly larger sums to other countries in the region: $22.5 billion to Saudi Arabia, $13 billion to Iraq, $4.6 billion to Kuwait, $1.8 billion to Qatar, $19.3 billion to the United Arab Emirates (UAE), and $2.5 billion to Oman. Even China's investment in Bahrain, a relatively small economy, exceeded twice the level of Chinese capital directed to Iran. This discrepancy highlights a strategic recalibration in Beijing's regional economic priorities, revealing that Iran, while politically significant, does not constitute the principal focus of China's Middle Eastern or Eurasian engagement strategy. Moreover, Tehran has expressed frustration with certain diplomatic positions taken by China. In a recent meeting with Arab states, China endorsed a communiqué that contested Iran's control over three small islands in the Persian Gulf, also claimed by the UAE. In response, Iran summoned the Chinese ambassador to Tehran to protest, but the Chinese Ministry of Foreign Affairs reiterated that Iran and the UAE should resolve territorial disputes through bilateral negotiations. This episode underscores the limits of Chinese support for Iran and demonstrates that Beijing is pursuing a cautious, economically-driven diplomacy rather than overtly favouring Tehran, even in matters of regional territorial disputes.

Within this context, the competition between India's Chabahar Port and China's Gwadar Port assumes particular significance. China has committed to investing $62 billion in Gwadar, reflecting its ambitions to establish a highly integrated regional logistics and trade hub. In comparison, India's investment in Chabahar remains below $500 million, reflecting a more measured, strategically calibrated approach. The projected capacities of the two ports illustrate the asymmetry in scale: by 2030, Gwadar is expected to handle approximately 400 million tons of cargo annually, whereas Chabahar's projected throughput is estimated at only 10 to 12 million tons. Despite this, the strategic importance of Chabahar for India cannot be measured merely by volume. The port's geographical location, providing a direct maritime link to Afghanistan and the Central Asian republics while bypassing Pakistan, imbues it with an inestimable value in India's long-term connectivity and regional influence strategy. Chabahar, therefore, is not merely a logistical infrastructure project; it is a critical instrument in India's broader geostrategic vision for Central Asia, linking trade, energy, and diplomatic engagement in a region where India's access is otherwise constrained.

Shaping India's Geopolitical Trajectory in Central Asia

Central Asia itself has emerged as a key geopolitical pivot in the contemporary international system. The region's significance is underscored by its location at the crossroads of Eurasia, connecting South Asia, the Middle East, and East Asia, and serving as a repository of abundant natural resources, particularly energy reserves. Major powers, including the USA, Russia, and China, actively pursue influence in the region, seeking to secure economic, political, and strategic advantages. Russia and China have long-established presences, with Moscow leveraging historical, cultural, and security ties, and Beijing pursuing extensive economic and infrastructural engagement through initiatives such as the Belt and Road Initiative (BRI). The West, and particularly the USA, has also renewed its attention towards Central Asia, recognising the region's potential as a counterbalance to Russian and Chinese influence, as evidenced by the September 2023 summit involving all five Central Asian heads of state and US President Joe Biden.

India's engagement in Central Asia has shown sustained improvement over the past decade. The establishment of strategic partnerships with individual Central Asian states reflects a nuanced approach that combines diplomacy, trade, cultural outreach, and security cooperation. Prime Minister Narendra Modi's visits to all five Central Asian countries in 2015 marked a symbolic and practical milestone in this process, reinforcing India's commitment to the region and signalling a willingness to assume a proactive role in Eurasian geopolitics. Through mechanisms such as the Connect Central Asia Policy, India seeks to strengthen bilateral and multilateral ties, foster economic integration, and build resilience against regional instability. These efforts include cooperation in counter-terrorism, energy security, education, culture, and infrastructure connectivity, all aimed at creating a durable strategic presence despite geographic constraints and competition from other major powers. India's centrality in Central Asia's evolving geopolitical architecture is further reinforced by its investment in Chabahar Port, which serves as a critical gateway to the region. By enhancing trade connectivity with Afghanistan and the Central Asian republics, Chabahar provides India with a strategic foothold in a region historically dominated by Russia and increasingly influenced by China. While Chinese investment in Gwadar dwarfs Indian expenditure at Chabahar in financial terms, India's strategic advantage lies in the port's ability to circumvent Pakistani control and directly connect to regional markets. India's diplomatic and economic engagement with the Central Asian republics is thus intrinsically linked to its ability to operationalise infrastructure projects such as Chabahar and the International North-South Transport Corridor (INSTC), ensuring access to energy, trade, and regional influence.

The broader implications of India's Central Asia policy are significant. By deepening engagement with Kazakhstan, Uzbekistan, Turkmenistan, Tajikistan, and Kyrgyzstan, India is consolidating relationships with nations that are economically dynamic, resource-rich, and strategically located. These partnerships allow India to participate in the region's energy security, counter-terrorism initiatives, and infrastructural development, while also expanding its cultural and educational influence through scholarships, capacity-building programmes, and people-to-people exchanges. India's involvement complements its long-standing strategic partnership with Russia and aligns with its desire to maintain a stable regional environment, counterbalance China's influence, and mitigate risks associated with volatility in Afghanistan and Pakistan. India's approach is carefully calibrated to maximise regional impact while maintaining positive relationships with all major powers engaged in Central Asia. Through diplomatic finesse, New Delhi has positioned itself as a constructive actor in multilateral frameworks such as the SCO, while simultaneously developing bilateral partnerships that leverage trade, energy, and cultural links. The combination of multilateral and bilateral engagement ensures that India remains relevant in a competitive environment dominated by larger powers, while creating avenues to exercise strategic influence in an area critical to regional stability and economic growth.

The emerging picture is one of a region increasingly recognised for its geostrategic and economic significance, with India steadily advancing its presence through a combination of diplomacy, investment, and connectivity initiatives. By linking Chabahar Port to the broader Central Asian region, India not only strengthens trade routes but also signals its long-term commitment to Eurasian stability and development. In this context, India's proactive engagement is likely to expand in the years ahead, solidifying its role as a trusted partner for Central Asian states and enhancing its strategic footprint in a region poised to play a central role in twenty-first century geopolitics. India's methodical approach, anchored in careful diplomacy, infrastructure development, and cultural outreach, positions it to leverage opportunities arising from both the evolving dynamics of great-power competition and the growing aspirations of Central Asian republics. This strategy, executed with patience and foresight, ensures that India's influence in Central Asia will continue to grow, translating diplomatic engagement into tangible economic, political, and strategic dividends in the years to come.

References

1. Khalid, A. (2012). *Central Asia: A New History from the Imperial Conquests to the Present.* Princeton University Press.
2. Supyaldiyarov, I. (2024). 'Charting new (old) paths: Unravelling India-Kazakhstan ties in Eurasian geopolitics.' *Electronic Journal of Social & Strategic Studies,* Special Issue, July 2024.
3. Joshi, N. (ed.). (2010). *Reconnecting India and Central Asia: Emerging security and economic dimensions.* Central Asia-Caucasus Institute & Silk Road Studies Program/Pentagon Press (Indian edition).
4. Mohan, C. R. (2025). *India and the Rebalancing of Asia* (Adelphi/Brookings/Routledge). Routledge.
5. Weitz, R. (2008). *Kazakhstan and the New International Politics of Eurasia* (Silk Road Paper). Central Asia-Caucasus Institute & Silk Road Studies Program.
6. Pradhan, R. (2022). "India-Kazakhstan energy relations.' *Energy Policy/Regional Studies Journal*, 6(2), 145–163.
7. Hunter, S. T. & Lewis, D. (eds.). (1999). *Central Asia: Political and Economic Challenges in the Post-Soviet Era.* Westview Press.

8. Sajjanhar, A. S. (2013). 'India–Kazakhstan relations: Challenges and opportunities.' *India Review*/Ministry of External Affairs Brief, 2013.
9. Olcott, M. B. (2002). *Central Asia's Second Chance.* Carnegie Endowment for International Peace.
10. Grant, B. & Mikoyan, A. (eds.). (2010). *Energy and Geopolitics in Central Asia and the Caucasus.* Routledge.
11. Vanderhill, R. (2020). 'Between the bear and the dragon: Multivectorism in Kazakhstan.' *International Affairs*, 96(4), 975–993.
12. Mohapatra, N. K. (2021). 'Geopolitical dimension of India's relations with Central Asia.' *Strategic Analysis Journal,* 45(3), 201–220.
13. Omelicheva, M. Y. (2018). 'Kazakhstan's multi-vector foreign policy and the management of great-power rivalry.' *Post-Soviet Affairs*, 34(5), 375–398.
14. Contessi, N. P. (2019). 'Taking stock of Kazakhstan's foreign policy, 1992–2019.' In *Eurasian Regional Studies* (book chapter), 2019.
15. Cornell, S. E. (2024). 'Kazakhstan and the rise of middle powers in Central Asia.' *Silk Road Studies/Central Asia Caucasus Analyst*, July 2024.
16. Shishkin, P. (2012). 'Central Asia's crisis of governance.' *Asia Policy*/Columbia Working Paper, 2012.
17. Cooley, A. (2012). *Great Games, Local Rules: The New Great Power Contest in Central Asia.* Oxford University Press.
18. Starr, S. F. (2013). *Lost Enlightenment: Central Asia's Golden Age from the Arab Conquest to Tamerlane.* Princeton University Press.
19. Laruelle, M. (2017, March). *Assessing Russia's normative agenda in Central Asia* (Bishkek Project memo). Bishkek Project/Eurasianet.
20. Cummings, S.N. (2012). *Understanding Central Asia: Politics and Contested Transformations.* Routledge.
21. Kaushiki, N. (2013). 'The New Great Game and India's Connect Central Asia Policy: Strategic Perspectives and Challenges.' *Journal of International and Area Studies,* 20(2), 83–100.
22. Frankopan, P. (2015). *The Silk Roads: A New History of the World.* Bloomsbury.

2

Analysis of Kazakhstan's Geopolitical Position

Prof. Fatima Kukeyeva

Introduction

The geopolitics of Kazakhstan is a subject of both theoretical and practical significance. Studying this topic offers insights into the country's specific characteristics and enables forecasting of processes in Kazakhstan's domestic and foreign policy. Despite its relevance, the geopolitics of Kazakhstan, as well as that of the broader Central Asian region, remains underexplored or examined only in a fragmented manner. This is largely due to Kazakhstan's unique geopolitical location at the crossroads of Europe and Asia, making it one of the most complex countries in the post-Soviet space to analyze (Brzezinski, 1997).

The complexity of such an analysis can be attributed to several factors: the complexity of regional dynamics, the rapid changes in geopolitical conditions, and the lack of a unified theoretical framework. Although Kazakhstan has a centuries-long history, including the Kazakh Khanates of the 15th century and the periods of colonisation by the Russian Empire and subsequent incorporation into the Soviet Union, it is a relatively young state in terms of independence. The lack of an extensive historical perspective, combined with the complex interplay of geopolitical interests, both from neighbouring states and from extra-regional actors, significantly complicates a deep analysis of Kazakhstan's geopolitical preferences.

The geopolitical environment in Central Asia is shaped not only by the traditional interests of neighbouring states such as Russia, China, and other Central Asian countries, but also by the involvement of external players such as the USA, the European Union, and India, all seeking to strengthen their positions in the region (Menon, 2003). These variables create a multilayered environment in which each country pursues its strategic objectives, often competing for influence, resources, and trade routes. Positioned at the centre of these processes, Kazakhstan is compelled to balance among diverse external and internal factors, making its geopolitical preferences neither obvious nor unequivocal.

One of the key reasons for the complexity of studying Kazakhstan's geopolitics lies in the unique and multifaceted regional dynamics of Central Asia, a historically and culturally rich territory that encompasses numerous civilisations and peoples. For millennia, this region has served as a crossroads of cultures, trade routes, and political interests, leaving a profound imprint on its geopolitical landscape (Mackinder, 1904). Understanding Kazakhstan's geopolitical preferences requires consideration of this historical depth.

Central Asia has long been a space of interaction between diverse cultural and civilisational influences. Since antiquity, the routes of the Great Silk Road traversed the region, facilitating not only trade flows but also the exchange of ideas and religions, including Islam, Christianity, and Buddhism. This process shaped a unique and diverse cultural and ethnic fabric, resistant to simplistic categorisations and divisions.

Moreover, Kazakhstan's geographical position grants it a strategically important role, located at the intersection of the interests of major world powers and regional actors. The country has become an arena of geopolitical influence and competition involving Russia, China, Iran, as well as the EU, the USA, and India (Kleveman, 2004). This means that Kazakhstan's geopolitics cannot be considered in isolation from broader global and regional political processes, adding further complexity to the study.

In addition, Kazakhstan's policy must take into account not only traditional historical and cultural factors, but also current challenges such as security concerns, economic integration, environmental issues and instability in neighbouring states, notably Afghanistan (ICWA, 2022). These factors influence the country's decision-making and strategic choices, making the analysis of its geopolitical preferences exceptionally complex and multidimensional.

One of the main reasons for the complexity of studying Kazakhstan's geopolitics is the rapid changes in the geopolitical configuration of the region following the collapse of the Soviet Union. This historical moment became a starting point for profound transformations in the political, economic, and social spheres, both across the post-Soviet space and in the global context (Zhiltsov, 2025). As one of the largest and most strategically important states in Central Asia, Kazakhstan found itself at the epicentre of these shifts, which complicates the development of long-term forecasts and models.

After the dissolution of the USSR, Kazakhstan faced a new reality: independence, the necessity of formulating a foreign policy in a multipolar world, and the search for optimal forms of cooperation with a range of global and regional actors, including Russia, China, the USA, and the European Union (Brzezinski, 1997). Moreover, the rapid development of integration processes, such as the Eurasian Economic Union (EAEU) and the Shanghai Cooperation Organisation (SCO), alongside the growing influence of factors such as new economic and military alliances, exerts a significant impact on the political and economic stability of the region (Zhiltsov, 2025).

The absence of a unified theoretical framework for analyzing Kazakhstan's geopolitics significantly complicates research in this field. Classical geopolitical theories, such as those of Halford Mackinder (1904), Nicholas Spykman (1944), and Zbigniew Brzezinski (1997), were developed in the context of other world regions and focused primarily on major global powers. However, their applicability to Central Asia raises questions. Kazakhstan does not constitute the classic 'Heartland' in Mackinder's interpretation, though its role as a central state at the crossroads of diverse cultures complicates the direct application of traditional approaches.

Furthermore, Central Asia has its own distinctive historical and cultural dynamics. The diversity of cultural and historical factors necessitates the development of new approaches that account for both the interaction and rivalry among these cultures. The inability to directly apply classical theories is also linked to the dynamic and volatile nature of the region's geopolitical situation (Spykman, 1944).

When developing new approaches, it is essential to examine the key features of the Republic of Kazakhstan's geopolitics. First is Kazakhstan's multi-vector foreign policy. In the 1990s, following independence, Kazakhstan's foreign policy evolved into the doctrine of 'Kazakhstan's multi-vector diplomacy,' first articulated by President Nursultan Nazarbayev in his article 'Strategy for the Formation and Development of Kazakhstan as a Sovereign State' (Nazarbayev, 1992).

By framing foreign policy as multi-vector, Nazarbayev emphasised the importance of balancing relations with major global powers while strengthening ties with regional partners. This approach sought to ensure Kazakhstan's sovereignty and create conditions for sustainable development and security in a complex geopolitical environment.

One of the main objectives of multi-vectoralism is to ensure national security and sovereignty. Kazakhstan successfully resolved all territorial issues with its neighbouring states, signing treaties on the delimitation of state borders (Ayagan, 2014). Kazakhstan has also acted as the initiator of major initiatives in international and regional security, most notably the creation of the Conference on Interaction and Confidence-Building Measures in Asia (CICA, n.d.).

Multi-vectoralism enabled Kazakhstan to pursue an independent foreign policy, establishing relations with both global and regional powers. As the Indian Council of World Affairs (2022) noted, Kazakhstan's multi-vector diplomacy has helped the state maintain balanced relations with Russia, China, the USA, and the European Union while protecting its sovereignty.

Economically, multi-vectoralism was crucial for survival during early independence. The development of oil infrastructure projects such as the Kazakhstan-China oil pipeline (Kazakhstan-China Pipeline, n.d.) strengthened export capacity and diversified trade routes. This was complemented by Kazakhstan's active participation in the CIS Free Trade Area and later the EAEU (Zhil͡tsov, 2025).

In addition, Kazakhstan's economy remains heavily dependent on commodity exports, primarily hydrocarbons (APK News, 2024). According to QazTrade (2025), raw materials made up 63.3 per cent of exports in 2024, while high value-added products accounted for only 13.5 per cent. Similarly, Inbusiness.kz reported growth trends in exports but noted continued dependence on raw materials (Tatarinova, 2024). *The Times of Central Asia* (2025) also highlighted a threefold increase in high-tech exports, signalling gradual diversification.

Investment remains concentrated in the extractive sector – 90 per cent of foreign portfolio investments in 2024 were directed there (Nurasheva et al., 2024). President Kassym-Jomart Tokayev (2023) emphasised the need for diversification, stating that Kazakhstan's development requires reducing dependence on mineral extraction.

Kazakhstan's strategic geographic location at the crossroads of Europe and Asia also defines its foreign policy and economic orientation. Dependence on oil and gas exports reinforces cooperation with major buyers such as China and Russia, which limits foreign policy flexibility. Active participation in economic alliances such as the EAEU and SCO helps expand markets but may deepen dependence on major powers (Tokayev, 2023).

Theoretical perspectives such as geopolitical orientation and state gravitational pull provide useful tools for analyzing Kazakhstan's strategic behaviour (MacDonald, 2021). Throughthis lens, Kazakhstan maintains close ties with Russia through the EAEU, with China through the Belt and Road Initiative, and with the West through the OSCE and other programs (Cooper, Higgott, & Nossal, 1993).

Positioning itself as a 'middle power,' Kazakhstan employs its gravitational pull to exert influence across Central Asia. By combining multi-vector diplomacy, strategic geography, and stable governance, Kazakhstan has established itself as a balancing actor among the world's major powers (Cooper et al., 1993). Preserving sovereignty, advancing multi-vector policy, and strengthening regional leadership remain key priorities for ensuring long-term prosperity.

References

1. APK News. (2024). Kazakhstan's economic growth remains heavily dependent on commodity exports, particularly hydrocarbons. Retrieved from [https://apk-news.kz] (https://apk-news.kz)
2. Ayagan, B. (2014, May 12). Defining the new state borders in 1990–2005 as key foundation of statehood. *The Astana Times*. [https://astanatimes.com/2014/05/defining-new-state-borders-1990-2005-key-foundation-statehood/?utm_source=chatgpt.com] (https://astanatimes.com/2014/05/defining-new-state-borders-1990-2005-key-foundation-statehood/?utm_source=chatgpt.com).
3. Brzezinski, Z. (1997). *The grand chessboard: American primacy and its geostrategic imperatives*. New York: Basic Books.
4. CICA. (n.d.). Conference on Interaction and Confidence Building Measures in Asia. Retrieved from [https://www.s-cica.org/] (https://www.s-cica.org/).
5. Cooper, A. F., Higgott, R. A., & Nossal, K. R. (1993). *Relocating middle powers: Australia and Canada in a changing world order*. Vancouver: UBC Press.
6. Indian Council of World Affairs. (2022, December 19). 'Kazakhstan's multi-vector foreign policy: Prospects and challenges.' ICWA. [https://www.icwa.in/show_content.php? lang=1 &level=3&lid=7037&ls_id=11092] (https://www.icwa.in/show_content.php?lang=1&level=3&lid=7037&ls_id=11092
7. Kazakhstan-China Pipeline. (n.d.). History. Kazakhstan-China Pipeline LLP. Retrieved September 4, 2025, from [https://www.kcp.kz/company/history?language=en#:~:text= Atasu-Alashankou%20crude%20oil%20pipeline,ever%20built%20in%20independent%20 Kazakhstan] (https://www.kcp.kz/company/history?language=en#:~:text=Atasu-Alashan kou%20crude% 20oil%20pipeline,ever%20built%20in%20independent%20Kazakhstan).

8. Kleveman, L. (2004). 'The new great game: Blood and oil in Central Asia'. London: Atlantic. [https://archive.org/details/newgreatgamebloo0000klev] (https://archive.org/details/newgreatgamebloo0000klev).
9. MacDonald, A. (2021). 'Developing a Canadian Indo-Pacific geopolitical orientation.' *Canada's Journal of Global Policy Analysis*. [https://doi.org/10.1177/00207020221083243] (https://doi.org/10.1177/00207020221083243).
10. Mackinder, H.J. (1904). 'The geographical pivot of history.' *The Geographical Journal*, 23(4), 421–437.
11. Menon, R. (2003). 'The new great game in Central Asia.' *Survival*, 45(2), 187–204. [https://doi.org/10.1080/00396330312331343255] (https://doi.org/10.1080/00396330312331343255).
12. Nazarbayev, N.A. (1992, May). 'Strategy for the formation and development of Kazakhstan as a sovereign state.' *Kazakhstanskaya Pravda*.
13. Nurasheva, K.K., Kulyanda, K. and others. (2024). 'Capital inflow and investment attractiveness of Central Asian countries (on the example of Kazakhstan).' *International Economics*, 180, 161–175. [https://doi.org/10.1016/j.inteco.2024.05.006] (https://doi.org/10.1016/j.inteco.2024.05.006).
14. QazTrade. (2025, August 26). 'The country is increasing its export potential in the new global reality. QazTrade Trade Policy Development Centre JSC. [https://qaztrade.org.kz/eng/the-country-is-increasing-its-export-potential-in-the-new-global-reality] (https://qaztrade.org.kz/eng/the-country-is-increasing-its-export-potential-in-the-new-global-reality).
15. Spykman, N.J. (1944). *The geography of the peace*. New York: Harcourt, Brace and Company.
16. Tatarinova, K. (2024). 'Kazakhstan's export and import: Trends and forecasts.' Inbusiness.kz. Retrieved from [https://inbusiness.kz/ru/news/eksport-i-import-kazahstana-trendy-i-prognozy] (https://inbusiness.kz/ru/news/eksport-i-import-kazahstana-trendy-i-prognozy).
17. *Times of Central Asia*. (2025, September 4). 'What drives Kazakhstan's threefold growth in high-tech exports.' [https://timesca.com/what-drives-kazakhstans-threefold-growth-in-high-tech-exports/] (https://timesca.com/what-drives-kazakhstans-threefold-growth-in-high-tech-exports/).
18. Tokayev, K.-J. (2023, September 1). Address by the President of the Republic of Kazakhstan Kassym-Jomart Tokayev to the people of Kazakhstan. Akorda. [https://www.akorda.kz] (https://www.akorda.kz).
19. Tokayev, K.-J. (2023, September 1). Economic course of a Just Kazakhstan [State-of-the-Nation Address]. Akorda. [https://www.akorda.kz/en/president-kassym-jomart-tokayevs-state-of-the-nation-address-economic-course-of-a-just-kazakhstan-283243] (https://www.akorda.kz/en/president-kassym-jomart-tokayevs-state-of-the-nation-address-economic-course-of-a-just-kazakhstan-283243).
20. Zhilt͡sov, S.S.(2025) 'Eurasian integration: Analysis of key documents of the member states of the integration association.' *Post-Soviet Issues*, 12(2), 135–150. [https://doi.org/10.24975/2313-8920-2025-12-2-135-150] (https://doi.org/10.24975/2313-8920-2025-12-2-135-150).

3

Kazakhstan's Relations with Global Powers and Regional Actors

Prof. Fatima Kukeyeva

Introduction

In the context of a rapidly evolving global landscape, Kazakhstan seeks to adapt its foreign policy to ensure sustainable development and to strengthen its role on the international stage. The concept of multi-vector diplomacy, which remains a cornerstone of the country's foreign policy, entails diversification of international partnerships and the maintenance of balanced relations with key global and regional actors (Republic of Kazakhstan, 2020). Within this framework, particular importance is attached to the Central Asian, American, European, Russian and Chinese vectors of Kazakhstan's foreign policy (Republic of Kazakhstan, 2020).

The Central Asian Vector of Kazakhstan's Foreign Policy

The Foreign Policy Concept of the Republic of Kazakhstan for 2020-2030 marks a shift from a predominantly country-specific to a more regionally oriented approach (Republic of Kazakhstan, 2020). Kazakhstan positions itself as a regional leader, setting certain standards and a pace for the development of 'Central Asia 2.0,' without seeking a dominant role (Akorda, 2024). Astana's policy aimed at enhancing cooperation within the region is shaped by both internal and external economic and political factors. This strategy is facilitated by the open nature of Kazakhstan's economy and its integration into the global economic system at various and interconnected levels: intra-regional cooperation (deepening ties with the five Central Asian states), inter-regional engagement (cooperation between the region and its neighbours), and global economic integration (embedding the region and its surroundings into the world economic system) (Digital Kazakhstan, n.d.; AIFC, 2024).

Deepening Ties with the Five Central Asian States: Kazakhstan consistently strengthens cooperation with the states of Central Asia, Uzbekistan, Kyrgyzstan, Tajikistan, Turkmenistan, and to a more limited extent, Afghanistan. These relations span a broad range of areas, including trade and economic cooperation, transport connectivity, water and energy collaboration, as well as regional security (Akorda, 2024; Ministry of Foreign Affairs of the Republic of Kazakhstan, 2024).

Trade and Economic Cooperation: Kazakhstan is the largest economic actor in Central Asia, and its trade ties with neighbouring states have been growing steadily (24.kz, 2025). For example, trade turnover between Kazakhstan and Uzbekistan has been increasing in recent years, exceeding USD 5 billion, with both countries setting a target to raise this figure to USD 10 billion (Timesca, 2024). Kazakhstan also plays a key role in ensuring regional food security by supplying grain, flour, and other agricultural products to Kyrgyzstan, Tajikistan, and Uzbekistan (KAZAKH INVEST, 2024).

Transport and Logistics: The development of transport infrastructure is a crucial element of cooperation. Kazakhstan actively participates in the construction and modernisation of regional transport corridors (AIFC, 2024). Key projects include: the Western China-Western Europe Road and rail corridor, which facilitates seamless trade within the region (Khorgos, 2017); the Khorgos International Centre for Boundary Cooperation, which plays a vital role in goods transit between China and Central Asia (Khorgos, 2017); and modernisation of border checkpoints such as the 'Saryagash' railway crossing (UzDaily, n.d.). Kazakhstan's investments in transit infrastructure support regional connectivity and position the country as a logistics hub (Knyazeva, 2024; Avdaliani, 2024).

Water and Energy Cooperation: Joint management of water resources is one of the key issues in Kazakhstan's relations with its neighbours, particularly Kyrgyzstan and Tajikistan, which possess significant hydropower reserves. Kazakhstan advocates stronger coordination within international frameworks such as the Interstate Commission for Water Coordination to ensure equitable distribution of the Syr Darya and Amu Darya River resources (Guo et al., 2016). Cooperation with Uzbekistan in modernising irrigation systems is also essential (Guo et al., 2016).

Regional Security and Stability: Kazakhstan plays an active role in promoting regional stability, particularly in the light of challenges related to Afghanistan. In this regard, Astana participates in programs to provide food and humanitarian aid to Kabul, as well as in joint initiatives to combat extremism and cross-border crime within the CSTO and SCO frameworks (Ministry of Foreign Affairs of the Republic of Kazakhstan, 2024; Avesta, 2024).

Political Coordination and Regional Consolidation: Kazakhstan actively promotes regional dialogue platforms, such as Consultative Meetings of Central Asian Heads of State. These meetings help build trust among countries, advance joint economic projects, and coordinate positions on key issues, including trade, ecology, and security (Akorda, 2024). Thus, Kazakhstan plays a pivotal role in shaping a new model of regional cooperation – 'Central Asia 2.0' – in which the states of the region aim for greater autonomy, deeper economic integration and enhanced influence on the international stage (Republic of Kazakhstan, 2020).

Kazakhstan's Role in Cooperation between Central Asia and its Neighbours

Kazakhstan plays a pivotal role in advancing cooperation between Central Asian states and their neighbouring partners, including China, Russia, the Caspian littoral states, South Asia, and the European Union. This engagement is rooted in the country's multi-vector foreign policy, which is oriented towards strengthening economic linkages, developing transport connectivity and coordinating on security and sustainable development issues (Republic of Kazakhstan, 2020; EU & Kazakhstan, 2015).

Kazakhstan as a Transport and Logistics Hub: Kazakhstan serves as the infrastructural backbone for integrating Central Asia into global markets (AIFC, 2024).

Key strategic routes include the Trans-Caspian International Transport Route (TITR) which provides a strategic pathway for Central Asian exports to Europe via the Caspian Sea and the South Caucasus (Knyazeva, 2024; Avdaliani, 2024); the China-Kazakhstan-Europe corridor as part of the Belt and Road Initiative (BRI) (Tokayev, 2025; KAZAKH INVEST, 2024); and the Kazakhstan-Turkmenistan-Iran-Turkey railway connecting Central Asia to the Persian Gulf and the Mediterranean (AIFC, 2024).

Economic Cooperation and Trade Initiatives: Kazakhstan acts as the principal economic bridge between Central Asia and external partners.

Kazakhstan-China: Bilateral trade exceeded $30 billion in 2024, with Kazakhstan serving as a leading supplier of oil, uranium, and agricultural products to China. Infrastructure modernisation projects are being implemented under the BRI framework agreements (Forbes.kz, 2024; KAZAKH INVEST, 2024).

Kazakhstan-Russiaties continue via EAEU mechanisms while Kazakhstan seeks to channel Russian investments regionally (AFK Analytical Centre, 2024; Russian International Affairs Council, 2022).

Kazakhstan-EU: Within the framework of the Enhanced Partnership and Cooperation Agreement (EPCA), Kazakhstan strengthens trade ties between the EU and Central Asia, particularly in energy and critical raw materials (uranium, rare earth metals). (European Union & Republic of Kazakhstan, 2015; Gusseinov, 2024).

Kazakhstan-South Asia: Kazakhstan is expanding cooperation with Pakistan, India, and Afghanistan, using Iranian ports to access the Indian Ocean. Projects include uranium and agricultural exports to India.

Water and Energy Cooperation: Kazakhstan is engaged in addressing Central Asia's water challenges in coordination with neighbouring states, including transboundary river issues with China (Guo et al., 2016), and in joint energy projects with Uzbekistan and Kyrgyzstan aimed at balancing water and energy needs (UNECE, 2025).

Regional Security and Diplomatic Coordination: Kazakhstan actively contributes to regional security arrangements within the SCO on counter-terrorism, drug-trafficking prevention, and cybersecurity (Ministry of Foreign Affairs of the Republic of Kazakhstan, 2024). Within the CSTO, Kazakhstan participates in collective security efforts while balancing domestic political sensitivities (Republic of Kazakhstan, 2020). Through 'Central Asia +' platforms (C5+1, B5+1) and engagement with the EU, China, India, and Gulf states, Kazakhstan fosters multilateral cooperation to address security, economic, and sustainable development agendas (U.S. Embassy in Kazakhstan, 2025; Atameken, n.d.; Associated Press, 2025).

Kazakhstan's Role in Integrating Central Asia and its Surroundings into the Global Economic Space: Kazakhstan plays a central role in promoting the integration of Central Asia and its neighbouring regions into the global economy, acting as the region's transport, trade, and investment hub (AIFC, 2024; UNECE, 2025). Amid growing geopolitical turbulence, Kazakhstan has strengthened its position as a mediator between different economic blocs, creating opportunities for sustainable regional growth and inclusion in global value chains (Republic of Kazakhstan, 2020; Zipatolla, 2025).

Kazakhstan as a Transit Hub for Central Asia: The development of transport and logistics routes connecting Central Asia to world markets is a major driver of regional integration. TITR offers an alternative to Russian transit corridors while BRI land routes channel much China-Europe overland trade through Kazakhstan (Knyazeva, 2024; Tokayev, 2025). Kazakhstan has also explored rail corridors through Iran to access the Indian Ocean and South Asian markets (AIFC, 2024).

Central Asian Energy Hub: Kazakhstan exports electricity and hydrocarbons to China, Uzbekistan, Kyrgyzstan, Russia, and EU member-states, facilitating integration into global energy markets (UNECE, 2025; European Union & Republic of Kazakhstan, 2015). Energy cooperation and export route diversification remain high priorities (U.S. Department of State, 2019).

Kazakhstan as an Investment Magnet in Central Asia: Kazakhstan not only attracts foreign investment but also channels it into neighbouring countries via FDI and state-led initiatives such as Kazakh Invest and investment funds focused on infrastructure, extractives, and agriculture (KAZAKH INVEST, 2024; AFK Analytical Centre, 2024). In 2022, Kazakhstan led the region in attracting FDI and launched funds to support regional cooperation (AFK Analytical Centre, 2022).

Integrating Central Asia into the International Trading System: Kazakhstan advances regional interests in the WTO, EAEU, and other international organisations, facilitating market access for Central Asian goods and integrating agricultural and mineral exports into global supply chains (Republic of Kazakhstan, 2020; U.S. Department of State, 2019).

Technological and Digital Transformation of the Region: Kazakhstan is emerging as an innovation hub for the region with initiatives such as Astana Hub and the Digital Kazakhstan program that support start-ups and digital transformation (Digital Kazakhstan, n.d.; AIFC, 2024). Partnerships with global tech firms and targeted AI and blockchain projects are also underway (KAZAKH INVEST, 2024; Vakhabov, 2025).

Kazakhstan as a Centre of Regional Diplomacy and Economic Coordination: Kazakhstan promotes initiatives that strengthen cooperation between Central Asia and leading global economic centres, including the C5+1 format with the USA, the EU's New Strategy for Central Asia, and engagement via SCO mechanisms (U.S. Embassy in Kazakhstan, 2025; European Union, 2024; Ministry of Foreign Affairs of the Republic of Kazakhstan, 2024).

Owing to its strategic geography, economic capacity, and active foreign policy, Kazakhstan functions as a bridge between Central Asia and its surrounding regions. By developing transport corridors, deepening economic cooperation, and engaging in diplomatic mediation, Kazakhstan contributes to transforming the region into an increasingly autonomous and influential actor on the global stage (Republic of Kazakhstan, 2020; UNECE, 2025).

The American Vector of Kazakhstan's Foreign Policy

The development of the expanded partnership between Kazakhstan and the USA is shaped by intensifying rivalry among global powers in Central Asia and by shifts in U.S. priorities at both regional and global levels (U.S. Department of State, 2019; U.S. Embassy in Kazakhstan, 2025). The C5+1 and B5+1 formats, along with the *U.S. Strategy for Central Asia 2019–2025*, serve as important tools that allow Kazakhstan to adapt to emerging challenges and leverage new opportunities for growth (U.S. Department of State, 2019; U.S. Embassy in Kazakhstan, 2025). Cooperation with the U.S. plays a critical role in modernising Kazakhstan's economy and advancing the country's digitalisation strategy. Kazakhstan's participation in Western scientific and technological initiatives accelerates digital transformation and facilitates integration into the global innovation ecosystem (KAZAKH INVEST, 2024; U.S. Department of State, 2019). Moreover, engagement with the USA is vital for regional and international security, enhancing national capabilities to counter cyber threats and terrorism (U.S. Department of State, 2019).

Evolution of Kazakhstan-USA Partnership: Bilateral relations have evolved from a strategic partnership to expanded strategic cooperation covering economic, security, and political dimensions (U.S. Department of State, 2019). Between 2010 and 2014, the U.S. reduced its regional presence, but later adjustments reinvigorated U.S. engagement through formats such as C5+1 (U.S. Department of State, 2019; U.S. Embassy in Kazakhstan, 2025).

Energy Cooperation: Energy remains central to U.S.-Kazakhstan interaction, with U.S. support for diversification of export routes, renewable energy, and critical mineral development. The Bureau of Energy Resources (ENR) cooperation, discussions on Trans-Caspian corridors, and U.S. investments in critical minerals underpin this area (U.S. Department of State, 2019; Geology.kz, 2024).

Critical Minerals Development: U.S. companies and institutions have stepped up activities in Kazakhstan's mining sector, supporting exploration and extraction of minerals critical to high-tech industries and renewable energy (Geology.kz, 2024). Joint initiatives with the USGS and private investment align with broader G7 objectives to reduce dependence on single suppliers (Geology.kz, 2024).

B5+1 and Economic Cooperation: The B5+1 mechanism aims to reduce barriers between Central Asian businesses and U.S. markets, fostering integration into global supply chains (Atameken, n.d.; U.S. Embassy in Kazakhstan, 2025). In 2025, reports indicated that the USA had become one of Kazakhstan's largest investors, reflecting expanding American interests in mineral, financial, education, and technology sectors (24.kz, 2025).

Geopolitical Context: U.S. engagement should be considered alongside China's and Russia's regional initiatives; Central Asian states remain shaped by external competition, and Kazakhstan uses multi-vector diplomacy to manage these pressures (Republic of Kazakhstan, 2020; Bittar, 2017).

Kazakhstan-U.S. relations represent an expanded strategic partnership across diplomacy, economics, security, science, and education but remain more limited in scale compared with the Russian and Chinese vectors. The C5+1 format offers a durable mechanism for engagement and a platform for future cooperation on technology and sustainable development (U.S. Department of State, 2019; U.S. Embassy in Kazakhstan, 2025).

Cooperation between the Republic of Kazakhstan and the European Union in the Context of the New Geopolitics

Relations between Kazakhstan and the EU develop within the *Enhanced Partnership and Cooperation Agreement* (EPCA) signed in 2015, which forms the legal and institutional basis for expanding trade, investment, and political dialogue (European Union & Republic of Kazakhstan, 2015). Despite active EU projects, the EU's geopolitical influence in Central Asia remains more limited than that of Russia or China because of remoteness, regulatory differences, and competing priorities (Gusseinov, 2024; Anceschi, 2024).

Trade: Although China became Kazakhstan's largest trading partner in recent years, the EU continues to be a major trade and investment partner – particularly for energy and critical raw materials such as uranium (European Union & Republic of Kazakhstan, 2015; Euronews, 2025).

Energy Cooperation: Energy cooperation was historically central to EU-Kazakhstan ties, with Europe absorbing a large share of Kazakh oil and uranium prior to recent global shifts; leading European firms retained stakes in Kazakh hydrocarbon projects (European Union & Republic of Kazakhstan, 2015; Reuters, 2015).

Connectivity and Strategic Initiatives: Concern about expanding Chinese influence has prompted the EU to propose Global Gateway as a sustainable alternative to the Belt and Road Initiative. Kazakhstan's transit potential means it is strategically important to both initiatives (European Union, 2024; Zipatolla, 2025).

The EU-Kazakhstan relationship is pragmatic and centred on investment, trade diversification, green energy, and standards transfer; the EPCA and EU programs such as Global Gateway provide mechanisms for deepening cooperation (European Union & Republic of Kazakhstan, 2015; European Union, 2024).

The Russian Vector in Kazakhstan's Foreign Policy

Russia remains a central pillar of Kazakhstan's foreign policy due to geography, history, economic ties, and cultural links (Republic of Kazakhstan, 2020; Russian International Affairs Council, 2022). Kazakhstan pursues close cooperation with a degree of distance to avoid excessive dependence on Moscow (Republic of Kazakhstan, 2020).

EAEU and Economic Dependence: Membership in the Eurasian Economic Union offers Kazakhstan market access and investment linkages but also creates asymmetries – e.g., trade imbalances and logistical reliance on Russian infrastructure (AFK Analytical Centre, 2024; AFK Analytical Centre, 2022). Approximately 91 per cent of Kazakhstan's oil exports transit via the Caspian Pipeline Consortium route to Novorossiysk, illustrating logistical reliance that exposes Kazakhstan to external disruptions (AFK Analytical Centre, 2024).

Impact of Sanctions: Western sanctions on Russia have disrupted production chains and access to machinery and components that used to flow through Russia, affecting Kazakhstan's industrial sectors and GDP growth projections (Moody's; Renaissance Capital cited in AFK Analytical Centre, 2022; AFK Analytical Centre, 2024).

Allied Relations and Security: Kazakhstan's participation in the CSTO and other security frameworks reflects continuing defence ties with Russia, but domestic debates question whether such arrangements constrain Kazakh sovereignty (Republic of Kazakhstan, 2020; Svoboda, 2022). Notably, Kazakhstan's refusal to recognise the self-proclaimed DNR and LNR underscored a commitment to international law and independent policymaking (Svoboda, 2022).

Contemporary Kazakhstan-Russia relations are reshaped by sanctions, geopolitical shifts, and the imperative for Kazakhstan to diversify its external economic ties while preserving regional stability and balanced relations with other global powers (Republic of Kazakhstan, 2020; RIAC, 2022).

The Chinese Vector of Kazakhstan's Foreign Policy

In the 2020-2030 Foreign Policy Concept, Kazakhstan defines relations with China as a 'comprehensive strategic partnership,' actively attracting Chinese investment and participating in joint infrastructure and industrial projects (Republic of Kazakhstan, 2020; Akorda, 2019). Since 2022, China's role in Central Asia has grown, reflected in intensified BRI activity and SCO cooperation (China Today, 2022; Avesta, 2024).

Political Dimension: Kazakhstan-China relations promote regional stability and integration favourable to China's border security goals (Ministry of Foreign Affairs of the Republic of Kazakhstan, 2024; Bittar, 2017).

Economic Dimension: China's engagement aims to unlock regional potential through bilateral trade, investment, and integration with Kazakhstan's NurlyZhol program and BRI (Tokayev, 2025; KAZAKH INVEST, 2024). Large commercial packages and investment pledges have been reported in recent years (KAZAKH INVEST, 2024; Reuters, 2015).

Challenges and Constraints: Cooperation is constrained by domestic anti-Chinese sentiment, transboundary water disputes, migration concerns, and risks of overdependence on Chinese investment – with public debates about labour flows and environmental impacts (Woods & Baker, 2022; Eco-Business, 2020).

Chinese Model and Influence: China's development model draws interest as a pragmatic reference for growth and stability, but Moscow's weakening or sanctions-induced pressures could accelerate China's economic predominance – raising strategic balance concerns for Kazakhstan (Bittar, 2017; China Today, 2022).

Integration with the BRI: Kazakhstan's geographic role and infrastructural projects make it a key BRI partner; the NurlyZhol program aligns with BRI goals and has attracted major Chinese investments (KAZAKH INVEST, 2024; Khorgos, 2017).

Key Areas of Cooperation and Risks: Transit corridor construction, joint industrial projects, high-tech cooperation, and agro-industrial investments have all expanded (KAZAKH INVEST, 2024; Vakhabov, 2025). Yet concerns remain about technology transfer, employment of local labour, and environmental safeguards; policy recommendations urge shifting from a 'resources-for-investment' model to 'market access-for-technology and training' models and stronger regulation of foreign participation (KAZAKH INVEST, 2024; Woods & Baker, 2022).

Conclusion

While China provides investment and connectivity benefits, Kazakhstan seeks to mitigate long-term risks through regulatory measures ensuring technology transfer, local employment, and environmental protection (Republic of Kazakhstan, 2020; KAZAKH INVEST, 2024). Kazakhstan positions itself as a leader setting the standards and pace of development in Central Asia, aiming to strengthen regional cooperation and address shared challenges while developing partnerships with the USA, European Union, Russia, and China. Adhering to the principle of multi-vector diplomacy, Kazakhstan strives to consolidate its international position by fostering cooperation with a diverse range of global and regional actors and by balancing economic opportunity with sovereignty, environmental sustainability, and technological development (Republic of Kazakhstan, 2020; UNECE, 2025; KAZAKH INVEST, 2024).

References

1. Akorda. (n.d.). On the Foreign Policy Concept of the Republic of Kazakhstan for 2020-2030. [https://www.akorda.kz/ru/legal_acts/decrees/o-koncepcii-vneshnei-politiki-respubliki-kazahstan-na-2020-2030-gody] (https://www.akorda.kz/ru/legal_acts/decrees/o-koncepcii-vneshnei-politiki-respubliki-kazahstan-na-2020-2030-gody)
2. TimesCA. (2024). 'Kazakhstan and Uzbekistan to increase bilateral trade.' [https://timesca.com/kazakhstan-and-uzbekistan-to-increase-bilateral-trade/?utm_source=chatgpt.com] (https://timesca.com/kazakhstan-and-uzbekistan-to-increase-bilateral-trade/?utm_source=chat gpt.com)
3. Khorgos. (2017, January 11). MTK 'Western China-Western Europe'. [https://khorgos.biz/ru/info/article/74] (https://khorgos.biz/ru/info/article/74)
4. UzDaily. (n.d.). On the modernization of the 'Saryagash' railway crossing. [https://www.uzdaily.uz/ru/na-granitse-kazakhstana-i-uzbekistana-modernizirovali-zhd-perekhod-saryagash/] (https://www.uzdaily.uz/ru/na-granitse-kazakhstana-i-uzbekistana-mod ernizirovali-zhd-perekhod-saryagash/)
5. Akorda. (2024, August 9). Under the chairmanship of Kassym-Jomart Tokayev, the VI Consultative Meeting of Central Asian Heads of State took place. [https://www.akorda.kz/ru/ pod-predsedatelstvom-kasym-zhomarta-tokaeva-sostoyalas-vi-konsultativnaya-vstrecha-glav-gosudarstv-centralnoy-azii-971327] (https://www.akorda.kz/ru/pod-predsedatelstvom-kasym-zhomarta-tokaeva-sostoyalas-vi-konsultativnaya-vstrecha-glav-gosudarstv-centralnoy-azii-971327).

6. AIFC. (2024). Transport and logistics sector of Kazakhstan (April 2024). [https://aifc.kz/wp-content/uploads/2024/07/2.2-transportno-logisticheskaya-otrasl-kazahstana-aprel-2024.pdf] (https://aifc.kz/wp-content/uploads/2024/07/2.2-transportno-logisticheskaya-otrasl-kazahstana-aprel-2024.pdf).
7. Knyazeva, T. (2024, May 27). 'Kazakhstan's role in shaping Trans-Caspian transport route.' *The Astana Times*. [https://astanatimes.com/2024/05/kazakhstans-role-in-shaping-trans-caspian-transport-route/] (https://astanatimes.com/2024/05/kazakhstans-role-in-shaping-trans-caspian-transport-route/).
8. Avdaliani, E. (2024, May 30). 'Europe's big bet on the Trans-Caspian transport corridor.' *Diplomatic Courier*. [https://www.diplomaticourier.com/posts/europes-big-bet-on-the-trans-caspian-transport-corridor---emil-avdaliani] (https://www.diplomaticourier.com/posts/europes-big-bet-on-the-trans-caspian-transport-corridor---emil-avdaliani).
9. Forbes.kz. (2024). 'Kazakhstan-China trade turnover increased by 30% in a year.' [https://for bes.kz/articles/tovarooborot_mejdu_kazahstanom_i_kitaem_vyiros_na_30_za_god] (https://for bes.kz/articles/tovarooborot_mejdu_kazahstanom_i_kitaem_vyiros_na_30_za_god).
10. Guo, L., Zhou, H., Xia, Z., & Huang, F. (2016). 'Evolution, opportunity and challenges of transboundary water and energy problems in Central Asia.' *Springer Plus*, 5(1), 1918. [https://doi.org/10.1186/s40064-016-3588] (https://doi.org/10.1186/s40064-016-3588).
11. Vakhabov, J. (2025, June 17). 'Connectivity impulse.' *China Daily*. [https://www.china daily.com.cn/a/202506/17/WS6850aabca310a04af22c69b5.html] (https://www.chinadaily.com.cn/a/202506/17/WS6850aabca310a04af22c69b5.html).
12. Azertag. (2025, April 1). Kassym-Jomart Tokayev: Kazakhstan ensures 90% of overland trade between Europe and China. [https://azertag.az/ru/xeber/kasym_zhomart_ tokaev_ kazahstan_ obespechivaet_90_procentov_suhoputnoi_torgovli_mezhdu_evropoi_i_kitaem-3480979] (https://azertag.az/ru/xeber/kasym_zhomart_tokaev_kazahstan_obespechivaet_90_procentov_suhoputnoi_torgovli_mezhdu_evropoi_i_kitaem-3480979).
13. United Nations Economic Commission for Europe (UNECE). (2025). Energy policy brief: Kazakhstan. [https://unece.org/sites/default/files/2025-01/Energy%20Connectivity-Kazakh stan%20Policy%20Brief.pdf] (https://unece.org/sites/default/files/2025-01/Energy%20Con nectivity-Kazakhstan%20Policy%20Brief.pdf).
14. Zipatolla, S. (2025, May). Rethinking EU strategy in Central Asia: Achieving long-term success for the Middle Corridor (DGAP Policy Brief No. 12). German Council on Foreign Relations (DGAP). [https://dgap.org/en/research/publications/rethinking-eu-strategy-central-asia] (https://dgap.org/en/research/publications/rethinking-eu-strategy-central-asia).
15. Digital Kazakhstan. (n.d.). Digital Kazakhstan program. [https://www.gov.kz/memleket/entities/mdai/activities/14764?lang=ru] (https://www.gov.kz/memleket/entities/mdai/activities/14764?lang=ru).
16. U.S. Embassy and Consulate in Kazakhstan. (2025). C5+1. [https://kz.usembassy.gov/ru/c51/] (https://kz.usembassy.gov/ru/c51/).
17. Associated Press. (2025, April 4). 'EU leaders hold their first summit with Central Asian states.' *AP News*. [https://apnews.com/article/uzbekistan-central-asia-eu-samarkand-summit-2a3b1408 8999fe72eb60e1b4417fac60] (https://apnews.com/article/uzbekistan-central-asia-eu-samarkan d-summit-2a3b14088999fe72eb60e1b4417fac60).
18. Ministry of Foreign Affairs of the Republic of Kazakhstan. (2024, October 4). Opredsedatel'stveRespubliki Kazakhstan v Shankhaiskoiorganizatsiisotrudnichestva. [https://www.gov.kz/memleket/entities/mfa-vilnius/press/news/details/615933?lang=ru] (https://www.gov.kz/memleket/entities/mfa-vilnius/press/news/details/615933?lang=ru).
19. Atameken. (n.d.). B5+1 removes barriers between Central Asian and U.S. businesses. [https://atameken.kz/ru/news/51579-b--razrushaet-bar-ery-mezhdu-biznesom-central-noj-

azii-i-ssha] (https://atameken.kz/ru/news/51579-b--razrushaet-bar-ery-mezhdu-biznesom-central-noj-azii-i-ssha).

20. U.S. Department of State. (2019). U.S. Strategy for Central Asia 2019–2025: Advancing sovereignty and economic prosperity. [https://kz.usembassy.gov/u-s-strategy-for-central-asia-2019-2025-advancing-sovereignty-and-economic-prosperity] (https://kz.usembassy.gov/u-s-strategy-for-central-asia-2019-2025-advancing-sovereignty-and-economic-prosperity).
21. Geology.kz. (2024, July 18). Kazakhstan and the U.S. cooperate on prospective rare metals exploration. [https://geology.kz/ru/news/1776] (https://geology.kz/ru/news/1776).
22. Geology.kz. (2024, July 18). Kazakhstan and the U.S. cooperate on prospective rare metals exploration. [https://geology.kz/ru/news/1776] (https://geology.kz/ru/news/1776).
23. Geology.kz. (2025, January 20).U.S.–One of Kazakhstan's largest trading partners. [https://24.kz/ru/news/economyc/690865-ssha-odin-iz-krupnejshikh-torgovykh-partnerov-kazakhstana] (https://24.kz/ru/news/economyc/690865-ssha-odin-iz-krupnejshikh-torgovykh-partnerov-kazakhstana).
24. European Union & Republic of Kazakhstan. (2015). 'Enhanced Partnership and Cooperation Agreement between the European Union and its Member-States, of the one part, and the Republic of Kazakhstan, of the other part. *Official Journal of the European Union.* [https://assets.publishing.service.gov.uk/media/5a74a402e5274a56317a5f30/EU.2.2016_Kaza_WEB.pd] (https://assets.publishing.service.gov.uk/media/5a74a402e5274a56317a5f30/EU. 2.2016_Kaza_WEB.pd).
25. Gusseinov, E. (2024, May 23). 'Evaluating EU's Central Asia strategy: Five-year mark and future expectations.' *The Astana Times.* [https://astanatimes.com/2024/05/evaluating-eus-central-asia-strategy-five-year-mark-and-future-expectations/?utm_source=chatgpt.com] (https://astanatimes.com/2024/05/evaluating-eus-central-asia-strategy-five-year-mark-and-future-expectations/?utm_source=chatgpt.com).
26. Anceschi, N. (2024). 'Central Asia in the EU focus: Strategies of the union's largest economies in the region.' *Eurasia Today.* [https://eurasiatoday.ru/tsentralnaya-aziya-v-fokuse-es-strategii-krupnejshih-ekonomik-evrosoyuza-v-regione/] (https://eurasiatoday.ru/tsentralnaya-aziya-v-fokuse-es-strategii-krupnejshih-ekonomik-evrosoyuza-v-regione/).
27. Euronews Russia. (2025, June 3). Kazakhstan strengthens its position in the global market through oil production growth. [https://ru.euronews.com/business/2025/06/03/kazahstan-ukreplyaet-svoi-pozicii-na-mirovom-rynke-rostom-dobychi-nefti] (https://ru.euronews.com/business/2025/06/03/kazahstan-ukreplyaet-svoi-pozicii-na-mirovom-rynke-rostom-dobychi-nefti).
28. European Union. (2024, July 2). EU Global Gateway in Central Asia: Investment, competitiveness and trade conference. (Accessed November 21, 2024). [https://astana.embaix adaportugal.mne.gov.pt/ru/o-] (https://astana.embaixadaportugal.mne.gov.pt/ru/o-).
29. AFK Analytical Centre. (2024). Trade imbalance with Russia expanded by nearly one-third in 2024. [https://afk.kz/ru/analytics/prochie-analiticheskie-materialyi/obzor-tovarooborota-rk-rf. html] (https://afk.kz/ru/analytics/prochie-analiticheskie-materialyi/obzor-tovarooborota-rk-rf.html).
30. AFK Analytical Centre. (2022). *'Renaissance Capital' retains Kazakhstan's 2022 GDP growth forecast at 5.3%*. [https://afk.kz/ru/analytics/prochie-analiticheskie-materialyi/obzor-tovaroo borota-rk-rf.html] (https://afk.kz/ru/analytics/prochie-analiticheskie-materialyi/obzor-tovaroo borota-rk-rf.html)
31. Republic of Kazakhstan. (2020, March 6). On the concept of foreign policy of the Republic of Kazakhstan for 2020–2030 (Decree No. 280). Presidential Executive Office of the Republic of Kazakhstan.

32. Russian International Affairs Council (RIAC). (2022). Russia and Kazakhstan: Is it difficult to be allies in the modern world? RIAC – Analytics and Comments. [https://russiancouncil.ru/ analytics-and-comments/rossiya-i-kazakhstan-slozhno-li-byt-soyuznikami-v-sovremennom-mire] (https://russiancouncil.ru/analytics-and-comments/rossiya-i-kazakhstan-slozhno-li-byt-soyuznikami-v-sovremennom-mire).
33. Radio Svoboda. (2022, June 17). Tokayev: Kazakhstan ne priznaet 'kvazigosudarstvennye' 'DNR' i 'LNR'. [https://www.svoboda.org/a/tokaev-kazahstan-ne-priznaet-kvazigosudarstve nnye-dnr-i-lnr-/31903338.html] (https://www.svoboda.org/a/tokaev-kazahstan-ne-priznaet-kvazigosudarstvennye-dnr-i-lnr-/31903338.html).
34. China Today. (2022, October 22). Role of Kazakhstan in implementing the Belt and Road Initiative: Achievements and prospects. [http://www.kitaichina.com/rxinwen/202410/ t20241022_800381245.html] (http://www.kitaichina.com/rxinwen/202410/t20241022_800381245.html).
35. Bittar, Y. (2017). China's expanding energy and geopolitical linkages with Central Asia and Russia: Implications for businesses and governments (Policy Paper PP-17/09). OCP Policy Centre. [https://www.policycenter.ma/sites/default/files/OCPPC-PP1709_0.pdf] (https://www. policycenter.ma/sites/default/files/OCPPC-PP1709_0.pdf).
36. Akorda. (2019, September 11). Meeting with representatives of the Chinese business community. [https://www.akorda.kz/ru/events/international_community/foreign_visits/kasym-zhomart-tokaev-vstretilsya-s-predstavitelyami-delovyh-krugov-knr?utm_source=chatgpt.com] (https://www.akorda.kz/ru/events/international_community/foreign_visits/kasym-zhomart-tokaev-vstretilsya-s-predstavitelyami-delovyh-krugov-knr?utm_source=chatgpt.com).
37. Bittar, Y. (2017). China's expanding energy and geopolitical linkages with Central Asia and Russia: Implications for businesses and governments (Policy Paper PP-17/09). OCP Policy Centre. [https://www.policycenter.ma/sites/default/files/OCPPC-PP1709_0.pdf] (https://www. policycenter.ma/sites/default/files/OCPPC-PP1709_0.pdf).
38. Avesta. (2024, July 2). China-Kazakhstan partnership elevates SCO cooperation to a new level. [https://avesta.tj/2024/07/02/partnerstvo-kitaya-i-kazahstana-vyvodit-sotrudnichestvo-v-ramkah-shos-na-novyj-uroven/?utm_source=chatgpt.com] (https://avesta.tj/2024/07/02/partnerstvo-kitaya-i-kazahstana-vyvodit-sotrudnichestvo-v-ramka h-shos-na-novyj-uroven/?utm_source=chatgpt.com).
39. Reuters. (2015, September 1). Kazakh leader says $23 billion in economic deals agreed with China. [https://www.reuters.com/article/kazakhstan-china/update-1-kazakh-leader-says-23-bi llion-in-economic-deals-agreed-with-china-idUSL5N1172V620150901] (https://www.reuters.com/article/kazakhstan-china/update-1-kazakh-leader-says-23-billion-in-economic-deals-agreed-with-china-idUSL5N1172V620150901)
40. KAZAKH INVEST. (2024, June). Kazakhstan and China signed 58 commercial documents worth over $24 billion. [https://invest.gov.kz/media-center/press-releases/kazakhstan-and-china-signed-58-commercial-documents-worth-over-24-billion/?utm_source=chatgpt.com] (https://invest.gov.kz/media-center/press-releases/kazakhstan-and-china-signed-58-commerci al-documents-worth-over-24-billion/?utm_source=chatgpt.com).
41. Woods, E., & Baker, T. (2022, May 5). Public opinion on China waning in Central Asia: Even as China's economic influence expands, a credibility gap looms in Central Asia. [*The Diplomat*. [https://thediplomat.com/2022/05/public-opinion-on-china-waning-in-central-asia/?utm_source=chatgpt.com] (https://thediplomat.com/2022/05/public-opinion-on-china-waning-in-central-asia/?utm_source=chatgpt.com).
42. Eco-Business. (2020, February 25). Central Asian NGOs raise concerns about BRI projects. [https://www.eco-business.com/news/central-asian-ngos-raise-concerns-about-bri-projects/?utm_source=chatgpt.com] (https://www.eco-business.com/news/central-asian-ngos-raise-concerns-about-bri-projects/?utm_source=chatgpt.com).

4

India's Geopolitical Strategy Amidst Global Turbulence

Amb. Ashok Sajjanhar

Introduction

The world is going through extraordinary and unprecedented changes. Change is the order of nature but the transformations that the world has witnessed over the last few years have been qualitatively and quantitatively different in nature, scope and pace than those experienced in any similar previous period.

Some of the most significant changes over the last several years include the collapse of bipolarity, the transient rise of unipolarity, the upswing in multipolarity signalled by the ascent of China and other emerging economies like India, Brazil, Indonesia, African nations, etc., decline in multilateralism, surge in terrorism, weaponisation of interdependence with economic ties becoming tools for coercion (trade wars, sanctions), emergence of Technology as Power, with competition for dominance in AI, semiconductors, rare earth minerals and magnets, 5G becoming central to national power, etc.

In essence, the world has moved from a predictable, albeit tense, Cold War bipolarity to a fluid, contested system defined by rising powers, intertwined economies, technological competition, and challenges to traditional state power.

In a somewhat more proximate time frame, the world and India have witnessed the onslaught of the COVID-19 pandemic in 2020 which devastated several countries around the globe, the departure of U.S. and NATO forces from Afghanistan in 2021, the political and economic crisis in Sri Lanka in

2022, the unexpected aggression by Russia of Ukraine in February 2022 and its continuation for close to four years with no end in sight, the violent change of government in Bangladesh in August, 2024, the onset and continuation of the Israel-Hamas conflict since October, 2023, the changeover of government in the Maldives by an ostensibly anti-India dispensation in November, 2023, and many more, with the latest being the assumption of power by Donald Trump as the President of USA in January 2025 and the huge shocks he has dealt to the steadily expanding and growing ties between India and the USA over the last twenty-five years.

India has been able to effectively deal with the challenges that have come its way through the use of policies based on *Vasudhaiva Kutumbakam* (The World Is One Family), Multialignment and Strategic Autonomy.

India's Economic Rise

India has been successful in implementing these strategies because of two fundamental advantages it has been endowed with.

One, India's economy has grown significantly over the last 11 years. When the Prime Minister Narendra Modi-led government came to power in 2014, India's economy was the 10th largest in the world. Today it is the 4th largest with prognosis to emerge as the third largest by 2027. Today, India is the fastest growing major economy with its GDP growth registering impressive figures of 8.2 per cent and 7.8 per cent over the last two quarters. India is expected to grow from a US$4 trillion economy today to US$10 trillion by 2035.

India's increased economic capacity has helped it in multiple ways. It has been able to provide a better standard of living to its people. It has been able to improve its infrastructure, both physically and socially, in terms of health, education, roads, highways, ports, airports, etc. It has also been able to apportion a larger quantum of funds towards its military preparedness, moving in the direction of increasingly becoming *atmanirbhar* (self-sufficient) in defence preparedness, improving and expanding its roads, tunnels, bridges, etc., infrastructure in the border areas to safeguard and ensure its security and territorial integrity. Secondly, it has increased India's capacity to play a much more active role in global affairs and lend a helping hand in times of need to its strategic partners. During the COVID-19 pandemic, India went out of its way to supply medicines and vaccines, both Covishield and Covaxin, to its strategic partners, particularly from the Global South. India provided the necessary medicines, most of them gratis, to more than 150 countries, and supplied more than 300 million vaccine doses under its Vaccine Maitri (Vaccine Friendship) initiative to more than 100 countries. Because of its economic heft and capability, India could come to the assistance of Sri Lanka to the tune of US$4.5 billion when the latter's coffers were empty in 2022 and to the support of Afghanistan, Maldives, etc. when these countries had their backs against the wall. This has also enabled India to emerge as the First Responder in times of need and when calamities like earthquakes, floods, etc., have struck in our neighbourhood and beyond.

The Leadership Advantage

The second significant contributor to India's evolution as a major global power in recent years is the bold, decisive and visionary leadership of Prime Minister Narendra Modi. This has stood India in good stead in successfully dealing with the challenging and difficult times that it has faced, both internally and externally, over the last several years. India was able to provide the underprivileged sections of its society with adequate food rations while confronting the scourge of the COVID-19 pandemic. This government support continues even till now providing a cushion to about 800 million citizens for their nutrition as they deal with the new challenges and problems that they are required to contend with.

While firmly and decisively dealing with the continuing challenges, PM Modi has provided an aspirational objective of attaining Viksit Bharat 2047 (Developed India 2047) by the time India celebrates the centenary of its independence in 2047. It is expected that if India were to grow at 8-9 per cent per annum, its economy would reach US$30 trillion by that date which would enable its people to have a much higher standard of living than at present. For this, India will need to become a technological leader. To achieve this, India is focusing in a big way on advancing in AI, Quantum Computing, Robotics, Semiconductors, etc., to stay ahead in the march of global technological leadership.

On the external front, India, under PM Modi, has categorically stated that it will go to any extent to safeguard and protect the security and wellbeing of its people and territorial integrity of its borders. The firm action taken by India against the intrusions by China in the Eastern Ladakh area in 2014, in the Doklam sector of Bhutan in 2017 and in the Galwan region of Ladakh in 2020 has sent out a strong and clear message to China that India will no longer tolerate the practice of salami slicing that China has resorted to in the past. On the western front, by resorting to surgical strikes (2016), air strikes on the Balakot camp (2019) and Op Sindoor (2025), India has made it abundantly clear that it will not succumb to the threat of terrorism, of nuclear blackmail and that every cross-border act of terror will be treated as an act of war.

India has also stood firm against the coercive tactics of US President Donald Trump to reduce its tariffs on agricultural products like dairy items (milk, cream, yogurt, cheese), GMOs, cereals, pulses and oilseeds, sugar, onions, almonds, etc., to protect the livelihoods of its farmers and ensure food security. It has also refused to be coerced to acknowledge that Donald Trump had any role to play in the cessation of hostilities in Op Sindoor on 10 May 2025. India's consistent stance has been that India agreed to the ceasefire when Pakistan begged it to do so after the latter's airfields and other strategic assets were decisively demolished on 10 May 2025.

In the context of the Russia-Ukraine conflict, India has made it clear that it is in favour of a negotiated settlement through Dialogue and Diplomacy. It has however not wilted under the Western, particularly U.S., pressure to stop importing oil at concessional rates from Russia to safeguard its national interests to provide energy at affordable rates to its 1.4 billion nationals.

India demonstrated its Strategic Autonomy by PM Modi visiting Russia twice in 2024, attending the SCO Summit in Tianjin, China, in September 2025, and extending a warm and enthusiastic welcome to Russian President Vladimir Putin to India for the 23rd India-Russia Annual Summit in December 2025 and taking the relations to a new high by declaring to provide a quantum jump to bilateral trade, defence and technological cooperation. In parallel to this, India announced that European Commission President Ursula von der Leyen and President of the European Council Antonio Costa will be the Chief Guests at India's Republic Day celebrations in January, 2026. This is a vivid demonstration of India's policy of multi-alignment.

The Path of *Vasudhaiva Kutumbakam*

While delivering his first address to the UN General Assembly session in September 2014, immediately after assumption of power, Prime Minister Narendra Modi invoked the spirit of *Vasudhaiva Kutumbakam* as the guiding philosophy of India's foreign policy. This principle has continued to inform all of India's policy actions, particularly its ''Neighbourhood First'' policy by which it has sought to reach out unilaterally and non-reciprocally to its neighbouring countries. This has yielded rich dividends in deepening trust and expanding its ties with most of its neighbours including Sri Lanka, Maldives, Bhutan, Nepal, Bangladesh (till July, 2024), Afghanistan, etc. The fact that India's relations with some countries like Pakistan and Bangladesh (from

August 2024) have been rocky and tense is not for want of trying by India but because of the internal domestic politics of those countries. With China also, India went out of its way to have normal and stable ties and to realise the full potential of their bilateral relations as two large economies and ancient civilisations. However, China's inexplicable aggressive policies in 2020 leading to the Galwan conflict led to a hiatus and standoff for more than four years. India steadfastly withstood its ground, not succumbing to the Chinese pressure of deploying 50-60,000 troops in the border areas, contrary to agreements signed between the two countries. A bilateral meeting between PM Modi and Chinese President Xi Jinping in October 2024 in Kazan, Russia, began the gradual process of normalisation of bilateral ties. India has consistently maintained that bilateral ties can improve only on the basis of the three 'mutuals': mutual sensitivity, mutual respect and mutual interest.

India's policy of *Vasudhaiva Kutumbakam* witnessed its fullest expression during India's chairmanship of the G20 in 2023. India not only adopted the motto of 'One Earth, One Family, One Future'' for its presidency but also made sure that all decisions and results emanating from the deliberations among the G20 members and the invited guest countries fully reflected this commitment. This became obvious on the first day of the Summit itself when India announced the decision of the G20 membership to invite the African Union (AU), a grouping of 54 African countries, as the 21st member of the G20. This issue had been on the back-burner of the G20 deliberations for the last several years but it fell upon India, with its commitment to the interests of the Global South, to bring this to fruition.

In addition, to focus on the interests, concerns, aspirations and challenges of the developing countries, PM Modi organised the first Voice of the Global South Summit (VOGSS) within a few weeks of taking over charge of the G20. About 125 developing countries of the level of Presidents, Vice Presidents, PMs and Ministers participated in this virtual Summit. All their concerns including food and energy security, debt relief, women's empowerment, infrastructure financing, functioning of the MDBs, economic instability, climate vulnerability, and lack of representation in global governance institutions were taken on board in discussions and the final outcome enshrined in the New Delhi Leaders' Declaration in September 2023. India organised the Second VOGSS in November 2023 to inform the members of the Global South about the decisions of the G20 and how their concerns and aspirations had been fully reflected in the final document adopted by the G20 member-states. India has continued to articulate the concerns and ambitions of the Global South by holding the third VOGSS in August, 2024, and raised the problems and challenges faced by the developing world in all multilateral and plurilateral fora.

Multi-Alignment and Strategic Autonomy

India's policies of multi-alignment and strategic autonomy are two sides of the same coin. Both of these are supported by India's active diplomatic profile, and greater economic, political, strategic, military and human capacity. In addition to these elements of hard power which India has continued to strengthen over the last more than a decade, India has also expanded its soft power through greater popularisation of yoga (177 countries co-sponsored India's resolution to declare 21 June as the International Day of Yoga in 2014), Indian dance, music, culture, Bollywood films, Ayurveda, traditional medicine, democratic values, cuisine, spiritual heritage (Hinduism, Buddhism), development cooperation, strong and active diaspora, etc.

In the current-day conflicts, India is one of the very few countries, if not the only country, to have good relations with both the West (USA, EU, Japan, Australia) and the main protagonist, Ukraine, as well as Russia, and also with Israel as well as Palestine, Iran and other West Asian countries. In the context of the Russia-Ukraine conflict, India has stated categorically that its policy is not of neutrality. It stands on the side of peace and wants an end to the conflict as quickly as possible on the basis of dialogue and diplomacy. India has strongly articulated this stance as the continuation of the conflict has a harmful impact in the areas of increasing debt, food and energy security, etc., on developing countries. It has stated clearly that disputes can never be solved on the battle field but only at the negotiating table.

Some analysts commit the serious error of equating multi-alignment with transactionalism. Nothing could be further from the truth. The two concepts represent fundamentally different approaches to international relations and cooperation. While both involve engaging multiple partners, multi-alignment is a strategic approach to build diverse, long-term geopolitical and economic resilience by engaging various global powers (USA, Russia, China, EU) based on shared interests, aiming for strategic autonomy and navigating a multipolar world. Transactionalism, on the other hand, focuses more narrowly on quick, bilateral, short-term deals for immediate gains, often degrading complex multi-alignment for simpler, self-interested transactions – a pattern that could be associated with recent U.S. foreign policy positions. Multi-alignment seeks broad, deep engagement across issues (energy, defence, trade), not just single deals, making it more complex and non-transactional.

The key objective of multi-alignment for India is strategic autonomy, leading to reduced geopolitical risk and broader influence in a multipolar world. It embodies a proactive, complex, issue-specific cooperation with multiple, often competing, global poles (USA, China, Russia, EU). For example, India partnering with Russia on energy/arms and strategic manoeuvrability, while engaging with the USA on trade, defence and tech, and collaborating with Europe on climate, technology and markets will fall squarely under this policy of multi-alignment. Multi-alignment is not just about hedging options; it's about actively shaping relationships for national interest on a long-term basis, moving beyond ideological constraints.

Multi-alignment acknowledges the complex, interconnected nature of global issues (trade, climate, technology, security), requiring broad engagement, while transactionalism favours transient, short-term bilateral deals. Multi-alignment is a nuanced geopolitical, long-term strategy for rising powers like India to navigate great power competition without choosing sides, whereas transactionalism can be seen as a short term, self-interested approach to foreign policy. Transactionalism represents rejection of shared, multilaterally accepted norms: It tends to downplay long-term partnerships and international rules in favour of specific, one-off deals.

India's multi-alignment strategy is best illustrated by India's expanding and robust ties with Europe, Japan, Australia, etc. (USA has not been included in the list on account of the considerable stress brought into this relationship by President Trump's trade and strategic policies over the last six months since June 2025) on the one hand, and the time-tested and trusted relations with Russia (and normalising relations with China) on the other. This is also evident from India's membership of the BRICS on one side and the Quad on the other, from India's ties with SCO members on the one hand and the regular and constant invitation to PM Modi to participate in the G7 meetings for the last seven years since 2019 on the other. The West, particularly the USA, wants that India disengage itself from Russia in energy and defence-related deals. It needs to understand that India is a determined and committed partner of the West, and that a strong and independent India is a better strategic ally than a subservient one.

Major Challenges

India's most formidable geo-political challenge in the immediate future and long-term is the aggressive stance of China as it seeks to emerge as the unipolar power in Asia and to reduce India to a subordinate status. Its border dispute with India, its military, intelligence, strategic and economic support to Pakistan, the Tibet issue, its weaponisation of its critical minerals and supply chains, and creation of a 'necklace of pearls' around India to contain its rise are significant challenges.

The threat emanating from Pakistan is of comparatively lesser significance. India is well equipped to deal with it effectively. India will however have to keep a close watch on Pakistan's machinations as its Army Chief, Asim Munir, and its political leadership would have been made even more reckless and adventurous than in the past by the excessive and exorbitant support and praise heaped on them by President Trump.

Bangladesh has emerged as a potent challenge in recent months in areas of border security, rising Islamist extremism, increasing minority attacks, and shifting geopolitical alignments, particularly its growing ties with Pakistan, Turkey and China, against India's interests. India is pursuing a balanced strategy that prioritises diplomacy, security enhancements, and economic leverage while eschewing escalation. India needs to deploy advanced surveillance like drones and AI-monitored fencing along the 4,000-km plus border to curb infiltration, smuggling, and terror threats from radical groups. It should leverage Bangladesh's trade dependencies by conditioning connectivity projects on stability commitments. Bangladesh needs to adopt a balanced foreign policy, keep a lid on insurgency and extremism, and do more to curb cross-border smuggling and illegal migration. Assuaging Indian security concerns will be paramount for putting the relationship on the right track, and making it a source of stability in the years ahead.

One of the most unexpected and vexing problems to have emerged in recent months is India's relations with the USA which had been cruising along on a steady upward trajectory since 2000. While India was among the most enthusiastic to welcome Trump's second incarnation based on its experience of dealing with him in his first term, India-US relations suddenly and unexpectedly plummeted in June 2025. For decades, the USA and India have built a steadily deepening partnership, forged by shared strategic interests, economic ties, and growing defence cooperation. Recent actions by the Trump Administration have jeopardised that hard-earned trust by actions and rhetoric that cut deeper than the usual strains on the U.S.-India relationship. The Trump

Administration's 50 percent tariff on goods from India, President Donald Trump's claiming credit for achieving a ceasefire between India and Pakistan, and a controversial meeting with the Pakistani army chief in the Oval Office with a strong outreach to Pakistan, serve to fundamentally erode the trust built over decades, and play into India's deepest historic reservations about the reliability of the relationship. At a moment when the U.S.-India partnership is more important than ever, this breach takes on added significance.

India has stood firm in the face of Trump's provocative rhetoric and bullying tactics. It is expected that bilateral ties which are characterised as "comprehensive global strategic partnership" will stabilise in the coming weeks and months. It is encouraging that barring the issue of trade and Pakistan, bilateral ties in the areas of defence, military exercises, exchange of delegations, etc., have been proceeding seamlessly. It is in the mutual interest of both countries as well as in the interest of peace, security and stability in the Indo-Pacific to have robust, stable and dynamic ties between the two countries. While India continues to negotiate on all outstanding issues with the USA in good faith, it is hoped that this realisation will dawn, sooner rather than later, on President Trump also who will start working towards normalising relations between the two countries. It is not certain whether Trump's policies will continue to govern India-US ties only during the current term of his administration or similar policies will inform the US attitude towards India after 2029 also. While working towards optimum results in bilateral India-US relations, India will have to insulate itself against outcomes which might not be ideal from its perspective.

Conclusion

To contend with the geo-political and geo-economic challenges that confront India under the current global strategic, security and economic architecture, the most imperative requirement is to maintain India's consistent technological and economic growth at 8-9 per cent per annum so that India reaches a respectable figure of US$30 trillion by the time it celebrates the centenary of its independence in 2047. This will not only help it to provide a better standard of living to its people but also make adequate funds available to significantly enhance its defence preparedness and improve its infrastructure in the border areas as well as throughout the country.

The USA will continue to be India's most significant economic, defence and technological partner for the foreseeable future. The level of trust that had been steadily growing and strengthening has been deeply eroded and will take a long time to recover and get restored. In the meantime, it will be incumbent upon India to diversify away from the USA in the area of markets, defence supplies, and critical and emergent technologies. Some of the most attractive partners in this sphere would be the EU with which India is on the verge of concluding an FTA, with the UK with which India has recently finalised an FTA, with Japan, Australia, Africa, ASEAN and other like-minded countries.

India's partnership with Russia is also very vital and critical and needs to be nurtured notwithstanding the fact that its suitability as a big market, or source of cutting-edge technology (except in the area of defence) is somewhat limited and questionable.

In addition to new initiatives like the "Neighbourhood First" Policy which has yielded rich dividends in terms of expanding and strengthening relations with its neighbours, PM Modi has launched several more fresh initiatives. Some of the most significant of these are the 'Engage West' policy to reach out to the countries in West Asia, the "C5 plus India" to deepen and enhance relations with our extended neighbourhood of Central Asia, as well as the 'Act East Policy' to raise and revitalise ties with ASEAN member-states and those of Far East Asia. India has paid special attention to relations with Africa and Latin America which are emerging as new centres of economic and technological dynamism. Several new embassies have been established on the African and South American continents as also in Central and Eastern Europe, making up for the years of neglect of these regions. Significantly, India's senior leadership has invested considerable political capital in reaching out to these regions by visiting these countries often and also welcoming their leaders and ministers to India.

India's global power and influence has expanded significantly over the last decade. It will continue to grow in the coming years. As India has successfully and effectively confronted the several gray and black swan events that it has encountered in recent years, it can look with hope, confidence and determination to deal with any fresh challenges that come its way in the coming months and years.

5

Multilateral Engagements in Indo-Kazakh Relations

Dr. Anita Sengupta

The term 'multilateral' can refer to an organising principle, an organisation or simply an activity. Any of the above can be considered multilateral when it involves cooperative activity among many countries. 'Multilateralism' as opposed to 'multilateral' is a belief that the activities ought to be organised on a universal, or at least a many-sided basis for a 'relevant' group. It may be a belief both in the existential sense of a claim about how the world works and in the normative sense that things should be done in a particular way. As such, multilateralism is 'designed' to promote multilateral activity. It combines normative principles with advocacy and existential beliefs. The debate on multilateralism, defined in the broadest sense as international cooperation among more than two states in the international arena, re-emerged in the light of the pervading unilateralist impulse emanating from the Bush administration (Schlesinger, 2005). While a debate on the reform of the United Nations, as the principal global multilateral forum, had been an ongoing process, multilateral approach towards regional issues, particularly security issues, with emphasis on confidence building, preventive diplomacy and conflict resolution, are being increasingly accepted as significant to the maintenance of regional security and promotion of regional development.

Multilateral confidence-building measures reflect the belief that through regularised dialogue and consultation, existing and potential conflicts can be effectively managed without the necessity of recourse to coercion. It is pointed out that multilateralism is distinctive, not merely because it coordinates national policies in groups of three or more states, which is something that other organisational forms also do, but additionally because it does so on the basis of certain principles of ordering relations among states (Ruggie, 1993). However, an understanding of multilateral initiatives remains incomplete without a close reading of how regions perceive their 'national' and 'regional' security. Underlying these national priorities are a set of assumptions about the security of the state and how shifting alliances with other states can best preserve this. This rather realistic understanding of the situation, of course, is not without its problems, not the least of which is that states often do not act as unitary and rational actors. In actual situations, state decisions are often determined by the interplay of domestic and international factors and influenced by partisan interests.

Situated in the heart of Asia the most persistently pursued goal for the first Kazakh President Nursultan Nazarbayev since the country gained independence in 1991 has been to promote integration at various levels within Central Asia and the former Soviet space, but also within global markets and institutions. He has since been applauded for attempting to bring the benefits of globalisation to Kazakhstan. Nazarbayev's intense support for globalisation partly results from his perception that Kazakhstan would benefit from enhanced ties with other countries and organisations. In his view insufficient integration has prevented Kazakhstan and its neighbourhood from assuming their natural status as the linchpin of global governance. In the economic sphere, greater integration would allow Kazakhstan and other neighbouring states to better exploit their natural resources and pivotal location. Kazakhstan's ability to realise its potential as a natural crossroad for east-west and north-south commercial trade depends on reducing obstacles to the free flow of goods and people among the Eurasian nations. Deeper economic integration would also make these countries more attractive to foreign investors and enhance collective leverage with external actors. In the security realm, greater integration would provide Kazakhstan with room to manoeuvre among the great powers active in the region and reduce the risks of becoming a pawn in the emerging great power condominium. It would also help them coordinate their responses to regional economic, political and security problems. There is emphasis on the fact that instability provides opportunities for external meddling and conflicts can spill across borders, either directly or through refugee flows that discourage international capital markets from investing in the region.

It was also argued that regional integration would help avert potential inter-ethnic and inter-confessional discord among Kazakhstan's heterogeneous population. The country claims to be home to more than a hundred distinct ethnic minority groups. The government promotes religious harmony at home and abroad. However, large minorities, including significant numbers of ethnic Russians, mean that Kazakhstan would not remain indifferent to developments in the neighbourhood. Kazakh leaders argue that their country's strong economic development, market reforms and commitment to regional prosperity make it the most important factor in regional economic integration mechanisms among Eurasian states. In addition to global and regional integration, President Nazarbayev also called for a geographically narrower but functionally deeper union of Central Asian states that would entail the sharing of water and energy resources, improvements in the regional transportation infrastructure, establishment of common customs and trading tariffs, mechanisms to respond collectively to environmental threats and natural disasters and support for region-wide tourist networks. Nazarbayev supported the transition from a free-trade-zone to a customs union and economic union with supporting political institutions. Within Eurasia and beyond, Nazarbayev, as the first Kazakh President of independent Kazakhstan, sought to make Kazakhstan a 'transcontinental economic bridge' and a 'regional locomotive' of economic development. Kazakh officials promoted closer regional transportation, pipeline and communication networks, reducing customs and other man-made barriers to trade, encouraging tourism and other non-governmental exchanges while strengthening relations governing labour mobility in Eurasia and promoting Kazakh private investment in other Eurasian economies.

This chapter begins by examining Kazakh efforts at creating and sustaining multilateral initiatives within Central Asia and then moves on to an examination of the specific multilateral initiatives that include India.

Regional Multilateral Initiatives

It is generally accepted that the purpose of any regional organisation is twofold: the acceleration of economic development and the reinforcement of regional stability and security. The role of multilateral regional initiatives on a Central Asian level as primary providers of security has not been rated very high. It has been observed that such initiatives have been unable to convey hard defence guarantees, create joint military units, negotiate arms reductions or enforce the end of overt conflicts. However, a correct assessment of these initiatives would have to begin with noting their existential significance as groups of states that recognise themselves as sharing some elements of community and can define their national identity as complementary rather than adversarial to their neighbours. Regular meetings and the creation of personal ties encourage *esprit de corps* and may help to defuse a crisis. In fact, non-traditional security issues like environment, defence against pollution, water management, drug smuggling, organised crime, migration and refugees have provided more useful areas for regional discourse. In addition, there have been attempts at economic cooperation with an understanding that economic development is conducive to the security of the region (Meiirzhan, 2000).

It is undeniable that compared to the more successful of regional multilateral efforts, a great deal remains to be achieved (Sengupta, 2004). However, prior to any critical evaluation of these efforts, it is crucial to keep in mind that in a number of indirect ways both development and stability have been contributed to by these regional processes. Representative of this are the numerous agreements that have been made regarding environmental degradation. This is a case that in the Central Asian region could lead to regional instability and also affect economic development. This is particularly so since the ecological crisis in the Central Asian region overlays and aggravates a structural, economic and social crisis. Central Asia is a developing region, characterised by a high share in agricultural production, low industrialisation, mass unemployment and a high population growth. With the standard of living considerably below the Soviet average, it was extremely dependent on the subsidies from the centre. The disintegration of the Soviet Union meant the beginning of a new process of nation-building in the region and a redefinition of political and cultural identities. It also saw the emergence of a new international water basin, the Aral, with all consequent consequences for the political, ethnic and economic relations between the states. The entire political geography changed and once shared natural resources that were controlled by central directions became the 'national wealth' of the newly independent states. Rivers became national borders and the division into up and down stream riparian became politically relevant. While it is accepted that environmental issues are unlikely to be the primary cause of conflict, it is also argued that they play a complex role in shaping relations among states. And here the success of regional initiatives in the Central Asian region cannot be denied. Speaking at the Carnegie Endowment for International Peace, Dr. Kadir Gulomov, Minister of Defence in Uzbekistan, noted that security has many aspects. Efforts to promote regional cooperation through the use of water and energy resources are an important way to reduce tensions in the area (Carnegie Endowment, 2000).

Within Central Asia, the Kazakh commitment to multilateral initiatives has been the strongest. This commitment has extended not just within the Central Asian region but also on a broader Eurasian level. On a practical level Kazakh effort at integration on a Eurasian level has involved numerous initiatives. Kazakhstan has emerged as a leader in efforts at the promotion of regional economic and political integration in Eurasia. Under President Nursultan Nazarbayev, Kazakhstan has followed a foreign policy that has sought to maintain good relations with the most important external powers. In addition, there has been an attempt to strengthen ties with countries of Central Asia and the Caspian Sea basin. Kazakhstan also plays a prominent role in most of Eurasia's international institutions and organisations like the Commonwealth of Independent States, the Collective Security Treaty Organisation, the Eurasian Economic Community, the Shanghai Cooperation Organisation, the North Atlantic Treaty Organisation and the Organisation for Security and Cooperation in Europe. In line with this, the President has stated the objective of making Kazakhstan a 'transcontinental economic bridge.' He emphasised this when he noted, 'Occupying the position midway between Europe and Asia and serving as a lively arena for economic and political contacts, Kazakhstan is nowadays able to act as a link in the chain connecting the two great civilisations of East and West' (Nazarbayev, 1995, November 15).

In keeping with this, there have been efforts at improving regional transportation, pipelines and communication networks, reducing customs and other man-made barriers to trade, encouraging tourism and other non-governmental exchanges, while strengthening labour mobility in Eurasia and promoting Kazakh private investment in other Eurasian economies. The strong Kazakh support for regional integration results in part from a recognition that Kazakhstan will benefit from enhanced ties among Eurasian countries. There is also a conviction that through this integration at the Eurasian level, Kazakhstan and its neighbours will achieve greater room to manoeuvre among great powers active in the region and reduce the risk of their becoming dependent on any one supplier, customer or market. The increase in regional prosperity that economists predict will ensue from this integration would help Kazakhstan expand its economic activities and realise its potential as a natural crossroads for east-west and north-south commercial links based on the reduction of man-made political and economic obstacles to the free flow of goods and people among Eurasian nations. It has been argued that Kazakhstan's geography allowed it to exercise decisive influence in two of Eurasia's most important sub-regions: Central Asia and the Caspian Sea (Weitz, 2008).

In addition, Kazakhstan has presented repeated proposals for a Eurasian Union covering a range of cooperative endeavours in the areas of politics, economics and security. The idea of a Eurasian Union was conceived in the mid-1990s and was intended to promote economic, social and, to a limited degree, political integration across the post-Soviet space. The Eurasian Union was conceived with the idea of first establishing a customs union and a common economic space and to enable the citizens of the post-Soviet successor states to travel visa-free across newly-erected borders. President Nazarbayev argued that the Commonwealth of Independent States had been impotent. In contrast, the Eurasian Union would be empowered and legitimized by an executive committee and a parliament. The effort would be to erect an effective institutional framework for economic integration and mutual security in order to avoid unnecessary expenses of border control. President Nazarbayev argued that much of the world is integrating and in the post-Soviet space this integration should work better since till recently it was an integrated economic space. While this initiative failed, President Nazarbayev reaffirmed his commitment to a union launching a new initiative in April 2007 that focused on borders and water management issues that had long complicated relations among the Central Asian states and matters that could only be resolved collectively. The November 2007 decision to award Kazakhstan the chairmanship of the Organisation for Security and Cooperation in Europe (OSCE) in 2010 recognises the country's growing importance in Eurasia. Kazakh officials have characterised this as an endorsement of their country's successful economic and political reforms, its leading role in Europe and Central Asia and its contribution as a bridge between the former Soviet republics and other OSCE members.

On the broader international front, the rhetorical significance of the Eurasian Union is stated as a self-evident move. The President argues, "It is absolutely clear to us that the main tendency in world development today is global integration, and the inspiring example of the member-countries of the European Union is finding support in the most varied regions of the world. Moves towards unification are evident in the countries of Latin America, Southeast Asia and the Near East. Along the same lines is the idea, advanced by Kazakhstan and having many adherents beyond its frontiers, for the creation of a Eurasian Union on the territory of the former Soviet Union. This not only pursues obvious economic objectives but also assumes the integration of the former Soviet Republics in the fields of science, culture, education and information. I feel sure that in the next century and beyond, the united subcontinent of Europe and Asia must develop as a single unit for the future of our children and our descendants and that there will come a day when Europe and Asia will develop together, drawing upon their huge natural and human resources" (Nazarbayev, 1995, November 15).

The Eurasian idea is therefore presented as the ideal for the future, not just on a political and economic level but also at a cultural level. President Nazarbayev called for the establishment of a Eurasian research centre that will focus on the unique spiritual heritage of the Eurasian people. Consultative meetings between the heads of Central Asian states in recent years are a testament to the fact that the significance of regional cooperation and integration is clearly recognised. While border agreements have seen tangible results with Kyrgyzstan, Uzbekistan and Tajikistan concluding a trilateral agreement in March 2025, the creation of a Special Economic Zone to boost trade at Korkyt Ata Special Economic Zone by Kazakhstan and infrastructure projects with Kyrgyzstan signal the significance of regional cooperation for development. The Central Asia 2040 agreement, signed by the heads of state of Central Asia along with President Tokayev, similarly outlined prospects for development and cooperation.

India-Kazakh Multilateral Engagements

India's trans-continental connections to its northwest predates the age of globalisation with historically located networks that re-orient conventional cartographies and spatial configurations. For India, the contemporary connection to the wider Central Asian region had been formally visualised through the Connect Central Asia Policy launched in 2012 as an alternative infrastructure and transport connectivity plan that sought to enhance trade and educational rights and encourage expanded joint commercial and security initiatives with Central Asia. It is also an initiative to include the states in the North-South Transport Corridor with the aim to involve Central Asian states wherever possible and, with this in mind, expand land routes to include Armenia, Kazakhstan and Turkmenistan. India faces connectivity challenges regarding land routes to Afghanistan and Central Asia, which limit direct communications and part of the effort to relieve these connectivity bottlenecks has been through greater emphasis on participation in multilateral organisations, the SCO being an example.

The 16th SCO Summit held in Tashkent, Uzbekistan, on June 23-24, 2016, concluded the process of inclusion of India and Pakistan as permanent members in the SCO. India's own decision for entry into the Shanghai Cooperation

Organisation was through a much-debated process where the advantages and disadvantages of membership in a multilateral forum that would include not just Russia and China but also Pakistan has been subject to intense scrutiny not just by commentators from within India but also globally. A recent rather positive editorial begins with the argument that entry into the SCO opens up opportunities for India to its north (*Times of India*, 2017). A refreshing change from many others that have argued that 'look north/northwest' would never be a viable policy option for India given the intractable position of Pakistan and the continuing conflicts in Afghanistan that make 'Look/Act East' the only available Indian alternative. The editorial goes on to argue that entry into the SCO would provide opportunities in three key areas. First, the SCO would become a forum where Pakistan could be held accountable for its terrorism; secondly, it could be a forum for negotiation of India's relations with China and, finally, it would resolve the issue of non-contiguity with the Central Asian region by opening up lines of communication through Pakistan and Afghanistan.

Connectivity, therefore, played a large part in the Indian decision to apply for membership with the general agreement that, for India, joining the SCO was about 'raising its stakes in Central Asia,' of greater connectivity to a wider resource-rich region and an opportunity to work on common issues of concern. This, in conjunction with Iran's SCO membership, would ensure that India would be able to move towards developing a platform for trade and transit through Bandar Abbas and Chabahar, eventually linking with the North-South Corridor. There also remains the possibility of the SCO acting as guarantor for projects like the Turkmenistan-Afghanistan-Pakistan-India pipeline (TAPI) and the Iran-Pakistan-India pipeline (IPI), which have been in the pipeline for a number of years. This would also provide a useful interface for interaction with Afghanistan and its neighbourhood. However, there is also the counter-argument that SCO engagement need not be overemphasised as bilateral engagement with the Central Asian states works just as well, as illustrated by the uranium supply deal with Kazakhstan during Prime Minister Modi's visit. The Indian alternative through 'Connect Central Asia' that was projected as the policy initiative on the West that would complement its Look/Act East Policy with emphasis on the four 'Cs' – commerce, connectivity, consular and culture – however, could not match the Chinese engagement either economically or in political terms.

In 2022, all five Central Asian Presidents were invited to be part of the Republic Day celebrations in New Delhi on 26 January. While COVID-19 restrictions meant that they could not attend in person, on 27 January 2022 a virtual India-Central Asia Summit between Prime Minister Modi and the leaders signalled three facts: first that the relationship was now integral to India's neighbourhood policy; second, that it was moving in a more structured direction with the establishment of a Secretariat and third, the relationship was now part of a larger vision to re-connect. Connectivity, trade and developing a framework for co-operation on the Afghan situation were part of the Summit agenda. Afghanistan, of course, is a crucial for connect between the regions and, unfortunately, the present political situation complicates matters. As a reflection of this, joint working groups on Afghanistan have been constituted. There was a proposal to make the Summit a permanent yearly event with a permanent Secretariat for greater engagement at the ministerial level, a change from the foreign-minister level at which India-Central Asia summits currently exist. The hosting of the Summit elevates the bilateral relations that India has with the states to a formal multilateral level. It also indicates a move towards creating a regional connectivity network that has often been a challenge for both South Asia and Central Asia, given its poor infrastructure, problematic diplomatic relations and limited formal trade. It is also significant that the Summit was not an isolated engagement as it followed the Delhi Regional Security Dialogue which was hosted in New Delhi in November 2021.

A very significant multilateral effort on a Pan-Asian level initiated by the Kazakh President, Nursultan Nazarbayev, is the Conference on Interaction and Confidence Building in Asia (CICA). The CICA vision for security in Asia elaborates on multilateral approaches towards promoting peace and security and visualises itself as the forum for dialogue, consultation and adoption of decisions and measures on the basis of consensus on security issues in Asia. CICA originated with the idea that there was a necessity for a pan-Asiatic system of security, which, while addressing problems of security and confidence building, would also keep in mind cultural origins, national peculiarities and the complicated history of the relationship among them. The purpose behind the initiative was the creation of a system of security in Asia where safety would be guaranteed by the whole complex of measures. CICA has been involved in dialogue over three groups of issues: military-political affairs, socio-economic development and humanitarian concerns. CICA identifies certain elements as challenges to security and seeks to find ways to eliminate them. In this context, it resolves to support efforts for the elimination of weapons of mass destruction, to ensure the establishment of nuclear-free zones, to curb excessive accumulation of conventional armaments, condemn terrorism, not to render any assistance to separatist movements in other states, reject the use of religion as a pretext for terrorists and separatists, emphasise the significance of curbing the movement of illicit drugs and corruption. In the context of achieving these objectives, the CICA will take necessary steps for the elaboration and implementation of measures aimed at enhancing cooperation and creating an atmosphere of peace, confidence and friendship. All states are encouraged to resolve their disputes peacefully through negotiations in accordance with the principles enshrined in the UN Charter and International Law (Laumulin, 2002; Ashimbaev et al., 2003.

The most significant aspect of CICA is its membership, which includes not just the Central Asian states and the two Eurasian powers, Russia and China, but also major South and Southeast Asian powers. In addition, it includes the USA as an observer. This is significant as the reality of US presence and interest in the region cannot be wished away. Members include Afghanistan, Azerbaijan, China, Egypt, India, Iran, Israel, Kazakhstan, Kyrgyzstan, Mongolia, Pakistan, the Palestinian National Administration, Russia, Tajikistan, Thailand, Turkey and Uzbekistan. Thailand was accepted as the seventeenth member in 2004 and the Republic of Korea as the eighteenth member in 2006. Observers of CICA are Vietnam, Indonesia, Korea, Malaysia, USA, Ukraine, and Japan. Other observers are international organisations like the United Nations, Organisation of Security and Cooperation in Europe and the League of Arab States.

The multilateral basis of the CICA is evident in the first principle enshrined in the Declaration at the Second Summit of the CICA in Almaty in 2006. It notes

> "We are convinced that multilateral cooperation based on the principles enshrined in the Charter as well as the Principles Guiding Relations among States and in the Almaty Act, is more necessary today than ever for maintaining international peace and security. To this end, we will intensify our efforts to develop a forum for political dialogue through elaborating common approaches to security on the basis of consensus" (*The Astana Times*, 2025).

In addition, there are other multilateral initiatives and dialogues in which both India and Kazakhstan are a part. The first India-Central Asia Summit was a reflection of India's growing engagement with the Central Asian countries, which are a part of India's 'Extended Neighbourhood.' The inception of the India-Central Asia Dialogue at the Foreign Ministers' level, the third meeting of which was held in New Delhi from 18 to 20 December 2021, provided an impetus to India-Central Asia relations. On 27 January 2022, a virtual India-Central Asia Summit was held with leaders of Kazakhstan, Kyrgyzstan, Uzbekistan, Tajikistan and Turkmenistan. The Summit focused on cooperation, consistent engagement and regional connectivity while focusing on all-round regional development and transparency. The Summit reflects India's renewed engagement with an extended neighbourhood, which now looks not just eastwards but also towards the northwest. It also reflects a willingness on the part of the Central Asian leadership to engage with India through an alternative multilateral format in addition to the SCO, of which India and the Central Asian states are already a part along with Russia and China (*The Indian Express*, 2022).

The BRICS, where Kazakhstan recently became a partner-state, is another organisation where both India and Kazakhstan are members. BRICS emerged from a market-driven intellectual inspiration to bring together a group of states with diverse history, size, economic profiles, political systems, national preferences and strategic cultures for what was aspired to be a meeting of equitable partners for a just and fair management of the global community of nations. The anticipation of a 'just, fair and equitable order' still seems to be the abiding expectation from the group, along with policy coordination that would restructure outmoded economic and political institutions and global governance structures in a world that seems to be rapidly moving towards de-globalisation (particularly due to decisions from its most vocal proponents in the West). While commitment to 'enhancement of the voice and representation of BRICS economies in global economic governance' is duly articulated in each Summit, the intensifying competition over common strategic spaces, the drifting apart of long-term relationships and global political and economic instability has brought into question the significance of institutions like BRICS that work on a multilateral format and depend on consensus for decisions. BRICS was created with the anticipation that since all member states were interested in a more equitable economic and political order, they would become the harbinger of a new matrix of global governance in politics, trade, energy and climate change. At the Rio Summit in 2025, Kazakh Deputy Prime Minister and Foreign Minister Murat Nurtleu underlined Kazakhstan's commitment to promoting a just, inclusive, and sustainable world order based on the UN Charter and international law. Nurtleu also emphasised Kazakhstan's interest in deepening economic cooperation with BRICS countries and advancing digital technologies (*The Astana Times*, 2025).

Conclusion

India's relations with Kazakhstan incorporate both bilateral initiatives as well as common engagement in multilateral forums. This engagement is mutual, with India supporting Kazakhstan's initiatives at CICA and Kazakhstan supporting India's permanent membership in an expanded UNSC. In a global scenario where partnership and engagement within the Global South is increasingly becoming significant in seeking an equitable political and economic order through championing multipolarity and fairness in global governance, the relationship assumes new importance in the face of the ongoing flux within the global system.

References

1. With the change in the US administration, the focus has increasingly been on the need to be more oriented towards multilateralism, a need that arises not only from the nature of many contemporary issues and problems and the evolution of international diplomatic process but also from the necessity of rebuilding goodwill, soft power and the influence lost during the Bush administration. See, for instance, Karns (2008).
2. Meiirzhan elaborates on the role of the Central Asian Economic Union in this regard in his article, 'Regional Security as a System Factor in Central Asian Integration.' See Meiirzhan (2000).
3. For a detailed discussion, see Sengupta (2004).
4. 'Take the plunge: Entry to SCO opens up opportunities for India to look North,' *Times of India*, 12 June 2017, at http://blogs.timesofindia.indiatimes.com/toi-editorials/take-the-plunge-entry-to-sco-opens-up-opportunities-for-india-to-look-north/ accessed 26 July 2017.
5. For a detailed analysis of CICA, see Laumulin (2002) and Ashimbaev et al. (2003).
6. From the Declaration at the Second Summit of the Conference on Interaction and Confidence Building Measures in Asia, Almaty, June 17, 2006.
7. Editorial. 'India-Central Asia Summit Focused on Overland Connectivity, Security. Both Sides Need to Turn Political Wills into Outcomes.' *The Indian Express*, 29 January 2022, https://indianexpress.com/article/opinion/editorials/india-central-asia-summit-overland-connectivity-security-7746546/.
8. Dana Omirgazy. 'Kazakhstan Takes Seat at BRICS Summit in Rio de Janeiro as Partner Country', *The Astana Times*, 8 July 2025, https://astanatimes.com/2025/07/kazakhstan-takes-seat-at-brics-summit-in-rio-de-janeiro-as-partner-country/
9. Ashimbaev, M. et al. (eds.). (2003). *New Challenges and New Geopolitics in Central Asia after September 11*. Almaty: Kazakhstan Institute for Strategic Studies.
10. Boucher, Richard A. (2006, September). 'South and Central Asia.' *Foreign Policy Agenda*, September 2006.
11. Buyukakinci, Erhan. (2000, March–May). 'Patterns of Integration in Central Asia.' *Perceptions*, 5 (I).
12. Carnegie Endowment for International Peace.(2000, November 3). *Meeting Report*, 2 (8). www.ceip.org/files/events/gulomov.asp?EventID==218.
13. Dieter, Heribert. (1996). 'Regional Integration in Central Asia: Current Economic Position and Prospects.' *Central Asian Survey*, 15 (3/4).
14. Ismagambetov, Talgat. (2003). 'Some Geopolitical Peculiarities of Central Asia, Past and Present.' In Sally N. Cummings (ed.), *Oil, Transition and Security in Central Asia*. London and New York: Routledge-Curzon.

15. Karns, Margaret P. (2008). 'Multilateralism Matters Even More.' *SAIS Review*, 28 (2).
16. Kubicek, Paul. (1997). 'Regionalism, Nationalism and Realpolitik in Central Asia.' *Europe-Asia Studies*, 49 (4).
17. Laumulin, Murat. (2002). *The Security, Foreign Policy, and International Relationship of Kazakhstan After Independence, 1991-2001*. Almaty: Kazakhstan Institute of Strategic Studies and Friedrich Ebert Shiftung.
18. Meiirzhan, Mashan. (2000). 'Regional Security as A System Factor in Central Asian Integration.' In Jasjit Singh (ed.), *Peace and Security in Central Asia*. New Delhi: IDSA.
19. Nazarbayev, Nursultan. (1995, November 15). *Address by H. E. Mr. Nursultan Nazarbayev, President of the Republic of Kazakhstan to the twenty-eighth session of the General Conference of the United Nations Educational, Scientific and Cultural Organisation*, Paris.
20. Ruggie, John Gerard (ed.). (1993). *Multilateralism Matters. The Theory and Praxis of an Institutional Form*. New York: Columbia University Press.
21. Samaddar, Ranabir. (1996). *Whose Asia Is It Anyway: Region and the Nation in South Asia*. Calcutta: Pearl Publishers for Maulana Abul Kalam Azad Institute of Asian Studies.
22. Schlesinger, Stephen. (2005). 'The United States and the World: Is a Return to Multilateralism Possible?' In C. Uday Bhaskar et al. (eds.), *United Nations: Multilateralism and International Security*. Delhi: Shipra Publications.
23. Sengupta, Anita. (2004). 'Region, Regionalisation, Regionalism: The 'Myth' of TsentralnayaAziia Revisited.' In K. Warikoo and Mahavir Singh (eds.), *Central Asia since Independence*. New Delhi: Shipra.
24. Weitz, Richard. (2008, July). 'Kazakhstan and the New International Politics of Eurasia.' *Silk Road Paper*. Central Asia-Caucasus Institute and Silk Road Studies Programme. www.silkroadstudies.org.

SECTION II

State, Nation-Building and Political-Economic Development

6

State and Nation-Building in Kazakhstan: Issues and Challenges

Dr. Pramod Kumar

The post-Soviet transformation of Kazakhstan represents one of the most complex and multidimensional cases of state and nation building in the contemporary world. Since independence on December 16, 1991, Kazakhstan has navigated the gentle balance between building effective governance institutions along with national identity from its ethnically diverse population. The process of state-building and nation-building in Kazakhstan has been characterised by significant institutional development, societal transformation demographic shifts and economic transformation that continue to shape the country's development path.

Kazakhstan, the world's largest landlocked country and the ninth-largest by land area, emerged from the shadows of the Soviet Union to declare its independence. This momentous occasion marked the beginning of a profound transformation for the nation, which had been significantly influenced by Soviet policies that emphasised centralised governance and ethnic homogenisation with over 130 ethnic groups living together in its vast territory (Sajjanhar, 2013).

Kazakhstan faced the dual challenge of building a unified nation while managing a diverse demographic landscape. Kazakhstan's nomadic past, which includes elements from the historic Silk Road as well as a combination of Turkic, Persian, Mongol, and Russian customs, is fundamental to the country's cultural identity (Kaushik & Khalfin, 1970). The majority of Kazakhs were nomadic prior to the Soviet era. Traditional instruments like the dombra, oral poetry in Kazakh, and unusual customs like yurt dwelling continue to represent nomadic culture (Syzdykova et al., 2024). The legacy of the Soviet era, characterised by policies of industrialisation and forced migration, created a unique context for the state-building and nation-formation processes in the post-Soviet period (Narottum, 2006).

From the beginning, Kazakhstan's leaders recognised the importance of establishing a stable political framework that could assist economic development and social unity. It is the richest country in Central Asia due to its massive reserves of gas, oil, and mineral resources and its growing significance in geopolitics as well as its expanding economic importance, development outlook, and stable politics and economy (Yilmaz, 2017). Nursultan Nazarbayev, the country's first president, played a crucial role in shaping the political landscape, adopting a pragmatic approach that balanced the need for strong centralised governance with efforts to foster democratic institutions. The Constitution adopted in 1995 laid the groundwork for these institutions, promoting principles such as democracy, the rule of law, and respect for human rights (Kemelova, 2025). However, the realisation of these principles has often been marred by accusations of political consolidation and limited political pluralism, leading to on-going debates about the nature of governance in Kazakhstan.

The process of nation-building in Kazakhstan has also been profoundly influenced by the interplay between ethnic identity and state policies. The government has sought to promote a singular Kazakh identity, emphasising the Kazakh language, culture, and historical narratives, while also recognising the rights of minority populations (Yerekesheva, 2020). This attempt reflects the complexities of creating a unified national identity in a country characterised by its ethnic diversity (Brown, 2024). The challenge lies in balancing the promotion of a dominant national identity with the need to integrate the various ethnic groups that contribute to the nation's cultural richness.

Economically, Kazakhstan has undergone a significant transformation since independence, shifting from a centrally planned economy to a market-oriented model. The country's abundant natural resources, particularly in the oil and gas sectors, have played a pivotal role in driving economic growth and attracting foreign investment (Cornell et al., 2021a). However, this reliance on resource extraction has also raised concerns about economic diversification and sustainability. As the country navigates these economic challenges, social transformations have accompanied the shifts in political and economic spheres, impacting the lives of ordinary citizens and reshaping societal values.

Kazakhstan's geopolitical position further complicates its state-building efforts. It has overlapping borders of both Europe and Asia. Kazakhstan has pursued a multi-vector foreign policy aimed at the development of relationships with major powers, including Russia, China, and Western nations (Gaur, 2024). This strategy has been instrumental in promoting national security and economic cooperation, but it also poses challenges as the country seeks to assert its independence and navigate regional dynamics.

In the light of these factors, this chapter aims to provide a deeper understanding of state-building and nation-building in Kazakhstan since 1991. By exploring the historical context, institutional development, and societal transformations, this research seeks to understand the complexities and nuances of Kazakhstan's unique path towards nationhood. It will also examine the ongoing challenges and opportunities that drive this country to strengthen its state institutions, promote national unity, and ensure sustainable development in the years to come.

Foundations of State-Building and Nation-Building in Kazakhstan

Soviet Nationality Policies and its Implications

It is a well well-known fact that state and state apparatus existed before the Soviet era. Rather than going into deep history, this author considers the state-building and nation building analysis from the Soviet past in this chapter. The Soviet period represented a fundamental change in Central Asian cultural identity formation. The policy of *korenizatsiya* (indigenisation) of 1927-1928 initially promoted Kazakh language and culture, recruiting ethnic Kazakhs to administrative and party positions while developing national forms of expression. This policy aimed to create 'national in form, socialist in content' identities that would ultimately merge into a unified Soviet nation (Dadabaev & Komatsu, 2016). Through the process of national delimitation in the 1920s and 1930s, the Soviet authorities created modern Central Asian national identities by drawing territorial boundaries based on ethnic groups that largely persist today. These processes elaborate the systematic creation of national languages, literatures, and cultural institutions designed to subordinate national identities within the Soviet framework (Sengupta, 2017).

However, the reversal of *korenizatsiya* by the late 1930s initiated a systematic Russification campaign that had profound consequences for Kazakh identity. The policy shift declared ethnic Russians as 'first among equals' and placed them as culturally superior guides for 'backward' peoples. The impact on education was particularly severe, with only two Kazakh-language schools remaining in Almaty by the late Soviet period. This 'russification of the masses' was arguably more successful in Kazakhstan than in any other Soviet republic, creating what scholars term a 'deep sense of insecurity' in modern Kazakh identity (Bourdais Park et al., 2023).

The Soviet nationality policy produced paradoxical results in Central Asia. While officially promoting national cultures, Soviet authorities simultaneously worked to weaken traditional social structures and religious practices that formed the basis of pre-Soviet identity (Bourdais Park et al., 2023). The creation of uniform literary languages, educational systems, and cultural institutions nurtured modern national consciousness. On the other side, they started undermining traditional forms of identity based on tribal, regional, and religious affiliations (Kaushik & Khalfin, 1970).

The Soviet approach to Central Asian identity involved selective preservation and transformation of cultural elements. Traditional arts like carpet weaving, music, and dance were maintained and even promoted, but religious practices were suppressed and nomadic lifestyles were forcibly sedentarised. This selective cultural policy created hybrid identities that combined Soviet modernisation with conserved elements of traditional culture (Ubiria, 2015).

Soviet Legacy and the Path to Kazakhstan's Independence

Kazakhstan's incorporation into the Soviet Union began with the establishment of the Kirghiz Autonomous Soviet Socialist Republic (ASSR) in 1920, which was later renamed the Kazakh ASSR in 1925. It was elevated to the status of a union republic on December 5, 1936, becoming the Kazakh Soviet Socialist Republic (Kazakh SSR). This period saw significant demographic changes due to policies of forced collectivisation and settlement, which aimed to transform the largely nomadic Kazakh population into a settled agricultural society (Sengupta, 2017). These policies led to catastrophic consequences, including the Kazakh famine of 1930-1933, which resulted in the deaths of between one and two million people (Bureau of South and Central Asian Affairs, 2008).

It is difficult to determine the exact percentage of Kazakhstanis who have a nostalgic perspective of the Soviet era, considering it to be very different from Russian colonial authority. Although there are certainly Kazakhs who share this opinion, it appears to be more prevalent among non-Kazakhs (and not only ethnic Russians) than among ethnic Kazakhs. These Kazakhs are typically those who grew up on state or collective farms that did not successfully transition to commercial agriculture, were close to or at pension age at the time of the Soviet Union's collapse, and struggled to adjust to the end of the social welfare state. This group also occasionally includes former military personnel, doctors, and teachers, who lament the loss of the respect and comparatively higher pay they once had as members of these professions, as well as the social mobility they perceived as a characteristic of Soviet authority. Former members and activists of the Communist Party are also frequently included in this group. They believe that Kazakhstan's political philosophy should incorporate more of the traditional socialist principles, and for non-Kazakhs, more of the traditional internationalist doctrine. (M. Olcott, 2011a)

Kazakhstan's territory was significantly shaped during the Soviet era, where it was established as an autonomous republic and later as a union republic within the USSR. The borders that define Kazakhstan today were largely drawn during this period, with ethnic considerations influencing territorial demarcations. The legacy of Soviet governance created a unique backdrop for nation-building efforts post-independence, as Kazakhstan emerged as one of the fifteen republics following the dissolution of the Soviet Union in 1991. (Kadyrzhanov, 2023). Kazakhstan's historical context is deeply rooted in its experiences under Soviet rule, which significantly shaped its national identity and institutional framework. The evolution of Kazakhstan from a Soviet republic to an independent nation is marked by key events and policies that influenced its demographic, political, and cultural landscape.

The Kazakh ruling class was closely integrated into the top levels of the Soviet hierarchy throughout the Soviet era. Dinmuhamed Kunayev, a long-time full member of the Politburo (the inner political circle of the Kremlin) and a close colleague of the former Soviet leader, Leonid Brezhnev, was actually the sole representative of the CARs. The 'Kazakhstan Affairs', Gorbachev's anti-corruption campaign, was the only time Almaty's relations with Moscow deteriorated. However, during the second phase of Gorbachev's rule, Kazakhstan's leaders were heavily involved in Moscow politics and backed Gorbachev's efforts to maintain the USSR's integrity (Shakenov et al., 2024). When three Slavic republics – Russia, Belorussia, and Ukraine – excluded them from a discussion on the future of the Soviet Union and even failed to consult them on the decision to dissolve the USSR unconditionally, they were taken aback. Following independence, Kazakhstan's old Soviet name has been essential to control a peaceful political and economic transition, where the president's character was supreme. President Nazarbaev, who served as Prime Minister from 1984 to 1989, was elected in 1989 on behalf of the pragmatic and somewhat nationalistic Kazakh elite. His generation was raised under the unique conditions of Kazakhstan and was a direct result of Soviet social engineering (Abazov, 1998a).

The majority of the President's staff came from the Soviet nomenclatura's industrial managerial class. Even though it was the Soviet command economy, the President and his high-ranking appointees had the training and experience to manage the economy, unlike the professional Party officials. Nazarbaev's predecessor left him with a respectable rapport with President Yeltsin and the conservative elite in Russia. However, there has been a very bad relationship with the young reformers and the group of Russian nationalists (Brown, 2024).

The post-Soviet period witnessed a remarkable revival of Islamic religious practices and cultural expressions that had been suppressed during the Soviet era. Thousands of mosques were reopened or newly constructed, and pilgrimage to Mecca resumed on a large scale. Islamic education experienced a significant expansion. This religious revival characterised both genuine cultural restoration and strategic political positioning by post-Soviet elites (Ubiria, 2015). The Ruling Elites were seeking to distinguish their societies from Russian influence. Traditional cultural practices experienced a significant revival during this period. They started celebration of pre-Islamic festivals like Navruz, the restoration of traditional crafts, and the promotion of indigenous languages. Governments throughout Central Asia invested heavily in cultural institutions designed to preserve and promote national heritage. They also started constructing new national narratives that emphasised continuity with pre-Soviet traditions (Sengupta, 2017).

The complex political climate in the republic has made Kazakhstan's political and socio-economic circumstances especially challenging. In the northern oblasts of Kazakhstan, where ethnic Russians made up the majority, separatist sentiments were on the rise. A strong public dispute about the status of Russian and Kazakh languages further exacerbated the issue (BINICI, 2022). The dissolution of the Soviet Union in 1991 presented Kazakhstan with a critical juncture. In the middle of the political turmoil and economic decline of the late 1980s, the Kazakhstani leadership, led by Nazarbayev, moved swiftly to assert the nation's independence. On December 1, 1991, Kazakhstan held its first presidential elections, with Nazarbayev emerging as the clear winner (Nohlen et al., 2001, p. 408). The formal declaration of independence followed on December 16, marking a pivotal moment in Kazakhstan's history and the beginning of its journey as a sovereign nation.

Institutional Development and Political Evolution

In the aftermath of independence, Kazakhstan faced the urgent task of establishing a functioning political system and state institutions. The 1995 Constitution was a significant milestone in this regard, outlining the framework for governance and asserting the principles of democracy and human rights (The Republic of Kazakhstan, Astana, 'Akorda' Presidential Palace). The initial years of independence were marked by economic turmoil, hyperinflation, and social unrest. The government recognised that effective state institutions were essential for maintaining stability and promoting economic growth. As a result, the Kazakhstani leadership focused on strengthening executive power, centralising authority, and creating a coherent administrative structure (Abazov, 1998b). This included the establishment of a bicameral parliament, the Senate and Mazhilis, which were designed to represent various interests within society.

The early years of independence were marked by the consolidation of power under President Nursultan Nazarbayev, who emphasised a strong presidential system to ensure stability in a nation characterised by ethnic diversity. The establishment of a new constitution and legislative framework aimed to unify various ethnic groups under a singular Kazakh identity while promoting civic nationalism. This approach laid the groundwork for institutional development that would evolve further under subsequent leadership, particularly during Kassym-Jomart Tokayev's presidency starting in 2019. Tokayev's administration has sought to address calls for reform and greater civic engagement, responding to societal demands for transparency and accountability (Melich & Adibayeva, 2013).

The establishment of institutions such as the Assembly of People of Kazakhstan in 1995 was instrumental in addressing ethnic diversity and fostering inter-ethnic dialogue. This body aimed to promote tolerance and understanding among the various ethnic groups residing in Kazakhstan. In addition to guaranteeing equal rights and freedoms for the nation's people, one of the body's objectives was to preserve social harmony and stability between different ethnic and religious groups. In addition to guaranteeing equal rights and freedoms for all the nation's people, the organisation sought to preserve inter-ethnic and inter-faith harmony and stability in society (Sharipova & Shormanbayeva, 2024). However, the challenge of balancing a dominant

Kazakh identity with the integration of other ethnic communities remained a contentious issue, particularly as some minority groups expressed concerns over potential marginalisation.

(a) **Constitutional Framework**: Kazakhstan's first post-independence constitution was adopted in 1993, marking a significant departure from the Soviet-era legal framework. This constitution established the foundations of a unitary republic with a strong executive branch. However, it was the 1995 constitution that solidified the presidential system, granting extensive powers to the president while outlining the roles of the legislative and judicial branches (Nurakhamet, 2019). Over a period of time, amendments have been introduced to mitigate executive supremacy and enhance legislative authority. Notably, constitutional amendments in 2017 (*2017 Constitutional Reform in Kazakhstan*, n.d.; Pistan, 2017) and 2022 aimed to reduce presidential powers and increase checks on executive authority, including the re-establishment of a constitutional court and greater autonomy for local leaders (*In Kazakhstan, Constitutional Council to Consider President's Amendment Proposals*, n.d.).

(b) **Legislative Structure**: Kazakhstan operates under a bicameral legislature consisting of the Senate and the Mazhilis (Assembly). The Senate comprises members elected indirectly by regional assemblies and those appointed by the president, while the Mazhilis includes representatives elected through both proportional representation and single-seat constituencies. This structure allows for a degree of representation across various demographics, although concerns about the effectiveness and independence of these bodies persist. The legislative process is designed to facilitate checks and balances; however, historically, it has often aligned closely with presidential initiatives, limiting its role as an independent actor in governance (United States Bureau of Citizenship and Immigration Services, 1994).

(c) **Local Governance**: The local governance framework in Kazakhstan has undergone significant changes since independence. Initially, local governments retained some decision-making powers inherited from the Soviet system. However, subsequent reforms have aimed at centralising authority within the executive branch. The *akims* (local governors) serve as representatives of the president at local levels, which has often resulted in diminished local autonomy. Recent efforts have focused on decentralisation, aiming to enhance accountability and responsiveness of local governments to their constituents. These reforms are crucial for addressing regional disparities and fostering civic engagement.

(d) **Political Dynamics**: The political landscape in Kazakhstan has been shaped by its leadership transitions and responses to public demands for reform. Under Nursultan Nazarbayev's presidency, political power was concentrated at the top, with limited space for opposition parties. However, following Tokayev's rise to the presidency in 2019, there has been a visible shift towards reforming political institutions. Tokayev's administration has initiated constitutional amendments aimed at reducing nepotism and enhancing legislative power (*Kazakhstan*, Chatham House report, 2023). This transition represents a critical juncture for Kazakhstan as it seeks to balance stability with democratic aspirations.

Nation-Building in Post-Soviet Kazakhstan

The process of nation-building in Kazakhstan since its independence in 1991 has been a multifaceted attempt, shaped by historical legacies, ethnic diversity, and the aspirations of its leadership. This section examines the key elements of Kazakhstan's nation-building efforts, focusing on the roles of territory, identity, and governance in shaping an interconnected national narrative. Nation formation in Kazakhstan has involved navigating the complexities of ethnic diversity while promoting an inter-related national identity. This dual focus is critical for fostering social cohesion in a multi-ethnic society where historical grievances and economic disparities persist (Aitymbetov et al., 2015).

Doctrine of National Unity and Managed Multiculturalism

The 2009 Doctrine of National Unity represented Nazarbayev's most ambitious attempt to reconcile ethnic and civic approaches to identity. The doctrine envisioned Kazakhstan as a 'multicultural melting pot' where every citizen was primarily a 'Kazakhstani' rather than identified by ethnic origin. Three key principles guided implementation: 'one country, one destiny', 'various origins, equal opportunities,' and 'development of a national spirit' ('Kazakhstan's Ethnic Policy 1991-2021,' 2021).

However, the doctrine faced resistance from Kazakh nationalists who argued that the Kazakh language was losing ground to Russian and required greater prominence. The 'National Patriots' movement criticised policies that they perceived as insufficient protection for Kazakh cultural identity. In response, modifications were made to the final version to address these concerns, demonstrating the limits of top-down identity construction (Burkhanov, 2020). The doctrine's mixed reception illustrates the fundamental tension in Kazakhstan's nation-building project. While officially promoting civic nationalism, the state simultaneously reinforced ethnic Kazakh privilege through constitutional provisions, language policies, and symbolic representations. This contradiction reflects what one analysis terms the 'inevitable' dilemma between civic Kazakhstani and ethnic Kazakh conceptions of nationhood (Kadyraliyeva et al., 2019).

Kazakhstan's territorial identity was largely established during the Soviet era, when the borders of the Kazakh SSR were delineated based on ethnic considerations. Upon gaining independence, Kazakhstan inherited these borders, which became the foundation for its national identity. The geographical expanse of Kazakhstan is not only significant for its economic potential but also plays a crucial role in fostering a sense of belonging among its diverse population. The recognition of Kazakhstan as the homeland for ethnic Kazakhs is reflected in its official name and national symbols, emphasising the core nation's historical connection to the land (Kadyrzhanov, 2023).

The quest for a national identity has been a central theme in Kazakhstan's post-Soviet state-building process. The diverse ethnic composition of the country presented both opportunities and challenges in forging a cohesive national identity. The government initiated several policies aimed at promoting a unified Kazakh identity while recognising the rights of minority groups (Brown, 2024). These policies included the promotion of the Kazakh language in education and public life, the revival of traditional cultural practices, and the celebration of national holidays.

The concept of a 'core nation' is essential in understanding Kazakhstan's nation formation. Ethnic Kazakhs are recognised as the titular nation, forming a demographic majority and holding a significant place in the political and cultural landscape. This status has been reinforced through various state policies aimed at promoting Kazakh language and culture while also acknowledging the contributions of other ethnic groups within the country. The government's emphasis on Kazakhization reflects an effort to solidify national identity while navigating the complexities of a multi-ethnic society (Melich & Adibayeva, 2013). Cultural policies, including the promotion of Kazakh history and the establishment of cultural institutions, played a vital role in shaping national consciousness. The government's focus on reviving Kazakh traditions and promoting national pride contributed to a growing sense of belonging among citizens.

In the immediate aftermath of independence, Kazakhstan undertook several initiatives to establish itself as a sovereign state. These included creating state symbols, establishing citizenship laws, and forming independent institutions. The relocation of the capital from Almaty to Nur-Sultan (formerly Akmolinsk) was a strategic decision aimed at fostering national unity and enhancing geopolitical stability. This move symbolized a new beginning for Kazakhstan, allowing it to position itself as a modern state capable of integrating its diverse regions (Bulatkulova, 2021).

Kazakhstan's approach to governance has evolved from an elite-driven model towards a more inclusive civic identity. While initial nation-building efforts were largely top-down, recent administrations have increasingly recognised the importance of civic engagement in fostering national unity. President Kassym-Jomart Tokayev's vision for 'New Kazakhstan' emphasises democratic reforms and greater public participation in governance, reflecting an acknowledgement of societal demands for accountability and transparency (Narottum, 2006). This shift is crucial for building a progressive national identity that resonates with all citizens.

Societal Transformation in Post-Soviet Kazakhstan

Since gaining independence in 1991, Kazakhstan has undergone profound societal transformations that reflect its complex historical legacy, economic shifts, and evolving cultural dynamics. This section explores the key aspects of these transformations, including demographic changes, economic development, social welfare reforms, and the interplay of ethnic identities (Yilmaz, 2017). The societal transformation in post-Soviet Kazakhstan has been a complex and multifaceted process, shaped by rapid economic changes, demographic shifts, evolving social values, and the quest for a cohesive national identity. This section explores the key dimensions of societal transformation, including economic reforms, urbanisation, changes in social structures, and the emergence of civil society.

Urbanisation and Demographic Shifts: The post-independence period has witnessed significant demographic changes in Kazakhstan, particularly in urbanisation patterns. The influx of rural populations into urban areas has transformed the social landscape, creating new challenges related to housing, infrastructure, and public services ('Nation-Building Reset in Kazakhstan,' 2023).

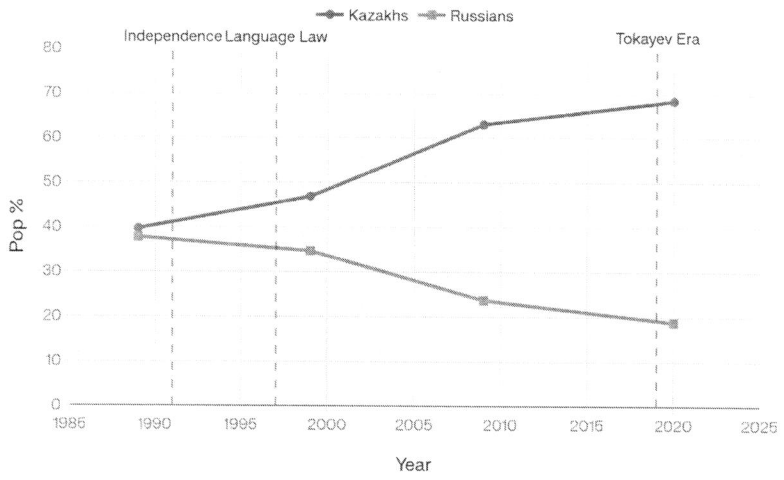

Kazakhstan's State and Nation Building Trajectory: Demographic Shifts, Political Milestones, and Economic Diversification (1989-2025)

Kazakhstan, like the majority of the world's countries, is thought to be becoming more urbanised. In Kazakhstan as well as in most other regions of the world, the migration of people from rural to urban areas has long been a significant global trend. Nearly fifty-eight percent of Kazakhstan's population presently resides in urban areas, according to UN projections. This is in line with the fifty-six percent global average rate of urbanisation. Nevertheless, rather than being a typical nation with moderate rates of urbanisation, Kazakhstan seems to be an anomaly when it comes to the dynamics of urbanisation. It is surprising to learn that despite having a relatively average proportion of the population living in cities, Kazakhstan has become much more urbanised over the past few decades than other developing nations. However, because of its slower rate of urbanisation than most other nations, Kazakhstan has finally become an average nation (Shakenov et al., 2024). Cities like Almaty and Nur-Sultan (formerly Astana) have experienced rapid growth, becoming hubs of economic activity, cultural exchange, and political engagement. Kazakhstan welcomed a substantial influx of ethnic Kazakh immigrants (oralmans) from neighbouring countries, which helped to reshape the demographic landscape and reinforce the Kazakh identity within the nation (M. Olcott, 2011b; M. B. Olcott et al., 2015). The urbanisation process has also resulted in a shift in societal values and lifestyles. As urban centres become more cosmopolitan, the traditional norms and customs of rural communities are being challenged.

Language Policy and Cultural Frameworks

Language policy became a central battleground for competing visions of national identity. The 1989 Language Law designated Kazakh as the sole state language while relegating Russian to the status of 'language of interethnic communication'. However, implementation proved challenging given that Russian remained the lingua franca for most of the population, including many ethnic Kazakhs ('Kazakhstan's Ethnic Policy 1991-2021,' 2021). The practical limitations of language policy reflected deeper structural challenges. Despite official promotion of Kazakh, Russian maintained dominance in education, media, and economic spheres. By 2020, only about two-thirds of the population were believed to speak fluent Kazakh, with Russian still serving as the primary language in major cities. This linguistic divide reinforced ethnic boundaries while complicating efforts to build a unified civic identity (Shakenov et al., 2024).

President Nazarbayev's response involved what he termed 'pragmatic' language policies, including the 2007 'Trinity of Languages' initiative promoting Kazakh, Russian, and English as priority languages. However, this initiative received limited support due to slow progress in Kazakh language development and resistance from nationalist groups advocating for more aggressive Kazakhization (In *Kazakhstan, Constitutional Council to Consider President's Amendment Proposals*, n.d.).

Language Policy and Alphabet Reform

Language policy remains a contentious aspect of nation-building, reflecting deeper tensions between ethnic and civic conceptions of identity. While Kazakh serves as the state language, Russian continues to dominate in urban areas, higher education, and economic spheres. This linguistic divide reinforces ethnic boundaries and complicates efforts to build unified national identity. The proposed transition from Cyrillic to Latin script for Kazakh represents the most ambitious language reform since independence. Initially scheduled for completion by 2025, the initiative aims to distance Kazakhstan from Russian cultural influence while aligning with Turkic linguistic traditions. Supporters argue Latinisation will facilitate technological integration and strengthen pan-Turkic connections, while critics warn of enormous costs and potential social disruption (Syzdykova et al., 2024).

The alphabet debate encapsulates broader struggles over national identity. Nationalist advocates view Latinisation as essential for cultural decolonisation and authentic Kazakh identity formation. However, opponents, including many Russian speakers and pragmatic officials, emphasize practical challenges and potential negative impacts on inter-ethnic relations. The reform's ultimate implementation remains uncertain, reflecting continued ambivalence about the pace and scope of Kazakhization policies (Cornell et al., 2021b).

Economic Development: The country's rich natural resources, particularly in oil and gas, have been pivotal in driving economic development. Kazakhstan has become one of the leading oil producers in the region, with significant foreign investment in the energy sector (Asian Development Bank and the Islamic Development Bank, 2024). This influx of capital has facilitated infrastructural development, technological advancements, and the expansion of various industries, contributing to overall economic growth. However, the over-reliance on natural resources has raised concerns about economic diversification and vulnerability to global market fluctuations (Bank, 2017).

Kazakhstan's transition from a centrally planned economy to a market-oriented system has been one of its most significant societal transformations. The country initially faced severe economic challenges following independence, including hyperinflation and unemployment due to its integration with the collapsing Soviet economy. However, Kazakhstan quickly implemented economic reforms that attracted foreign investment, particularly in the oil and gas sectors (Cornell et al., 2021a; M. Olcott, 2011b; M. B. Olcott et al., 2015). The discovery of major oil reserves, such as the Kashagan field in 2000, marked a turning point for the economy. By diversifying its economy and establishing a national oil fund to manage revenues effectively, Kazakhstan transitioned into a middle-income country with a growing GDP. The share of industry in value added increased significantly during this time, reflecting a shift away from agriculture towards extractive industries and services (BTI 2024, n.d.; Bertelsmann Stiftung's Transformation Index (BTI) 2024).

Kazakhstan's economic transformation has been a crucial aspect of its state-building efforts. In the early years following independence, the government faced the daunting task of transitioning from a centrally planned economy to a market-oriented system. The privatisation of state-owned enterprises, coupled with the liberalisation of trade, aimed to stimulate economic growth and attract foreign investment. The government strategically positioned the oil and gas sectors as key drivers of economic development, capitalising on Kazakhstan's vast natural resources. The nation has seen substantial foreign investment and market-oriented reforms. However, political reform in Kazakhstan remains behind, despite the adage that many prosperous nations in Southeast Asia have adopted: "First the economy and then politics" (Wandel & Kozbagarova, 2009; Wandel & Kozbagarova, 2009). Despite the initial challenges of economic instability, including inflation and unemployment, Kazakhstan emerged as one of the fastest-growing economies in the region by the late 1990s.

Changes in Social Structures: Inheriting a Soviet-era social welfare system on the brink of collapse posed significant challenges for Kazakhstan. In response, the government undertook extensive reforms to modernise its social safety nets. These included overhauling the pension system to offer citizens choices between private and public plans and improving healthcare and education systems by allowing private sector participation alongside public services (Ruffin & Waugh, 1999; BTI 2024). Despite these efforts, disparities in service quality across different regions remain a concern. While access to social services has improved overall, there are still significant gaps that need addressing to ensure equitable access for all citizens (M. Olcott, 2011a).

Kazakhstan's ethnic diversity is both strength and a challenge in its nation-building efforts. The country is home to over 100 ethnic groups, with ethnic Kazakhs constituting the majority. The government has promoted a multi-ethnic identity while emphasising Kazakh culture and language as central to national identity. This approach aims to foster social cohesion among various ethnic communities while acknowledging their contributions to the nation (BTI 2024, n.d.; Bertelsmann Stiftung's Transformation Index (BTI) 2024). The commitment to building a secular state that respects multiple confessions has also played a role in maintaining stability amid ethnic diversity. The government's policies have focused on creating an inclusive environment where all citizens can participate in national life regardless of their ethnic background (Kazakhstan, n.d.; Chatham House Report, 2023).

The Rise of Civil Society: The emergence of civil society has been a notable aspect of societal transformation in Kazakhstan. Following independence, there has been a gradual increase in civic engagement and activism, as citizens seek to participate in the political process and advocate for their rights. The establishment of non-governmental organisations (NGOs) and grassroots movements has contributed to a more vibrant civil society, fostering discussions on issues such as human rights, environmental protection, and social justice. The customs of nomadic life are the foundation of Kazakhstan's civic society. In order to survive in the hostile Kazakh steppes, clan members needed to have strong familial ties and the support of one another. Tribal norms are still present today in the general preference for using family and community networks rather than institutional organisations to address issues and meet needs (Asian Development Bank). Nevertheless, civil society organisations continue to play a crucial role in raising awareness about social issues and mobilising public support for various causes.

Contemporary Challenges and the 'New Kazakhstan' Project

Tokayev's Reform Agenda and Democratic Transition

President Tokayev has positioned his administration as pursuing a 'New Kazakhstan' that breaks with strict practices while maintaining stability. The reform program includes political liberalisation, anti-corruption measures, and economic modernisation aimed at building what Tokayev terms a 'listening state' responsive to citizen demands (Singh & Srivastava, 2019).

Political reforms have included establishing the National Council of Public Trust as a platform for government-society dialogue and expanding opposition representation in parliament. For the first time, opposition parties received guaranteed committee chairmanships and the right to initiate parliamentary hearings. These changes reflect Tokayev's principle of 'different opinions, a unified nation' in contrast to previous rubber-stamp practices (Mkrtchyan, 2014). However, implementation has proven inconsistent with reform rhetoric. While some political prisoners have been released and protest laws liberalised, civil society organisations report continued restrictions on freedom of assembly and expression. The gap between announced reforms and actual practice reflects on-going tension between democratisation imperatives and elite preferences for controlled change (Hub, 2025).

Conclusion

Kazakhstan's post-Soviet transformation illustrates a complex and dynamic process of state-building and nation formation. Since gaining independence in 1991, the country has made notable strides in economic development, institutional evolution, and societal modernisation. These achievements include the establishment of a stable political framework, economic reforms that have driven growth and urbanisation, and the emergence of a new middle class alongside increased workforce participation by women. Yet, these developments exist alongside enduring challenges, highlighting the intricate balance between progress and obstacles in Kazakhstan's national journey.

The legacy of Soviet-era strict governance and the diverse ethnic make-up of Kazakhstan have presented unique challenges in forging a cohesive national identity. While Kazakhstan has worked to develop democratic institutions, strengthen civil society, and uphold the rule of law, progress remains uneven. Centralised governance continues to dominate, and the need for political pluralism, accountability, and citizen participation is critical for genuine democratic advancement. Economic reforms have reshaped societal structures and relationships, fostering significant social change. Urbanisation and modernisation have brought about new opportunities, but they have also accentuated regional disparities and inequalities. The integration of diverse ethnic communities remains a sensitive and ongoing process, underscoring the importance of inclusive policies that promote cultural preservation and social cohesion.

Kazakhstan's geopolitical positioning, with its multi-vector foreign policy, has played a pivotal role in shaping its national identity and societal dynamics. By balancing relationships with major powers while asserting sovereignty and pursuing economic growth, Kazakhstan has carved out a strategic role in the region. This approach has been instrumental in maintaining stability and fostering development, but it also requires continued diplomatic agility and focus on national priorities. Looking ahead, Kazakhstan faces several critical priorities: addressing socio-economic inequalities, strengthening democratic governance, and fostering a shared sense of national unity amidst its diversity. These efforts will require sustained commitment from both the government and its citizens. Enhancing civic engagement, promoting inclusive development, and ensuring the representation of all societal groups will be essential to building a resilient and equitable nation.

Finally, Kazakhstan's post-Soviet experience offers a convincing case study of the challenges and achievements in state-building and nation formation. As the country moves forward, its ability to reconcile historical legacies with contemporary aspirations will define its trajectory. Through a focus on democratic governance, economic diversification, and social cohesion, Kazakhstan has the potential to emerge as a resilient and inclusive nation, poised to lead as a pivotal player in Central Asia's future.

Kazakhstan's three-decade experience of state and nation building reveals both achievements and persistent challenges in managing the complex transition from a Soviet republic to an independent nation-state. The country has successfully maintained territorial integrity, escaped major ethnic conflicts, and achieved significant economic development along with building basic institutional frameworks for governance. The peaceful political transition following Nazarbayev's resignation and the management of the 2022 crisis demonstrate institutional resilience despite political consolidation legacies. However, fundamental tensions remain unresolved between ethnic and civic conceptions of nationhood, democratic aspirations and diversification goals and resource dependence. The demographic shift favouring ethnic Kazakhs has enabled more assertive cultural policies (Cornell et al., 2021b).

The 'New Kazakhstan' project under President Tokayev represents an opportunity to address these challenges. He initiated genuine democratic reforms, inclusive identity formation, and sustainable economic development. However, implementation requires overcoming deep-rooted elite interests, institutional weaknesses (Cornell et al., 2021a). The success of Kazakhstan's state and nation-building project ultimately depends on its ability to balance competing demands while building legitimate, effective, and inclusive institutions capable of serving all citizens regardless of ethnic origin or social status. As Kazakhstan continues to navigate these challenges, its success or failure in building a stable, prosperous, and democratic society will influence regional stability and provide lessons for other transitional societies facing similar dilemmas of identity, governance, and development in an increasingly global environment.

References

1. 2017 Constitutional Reform in Kazakhstan: Increasing democracy without political pluralism? (n.d.). Constitution Net. http://constitutionnet.org/news/2017-constitutional-reform-kazakhstan-increasing-democracy-without-political-pluralism. Accessed on August 31, 2025.
2. Abazov, R. (1998a). Practice of Foreign Policy Making: Formation of Post-Soviet Politics of Kazakhstan, Kyrgyzstan, and Uzbekistan. Almaty, Kazakhstan. Accessed November 27 (2021), 96–98.
3. Abazov, R. (1998b). Practice of Foreign Policy Making: Formation of Post-Soviet Politics of Kazakhstan, Kyrgyzstan, and Uzbekistan. Almaty, Kazakhstan. Accessed November 27 (2021), 96–98.
4. Aitymbetov, N., Toktarov, E., &Ormakhanova, Y. (2015). 'Nation-building in Kazakhstan: Kazakh and Kazakhstani identities controversy.' *Bilig*, 74, 1–20.
5. Bank, A. D. (2017, September 18). Building a Diversified and Sustainable Economy in Kazakhstan (Kazakhstan) [Text]. https://www.adb.org/news/features/building-diversified-and-sustainable-economy-kazakhstan. Accessed on 19 November 2024.
6. Bourdais Park, J., Adibayeva, A., & Saari, D. (2023). 'De-Sovietization, State-Building, and Re-Regionalization.' In J. Bourdais Park, A. Adibayeva, & D. Saari, *Politics of Regionalism in Central Asia* (pp. 43–81). Springer Nature, Singapore. https://doi.org/10.1007/978-981-99-4079-0_2. Accessed on 24 November 2024.
7. Brown, M. T. (2024). 'Kazakh Means Freedom'-Kazakh Language Policy and National Identity Before and During the Ukraine War. https://scholarcommons.sc.edu/senior_theses/684/. Accessed on 30 November 2024.
8. BTI 2024: Kazakhstan. (n.d.). BTI 2024. https://bti-project.org/en/reports/country-

dashboard?isocode=KAZ&cHash=eb00c1545e5c1984d9d511f8eaed47cb. Accessed on 31 August 2025.

9. Bulatkulova, S. (2021, December 13). 'Kazakhstan's Path to Building a Progressive Nation.' *The Astana Times*. https://astanatimes.com/2021/12/kazakhstans-path-to-building-a-progressive-nation/. Accessed on 10 July 2025.
10. Burkhanov, A. (2020). 'Multiculturalism and Nation-Building in Kazakhstan: Trends in Media Discourse, State Policy, and Popular Perceptions.' *Muslim World*, 110(1). Accessed on 19 July 2025.
11. Cornell, S.E., Starr, S.F., & Barro, A. (2021a). 'Political and economic reforms in Kazakhstan under President Tokayev.' Central Asia-Caucasus Institute & Silk Road Studies Program, https://Silkroadstudies. Org/Resources/211201Kaz-Reforms. Pdf Accessed on 11 October 2022.
12. Cornell, S.E., Starr, S.F., & Barro, A. (2021b). 'Political and economic reforms in Kazakhstan under President Tokayev.' Central Asia-Caucasus Institute & Silk Road Studies Program, https://Silkroadstudies. Org/Resources/211201Kaz-Reforms. Pdf Accessed on 11 October 2022.
13. Dadabaev, T., & Komatsu, H. (2016). *Kazakhstan, Kyrgyzstan, and Uzbekistan: Life and politics during the Soviet era*. Springer.
14. Gaur, P. (2024, July 9). *Navigating Kazakhstan's 'multi-vector' foreign policy in an evolving geopolitical landscape.* Indian Council of World Affairs. ICWA.
15. Hub, K. (2025, August 31). Transparency International Knowledge Hub (https://knowledgehub.transparency.org/) [Text/html]. Knowledge Hub; Knowledge Hub. https://knowledgehub.transparency.org/helpdesk/kazakhstan-overview-of-corruption-and-anti-corruption. Accessed on 18 March 2025.
16. In Kazakhstan, constitutional council to consider president's amendment proposals. (n.d.). ConstitutionNet. http://constitutionnet.org/news/kazakhstan-constitutional-council-consider-presidents-amendment-proposals. Accessed on 31 August 2025.
17. Kadyraliyeva, A., Mukhanbet, A., Saparova, Y., Zholdubaeva, A., Omirbekova, A., &Daribaeva, R. (2019). 'Multiculturalism in Kazakhstan'. *Utopía y Praxis Latinoamericana*, 24 (Esp.5), 208–217.
18. Kadyrzhanov, R. (2023). 'Territory as a Factor of Nation-Building in New Kazakhstan.' *Horizons: Journal of International Relations and Sustainable Development*, 23, 244–256.
19. Kaushik, D., & Khalfin, N.A. (1970). Central Asia in modern times: A history from the early 19th century. https://cir.nii.ac.jp/crid/1130282269139415296. Accessed on 19 August 2025.
20. *Kazakhstan: Tested by Transition | About the authors*. (n.d.). https://www.chathamhouse.org/2019/11/kazakhstan-tested-transition/about-authors. Accessed on 31 August 2025.
21. Kazakhstan's Ethnic Policy 1991-2021: What Needs to Change? (2021, December 20). *CABAR. Asia.* https://cabar.asia/en/kazakhstan-s-ethnic-policy-1991-2021-what-needs-to-change. Accessed on 19 August 2025.
22. Kemelova, F. (2025, August 16). 'Global Film School Helps Kazakh Industry Find its Groove.' *The Astana Times*. https://astanatimes.com/2025/08/global-film-school-helps-kazakh-industry-find-its-groove/. Accessed on 16 August 2025.
23. Melich, J., & Adibayeva, A. (2013). 'Nation-building and cultural policy in Kazakhstan.' *European Scientific Journal*, Vol. 2, 1-15. https://files01.core.ac.uk/download/pdf/236413119.pdf
24. Mkrtchyan, N. (2014). 'The notion of 'Kazakhness' behind the symbolic nation-building of Kazakhstan.' *CEU Political Science Journal*, 9 (1–2), 16–38.
25. Narottum, S.K. (2006). 'Politics of nation-building and state-formation in Kazakhstan.' *Pakistan Horizon*, 59(2), 49–71.
26. Nation-Building Reset in Kazakhstan: What Unites People? (2023, June 14). *CABAR. Asia.*

https://cabar.asia/en/nation-building-reset-in-kazakhstan-what-unites-people. Accessed on 14 June 2024.

27. Nohlen, D., Grotz, F., & Hartmann, C. (2001). *Elections in Asia and the Pacific: A data handbook* (vol. 2). Oxford University Press.
28. Nurakhamet, A.A. (2019, August). Laws of the Republic of Kazakhstan – Web-based resources. https://www.nyulawglobal.org/globalex/kazakhstan1.html. Accessed on 19 August 2025.
29. OECD Public Governance Reviews. (2017). 'Decentralisation and Multi-level Governance in Kazakhstan.. OECD Public Governance Reviews.
30. Olcott, M. (2011a). 'Kazakhstan at 20.' Carnegie Endowment for International Peace. https://carnegieendowment.org/research/2011/12/kazakhstan-at-20?lang=en. Accessed on 25 August 2025.
31. Olcott, M. (2011b, November 30). Kazakhstan's Soviet legacy. Centre of Asia. https://carnegieendowment.org/posts/2011/11/kazakhstans-soviet-legacy?lang=en. Accessed on 19== August 2025.
32. Olcott, M.B., Olcott, A., & Hajda, L. (2015). *The Soviet multinational state: Readings and documents*. Routledge London. https://cir.nii.ac.jp/crid/1130282272623666048
33. Ruffin, M.H., & Waugh, D.C. (1999). *Civil society in central Asia*. University of Washington Press.
34. Sajjanhar, A. (2013). 'India-Kazakhstan relations: Challenges and opportunities.' Indian Embassy in Kazakhstan. https://www.indembastana.gov.in/content/Ashok%20Sajjanhar.pdf. Accessed on 28 August 2025.
35. Sengupta, A. (2017). *Symbols and the Image of the State in Eurasia*. Springer Singapore. https://doi.org/10.1007/978-981-10-2392-7. Accessed on 28 August 2025.
36. Shakenov, A., Gabdulina, B., &Dronzina, T. (2024). 'Can the Kazakh Language Become a Fundamental Factor in the Nation-Building of Kazakhstan?' *Eurasian Research Journal*, 6(4), 95–117.
37. Sharipova, R., & Shormanbayeva, D. (2024). 'Ethnic Identification of the Younger Generation of Students and Interethnic Relations Among Students. *2024 IEEE 6th International Symposium on Logistics and Industrial Informatics (LINDI)*, 000245–000248. https://ieeexplore.ieee.org/abstract/document/10820379/. Accessed on 29 August 2025.
38. Singh, A.K., & Srivastava, D. (2019). 'Kazakhstan at the Crossroads: Democratic Imperatives, Leadership and Exigency of Transition.' *Journal of Central Asian Studies*. https://ccas.uok.edu.in/Files/93269b6c-7f53-4439-ae9a-3bdf55a4c649/Journal/6af342d0-704c-40d7-ae46-a91834c4a8e6.pdf.
39. Syzdykova, M.B., Abikenov, Z.O., Abdiramanova, A.T., &Ilyassova, E. (2024). 'Influence of Globalization on the Transformation of Kazakh Traditions and Culture: A Case Study of Southern Kazakhstan.' *Changing Societies & Personalities*. 2024, 8(4), 964–984.
40. Ubiria, G. (2015). *Soviet nation-building in Central Asia: The making of the Kazakh and Uzbek nations*. Routledge. https://www.taylorfrancis.com/books/mono/10.4324/ 9781315715551/soviet-nation-building-central-asia-grigol-ubiria. Accessed on 30 August 2025.
41. Wandel, J., & Kozbagarova, B. (2009). 'Kazakhstan: Economic transformation and autocratic power.' *Mercatus Policy Series*, Country Brief, 4. https://papers.ssrn.com/sol3/papers.cfm?abstract_id=1434522. Accessed on 31 August 2025.
42. Yerekesheva, L.G. (2020). 'Functions of Religion and Dynamics of Nation-Building in Kazakhstan and Uzbekistan.' *Muslim World*, 110(1).
43. Yilmaz, S. (2017). 'The role of the leadership of Nursultan Nazarbayev in Kazakhstan's stability.' *International Journal of Liberal Arts and Social Science*, 5(2), 61–72.

7

Economic and Political Development of Kazakhstan

Dr. Zhapar Zhuman

Introduction

Kazakhstan is the largest state in Central Asia, possessing a favourable geographical location, significant global achievements, and strategic innovativeness in the global economy and politics. Since declaring independence in 1991, the country has undergone major transformations in both political and economic spheres, adapting to global changes. The development process consists of several key stages that reflect the pursuit of stability, innovation, and leadership in the world economy and agenda.

Economic Development of Kazakhstan

After gaining independence, Kazakhstan faced a number of economic problems. The collapse of the Soviet economy, the devaluation of the national currency, inflation, and the decline in production became the main challenges for the new state. Infrastructure and many sectors of industry were in decline, and the heavy dependence on Soviet economic ties complicated the transition to a market economy. In response to the economic crisis, the government began implementing market reforms aimed at creating new economic structures, developing the private sector, and attracting foreign investment.

An important element was the privatisation of state property, which was intended to create private enterprises. Within the framework of the "Kazakhstan 2030 Strategy," adopted in 1997, goals were set to achieve sustainable economic growth, develop infrastructure, improve quality of life, and ensure political stability.

One of the first measures was the introduction of a new currency – the tenge, which became an important step in strengthening the national financial system. During this period, Kazakhstan embarked on market reforms aimed at privatising state-owned enterprises, liberalising prices, and creating conditions for attracting foreign investment. These measures made it possible to restore economic growth in the early 2000s, despite initial difficulties.

At the beginning of the 21st century, Kazakhstan demonstrated impressive economic growth, primarily due to its rich natural resources, such as oil, gas, coal, as well as metals and minerals. Privatisation and market liberalisation became the foundation of economic transformation. In particular, Kazakhstan took leading positions in oil production and export, which made it possible to significantly increase the volume of foreign investment.

The country's economy continued to develop, thanks to the stabilisation of the internal situation, the improvement of infrastructure, and the attraction of major global corporations to various sectors. Kazakhstan's economy became more competitive, and a policy of diversification began, aimed at developing non-resource sectors. However, this economic growth was not without risks. Heavy dependence on resource exports remained a vulnerability and global economic crises, such as the 2008 crisis, demonstrated how important it was to seek new directions for sustainable growth.

Economic growth in the post-crisis years in Kazakhstan was driven by the following factors:

- **Recovery growth** – expressed in the full or partial restoration of the production of goods and services, including the production of ferrous and nonferrous metals, electricity and heat energy, food products, building materials, textiles and garments, transport and communication services, and more.
- **Conjunctural growth** – linked to the development of industries whose products enjoy consistently high demand in the world market. In Kazakhstan's case, this primarily meant oil and gas extraction.
- **Systemic growth** – resulting from the introduction of new segments of goods and services production. This includes the development of small businesses, the financial sector, real estate and automobile trade, as well as the production of goods and services within the household sector.

- **Innovative growth** – occurring as a result of the implementation of the "Industrial-Innovative Development Strategy" in Kazakhstan, which is still in the early stages. So far, this factor has had only a minor impact on the country's economic development. The fastest innovative growth has been observed in areas such as telecommunications and information technology.

Between 2001 and 2005, Kazakhstan's economy maintained consistently high growth rates, averaging 10.2 per cent per year. Investment activity was strong, and the annual average growth in oil and gas condensate production in 2001–2005 reached 12 per cent.

As a result, state revenues began to flow in fully, creating the preconditions for eliminating arrears in payments to the population for pensions, social benefits, and wages for employees of state-funded organisations.

The second stage of implementing the Kazakhstan–2030 Development Strategy naturally continued the policy initiated in previous years, which was based on high rates of economic growth, macroeconomic stability, and the creation of conditions for transitioning to a model of sustainable economic development.

This policy was defined in the Strategic Socio-Economic Development Plan for 2001–2010, whose goals were:

- Building the foundation of a long-term competitive economy.
- Doubling the volume of Gross Domestic Product (GDP) by 2010.

Achieving these ambitious goals required a wide range of measures across all areas of state socio-economic policy.

Accordingly, the state assumed the role of the "loco-motive" of economic growth, creating conditions for transitioning to a sustainable development model. This model involved the active participation of the state in forming economic and political conditions that would stimulate the creation of transnational corporations capable of competing both domestically and abroad.

Since Kazakhstan's domestic market is relatively small, its long-term growth strategy has been directed towards forming an export-oriented model of development. From 2001 to 2003, work focused on eliminating state and enterprise debts, combating poverty, continuing reforms in the production, financial, and budgetary sectors, and ensuring further institutional transformation.

At the same time, efforts were made to establish a stable financial and fiscal system. The government concentrated on systemic measures to reduce inflation, create conditions for medium- and long-term lending of investment projects, and ensure budgetary stability amid sharp fluctuations in world oil prices, as well as to support the development of non-resource sectors.

The following contributed to these objectives:

- Creation of the National Fund of Kazakhstan and the Development Bank of Kazakhstan.
- Implementation of a capital amnesty.
- Adoption of laws on financial leasing, construction savings, mortgage lending, insurance activities, and the Tax Code.

This period of socio-economic transformation was characterised by rapid industrial growth, a sharp decline in unemployment, and an increase in real household incomes.

The implementation of priority measures within the Strategic Plan positively affected all areas of Kazakhstan's economy. Economic growth began nationwide, which improved the well-being of the population.

In 2003, two fundamental documents were adopted, defining the country's economic development up to 2015:

- The Industrial-Innovative Development Strategy of the Republic of Kazakhstan (2003–2015).
- The State Program for the Development of Oil and Gas Fields in the Kazakh Sector of the Caspian Sea until 2015.

These documents outlined the strategy for forming a model of sustainable development. In addition, a number of programs and legislative acts were adopted to enhance Kazakhstan's competitiveness, including:

- Formation and development of the national innovation system.
- Deepening of social reforms.
- Development of microcredit.
- Development of education for 2005–2015.
- Digitisation of vocational and secondary education institutions.
- Development of the space industry.
- Housing construction development.
- Development of the securities market.
- Development of the construction materials industry.
- Improvement of national standardisation and certification systems.
- Development of the road industry for 2006–2018.

The intention was to maintain high rates of economic growth over the long term through oil extraction and its transportation to world markets, while simultaneously creating conditions for the development of non-resource sectors that serve the oil and gas industry. Part of the government's oil revenues was also to be used for the structural renewal of the economy.

Government policy primarily aimed to create incentives for the development of new types of non-resource goods and services in the private sector.

Overall, the work to diversify the economic structure and improve the competitiveness of non-resource sectors focused on raising technical requirements for production and trade, increasing budgetary allocations for infrastructure, education, science, innovation, new technology transfer, and healthcare. In other words, it was aimed at developing human and produced capital. State institutions established under the Industrial-Innovative Development Strategy were given sufficient financial resources to finance investment projects and partially participate in the share capital of new enterprises.

One of the main priorities of economic policy was the development of small and medium-sized enterprises (SMEs). The government believed that SMEs, with their flexibility, mobility, and market responsiveness, should quickly find their place in the innovation economy. The state, in turn, had to create favourable conditions for entrepreneurship and direct its support to those SMEs with the greatest potential in terms of competitiveness and technological advancement.

This concept was seen as a transitional stage towards a new state policy of SME support and development, based on a cluster-network approach and a new ideology of state-business relations.

To achieve this goal, the following tasks were set:

- Creating a maximally transparent legal framework for SME development.
- Reducing bureaucracy and removing administrative barriers.
- Decreasing the shadow economy within SMEs.
- Transferring non-core functions of state-owned enterprises and joint-stock companies to the market environment, primarily to SMEs.
- Establishing a viable infrastructure system based on a cluster-network approach.
- Ensuring SME participation in the innovation economy.

In practice, this approach proved effective and produced positive results. Kazakhstan achieved certain successes in the liberalisation of political life.

Democratic institutions, political pluralism, and democracy have developed gradually.

By now, structural reforms in the economy are largely complete: state property privatisation has been carried out, and an economic environment meeting the standards of a developed market has been established. Kazakhstan became one of the first CIS states to be recognised by developed countries as a market economy.

Kazakhstan is also implementing the Industrial-Innovative Development Program until 2025, which provides for the development of non-resource sectors. Targeted government programs are successfully being implemented in various fields – housing and road construction, rural development, building the new capital, Astana, healthcare, and others. Reforms in social infrastructure, healthcare, and social security continue. The funded pension system functions successfully, with more than $5.1 billion accumulated in pension funds.

The Republic of Kazakhstan possesses rich mineral resources, vast agricultural lands, a skilled workforce, and significant industrial potential. Today, Kazakhstan has a functioning market economy. One of the key factors behind its success is its resource wealth – oil, gas, coal, uranium, and rare and precious metals. These resources play a decisive role in Kazakhstan's economy and export policy. Through hydrocarbon exports, Kazakhstan has become one of the largest exporters in Central Asia.

In recent years, oil and gas production in Kazakhstan has grown significantly. The main export destinations are Russia, China, and the European Union. With modern technologies in the oil and gas sector, Kazakhstan has greatly increased its production and export capacity.

In the face of global economic instability and challenges such as the transition to green energy, Kazakhstan recognises the need to diversify its economy. In recent years, the country has taken steps to reduce dependence on hydrocarbons and to develop high-tech and environmentally friendly industries. Today, Kazakhstan continues its policy of economic diversification, focusing on information technology, agribusiness, and renewable energy. These sectors are expected to significantly reduce dependence on oil and gas exports.

The country has also actively invested in the development of the digital economy and start-ups, hoping to increase the share of high-tech industries. Under the "Digital Kazakhstan" program, new technology and educational hubs are being created, providing young people with up-to-date knowledge and skills for a rapidly changing world. Kazakhstan also plans to develop a "green economy" and adopt cleaner technologies, which has become an important trend amid global climate change.

Currently, Kazakhstan is one of the world's largest wheat producers. The main agricultural regions are the northern and central parts of the country. Kazakhstan actively exports grain and produces meat, dairy, and other food products.

However, despite positive changes in the agricultural sector, there remain problems such as insufficient irrigation, low efficiency of agricultural enterprises, and a lack of investment in innovative technologies.

Economic diversification affects not only energy but also other important sectors such as agribusiness, automobile manufacturing, pharmaceuticals, and information technology. Programs like "NurlyZhol" (Light Path) aim to develop infrastructure, create new jobs, and increase the country's attractiveness to investors in new technologies.

Kazakhstan has set itself the task of modernising and diversifying its economy, reducing dependence on the raw materials sector. An important step on this path was the industrialisation program, announced in 2010, aimed at developing new industries and creating new jobs. Within the framework of this program, thousands of new production facilities were created, and production volumes in sectors such as mechanical engineering, chemical industry, metallurgy, and building materials increased several times over.

Significant efforts have also been directed towards the development of transport infrastructure. Kazakhstan is an important transit corridor between Europe and Asia, and the improvement of transport routes, including rail and road, has facilitated trade and increased foreign trade volumes. Kazakhstan is becoming a major player in the transport and logistics sector through infrastructure development and strategic projects such as railway modernisation, the development of international trade routes across its territory, and participation in the Silk Road program.

Kazakhstan is interested in attracting investment for the creation of new transit corridors and the development of the port of Aktau, which has become an important trade and logistics hub. In addition, Kazakhstan is actively developing cooperation with China under the Belt and Road Initiative, which involves large-scale infrastructure projects and the stimulation of trade between China and Europe through Central Asia. This cooperation opens new prospects for Kazakhstan's economy. The country will continue to strengthen its role as an international transport hub, improve connections with other countries, and consolidate its position within the Eurasian Economic Union and other international organisations.

Kazakhstan has significant potential for further economic growth. One of the key tasks for the coming years is the diversification of the economy and the development of non-resource sectors. The government is actively investing in innovative technologies and digitalisation, which will create new jobs and improve the country's competitiveness on the global stage.

Kazakhstan's economic development over the past decades has shown significant achievements, but the country continues to face many challenges. Diversification of the economy, development of high-tech and innovative industries, improvement of the investment climate, and raising the quality of life of the population will define Kazakhstan's future path. It is important for the country to effectively use its resources and opportunities to ensure sustainable growth and development amid global economic change.

Political Development of Kazakhstan

After gaining independence, Kazakhstan pursued a course of strengthening national security and stabilising the internal political situation. In the early years of independence, reforms were carried out to reinforce centralised power. The adoption of the new Constitution in 1995 established Kazakhstan as a presidential republic with strong presidential authority, which influenced all key political and economic processes.

Starting from the 2000s, Kazakhstan began actively implementing political reforms aimed at modernisation and state development. These reforms touched on various aspects – from the economy to the legal system – but were mainly focused on strengthening presidential power.

An important step was the introduction of a multiparty system, although this did not mean genuine political competition. Officially, several parties operated in the country, but the most influential remained the Nur Otan Party, founded by Nursultan Nazarbayev in 1999. It became the main political force supporting the president and his policies.

Another important milestone was the 2007 constitutional reform, which further strengthened presidential authority and expanded powers. At the same time, the fight against opposition movements intensified, along with restrictions on freedom of speech. Despite efforts to modernise the political system, Kazakhstan continued to remain an authoritarian state with limited political pluralism.

Domestic and external challenges continued to shape Kazakhstan's policy. Externally, Kazakhstan sought to maintain neutrality and develop close ties with major world powers – Russia, China, and the West – while balancing its foreign economic relations.

In 2019, Nursultan Nazarbayev resigned, handing the presidency to Kassym-Jomart Tokayev. This step marked an important stage in the country's political life, ensuring a smooth transition of power and the continuation of stability. The new president pledged reforms in political and social spheres, including improving human rights and strengthening the role of parliament.

Since taking office, Tokayev has initiated a number of political reforms, including legislative changes, improving conditions for political competition, and supporting civil society. His government continues to modernise the economy and raise the standard of living.

One important step has been the expansion of citizens' rights and freedoms, as well as strengthening the role of parliament and local authorities. Tokayev has declared his goal to develop inclusive, dialogue-based politics and to ensure transparency and accountability of state institutions. In response to public demands for political change, the 2021 elections were held, becoming an important stage in the country's political modernisation.

Over 30 years of independence, Kazakhstan has managed to solve many problems related to political and economic reforms, achieving significant progress towards building a democratic state with a market economy. This success was facilitated by well-defined priorities, balanced domestic and foreign policy, and consistency in achieving goals.

In terms of foreign policy, Kazakhstan actively develops both bilateral and multilateral cooperation, supporting integration within the CIS, EurAsEC, EAEU, SCO, and CSTO, while engaging with the UN, OSCE, and other international organisations. The country has no serious conflicts with any state.

Kazakhstan has played an important role as one of the initiators of the Shanghai Cooperation Organisation (SCO), the founder of the Conference on Interaction and Confidence-Building Measures in Asia (CICA), and host of the Congresses of Leaders of World and Traditional Religions in Astana. These efforts contribute to tolerance, interfaith and inter-ethnic harmony, and peace and stability in the region.

Kazakhstan's leadership believes that democratisation should develop gradually, preferably alongside rising living standards and the growth of civil society institutions. For this reason, economic reforms were prioritised over democratic reforms. The state has proceeded cautiously, adapting existing institutions and creating new ones in line with national characteristics.

This approach has proven effective, producing positive results. Kazakhstan has made progress in liberalising political life, with the steady development of democratic institutions, political pluralism, and democracy.

Kazakhstan's geographic position, as a link between Europe and Asia, plays a key role in its external economic and political strategy. The country actively participates in organisations and projects such as the UN, SCO, EAEU, and OSCE. It seeks a neutral stance in international conflicts while building ties with Russia, China, the USA, and the EU.

Kazakhstan also actively cooperates with neighbours – Russia and China – as well as the European Union, participating in numerous trade and economic projects. Domestically, its policy maintains stable relations with neighbours, which is vital for regional security. A milestone in foreign policy was its nuclear disarmament, when Kazakhstan became the first post-Soviet state to voluntarily renounce its nuclear arsenal.

Kazakhstan strives to maintain balance in foreign policy, building strong ties with both regional neighbours and global powers. Infrastructure, energy, and transit development strengthen the country's position in Central Asia and the world.

Conclusion

Kazakhstan continues to evolve as a politically independent and economically dynamic country, striving for a higher standard of living for its citizens. The prospects for economic and political development depend on its ability to effectively manage challenges related to social justice, political modernisation, and international integration.

Kazakhstan has successfully overcome the difficulties of transition, achieving stability and growth. Still, major tasks remain – diversifying the economy, improving social infrastructure, and strengthening civil society. Political stability remains an achievement, despite criticism over political restrictions.

Thanks to its strategic location, natural resources, and global ambitions, Kazakhstan has all the opportunities to remain an important and stable player in international politics and the world economy, actively participating in global projects and solving domestic challenges to raise the quality of life of its people.

References

1. Сейдуманов А.С. (2018) Политический процесс в Казахстане на современном этапе // Проблемы постсоветского пространства. Том5,-N°2, 2018. -С.181-190.
2. Ионова Е. (2018) Казахстан: тенденции политического развития. Россия и новые государства Евразии. -N°1, 2018. -С.68-81.
3. Жуман Жаппар (2024) Экономическое развитие Казахстана за годы независимости.
4. О концепции внешней политики Республики Казахстан на 2020-2030 годы. Астана, Акорда, N°280 6 марта 2020 года.

8

Economic and Political Development between India and Kazakhstan

Dr. Beena

ABSTRACT

India's economic and political development over the past three decades has transformed the country into a pivotal actor in regional and global geopolitics. As the world's fifth-largest economy and the largest democracy, India's growth story is not merely a tale of liberalisation and rising Gross Domestic Product (GDP) figures – it is a strategic recalibration of its role in the international order. This paper argues that India's economic resilience, technological advancements, and assertive foreign policy, rooted in the principles of strategic autonomy, have enabled it to expand its diplomatic and economic footprints, particularly in Eurasia. In this context, the India-Kazakhstan relationship stands as a compelling case of pragmatic cooperation, anchored in shared interests in energy, connectivity, and regional stability. Through platforms such as the India-Central Asia Dialogue and projects like the International North-South Transport Corridor (INSTC), India has sought to diversify its partnerships and reduce dependency on volatile maritime routes. Simultaneously, India's political evolution – marked by coalition stability, institutional reforms, and global aspirations as seen during its G20 presidency – reinforces its credibility as a reliable partner for Central Asian states like Kazakhstan. The paper concludes that India's development trajectory offers mutual benefits and strategic opportunities for bilateral engagement, especially as both nations navigate a shifting multipolar world.

Keywords: *Strategic Autonomy, India-Kazakhstan Relations, Economic Development, Regional Connectivity, Multipolar World Order*

Introduction

India and Kazakhstan have cultivated a dynamic and expanding economic relationship, anchored in mutual confidence and shared strategic interests. As India's most significant trading and investment partner in Central Asia, Kazakhstan plays a vital role in New Delhi's 'Connect Central Asia' policy. Kazakhstan, the world's ninth-largest country and the largest landlocked nation, holds immense geopolitical significance due to its vast geography spanning Europe and Asia and its proximity to major powers like Russia and China (CIA, 2021; Sajjanhar, 2013). Its rich energy reserves – including oil, natural gas, uranium, and coal – combined with a strategic location, make it a vital partner for India. New Delhi views Kazakhstan as critical for three reasons: its geo-strategic position, abundant energy resources, and economic potential. As India's domestic energy production remains insufficient relative to its population and growing consumption, it seeks reliable external partners like Kazakhstan to meet its energy demands (NITI Aayog, 2017; EIA, 2018). A significant milestone in this bilateral energy relationship was Prime Minister Modi's 2015 visit, which marked the launch of oil drilling in the Satpayev field. Moreover, India renewed its uranium supply deal that same year, securing 5,000 metric tons of nuclear fuel for 2015–2019 (MEA, 2015). Kazakhstan's broader Eurasian energy projects, including the Abai field and the Caspian basin, also offer future opportunities for India's involvement (Stobdan, 2020). Additionally, Kazakhstan's indirect link to the TAPI pipeline and India's full membership in the Shanghai Cooperation Organisation (SCO) have strengthened the strategic energy and regional partnership between the two nations.

To institutionalise and advance this partnership, the two countries established the India-Kazakhstan Inter-Governmental Commission (IGC) in 1993. This platform serves as the principal mechanism to promote collaboration across trade, industry, science and technology, energy, and culture. The Commission is co-chaired by India's Ministry of Petroleum and Natural Gas and Kazakhstan's Ministry of Trade and Integration, highlighting the centrality of energy and commerce in bilateral ties (Embassy of India, Nur-Sultan, 2024).

Over the years, nine Joint Working Groups (JWGs) have been formed under the IGC framework, covering areas such as counter-terrorism, defence and military-technical cooperation, hydrocarbons, textiles, information technology, and space. Recent developments include proposals to create three additional JWGs focused on Chabahar Port, pharmaceuticals, and healthcare, reflecting the evolving priorities in India-Kazakhstan cooperation.

To enhance business-to-business (B2B) engagement, the Federation of Indian Chambers of Commerce and Industry (FICCI) and the Chamber of International Commerce of Kazakhstan jointly operate a Business Council. This council facilitates investment dialogue and trade promotion between private sector stakeholders. The Agricultural and Processed Food Products Export Development Authority (APEDA) has also been active in promoting Indian agro-products in the Kazakh market, contributing to the diversification of trade baskets.

Regular participation in trade fairs, expos, and industrial delegations has strengthened commercial exchanges. The existing direct flight route between Delhi and Almaty has supported not only trade but also tourism and people-to-people contacts. Significantly, new direct flights between Delhi and Astana, announced to commence in May 2025, are expected to further deepen bilateral connectivity and economic engagement (MEA Annual Report, 2024; Embassy of India in Kazakhstan, 2024).

Political Development

India and Kazakhstan have shared strong political ties since India became one of the first countries to recognise Kazakhstan's independence in 1991. Formal diplomatic relations were established in February 1992, with embassies opened shortly thereafter – India in Almaty (1992) and Kazakhstan in New Delhi (1993). Following the relocation of Kazakhstan's capital to Astana (now Nur-Sultan), India moved its embassy there in 2007, further consolidating diplomatic presence (Embassy of India, Kazakhstan, 2024).

The historical connection dates back to the 1950s, with visits from Indian leaders such as Prime Minister Jawaharlal Nehru and Vice President Dr. S. Radhakrishnan. Since independence, Kazakhstan's President, Nursultan Nazarbayev, has visited India five times, notably as Chief Guest for India's Republic Day in 2009, where a Joint Declaration on Strategic Partnership was signed. Indian Prime Ministers, including P.V. Narasimha Rao, Atal Bihari Vajpayee, Dr. Manmohan Singh, and Narendra Modi have all visited Kazakhstan, with Modi's 2015 visit marking a significant boost to the strategic partnership (MEA, 2024).

The India-Kazakhstan Inter-Governmental Commission (IGC), established in 1993, plays a central role in advancing cooperation in energy, trade, science and technology, and culture. The 12th IGC meeting in 2015 also initiated plans for a new Joint Working Group on connectivity. Regular Foreign Office consultations at the deputy ministerial level further sustain dialogue on bilateral and global issues.

India and Kazakhstan collaborate actively in multilateral bodies such as the SCO, Conference on Interaction and Confidence-Building Measures in Asia (CICA), and the United Nations. Kazakhstan supports India's bid for a permanent seat on the UN Security Council and full membership in the SCO, while India backed Kazakhstan's non-permanent UNSC seat for 2017-18. Both nations also share a common stance against terrorism and advocate for a comprehensive international convention to combat it (Ministry of External Affairs, 2024).

India and Kazakhstan maintain regular Foreign Office consultations (FOC) at the Deputy Foreign Ministers or Secretary (West) level to discuss bilateral, regional, and global issues of mutual concern. The seventh round was held virtually in November 2020, led by Secretary (West) Vikas Swarup and Kazakhstan's First Deputy Foreign Minister Shakhrat Nuryshev. The eighth round was conducted physically in New Delhi on 13 February 2023, led by Secretary (West) Sanjay Verma and Kazakh Deputy Minister Kanat Tumysh (MEA, 2023).

Kazakhstan actively participates in the India-Central Asia Dialogue, launched in 2019 in Samarkand. The Dialogue has served as a key platform for regional cooperation. The second edition, held virtually on 28 October 2020, was co-chaired by India's EAM, Dr. S. Jaishankar and Kazakhstan's Foreign Minister, Mukhtar Tileuberdi. The third meeting took place in New Delhi (18–19 December 2021), followed by a joint interaction with PM Narendra Modi (MEA, 2021).

The first India-Central Asia Summit, held virtually on 27 January 2022, witnessed participation by Kazakh President Kassym-Jomart Tokayev. He emphasised collaboration in trade, green energy, IT, cybersecurity and proposed the establishment of Indian-led IT education and engineering institutions in Kazakhstan. Discussions also covered regional stability in Afghanistan (MEA, 2022). Subsequent India-CA engagements included the India-CA Energy Conference (FICCI, August 2022), the inaugural meeting of Security Council Secretaries in New Delhi (December 2022), youth exchange programs (November 2022, March 2024), and the first India-CA Culture Ministers' Meeting chaired by G. Kishan Reddy (April 2023). Other key developments include the first JWG meetings on Afghanistan (March 2023) and on Chabahar Port (April 2023), during which Kazakhstan invited India to join the North-South Transport Corridor roadmap (MEA, 2023).

India assumed the rotational SCO Presidency in September 2022, culminating in the virtual SCO Heads of Council Summit on 4 July 2023. During this tenure, significant high-level exchanges occurred, reinforcing India-Kazakhstan regional coordination (MEA, 2023).

India's evolving relationship with Kazakhstan is shaped by a convergence of strategic interests, particularly in the domains of regional security, energy cooperation, and people-to-people exchanges. Both countries share a common vision of a stable Central Asia, especially concerning instability in Afghanistan and narcotics trade routes. India's participation in platforms like CICA, founded by Kazakhstan, and Kazakhstan's consistent support for India's permanent UNSC seat, underscore their political alignment. Engagement also extends into cultural and educational spheres through initiatives like Indian Technical and Economic Cooperation (ITEC) and Indian Council for Cultural Relations (ICCR) scholarship programs, fostering people-to-people ties and enhancing India's soft power. Despite Kazakhstan's relatively small population, these exchanges offer meaningful strategic value. However, India must remain attentive to Kazakhstan's internal challenges, including democratic deficits and governance concerns, as it seeks to deepen its influence and cooperation in Central Asia.

Economic Development

India and Kazakhstan have institutionalised their economic engagement through the India-Kazakhstan Inter-Governmental Commission (IGC), the primary bilateral mechanism since 1993. Co-chaired by India's Petroleum and Natural Gas Minister and Kazakhstan's Trade and Integration Minister, the IGC facilitates collaboration in sectors like trade, energy, science, technology, and culture. The 14th IGC meeting held on 3 June 2022 in New Delhi reviewed progress across nine joint working groups (JWGs) on counter-terrorism, defence, hydrocarbons, space, and IT. In 2022, three new JWGs were proposed, focusing on Chabahar Port, pharmaceuticals, and healthcare, indicating an expanded scope for regional connectivity and health diplomacy. A key milestone was the first JWG meeting on transport, connectivity, and logistics in November 2019 in New Delhi, reflecting a shared interest in regional trade infrastructure (MEA, 2022; Embassy of India, Nur-Sultan).

Kazakhstan plays a pivotal role in India's energy security due to its extensive reserves of oil, natural gas, uranium, and coal, along with established export and refining infrastructure. Prime Minister Modi's 2015 visit marked a turning point with the launch of oil drilling in the Satpayev oil field and the renewal of a uranium supply agreement for 5,000 metric tons between 2015 and 2019. ONGC Videsh Limited (OVL) has also explored re-engaging with Kazakhstan's Abai oil block. Kazakhstan's significance extends to multilateral energy initiatives like the TAPI pipeline, designed to diversify regional energy routes. India's full SCO membership since 2017 further strengthened multilateral cooperation in energy and security (Stobdan, 2020; MEA, 2015; SCO Secretariat, 2023).

On March 11, experts from Kazakhstan and India convened at Maqsut Narikbayev University to discuss enhancing bilateral trade via the International North-South Transport Corridor (INSTC). The corridor aims to reduce transport time and costs, streamline supply chains, and boost technology-driven trade. Sanzhar Ualikhanov of Kazakhstan's Foreign Ministry highlighted the $2.4 billion worth of investment projects in the manufacturing sector in 2024, Indian investments totalling $460 million since 2005, and trade nearing $1 billion. He emphasised Kazakhstan's reliability as an energy partner and the strategic role of INSTC in transport.

Indian Ambassador T.V. Nagendra Prasad underscored Kazakhstan's importance in the region, pointing to transport infrastructure development, especially through Chabahar Port, as vital to strengthening trade efficiency and strategic ties. He encouraged Indian business investment, highlighting Kazakhstan's industrial potential and investor-friendly environment. Praising the INSTC, he noted that connectivity would remain central to bilateral relations. Ashok Sajjanhar of the Institute of Global Studies linked these developments to historical ties and current geopolitical disruptions, calling for greater political will and regional cooperation. He identified customs inefficiencies and infrastructure gaps as key obstacles. Professor Zhanat Momynkulov described Kazakhstan as India's 'closest ally' under the Connect Central Asia policy, calling it a 'crucial gateway' to the region and urging enhanced cooperation in IT, space, and energy sectors.

Beyond the well-established political and economic dimensions, India and Kazakhstan share several underexplored yet promising areas of cooperation that hold significant potential for future engagement. These include cultural diplomacy, education, defence collaboration, counter-terrorism, civil nuclear energy, space cooperation, environmental sustainability, digital development, and multilateral engagement. Historically, India and Kazakhstan are linked through ancient Silk Route connections, with Buddhism and trade contributing to early cultural exchanges. Contemporary efforts to revive these ties are visible through initiatives like the celebration of the 'Days of Indian Culture,' yoga festivals, and film screenings in Kazakhstan. The popularity of Indian films and yoga has cultivated cultural goodwill, making soft power a significant diplomatic tool. Furthermore, the two countries could establish a Buddhist heritage circuit, connecting Buddhist sites in Kazakhstan with Indian pilgrimage destinations, deepening civilisational ties (Ministry of External Affairs, 2023).

In the field of education, India has emerged as a preferred destination for Kazakh students, particularly in the fields of medicine and engineering. Programs such as the Indian Technical and Economic Cooperation (ITEC) have facilitated capacity-building for Kazakh professionals in areas like information technology, finance, and public administration. With the growing digital divide and the emphasis on skill-based learning, future cooperation may include the establishment of Indo-Kazakh academic institutions, expansion of digital learning platforms under India's Digital India initiative, and enhanced vocational exchanges (MEA, 2023). Additionally, defence collaboration has gained traction through regular military exercises like 'Prabal Dostyk,' which enhance interoperability and build trust between the armed forces. Kazakhstan also sends military officers for training at Indian defence institutions, and the potential for cooperation in counter-insurgency, peacekeeping, and cybersecurity remains substantial (Korybko, 2022).

Counter-terrorism and internal security cooperation represent another vital area of convergence. Both countries face challenges from radical extremism, particularly due to the destabilising influence of developments in Afghanistan. Given Kazakhstan's interest in preserving its secular and multi-ethnic identity, India's model of pluralism and coexistence offers a framework for engagement in counter-radicalisation programs. Intelligence sharing and joint participation in regional counter-terrorism forums such as the Shanghai Cooperation Organisation (SCO) have already laid the groundwork for deeper strategic collaboration (Pant & Sahu, 2022). On the energy front, while Kazakhstan is already a key uranium supplier to India and supports India's entry into the Nuclear Suppliers Group (NSG), future cooperation could include civil nuclear energy technology sharing, safety protocols, and collaboration on small modular reactors. Furthermore, both countries can partner on renewable energy, especially solar power, under the framework of the International Solar Alliance (ISA), where Kazakhstan is an active participant (MEA, 2023).

Space cooperation is another emerging frontier. Kazakhstan, inheriting significant Soviet-era infrastructure including the Baikonur Cosmodrome, presents opportunities for collaboration with India's space agency, ISRO, in areas such as satellite launches, data sharing, and capacity building. Joint space education and climate monitoring initiatives using satellite data could strengthen bilateral ties in the high-tech sector. Environmental cooperation also presents mutual benefits, as both countries grapple with challenges like desertification, climate change, and water scarcity. India's expertise in afforestation, solar-powered irrigation, and water management can complement Kazakhstan's environmental priorities, especially through initiatives under the UN Convention to Combat Desertification (UNCCD) (UNCCD, 2022).

Digital cooperation and technology transfer are increasingly relevant, with India's strengths in fintech, digital governance, cybersecurity, and e-commerce presenting appealing models for Kazakhstan. Initiatives like India Stack and the Unified Payments Interface (UPI) could be shared under a broader framework of South-South cooperation, facilitating inclusive digital transformation in Kazakhstan. Moreover, both countries have engaged actively in multilateral fora. Kazakhstan has supported India's participation in regional platforms such as the Conference on Interaction and Confidence Building Measures in Asia (CICA) and the SCO. India's observer status in the Eurasian Economic Union (EAEU) could eventually evolve into greater economic and strategic integration in the Central Asian region (Vinokurov, 2021).

Finally, tourism and connectivity constitute another area of underutilised potential. With Kazakhstan offering e-visa facilities and direct flights from major Indian cities, tourism in sectors like Ayurveda, medical treatment, and spiritual travel is growing. The development of a tourism corridor connecting Central Asia with India via Iran's Chabahar Port may enhance regional connectivity and economic interdependence. In conclusion, the India-Kazakhstan relationship is a multi-dimensional and evolving partnership, extending well beyond conventional economic and political ties. As both countries seek greater regional influence and resilience, these lesser-highlighted domains of cooperation will be instrumental in shaping a sustainable and comprehensive bilateral relationship.

Conclusion

India and Kazakhstan, as key players in South and Central Asia, respectively, possess immense untapped potential to foster a mutually beneficial and strategic partnership. As highlighted, the bilateral relationship has grown over the decades in spheres such as energy, trade, connectivity, multilateral cooperation, and regional security. However, this trajectory needs deeper alignment with evolving geopolitical realities and shared economic aspirations. Going forward, several key areas demand attention for the relationship to evolve into a truly strategic partnership.

First, enhancing economic engagement through a comprehensive economic cooperation agreement would institutionalise trade and investment flows. Despite the availability of rich energy resources in Kazakhstan and India's growing energy demands, the bilateral trade volume remains modest. India should prioritise long-term energy agreements, especially in the uranium and oil sectors, while Kazakhstan can benefit from India's expertise in pharmaceuticals, information technology, and space technology. Establishing joint ventures and special economic zones (SEZs) in Kazakhstan with Indian investment could help diversify its economy beyond hydrocarbons and enhance bilateral industrial collaboration.

Second, connectivity is the cornerstone of future cooperation. India must fast-track its engagement with the International North-South Transport Corridor (INSTC) and operationalise the Chabahar Port as a viable trade route to Central Asia. Joint investments in logistics and transport infrastructure can bridge the physical and economic distance, making trade more efficient and reliable.

Third, political collaboration needs to be institutionalised through structured dialogue. Regular summits, strategic dialogues, and parliamentary exchanges should be institutionalised to ensure sustained diplomatic engagement. Kazakhstan's role as a leading voice in Central Asia, combined with India's leadership in South Asia and multilateral forums like the SCO and CICA, provides a solid platform to promote regional stability, multilateral reform, and sustainable development.

Fourth, cultural diplomacy and people-to-people ties must be strengthened to support political trust. Enhanced academic exchanges, scholarships, cultural festivals, and tourism initiatives will foster mutual understanding and long-term goodwill.

Finally, both nations must collaborate on regional security and climate challenges, including counterterrorism, cybersecurity, water security, and green energy transition. With Kazakhstan championing green growth and India advancing its renewable energy leadership, cooperation in sustainable technologies, climate finance, and innovation can be a future pillar of cooperation.

In conclusion, India and Kazakhstan must recalibrate their partnership to reflect the complex dynamics of the 21st century. A forward-looking, multi-dimensional strategy focused on trade liberalisation, energy cooperation, connectivity, cultural syncrgy, and regional leadership will not only fortify bilateral relations but also contribute significantly to the stability and prosperity of the broader Eurasian region.

References

1. Central Intelligence Agency. (2021). *The World Factbook: Kazakhstan*. CIA. https://www.cia.gov/the-world-factbook/countries/kazakhstan/. Accessed on 25 February 2025.
2. NITI Aayog (2017). India Energy Security Scenarios 2047.
3. MEA (2015). India-Kazakhstan Joint Statements and Agreements.
4. Stobdan, P. (2020). India-Kazakhstan Relations: Beyond Energy.
5. Embassy of India, Nur-Sultan. (2024). India-Kazakhstan bilateral relations. URL: https://www.eoikazakhstan.gov.in/. Accessed on 20 February 2025.
6. Embassy of India in Kazakhstan. (2024). India-Kazakhstan cooperation updates. https://www.eoikazakhstan.gov.in/. Accessed on 9 February 2025.
7. Ibid.
8. Ministry of External Affairs (MEA), Government of India. (2024). Annual report 2023–24. https://www.mea.gov.in/annual-reports.htm. Accessed on 10 June 2025.
9. Ibid.
10. Ministry of External Affairs, India (MEA), Press Releases and Official Statements, 2020–2023.
11. Ministry of External Affairs (MEA), Government of India. (2021, December 19). 3rd meeting of the India-Central Asia Dialogue held in New Delhi. https://www.mea.gov.in/press-releases.htm?dtl/34682/3rd_meeting_of_IndiaCentral_Asia_Dialogue_held_in New Delhi. Accessed on 15 March 2025.
12. Ministry of External Affairs, India (MEA), Press Releases and Official Statements, 2020–2023.
13. Ibid.
14. Ministry of External Affairs (MEA), Government of India. (2022, June 3). 14th India-Kazakhstan Inter-Governmental Commission (IGC) meeting held in New Delhi. https://www.mea.gov.in/press-releases.htm?dtl/35350/14th_IndiaKazakhstan_InterGovernmental_Commission_meeting & Embassy of India, Nur-Sultan. (n.d.). *India-Kazakhstan Bilateral Relations*. Government of India. https://www.eoikazakhstan.gov.in/page/bilateral-relations/. Accessed on 4 May 2025.
15. Stobdan, P. (2020). India-Kazakhstan Relations: Beyond Energy.
16. Embassy of India, Kazakhstan. (2024, March 11). India–Kazakhstan expert discussion on enhancing trade via INSTC at MaqsutNarikbayev University. https://www.indembastana.gov.in/news_detail/?newsid=207. Accessed on 20 May 2025.
17. Institute of Global Studies. (2024). Discussion highlights on India-Kazakhstan trade and INSTC connectivity. https://globalstudies.in/events/india-kazakhstan-international-north-south-corridor. Accessed on 2 March 2025.

18. Ministry of Foreign Affairs of the Republic of Kazakhstan. (2024). Kazakhstan-India relations: Transport and trade cooperation. https://www.gov.kz/memleket/entities/mfa/press/news/details/675892?lang=en. Accessed on 18 April 2025.
19. Ministry of External Affairs (MEA). (2023). India-Kazakhstan Bilateral Relations. Government of India. https://www.mea.gov.in/.Accessed on 16 April 2025.
20. Ibid.
21. Korybko, A. (2022). 'India and Kazakhstan's Growing Strategic Partnership.' *Eurasia Review*. https://www.eurasiareview.com/.Accessed on 10 March 2025.
22. Pant, H.V., & Sahu, A. (2022). *India's Central Asia Engagement: Security and Strategic Dimensions*. Observer Research Foundation. https://www.orfonline.org/. Accessed on 19 March 2025.
23. Ministry of External Affairs (MEA). (2023). India-Kazakhstan Bilateral Relations. Government of India. https://www.mea.gov.in/. Accessed on 20 March 2025.
24. UNCCD. (2022). *Combating Desertification: India's Global Role*. United Nations Convention to Combat Desertification. https://www.unccd.int/. Accessed on 14 March 2025.
25. Vinokurov, E. (2021). *Eurasian Economic Union and India: Prospects for Integration*. Eurasian Development Bank. https://eabr.org/. Accessed on 15 March 2025.

9

History of Diplomatic Relations and Political Cooperation between Kazakhstan and India

Dr. Saniya Nurdavletova

Introduction

Diplomatic relations between the Republic of Kazakhstan and India have a long-standing and multifaceted history, built on mutual respect and shared interests. Kazakhstan, located at the heart of the Eurasian continent, and India, a leading country in South Asia, have maintained political, economic, and cultural cooperation for decades – cooperation that continues to develop in the 21st century. India attaches great importance to strengthening its relations with Central Asia, as evidenced by the initiative of the so-called 'New Silk Road' in Indian foreign policy, aimed at deepening cooperation with the Central Asian region. Political cooperation between Kazakhstan and India is progressing within the framework of a strategic partnership, which is being reinforced at various levels.

Over more than three decades of engagement, Kazakhstan and India have established strong political, economic, and cultural ties based on mutual respect and shared interests in the areas of security, trade, education and science. Despite geographical distance, Kazakhstan and India share common approaches to key issues on the international agenda, which has enabled them to build a productive and strategic partnership.

A special role in their relationship is played by cooperation within international organisations such as the United Nations, the Shanghai Cooperation Organisation (SCO), and others, where both countries actively support common interests and share experiences. An important step in deepening bilateral relations was the signing of several agreements, including a strategic partnership agreement as well as agreements aimed at expanding mutual exchange in the fields of culture, science, education, and trade.

The history of diplomatic cooperation serves as an example of the successful integration of the two countries into global processes. In recent years, relations between Kazakhstan and India have continued to strengthen, opening new horizons for further development. This section will examine the history of the establishment and development of political and diplomatic relations between the Republic of Kazakhstan and the Republic of India. *The section has been prepared as part of scientific project AR26100515 'Risk management strategies and strengthening Kazakhstan's foreign policy in the context of geopolitical challenges and regional instability'.*

Establishment and Development of Political and Diplomatic Relations

On January 31, 1992, Kazakhstan and India established official diplomatic relations, marking an important step in the development of bilateral ties. During the early years of Kazakhstan's independence, the two countries laid the foundation for multifaceted cooperation in political, economic, and cultural spheres.

In November 1993, the Embassy of the Republic of Kazakhstan was opened in New Delhi. In October 1993, the Embassy of India was opened in Kazakhstan. After relocating to Astana in November 2007, a consular office has continued to operate in Almaty. Since May 2021, the Ambassador of Kazakhstan to India has been Mr. N. Zhalgasbayev, who presented his credentials on July 7, 2021. Since June 2023, the Ambassador of India to Kazakhstan has been Mr. T.V. Nagendra Prasad, who presented his credentials on October 6, 2023.

During the same period, active efforts began to establish mechanisms for cooperation in various fields such as the economy, culture, science, and security. In the early years following the establishment of diplomatic relations, Kazakhstan and India focused on laying the groundwork for deeper political and diplomatic engagement. Kazakhstan actively sought ways to diversify its foreign policy and economic ties, while India, with its growing ambitions in Central Asia, aimed to strengthen its presence in this key region.

Overall, the political and diplomatic relations between Kazakhstan and India in the modern era can be conditionally divided into four stages.

The first decade (1992–2002) marked the establishment of political and legal relations between the two states. India was among the first countries to establish diplomatic relations with Kazakhstan on February 23, 1992, following Kazakhstan's independence. Since then, the two countries have engaged in close cooperation and developed mutually beneficial relations across a wide range of areas. A key milestone in the development of diplomatic ties was a series of high-level visits. In 1993, the First President of Kazakhstan, Nursultan Nazarbayev, paid an official visit to India. This visit was the first in the history of independent Kazakhstan and contributed significantly to strengthening bilateral political relations. In turn, the Indian side actively supported these ties at the political level. This marked an important step towards opening new prospects for cooperation between the two countries in areas such as the economy, culture, and security.

During this period, several key agreements were signed, including the 'Agreement between the Republic of Kazakhstan and the Republic of India on Cooperation in the Fields of Trade-Economic Relations, Science, and Technology,', and the 'Agreement between the Governments of the Republics on Cooperation in the Fields of Culture, Art, Education, Science, Mass Media, and Sports' (signed in New Delhi on February 22, 1992). In addition, on September 10, 1993, the 'Air Services Agreement' was signed in Almaty. Later, on December 9, 1996, in Delhi, the 'Agreement on the Promotion and Protection of Investments' was signed between the Government of the Republic of Kazakhstan and the Government of the Republic of India, as well as the 'Convention for the Avoidance of Double Taxation and the Prevention of Fiscal Evasion with Respect to Taxes on Income and Capital'.

Overall, from 1991 to 2002, several significant high-level meetings took place in 1992, the official visit of the First President of the Republic of Kazakhstan, N. Nazarbayev, to the Republic of India; in 1993 the official visit of Indian Prime Minister Narasimha Rao to Kazakhstan; in 1996, another official visit of President Nazarbayev to India; and in the same year, the official visit of Vice President of India K. Narayanan to Kazakhstan. In 1999, the Deputy Prime Minister and Minister of Foreign Affairs of Kazakhstan, K. Tokayev, paid an official visit to India, during which key areas of bilateral cooperation were discussed.

Overall, when characterising the first stage of the development of Kazakhstan-India relations, it is important to highlight the rapid establishment and strengthening of the legal and institutional framework across various areas of cooperation. In the early years following the establishment of diplomatic ties, the main focus was on developing political and economic relations. Kazakhstan and India exchanged visits by high-level officials and signed a number of agreements aimed at expanding trade, economic relations, and cultural ties.

The second period (from 2002 to 2011) was marked by the practical implementation of the legal agreements signed between the Republic of Kazakhstan and the Republic of India, as well as the formation and expansion of other promising areas of bilateral cooperation. A significant milestone in the development of bilateral relations during this period was the state visit of the First President of Kazakhstan, Nursultan Nazarbayev, to India from February 11 to 14, 2002. Taking place in the year of the 10th anniversary of diplomatic relations between the two countries, the visit received numerous positive responses from Indian political and business circles regarding the prospects and expansion of cooperation.

In 2003, Indian Prime Minister Atal Bihari Vajpayee visited Kazakhstan, which became a landmark event in deepening political and economic relations. In return, the President of India visited Kazakhstan in 2009, further confirming the mutual interest of both nations in advancing their partnership.

Overall, over the span of ten years, the friendly and mutually beneficial relations between India and Kazakhstan have stood the test of time. Fruitful meetings held both in India and Kazakhstan demonstrated the sincerity of the intentions of both nations to expand their partnership and opened new horizons for cooperation.

During this period, several high-level meetings took place: in 2002, the official visit of the First President of Kazakhstan, Nursultan Nazarbayev, to India, and in the same year, Indian Prime Minister Atal Bihari Vajpayee visited Kazakhstan within the framework of the CICA Summit.

The negotiations held and the agreements reached during these visits marked a qualitatively new level in bilateral relations and confirmed the shared positions of the two countries on key global issues and joint efforts to counter emerging global challenges. This was reflected in the political document signed in 2002 – the 'Joint Declaration on Strategic Partnership'.

The leaders of both countries identified priority areas for Kazakh-Indian cooperation and declared mutual support in advancing their respective national interests. This declaration marked a transition to a new stage of interaction between the two nations, including collaboration in priority sectors.

It is encouraging that since the early 2000s, political and diplomatic relations between Kazakhstan and India have begun to deepen. The 'Strategic Partnership Agreement' signed in 2002 became the foundation for strengthening bilateral ties, opening up opportunities for closer cooperation in the fields of energy, trade, and technology.

This period marked an important milestone in bilateral relations, particularly with the visit of the First President of Kazakhstan, Nursultan Nazarbayev, to India in 2006. As a result of this visit, several agreements were signed in the areas of trade, energy, science, and technology. Special attention was given to energy cooperation, particularly in the field of uranium extraction and processing. Kazakhstan is one of the world's largest producers of uranium, and India has shown a strong interest in cooperating in this sector for the development of its nuclear energy program.

Further high-level meetings followed: in 2008, Indian Vice President M. Hamid Ansari paid an official visit to Kazakhstan; in 2009, President Nazarbayev made a state visit to India. In 2010, the Minister of External Affairs of India, S.M. Krishna, visited the Republic of Kazakhstan.

On January 1, 2009, the 'Strategic Partnership Agreement' between Kazakhstan and India was signed. This document was a significant step towards strengthening bilateral relations and covered a range of areas including the economy, trade, culture, science, and technology. In the same year, the 'Agreement on Cooperation in the Peaceful Use of Atomic Energy' was also signed, which provides for the supply of uranium from Kazakhstan to India and cooperation in the field of nuclear energy.

In 2009, Kazakhstan and India signed the 'Strategic Partnership Agreement,' marking an important milestone in their bilateral relations. This agreement facilitated the expansion of cooperation in areas such as energy, economy, culture, defence, science, and technology. The strategic partnership also called for increased high-level reciprocal visits. Throughout the 2010s, bilateral relations continued to develop based on the agreements signed.

During this period, a Long-Term Program for Cooperation in the Field of Education was also signed, aimed at student and academic exchanges. This program is an important part of bilateral relations and helps strengthen ties between the two countries in the fields of science, technology, and cultural exchange. It is designed to support human capital development and foster deeper scientific and educational collaboration.

The third phase (2011-2020) marked a new momentum in Kazakhstan-India relations with the signing of the 'Treaty of Friendly Relations and Cooperation' in 2011. This document reinforced the strategic partnership between the two countries, including the development of cooperation in political, economic, and cultural spheres, as well as in security and scientific fields. It confirmed the mutual interest in deepening bilateral cooperation across a range of key areas.

During these years, trade and economic ties intensified. Kazakhstan became an important partner for India in Central Asia, and a number of agreements were signed in the areas of trade, investment, and finance.

In 2011, an official visit by the Prime Minister of the Republic of India, Manmohan Singh, took place in Kazakhstan. During this visit, a 'Treaty on Legal Assistance in Civil Matters' was signed in Astana. This treaty regulates the provision of legal assistance in civil matters between the two countries.

One of the key documents between the two countries was the 'Treaty of Friendly Relations and Cooperation' signed in 2011, which deepened political ties and allowed for expanded collaboration in the fields of security, defence, and scientific and technical exchange.

Kazakhstan actively supported Indian initiatives in international organisations such as the United Nations and the Shanghai Cooperation Organisation (SCO), while India supported Kazakhstan on matters related to nuclear security and other international issues.

In 2012, a visit by the First President of Kazakhstan, Nursultan Nazarbayev, to New Delhi resulted in the signing of new agreements, including those aimed at improving transport and logistics links as well as cooperation in agriculture.

In 2015, the two countries signed a 'Memorandum of Understanding,' which included agreements on cooperation in the fields of railways, logistics, education, and more.

These documents reflect the desire of Kazakhstan and India to strengthen bilateral relations and develop cooperation in various fields. During this period, collaboration in the cultural and humanitarian spheres began to flourish, along with more active participation by Kazakhstan and India in joint projects within the framework of the SCO.

In 2016, Indian Prime Minister Narendra Modi visited Almaty, during which several important agreements were signed. These included cooperation in the fields of high technology, trade, education and science, energy, as well as agreements in the areas of security and counter-terrorism. With each passing year, Kazakhstan and India have intensified their cooperation in the field of defence and security. This visit and the signing of the agreements marked an important step in strengthening bilateral ties.

The year 2017 was also significant, as it marked the decision to create the Kazakhstan-India Business Platform, which helped increase mutual investments and expand business relations. In 2017, an official visit of Indian President Narendra Modi to Kazakhstan also took place.

During this period, a number of high-level meetings were held: in 2013, the official visit of the Minister of Foreign Affairs of the Republic of Kazakhstan, Erlan Idrissov, to India; in the same year, the visit of the Minister of Foreign Affairs of India, Salman Khurshid, to Kazakhstan; in 2018, the visit of the Minister of Foreign Affairs of the Republic of India, Sushma Swaraj, to Kazakhstan; in 2019, the visit of Indian Minister of State for External Affairs, V. Muraleedharan, to Kazakhstan. In 2019 in New York, in 2020 in Moscow, in March 2021 in Dushanbe, and in July 2021 in Tashkent, Deputy Prime Minister and Minister of Foreign Affairs of Kazakhstan, Mukhtar Tileuberdi and held meetings with his Indian counterpart, Subrahmanyam Jaishankar. All these meetings gave new momentum to the development of political and diplomatic relations between Kazakhstan and India.

It is important to note that inter-parliamentary cooperation between the two countries has also been actively developing. In 2013, a delegation of Kazakhstani parliamentarians, led by the Chairman of the Committee on International Affairs, Defence and Security of the Mazhilis of the Parliament of the Republic of Kazakhstan, Maulen Ashimbayev, visited India.

In 2018, Kazakhstan and India celebrated the 25th anniversary of the establishment of diplomatic relations. As part of this occasion, several documents were signed to strengthen the strategic partnership.

In 2020, during the global COVID-19 pandemic, both countries demonstrated solidarity and began joint efforts to overcome the consequences of the pandemic. Kazakhstan supplied India with medical materials, while India provided assistance in medical research.

The fourth stage (from 2021 to the present) has become a period of deepened cooperation in areas such as information technology, the space industry, agriculture, and green energy. Kazakhstan is actively promoting itself as a partner in the field of alternative energy sources, which has attracted interest from India. Evidence of this is the participation of the President of the Republic of Kazakhstan, Kassym-Jomart Tokayev, in the First 'Central Asia–India' Summit held via video-conferencing in 2022, where key issues of cooperation were discussed.

Achievements and promising areas of cooperation were also discussed during the visits of Indian External Affairs Minister S. Jaishankar to Kazakhstan and Deputy Prime Minister and Minister of Foreign Affairs of the Republic of Kazakhstan, M. Tileuberdi, to New Delhi during the 3rd India-Central Asia Foreign Ministers' Dialogue in 2021.

In 2022, relations between Kazakhstan and India continued to develop, with a focus on global issues such as climate change, counter-terrorism, and strengthening international security. During the SCO Summit, both sides reaffirmed their commitment to further develop bilateral relations.

In 2022, two high-level visits took place – those of Indian Minister of State for External Affairs Meenakshi Lekhi to Kazakhstan, during which issues related to further cooperation in trade, energy, and the economy were discussed.

In 2023, the President of Kazakhstan, Kassym-Jomart Tokayev, participated in a number of joint events including the first online summit 'Voice of the Global South' and the SCO Summit, hosted by India in videoconference format. That same year, Deputy Prime Minister and Minister of Foreign Affairs of Kazakhstan, Murat Nurtleu, visited India as part of the SCO Foreign Ministers' Meeting. These meetings highlighted Kazakhstan's role in the SCO and its active engagement in the organisation's development.

In recent years, political and diplomatic relations between Kazakhstan and India have become more dynamic. Both countries maintain close ties within the SCO framework, where they actively discuss issues of security, trade, and sustainable development. Kazakhstan and India are actively working on the development of joint digitalisation projects and are strengthening cooperation in response to global challenges such as geopolitical instability and climate change. A number of agreements have been signed between the two countries in the fields of trade, investment, science and technology, as well as cooperation in combating terrorism and other global threats.

Thus, Kazakhstan and India continue to deepen their relations, moving from a strategic partnership to a more comprehensive and multilateral cooperation aimed at realising mutual interests in politics, economics, and culture.

Conclusion

Diplomatic relations between Kazakhstan and India have come a long way from the establishment of official ties in 1992 to the development of a strategic partnership in the 21st century. The two countries are actively expanding cooperation in various fields, such as economy, culture, defence, and energy. Mutual visits by the leaders of both nations have contributed significantly to strengthening bilateral relations.

Both countries also actively cooperate at the multilateral level within international organisations such as the United Nations, the SCO, the Conference on Interaction and Confidence-Building Measures in Asia (CICA), and others. They advocate for a stronger role of the UN and support its central position in international politics. Kazakhstan supports India in its efforts to expand its influence on the global stage, particularly regarding India's bid for permanent membership in the UN Security Council.

Kazakhstan and India support each other on major global and regional issues, such as security, sustainable development, and the fight against international terrorism. They closely collaborate on matters of regional security, especially in the context of Central and South Asia. Both nations advocate for the peaceful resolution of conflicts, the maintenance of stability, and countering terrorist threats.

India also supports Kazakhstan's initiative to host the Congress of Leaders of World and Traditional Religions and actively participates in its events. Regular meetings between Kazakhstan and India are held at all levels. Their increased frequency and substantive content reflect the dynamic development of bilateral cooperation.

Political cooperation between Kazakhstan and India continues to evolve, covering diverse areas and creating a strong foundation for further strengthening bilateral relations. In the future, Kazakhstan and India will continue to deepen their ties, overcoming geopolitical and economic challenges to ensure the sustainable development of their bilateral relationship. The dynamic development of a bilateral partnership based on equality, mutual respect, and mutual understanding demonstrates the shared approaches, views, and positions of Kazakhstan and India across various fields of interaction.

Thus, the evolution of political and diplomatic relations between Kazakhstan and India has gone through several important stages, beginning with the establishment of official ties and culminating in a deeper strategic partnership in recent decades.

References

1. Kukeeva, F.T., & Azimkhanov, K.N. (2013). 'Kazakhstan and India: Perspectives in cooperation.' *KazNU Bulletin. International Relations and International Law Series,* 3-4(63-64), 89-93.
2. О казахстанско-индийских отношениях. (n.d.). Retrieved from https://www.gov.kz/memleket/entities/mfa-delhi/activities/2126.
3. Sultanov, B.K., & Santanam, K. (n.d.). India and Kazakhstan: Perspectives of strategic cooperation. Retrieved from http://kisi.kz/img/docs/5315.pdf.
4. Назарбаев, Н. А. (2018). *Стратегия Казахстана в условиях глобальных изменений.* Алматы: Казахстан.
5. Гуриев, С., & Махмудов, Н. (2020). Экономическое сотрудничество Казахстана и Индии: Современные тенденции. *Журналмеждународныхотношений, 2,* 36-44.
6. Сагиндыков, Н. (2015). *История дипломатии Казахстана: 1991–2010 годы.* Астана: Казахстан.
7. Ministry of External Affairs of India. (2020). *India-Kazakhstan Bilateral Relations.* New Delhi.
8. О ратификации Конвенции между Правительством Республики Казахстан и Правительством Республики Индия об избежании двойного налогообложения и предотвращении уклонения от налогообложения в отношении налогов на доход и на капитал: Закон Республики Казахстан от 3 июля 1997 года № 147–1. (2002). *БюллетеньмеждународныхдоговоровРеспублики Казахстан,* 144, 35.
9. Ibrokhim, R. (2009, September 5). 'India-Kazakhstan relations: Challenges and prospects.' *Mainstream Weekly, XLVII* (38).
10. Ashok Sajjanhar (2013). India-Kazakhstan relations: Challenges and opportunities. https://www.gatewayhouse.in/india-kazakhstan-relations-challenges-and-opportunities/
11. The Diplomat. (2019). *Kazakhstan and India: Building strategic ties in Central Asia.* Retrieved from https://thediplomat.com.
12. India–Kazakhstan Relations. Embassy of India in Kazakhstan, 2009. https://www.indembastana.gov.in/content/India_Kazakhstan_Relations.pdf
13. Sajjanhar, A. (2013). India-Kazakhstan relations: Challenges and opportunities. Gateway House, Indian Council on Global Relations. November, 20.
14. Foshko, K. (n.d.). India-Kazakhstan: Looking beyond energy II. Retrieved from http://www.gatewayhouse.in/india-kazakhstan-looking-beyond-energy-ii/
15. Hussain, Z. (2009, January 16). 'Analysis: Indian-Kazakh energy ties deepen.' *Energy Daily.*
16. Соглашение между Правительством Республики Казахстан и Правительством Республики Индия о сотрудничестве в области культуры, искусства, образования, науки, средств массовой информации и спорта. (1992, февраль 22). *БюллетеньмеждународныхдоговоровРеспублики Казахстан,* 10, 62.
17. Baizakova, K., & Dwivedi, R. (n.d.). India-Kazakhstan perspectives: Regional and international interactions. Retrieved from http://www.centralasiasouthcaucasus.com/index.php?option=com_content&task=view&id=90.
18. Соглашение между Республикой Казахстан и Республикой Индия о сотрудничестве в области торгово-экономических отношений, науки и технологии. (1992, февраль 22). *БюллетеньмеждународныхдоговоровРеспублики Казахстан,* 10, 63.
19. Деловые круги Индии заинтересованы в развитии торгово-экономических связей с Казахстаном. (2024, сентября 19). *IBA Moscow.* Retrieved from http://iba-moscow.ru/cgi-bin/iba/news.

SECTION III

Economic Cooperation, Trade, Connectivity and Business Engagement

10

Economic Cooperation and Trade

Dr. Zhapar Zhuman

Introduction

Kazakhstan is the largest trading partner of India in Central Asia. In recent years, there has been steady growth in trade turnover between the two countries, especially in the sectors of energy, pharmaceuticals, information technology, and metallurgy. However, the volume of trade is still far from reaching its full potential.

Economic cooperation between Kazakhstan and India is of strategic importance and covers various areas, including energy, pharmaceuticals, agriculture, technology, and transport infrastructure. Despite the geographical distance, the two countries are developing trade and economic ties through regional and emerging mechanisms.

India's great power strategy plays a key role in shaping its Central Asian policy. Another dominant factor in India's Central Asian policy is the geopolitical dimension, with geographical remoteness being the main obstacle to establishing closer ties between India and Central Asia.

Thus, although the Modi government has strengthened its commitments to Central Asia and successfully joined the Shanghai Cooperation Organisation (SCO), constraints on further expanding India's influence in Central Asia remain unresolved in the absence of solutions to geopolitical challenges. In the future, India's policy in Central Asia will, on the one hand, seek regional partners to enhance its presence, and on the other, strive to build connections with regional countries through mechanisms of regional cooperation.

India's Economy

India is one of the fastest-growing economies in the world, driven mainly by the service sector, industry, and agriculture. Thanks to strong macroeconomic indicators, robust domestic demand, and favourable demographic trends, India has become the world's fifth-largest economy by nominal gross domestic product (GDP) (Table 1).

Table 1. The Five Largest Economies in the World by GDP

№	COUNTRY	GDP (BILLION DOLLARS)	GDP PER CAPITA (THOUSAND DOLLARS)
1	USA	28,783	85.37
2	China	18,536	13.14
3	Germany	4,590	54.29
4	Japan	4,112	33.14
5	India	3,942	2.73

Source: https://www.worldbank.org

The rapid growth of India's economy in recent years has been largely attributed to strong demand for its goods and services, coupled with significant industrial expansion. Historically, the Indian economy was more dependent on the agricultural sector; however, it has since evolved into a diversified system in which the services sector now accounts for the majority of activity and growth. India is increasingly recognised as a 'global player' within the international economic system.

Figure 1 illustrates the sectoral distribution of India's gross domestic product (GDP) over the period 2012–2022.

Figure 1. Sectoral distribution of India's GDP (2012–2022)

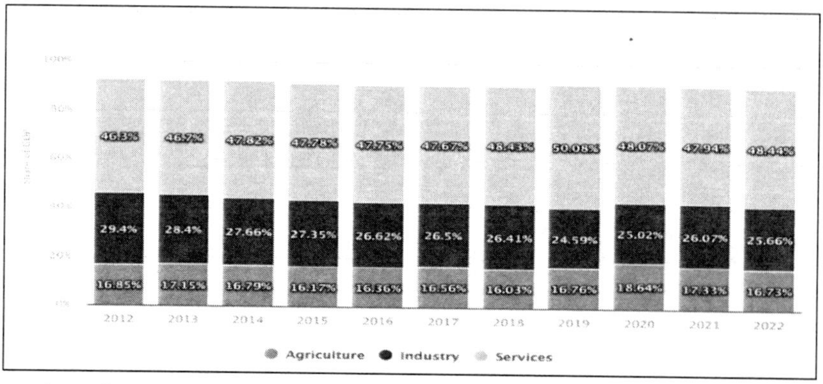

Source: https://www.statista.com/statistics/271329/distribution-of-gross-domestic-product-gdp-across-economic-sectors-in-india/

Agricultural Sector

India is the world's second-largest producer of fruits and a leading global producer of lemons, bananas, mangoes, papayas, and limes. Agriculture has traditionally been a primary source of income and revenue for the country; however, by 2022 its share of India's GDP had declined to 16.73 per cent. The agricultural sector faces several challenges, including inefficient infrastructure, limited irrigation, and a lack of adequate storage facilities and distribution channels. Forestry in India is regarded as a growing sector, responsible for producing fuelwood, fibreboard, pulp for paper, paper, and cardboard.

Industrial Production

The petrochemical industry represents a major business sector in India. It first appeared on the industrial landscape in the 1970s and experienced rapid expansion throughout the 1980s and 1990s.

India mines a significant quantity of precious stones and minerals, including iron ore, bauxite, and gold, as well as asbestos, uranium, and marble. In 2023, the country extracted 1,010.9 million tons of coal, 32.6 million tons of oil, and 62.6 billion cubic metres of natural gas. Additionally, India is among the world's largest producers of pharmaceuticals, automobiles, motorcycles, tools, tractors, and forged steel.

Business Services

The services sector in India has expanded from a modest share of GDP to approximately 48.4 per cent in 2022. The country benefits from a large pool of skilled, educated, and English-speaking professionals. Telecommunications, information technology, and software are among the leading service industries. Indian professionals are employed both domestically and in international corporations such as Yahoo, Google, Meta, and Microsoft.

Other components of India's services sector include power generation and tourism. The country continues to rely heavily on fossil fuels – coal, oil, and gas – yet it is steadily increasing its capacity in hydropower, wind, solar, and nuclear energy. In 2022, foreign exchange earnings from tourism amounted to USD 16.928 billion, contributing 5.9 per cent to India's GDP.

Exports and Imports

Over the past several decades, India has steadily expanded its exports, becoming one of the world's leading exporting nations. In 2023, India earned USD 437 billion from exports. The country's principal export commodities include leather and leather goods, petroleum products, precious stones and jewellery, pharmaceuticals, automobiles, and electronics. The main export destinations are the USA, the United Arab Emirates (UAE), the Netherlands, and Singapore.

Imports have also shown sustained growth, with a significant increase in the volume and variety of goods entering the country. In 2023, India's imports totalled USD 675 billion. The primary imports consist of crude oil, coal, diamonds, chemicals, rubber, electronics, and machinery, which together account for 82 per cent of the country's total imports. Imports play a vital role in supporting the development of India's economy.

China remains India's largest import partner, followed by Russia, the USA, the UAE, Saudi Arabia, Iraq, and other countries. Notably, the 'Make in India' initiative seeks to boost domestic production and reduce dependence on imports, particularly from China. Table 2 presents India's import and export data over the past five years.

Table 2. India's Imports and Exports, 2019–2023 (in USD billions)

Year	2019	2020	2021	2022	2023
Export	313.3	291.8	422	451.1	437.1
Import	474.7	394.4	613	715.9	675.4

Source: Ministry of Commerce and Industry of India (https://www.commerce.gov.in/trade-statistics/)

State of Trade between India and Kazakhstan

When considering India's trade with Central Asian countries as a whole, numerous challenges can be observed in bilateral trade relations. In 2000, the volume of India–Central Asia trade was approximately USD 80 million, and by 2014 it had increased to USD 1.2 billion. India's trade with Central Asia can be described as developing 'from scratch.' Although there was a decline in India's trade with the region between 2005 and 2009, the overall trend during this period remained upward. Moreover, over the last decade, India's trade with Central Asia has generally shown a surplus, in contrast to India's trade deficit with Southeast and East Asia. However, it should be noted that Central Asia has not been a major trading arena for India, particularly if the energy sector is excluded.

In 2004, the volume of India's trade with Central Asia amounted to USD 202.6 million, and by 2013 it had increased to USD 746.3 million, reflecting quantitative growth in bilateral trade. Nevertheless, India's share of trade with Central Asia in the country's overall trade decreased from 0.15 percent in 2004 to 0.09 percent in 2013. Among the reasons for the low level of bilateral trade between India and Central Asia are the issue of geographical connectivity and the lack of adequate information regarding bilateral trade relations (see Table 3).

Table 3. GDP of India and Kazakhstan, 2014–2023 (USD billion)

Year	**2014**	**2015**	**2016**	**2017**	**2018**
India	1950	2100	2280	2430	2590
Kazakhstan	182.2	184.39	186.42	194.06	202.02
Year	2019	2020	2021	2022	2023
India	2690	2530	2780	2970	3200
Kazakhstan	211.11	205.83	214.68	221.55	232.85

Source: https://www.worldbank.org.

Before examining the mutual trade between India and Kazakhstan, it is important to consider the economies of the two countries and their positions in global trade. Although there is a significant gap in the size of their economies (GDP), both India and Kazakhstan are among the fastest-growing Asian countries in terms of economic growth in recent years (see Figure 2).

Figure 2. GDP Growth Trends of India and Kazakhstan per cent (1992–2023)

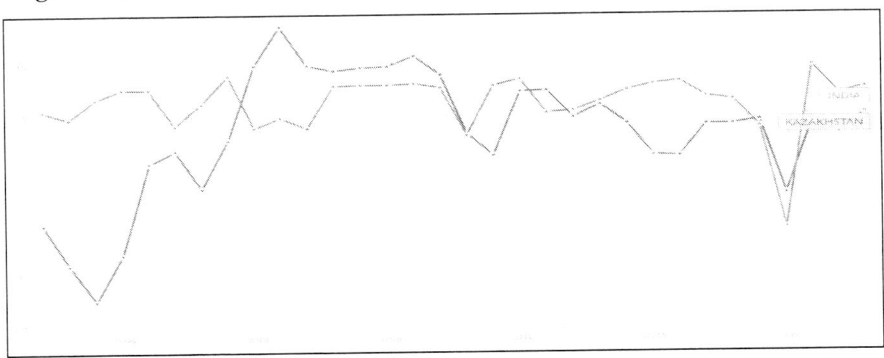

Source: https://data.worldbank.org/indicator/NY.GDP.MKTP.KD.ZG?end=2023&locations=KZ-IN&start=1992

This section concerns the shares of the analysed countries in global trade. In 2023, India's share of world exports amounted to 1.4 per cent, while its share of world imports reached 2.59 per cent. By contrast, Kazakhstan's share in both global exports and imports was less than 0.2 per cent. These figures indicate that both India and Kazakhstan still possess considerable potential for trade development. Kazakhstan is India's largest trading partner in Central Asia, and trade between the two countries has shown a consistent upward trend. Figure 3 illustrates the overall trade situation between India and Kazakhstan during the period 2014–2018.

Figure 3. Trade Trends between India and Kazakhstan (2014–2018)

Source: https://www.indembastana.gov.in/page/investment-statistics/

India's exports to Kazakhstan were lower than its imports from Kazakhstan during this period, highlighting India's dependence on Kazakhstani raw materials. Since nearly 80 percent of India's imports from Kazakhstan consisted of crude oil and petroleum products, the value of trade between the two countries declined sharply in 2015–2016 following the 2014 energy crisis (see Figure 4).

Figure 4. Composition of India's Imports from Kazakhstan, 2018.

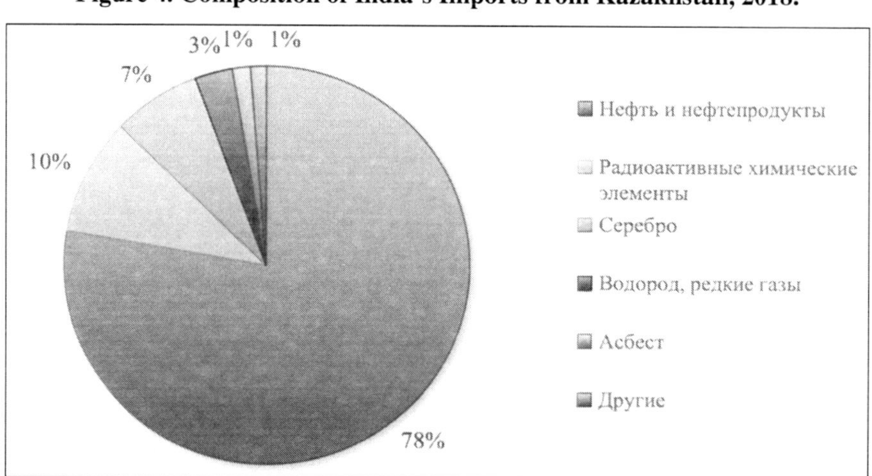

Source: https://www.indembastana.gov.in/page/investment-statistics/

The main goods exported from India to Kazakhstan in 2018 were pharmaceuticals, tea, telecommunication devices, stoves, and other household items (see Figure 5).

Figure 5. Composition of India's Exports to Kazakhstan, 2018

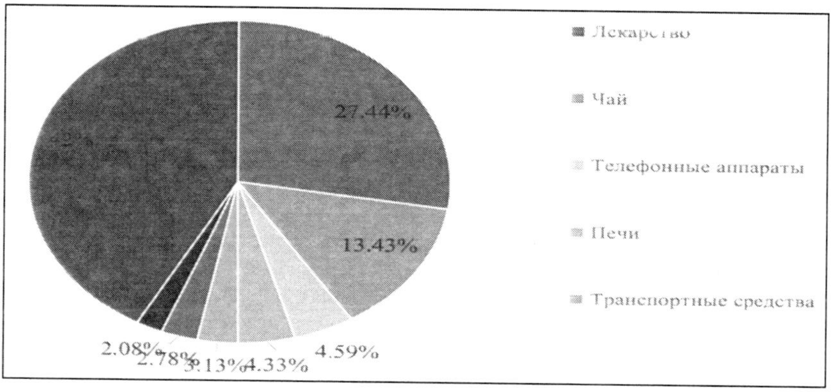

Лекарство
Чай
Телефонные аппараты
Печи
Транспортные средства
27.44%
13.43%
4.59%
4.33%
3.13%
2.78%
2.08%

Source: https://www.indembastana.gov.in/page/investment-statistics/

In 2019–2023, the total volume of India's exports to Kazakhstan did not change significantly compared to the previous period (see Figure 6). By contrast, India's total imports from Kazakhstan have been highly dependent on the international oil market. In 2022, due to the Russia-Ukraine conflict, India's imports of crude oil from Russia increased, leading to a substantial decline in imports of oil and petroleum products from Kazakhstan. Kazakhstan's crude oil exports decreased from 2.205 million tons in 2022 to 0.4 million tons in 2023.

Figure 6. Trade Trends between India and Kazakhstan (2019–2023)

Million USD$
2500
2000
1500
1000
500
0
2019
2020
2021
2022
2023
Экспорт из Индии в Казахстан
Импорт в Индии из Казахстан
Обшие суммы

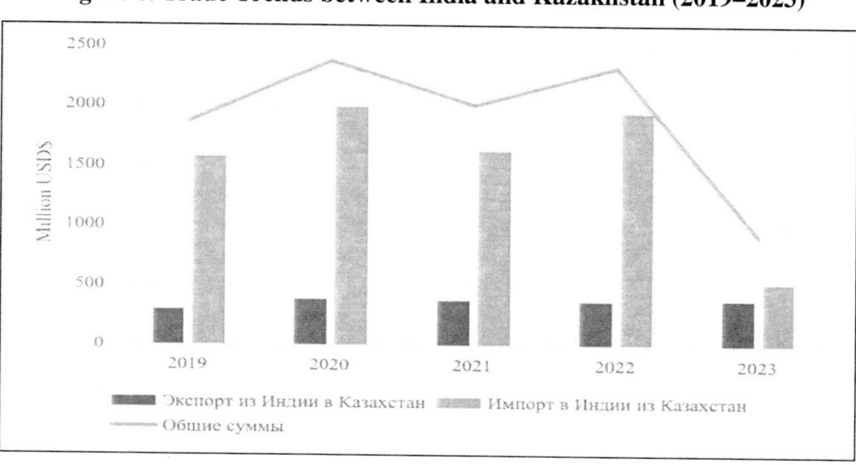

Source: https://www.new.stat.gov.kz.

Figure 7 presents the structure of India's imports from Kazakhstan in 2023. As the figure shows, the share of crude oil in India's imports from Kazakhstan declined to 50 per cent, while the share of inert gases and inorganic chemical products increased to 17 per cent.

Figure 7. Composition of India's Imports from Kazakhstan, 2023

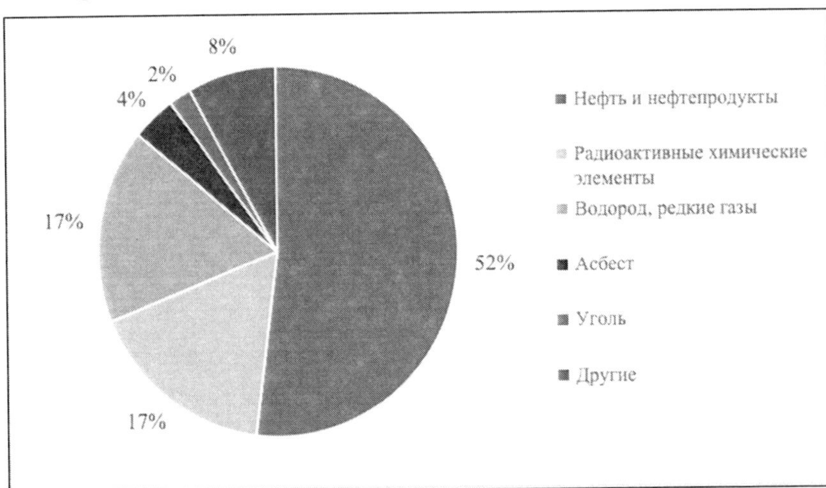

Source: https://www.new.stat.gov.kz

Compared to 2018, only minor changes were observed in India's main export commodities to Kazakhstan (see Figure 8).

Figure 8. Export structure from India to Kazakhstan in 2023.

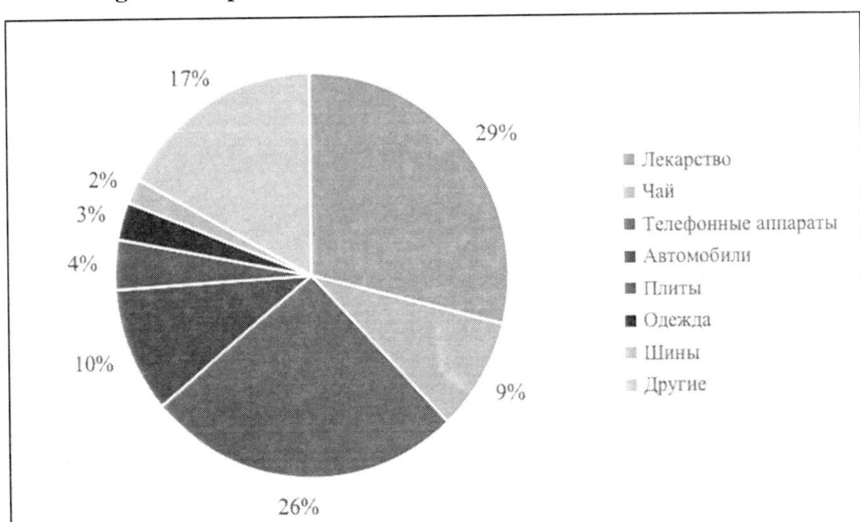

Source: https://www.new.stat.gov.kz.

Thus, India is undergoing a process of industrialisation and is in acute need of raw materials, which Kazakhstan, with its rich mineral resources, can provide. In this context, the largest share of India's imports from Kazakhstan consists of fossil fuels and various types of ores, which meet the growing needs of the population and industry.

In recent years, recognising the prospects for mutually beneficial cooperation, India and Kazakhstan have gradually strengthened their economic and political relations through the conclusion of a number of agreements on energy supplies, infrastructure development, and deeper economic and political integration. For instance, to expand energy cooperation, India and Kazakhstan have undertaken several measures to increase the supply of energy resources. In 2005, India's state-owned Oil and Natural Gas Corporation (ONGC) signed an agreement with the Kazakh national energy company KazMunayGas on cooperation in the oil and gas sector. In 2011, ONGC acquired a 25 per cent stake in the Satpayev oil block.

Looking ahead, Kazakhstan is prepared to expand trade turnover by increasing the export potential of 80 goods worth $609.5 million that can be supplied to the Indian market. According to forecasts, Kazakhstan has the capacity to increase the supply of metallurgical, chemical, food, and construction products. The main constraint on bilateral trade, however, remains transportation links. Both countries are discussing the possibility of investing in joint projects within the framework of the International Centre for Cross-Border Cooperation 'Khorgos' and the development of cross-border trade and economic hubs.

India's demographic context further reinforces this demand: with a population of 1.47 billion, the largest in the world, its domestic energy resources are insufficient. Although India accounts for 17 per cent of the global population, its share of coal, oil, and natural gas reserves stands at only 7 per cent, 0.4 per cent, and 0.6 per cent, respectively. Primary energy consumption in India in 2023 amounted to 39.02 exajoules, including 10.57 exajoules of oil (5,446 thousand barrels), 2.25 exajoules of natural gas, and 21.98 exajoules of coal. At the current rate of consumption, India's annual energy demand is expected to grow by 4.2 per cent by 2035. With the ongoing process of urbanisation, the country's energy consumption has shifted from direct fossil fuel use to electricity for cooking, heating, and lighting. Thus, energy trade remains a key area in India-Kazakhstan relations.

In the field of energy cooperation, India and Kazakhstan have signed significant agreements on nuclear energy and oil exploration. The 2011 Agreement on Cooperation in Nuclear Energy marked substantial progress in India's strategic partnership in the region. A new four-year agreement signed during this period envisaged Kazakhstan supplying 5,000 tons of enriched uranium to fuel India's 21 operating nuclear reactors, representing a new stage of energy cooperation.

Large-scale supplies of enriched uranium from Kazakhstan to India, which disrupted China's monopoly over Kazakh uranium exports, could potentially be reinforced by Russia's support for India in counter-balancing China's influence. Nevertheless, cooperation in nuclear materials may be constrained by geopolitical shifts, given the deepening alignment between Russia and China.

In 2011, OVL (ONGC Videsh Ltd.), a foreign subsidiary of India's state-owned ONGC, acquired a 25 per cent stake in the Satpayev oil block in the northern Caspian Sea, with the remaining 75 per cent held by Kazakhstan. After numerous delays, drilling commenced, and India committed $400 million in exploration investments.

Although India lacks close economic and trade ties with Kazakhstan due to the absence of direct geographical connectivity, these relations are vital for India's projection of 'soft power' and for enhancing its strategic role in Central Asia. Expanding economic cooperation, particularly in trade and energy, therefore represents an important tool for strengthening India's presence in Kazakhstan.

Investments in India and Kazakhstan

Against the backdrop of the reorganisation of global production chains, the opportunities and challenges of the 'Make in India' initiative are central to investors' attention. In order to assess the current state of investment in India, it is necessary to consider both the opportunities and risks associated with this initiative.

India has long faced a trade balance deficit. With economic development and rising per capita income, demand for imported goods such as electronics, machinery, and equipment continues to grow, thereby exerting pressure on foreign exchange reserves. The Government of India seeks to expand domestic production under the 'Make in India' initiative to meet domestic demand, increase exports, and reduce the long-term trade deficit.

Launched in 2014, 'Make in India' aims to promote industrial sector growth by improving the business environment, simplifying taxation, boosting investment, and encouraging technological innovation. The initiative covers sectors such as automobile manufacturing, aerospace, chemicals, and pharmaceuticals. In 2015, India introduced a phased manufacturing plan to incentivise local investment, replace imports, and raise import tariffs, especially in consumer electronics such as mobile phones and household appliances.

Driven by accelerating urbanisation, a growing working-age population, and the transformation of the economy towards services, India requires a further boost in infrastructure development. Nearly 70 per cent of announced infrastructure projects are in the energy sector, highways, railways, and urban facilities. In 2020, India launched the 'Self-Reliant India' *(Atmanirbhar Bharat)* program, aimed at strengthening domestic production and reducing dependence on imports.

Among the largest recent projects are Foxconn and Vedanta Resources' $19 billion plan to build one of India's first semiconductor plants, as well as a $5 billion green hydrogen project under a joint venture between Total Energies (France) and Adani Group (India).

Nevertheless, structural deficiencies remain. Road and rail transport in India are in poor condition, raising costs and delays. Energy supply remains unreliable, with power outages limiting manufacturing capacity and production.

In 2023, foreign direct investment inflows into South and Central Asia fell significantly, particularly in India and Kazakhstan. Sales resulting from mergers and acquisitions, which normally account for 10–15 per cent of total FDI in developing Asian economies, dropped by nearly $30 billion to $57 billion – roughly half of the overall decline in FDI in the region. Figure 9 illustrates investment dynamics in India and Kazakhstan over the past six years.

Figure 9. Investment Situation in India and Kazakhstan (2018–2023).

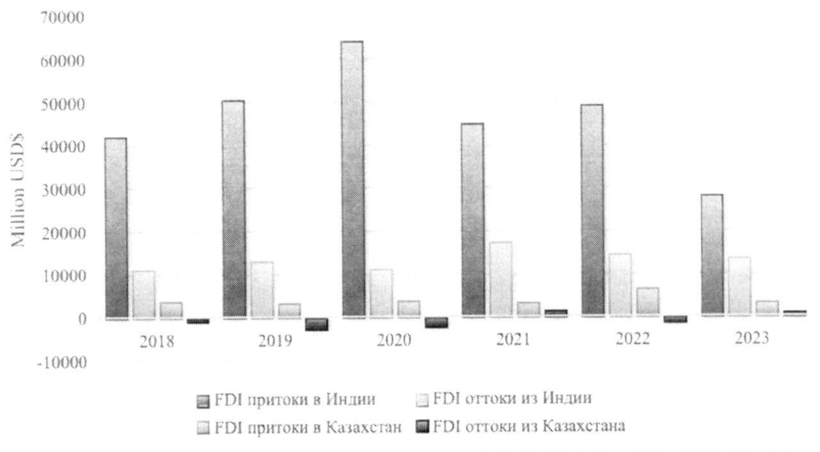

Source: World Investment Report 2024

With regard to Kazakhstan's investment profile, the largest volume of foreign direct investment (FDI) was directed towards the mining and metallurgical industries, which attracted USD 13,586 million. Within this sector, structural changes are evident: while the inflow of FDI into the metallic ore extraction segment increased, investment in coal extraction declined. More than USD 3.5 billion was invested in manufacturing, USD 3 billion in trade, USD 1.1 billion in transportation and storage, and over USD 1 billion in finance and insurance. The leading investors in Kazakhstan include the Netherlands (30.2%), the USA (23%), Switzerland (9.3%), China (7%), and Russia (5.8%).

India and Kazakhstan have significant potential to expand mutual investment through joint projects. In recent years, India has invested in agriculture, medicine, petrochemicals, healthcare, transport, logistics, tourism, and engineering. Kazakhstan remains India's principal trading partner among the Central Asian states. Kazakhstan's abundant natural energy resources make it a reliable partner for India in securing supplies of oil, gas, and other energy carriers. At the same time, India's large domestic market is of great interest to Kazakhstani exporters of goods and services. Currently, around 400 legal entities with Indian capital are registered in Kazakhstan, while the total inflow of Indian FDI into Kazakhstan over the past 25 years has exceeded USD 400 million.

Trade Relations between India and Kazakhstan

Kazakhstan occupies a strategic position as a gateway between Europe and Asia, offering significant potential for trade, investment, and growth. The country is endowed with substantial reserves of raw materials, including crude oil, natural gas, coal, gold, copper, aluminium, and iron. The increasing importance of hydrocarbons in the region has intensified competition among external powers. However, due to the geographic disconnection between India and Kazakhstan, the development of bilateral trade is likely to evolve not solely in the economic domain but within a geo-economic framework, largely through national projects aimed at strengthening regional cooperation.

In the future, India is expected to expand its engagement with Kazakhstan in the spheres of energy and trade, with active participation in oil extraction projects and uranium trade. Energy projects, in particular, will reduce India's dependence on hydrocarbon imports from the Middle East. The initiation and expansion of such projects will not only strengthen India's geo-economic presence but also translate into broader geopolitical influence.

India seeks to establish a more visible presence in Kazakhstan, making cooperation with the country a strategic imperative within India's Central Asia policy. Despite its potential status as a major power, India lags behind other key players in the region, including Russia, China, the European Union, and the USA. Although a rising power, India continues to face multiple domestic challenges that constrain its international projection.

Following the dissolution of the Soviet Union, Kazakhstan transitioned to an open economy and presented the international community with an entirely new market. With a relatively high level of economic development, vast economic potential, and an expansive market, Kazakhstan has become particularly important for India, which has experienced rapid economic growth in recent years. Available data indicate that since 2013, India-Kazakhstan trade has been characterised by a negative balance, with trade volumes, however, showing steady levels of cooperation.

India's significant economic interests in Kazakhstan necessitate the establishment of secure and uninterrupted trade routes with Central Asia. However, during the 2001–2002 India-Pakistan crisis, Pakistan closed its air corridors to Central Asia, making India's trade with the region dependent on bilateral relations with Pakistan. This situation increased the risks of India's trade with Central Asia. Consequently, to safeguard its economic interests in

Kazakhstan, India must develop new trade corridors that are not reliant on Pakistan.

The International North-South Transport Corridor (INSTC) represents such an initiative: a multimodal network spanning 7,200 kilometres to connect India with Russia via Iran, Europe, and Central Asia. The project is supported by 13 countries, including Kazakhstan, and is linked to the Iranian port of Chabahar, enabling India to transport Central Asian energy resources while bypassing Pakistan and Afghanistan.

Beyond trade, *energy security* remains a decisive factor in India's Central Asia strategy. As a major energy consumer with limited domestic reserves, India relies heavily on imports. Iran remains one of India's principal suppliers. In 2016, India – then the world's third-largest oil importer – sourced an average of 473,000 barrels per day from Iran, compared to 208,000 barrels per day in 2015. While Iran remains an important supplier, its domestic political instability necessitates diversification of India's supply sources. In this regard, Kazakhstan's substantial hydrocarbon reserves and India's growing demand for energy are mutually complementary, making the Central Asian energy corridor a critical component of India's strategic interests.

Conclusion

Kazakhstan, with its strategic geographic location and strong economic foundation, is a key partner for India. Kazakhstan's willingness to expand foreign economic cooperation, India's increasing demand for energy resources, and the complementary economic needs of both countries create a solid basis for further partnership. Both being Asian states, the rapid growth of one is likely to foster favourable conditions for the other, generating a spillover effect of development.

At the same time, the full potential of economic cooperation between India and Kazakhstan has yet to be realised, and numerous opportunities remain for expansion. India's membership in the Shanghai Cooperation Organisation (SCO) provides an important platform for dialogue and collaboration with Kazakhstan, facilitating exchanges, mutual understanding, confidence-building, and joint initiatives. This, in turn, supports the sustainable economic development of both states, particularly in addressing India's acute energy challenges.

Furthermore, engagement through international mechanisms significantly reduces the costs of bilateral cooperation and accelerates its development. International organisations create opportunities for India to deepen its interaction with Kazakhstan, enhance trust, and secure broader access to Central Asia. India's interest in strengthening economic cooperation with Kazakhstan, particularly in the energy sector, as well as in expanding access to the Kazakhstani market, can be more effectively pursued within the frameworks of the SCO and the Central Asia-India Summit.

References

1. Goldman Sachs. (2023). India to become the world's second-largest economy by 2075. – https://www.interfax.ru/world/911095 (https://www.worldbank.org.)
2. World Bank Group. https://www.worldbank.org.
3. Bureau of National Statistics of the Agency for Strategic Planning and Reforms of the Republic of Kazakhstan. https://www.new.stat.gov.kz.

11

Opportunities for Transport and Logistics Cooperation between Kazakhstan and India

Dr. Malik Augan

Clearly, one of the factors contributing to the growth of the intensity of economic ties of an interstate nature is the development of transport infrastructure. For this purpose, the implementation of state programs for the development of transport in Kazakhstan and India will be studied. This chapter attempts to study another direction of Kazakhstan's policy in creating a highly efficient logistics system and ensuring its integration into the Eurasian transport network, in particular South Asia, and specifically India.

Of the 30 geographically locked countries, Kazakhstan (3,750 km.), Kyrgyzstan (3,600 km.), Tajikistan (3,100 km.) and Uzbekistan (2,950 km.) are the most remote from the sea, and Turkmenistan (1,700 km.) occupies the eighth place.

The remoteness of Central Asia from sea routes is offset by the high transit potential of the region. To solve this problem, in 2006 Kazakhstan developed a Strategy for the development of the transport industry until 2015. Kazakhstan is the only country in the region that has adopted a comprehensive strategy for the development of the transport industry, aimed at creating the infrastructure of the transport and communication complex, consistent with the economic strategy of the state. The implementation of the strategic programme provides for the reconstruction of infrastructure facilities and the renewal of all types of vehicles.

In late 2014, Kazakhstan initiated the Nurly Zhol – the Way to the Future programme, aimed at implementing 15 infrastructure projects in the country's transport sector.

For a vast region remote from world markets, having a well-developed transport system with access to the outside world has become of crucial political and economic importance.

To develop trade and economic relations, the Central Asian countries have signed several agreements with China, Turkey, Iran, India and Pakistan. The most important of them are the China-Kazakhstan agreement on railway transportation (February 1992), the protocol on cooperation in the field of railway, road and maritime transport between China and Uzbekistan (March 1992), the Protocol on maritime transportation between Azerbaijan, Iran, Kazakhstan, Russia and Turkmenistan (April 1992), the agreement on Coordination of railway transport and cooperation in the field of transit transportation between Azerbaijan, Georgia, Turkmenistan and Uzbekistan (May 1996). The agreement on the creation of the North–South transport corridor (2000) between Russia, India and Iran, to which Kazakhstan subsequently joined, is important for the implementation of regional transport policy.

The first step towards the implementation of the concluded documents between Kazakhstan and China was the connection of the railways of the two countries in September 1990 in the area of Druzhba-Alashankou stations.

Kazakhstan is becoming an attractive overland transit route for cargo from the Chinese ports of Lianyungang, Qingdao, and Tianjin to Kyrgyzstan, Uzbekistan, Turkmenistan, Iran, Turkey, and ports in the Mediterranean and the Persian Gulf. Kazakhstan's transport infrastructure is becoming part of the global transport system and provides significant financial revenues to the budget of the state and transport companies, as well as the development of a competitive transport and logistics complex. Within the framework of this programme in 2006 Kazakhstan and China have reached an agreement on connecting the railways of the two countries along the Korgas (Kazakhstan)-Khorgos (China) line.

The completion of the Mashhad–Tejen railway in May 1996 connected the Turkmen and Iranian railways. In 2007, the heads of state of Kazakhstan, Turkmenistan and Iran signed a trilateral intergovernmental agreement on the construction of the Zhanaozen-Bolashak-Bereket-Etrek-Gorgan railway. The countries started construction in 2009 and completed it in 2014. This railway line creates new routes linking Kazakhstan and the Central regions of Russia with Turkmenistan, Iran, the countries of the Persian Gulf, South and Southeast Asia.

The development of transit sections of continental highways is of particular importance. Thus, Kazakhstan has upgraded the capacity of the Aktau seaport on the Caspian Sea, Iran has connected its railways with seaports in the Persian Gulf, and China has significantly rebuilt its railway network adjacent to Central Asia. The construction of a network of mutually complementary transcontinental, regional and local railways and highways allowed the Central Asian countries to gain access to both China and Iran, and through them to the outside world.

Kazakhstan and, to a lesser extent, Uzbekistan and Turkmenistan expect at least a small part of the huge cargo turnover that circulates between Asia and Europe to pass through their territory after the creation of the 8,500 km China–Europe transcontinental corridor. According to the General Administration of Customs of the People's Republic of China, China's trade turnover with the EU countries increased by 0.4% to $785.82 billion by the end of 2024, while the volume of Chinese exports to the Union increased by 3% to 516.46 billion and imports decreased by 4.4%, to $269.36 billion.

Due to the relative cheapness, the transportation of cargo by sea continues to be preferred.

The EU policy aimed at introducing a tax on hydrocarbon emissions from marine vessels starting in June 2012 may significantly correct this trend. China is heavily dependent on shipping. The tax on hydrocarbon emissions from marine vessels will directly affect the total cost of shipping and the cost of exporting Chinese goods. This innovation will also have an impact on the development of China's shipbuilding industry. China's shipping industry ranks fourth with a deadweight of more than 90 million tons.

However, on average, it takes approximately 56 days via sea, and land transportation routes can reduce travel time to 11-12 days.

All the main railways and highways of the Central Asian republics in Soviet times ran in a northerly direction and had no direct access to the outside world. The length of transport routes from the Pacific ports of China and Japan through Central Asia to Istanbul is much shorter compared to the Trans-Siberian Railway. Thus, the Tianjin-Istanbul route is shorter than the route through Russia by 1,286 km, Lianyungan-Istanbul by 2,350 km, Shanghai-Istanbul by 2,320 km, Hong Kong-Istanbul by 3,545 km, Yokohama-Istanbul by 2,350 km.

The transport route to some Pacific ports in East Asia from the main cities of Central Asia through Chinese territory is shorter than traditional communications through Russian territory: Almaty-Shanghai is almost 2.2 thousand kilometers, Tashkent-Shanghai is almost 900 kilometers shorter than the distance between these cities and Vladivostok. It is also fundamentally important that the distance between Almaty and the Pacific ports of China is almost equal to the length of the route from Almaty to the Baltic port of Riga and the Mediterranean port of Mersin.

The idea of creating a transport corridor connecting Asia and Europe through Central Asia is also being encouraged by leading international financial and economic institutions.

An important competitive advantage of Kazakhstan may be the construction of a railway line with a European/Chinese gauge (1435 mm, Russian/Soviet gauge of-1520 mm), which will reduce the travel time of goods and reduce transportation costs.

At the same time, if for Central Asia the restoration of the routes of the Great Silk Road is, first of all, the disclosure of the transit potential of the region, taking into account its advantageous geopolitical position, then for the initiators of the creation of the OBOR transport corridor it is also an important diplomatic step, since it contributes more to the formation of close integrated relations between the neighboring states of the region in the economic, political and humanitarian fields and promotes regional economic cooperation.

Central Asia is becoming a kind of bridge connecting the railways of Asian countries into a single network, while without South Asia. The revival of the Silk Road has ended the long-term isolation of Central Asia, the region has “opened up” and is turning into an important transit area for transcontinental trade.

Since the beginning of the Russian-Ukrainian conflict, the intensification of cooperation within the five countries of the region has become more pronounced, and political and economic relations with China and the countries of the Organisation for Economic Cooperation located on the southern borders of the region have become more frequent. Perhaps new geopolitical trends will lead to a change in the balance of power in the region and serve as an incentive for further institutionalisation.

According to the theory of the Russian researcher A.D. Bogaturov, Central Asia will turn out to be part of a larger region, apparently with the dominant role of China. According to the author, the political, military-strategic and economic contours of the new subsystem of international relations do not coincide with the division of the world into conditional geographical regions that has been established for many years in analytical traditions.

Bogaturov A.D. identified several reasons that contributed to the formation of a new regional subsystem. First, the collapse of the USSR led to the restoration of a powerful ethnodemographic, geographical, and political-strategic "bundle" of Pakistan-Afghanistan-Tajikistan-Uzbekistan, parts of which are extremely difficult, and sometimes even impossible, to untie "separately."

Secondly, the accelerated formation of the regional subsystem was facilitated by the emergence of a new western and northwestern vector of China's national security policy related to the threats of terrorism and China's interests in the energy resources of Central Asia. This has become one of the most important areas of Beijing's foreign policy, going far beyond a narrow regional strategy. This area of ensuring the country's security is integrated with the security policy of the coastal-island part of China from the Pacific Ocean. The territory of the People's Republic of China represents the binding core of China's unified security space-from the Pacific coast to the Caspian Sea.

Kazakhstan, being in the center of Eurasia, at the junction of large economic regions such as Russia, China and India, various civilisations and cultures, Kazakhstan is trying to integrate into the modern system of global political and economic interactions. By developing a modern transport infrastructure, Kazakhstan is becoming a connecting hub between the West and the East, through which continental and transcontinental transportation is carried out.

The range of destination countries for transit cargo flows through Kazakhstan is insignificant, mainly the countries of Central Asia and Afghanistan –85%, Russia and China-over 10%.

The average speed of cargo transportation along railway routes in Kazakhstan (44 kilometers per hour) is slightly lower than in China and Western countries (50-60 kilometers per hour).

To become one of the full-fledged centers of transcontinental and transit transportation between Europe and Asia, Kazakhstan needs to increase competitiveness in the international transport services market and develop Eurasian transport links due to the attractiveness of their land communications, paying significant attention to logistics.

Kazakhstan's advantageous location in terms of transport accessibility to the world's leading economies in the production of finished products and consumption of raw materials, its own Railway Transport Development Strategy and the implementation of the Intergovernmental Agreement on Dry Ports, which is an agreement within the framework of UNESCAP, make our country one of the actors in the development of an international integrated intermodal transport and logistics system. Systems in Asia and ensuring its connectivity with neighboring regions.

Based on the above, it can be seen that the main goal of Kazakhstan's transport policy is the further integration of national transport systems and logistics into Euro-Asian transport links.

The economic and geopolitical interests of Kazakhstan dictate the construction of new transport communications in the southern direction.

The transport corridors related to the so-called southern direction, including India, Kyrgyzstan, Tajikistan, Turkmenistan and Afghanistan, are the most complex and expensive in terms of cargo transportation costs. Kabul's active involvement in regional trade and transport infrastructure, and the announced railway projects across Afghanistan from a number of countries, primarily Uzbekistan, Kazakhstan, Turkey, and Turkmenistan, would seem to have great prospects. However, from the very beginning, the new South-Central corridor faces challenges due to high transportation costs and geopolitical instability. For example, to move a 20-foot container along the existing 75 km railway from Mazar-i-Sharif to Uzbek Termez, you will have to pay about 3,000 US dollars, which is much more expensive than moving the same amount of cargo from Uzbekistan to Russia (about 3,000 km). The permanent conflicts between India and Pakistan also do not give much optimism about this transport corridor.

At the same time, official and unofficial trade between India and Pakistan is growing, probably exceeding 10 billion US dollars. Positive dynamics are developing in the sphere of trade and transport and between Afghanistan and Pakistan. In recent years, the business climate in Afghanistan has been noticeably improving, which affects cross-border trade not only with South Asian countries, but also with Central Asian countries, primarily with Uzbekistan and Kazakhstan. This situation in Afghanistan gives hope for the country's involvement in international transport corridors. Close ties have already been established between the TRACECA countries and Afghanistan, although the country's transit potential is still not included in the transport routes of the organisation's program.

Despite significant transportation costs and geopolitical risks, the South-Central corridor holds substantial potential to significantly enhance Eurasian economic and cultural integration.

The trade and economic ties of the Central Asian countries with foreign markets through the Caucasus, Iran, Afghanistan and China are limited, so Kazakhstan pursues a policy of turning intra-continental restrictions into strategic transit opportunities. The factor of the impossibility of access to the sea pushes Kazakhstan to search for alternative logistics directions and infrastructural initiatives in foreign policy. The term "exit strategy" is used as an important means of overcoming this limitation. It is a set of policies and decisions adopted by the Government to overcome natural or political constraints in the international arena. Kazakhstan is implementing an "exit strategy" in this direction by diversifying foreign trade, creating transport and logistics hubs, and strategic partnerships with neighboring countries.

In October 2022, India developed a new National Logistics Policy to limit logistics costs to 5 percent of GDP. Due to the high logistics costs, about 14 percent, which is much higher than the global average, the cost of Indian producers' products is often not competitive in the global market. The main tasks of logistics will be to create a unified logistics interface platform, integrate a digital system, simplify and improve logistics.

In turn, the Government of India has launched the Gati Shakti programme as part of its national logistics policy, according to which various ministries will coordinate efforts to improve logistics in the country. Thanks to these measures, India ranked 38th in the Logistics Efficiency Index in 2023. This index was developed by World Bank experts and includes six indicators: the efficiency of customs services, the quality of infrastructure, competitive prices for international transportation, competence in logistics, tracking capabilities and timely delivery of goods.

The Logistics Performance Index 2024, compiled by the World Bank for 139 countries, is led by Singapore with 4.3 points and Afghanistan closes with 1.9. Of the countries with which Kazakhstan actively cooperates or is interested in cooperation in the transport sector, China, India and Turkey have the best indicators, respectively, 3.7 and 3.4 points. Kazakhstan and Georgia received 2.7 points each, Russia and Uzbekistan - 2.6 points, Tajikistan -2.5 and Iran, Kyrgyzstan and Pakistan –2.3.

Kazakhstan has no bilateral or multilateral agreements on railway transportation coordination with India. Negotiations on the creation of a special cargo terminal in one of India's western seaports, possibly Mumbai, for trade with Kazakhstan have been underway for a long time and are still under discussion. Kazakhstan had high hopes for the accession of India and Pakistan to the SCO and hoped to use the great potential of these countries in the transport sector.

The SCO Charter, adopted in 2002 at the St. Petersburg Summit, defines as one of the priorities the crucial role of transport and logistics cooperation between the organisation's member states in order to effectively use and improve their transport infrastructure and transit potential.

In India, maritime transport plays a significant role in international trade. Freight transport statistics show that approximately 70 percent of trade in value terms and more than 95 percent in volume terms is accounted for by sea.

India uses the advantages of the country's coastal location to develop its transport and logistics system. Thanks to the Arabian Sea, India is developing direct transportation to/from Europe, thereby avoiding transit traffic through Iran, Kazakhstan and Russia.

On July 14, 2022, the first I2U2 summit was held with the participation of the leaders of the participating countries: US President Joe Biden, UAE President Sheikh Mohammed bin Zayed Al Nahyan, Indian Prime Minister Narendra Modi and Israeli Prime Minister Yair Lapid. The appearance of I2U2 was largely made possible by the improvement of relations between a number of Arab countries and Israel, within the framework of the Abrahamic and Negev agreements. Economic issues, namely water supply, energy, healthcare, food security, space and transport, formed the basis of cooperation between the I2U2 member countries.

During the G20 summit in 2023, the leaders of India, the United States, Saudi Arabia and the European Union, chaired by India, agreed on the creation of a new transport corridor "India- Middle East-Europe" (India-Middle East-Europe Economic Corridor (IMEEC), which will connect India, Saudi Arabia, the United Arab Emirates, Jordan, Israel and the EU by sea and rail. Working groups have been set up to discuss the financial side of the project and create the necessary infrastructure. Whether this transport corridor with India's participation will become a challenge to the Chinese OBOR initiative will not be long in coming.

At one time, when Beijing officially invited India to join the Chinese OBOR initiative, it refused.

During the G20 summit in New Delhi, India tried to demonstrate a high level of partnership with the West, while, as a representative of the "global majority," combining this with the interests of the "global South."

The rivalry between China and India for leadership in the Global South, disagreements between states and their leaders and foreign policy orientations, different strategies in logistics and transport infrastructure affect the transport architecture of Central and South Asia and, more broadly, Eurasia. Cooperation between Kazakhstan and India in the transport and logistics sector demonstrates low efficiency and lack of prospects due to the multidirectional nature of their transport policies.

References

1. President of the Republic of Kazakhstan. (2006, April 12). On the Transport Strategy of the Republic of Kazakhstan until 2015 (Decree No. 86). *Kazakhstanskaya Pravda*. Almaty, Kazakhstan.
2. Government of Kazakhstan. (2015). *NurlyZhol-State Program for Infrastructural Development 2015–2019*. https://www.baiterek.gov.kz/en/activities/gos-programmy/nurly-zhol.
3. Li, B. (2012). Beijing Shang Bao (北京商报, Beijing Business Today). *Current Digest*, 1(6), 13–14.
4. United Nations. Economic and Social Commission for Asia and the Pacific. (2003). *Transit transport issues in landlocked and transit developing countries*. United Nations, New York.
5. Bogaturov, A.D. (2005). Central-Eastern Asia in contemporary international politics. *Vostok. Afro-aziatskiyeobshchestva: Istoriyaisovremennost*, 1, 102–118.
6. Idan, A., & Shaffer, B. (2011). *The foreign policies of post-Soviet landlocked states. Eurasian Geography and Economics,* 52(3), 241–263. https://doi.org/10.2747/1539-7216.52.3.241.
7. Rajan, V. C., & Krishnan, L. R. K. (2024). Significance and implications of National Logistics Policy of India. *Georgetown Journal of International Affairs*. https://gjia.george town.edu/.
8. World Bank. (2024). *Logistics Performance Index 2024*. http://lpi.worldbank.org/.
9. Shanghai Cooperation Organization. (2002). *Khartiya Shankhayskoyorganizatsiiso trudnichestva*. https://docs.cntd.ru/document/901858896.
10. Bhardwaj, N. (2023). Revolutionizing logistics in India: Top trends driving business operations in 2023.

12

Indo-Kazakhstan Business Prospects

Anil Sharma

Introduction

Kazakhstan is part of the India-Central Asia Dialogue, conceptualised at Samarkand on 12-13 January 2019. The first India-Central Asia Business Council Meeting, under this dialogue, was organised by the Federation of Indian Chambers of Commerce and Industry (FICCI), on 6 February 2020 in New Delhi. FICCI and the Chamber of International Commerce of Kazakhstan have set up a joint business council (JBC) to promote trade, economic and investment cooperation between the two countries. The fourth Council meeting was held on 5 June 2025 at New Delhi.

On a government-to-government basis, the India-Kazakhstan Inter-Governmental Commission (IGC) was established in 1993. It is the apex bilateral institutional mechanism for developing trade, economic, scientific, technological, industrial and cultural cooperation between the two countries and for that purpose several working groups have been established.

During the meeting between the Kazakh Foreign Minister (FM), Mr. Nurtleu, and the External Affairs Minister (EAM) of India, Dr. S. Jaishankar, held on the sidelines of the Council meeting on 5 June, the FM proposed intensifying business contacts to expand economic cooperation and further increase the volume of mutual trade. He also invited leading Indian companies to implement joint investment projects in industry, energy, transport, and logistics. He highlighted the importance of involvement of the business entities of both countries in developing business ties. The FM emphasised that "India is a reliable political, trade, and economic partner of Kazakhstan in South Asia, and our ties are developing steadily in a constructive direction."

India should seriously explore the business opportunities as referred and offered by Kazakh Foreign Minister Mr. Nurtleu. New deposits of rare earth metals estimating around one million tons of make Kazakhstan an important economic partner for India.

Kazakhstan and its major trade partners

1. Kazakhstan is the largest and most resource-rich country in the Central Asia region. It borders Russia, China, Kyrgyzstan, Uzbekistan, and Turkmenistan, as well as the Caspian Sea. It has a 20.6 million population, and its GDP in 2023 was USD 288 billion, which it aims to double by 2030. Its economy is dependent on oil, gas, uranium, coal, and gold. Kazakhstan's estimated oil reserves stand at 78 billion tons as of 2024, and it ranks 18th globally in gold reserves. It has the world's largest known uranium deposits, and 19 of the 34 types of raw materials needed for major economies, including uranium, titanium, copper, lithium, cobalt, tungsten, and many others. Holding 14 percent of the world's uranium reserves, Kazakhstan is the global leader in uranium production. In 2024, Kazakhstan produced 23,270 tonnes (approx.) of uranium. It is also a major exporter of oil and gas.

Kazakhstan's economy is heavily reliant on the extractive industry and financially dependent on international commodity prices, mainly oil, minerals and agricultural products. The high energy intensity of the Kazakh economy makes it the largest emitter of carbon dioxide in Central Asia and the 14th in the world with the carbon intensity of Kazakhstan's GDP two times higher than the world average and three times higher than the EU. Eightypercent of all CO_2 emissions in Kazakhstan come from the energy sector heavily dominated by coal generation.

2. The Russian Federation is amongst Kazakhstan's main trading partners. Despite a 13.2 percentage point decrease in its share since 2017, the Russian Federation remains the primary source of imports, accounting for 26.5 per cent of imports. China has partially replaced some of these imports, with its share increasing from 15.9 per cent to 27.4 per cent. Imports from the European Union decreased by three percentage points to 17.8 per cent.

In 2024, bilateral trade between Russia and Kazakhstan rose by nearly 3 percent, reaching USD 27.8 billion. Joint economic activities are also on the rise, with 171 collaborative projects currently underway. Interaction in the agribusiness sector remains an important area of bilateral cooperation. As of the end of last year, the trade turnover in this sphere grew by 4.5 percent and totalled USD 3.8 billion. Further discussions between the senior functionaries of the two governments were held to enhance areas of cooperation, including transit and transport infrastructure, agriculture, energy, environmental protection, space exploration, and cultural initiatives. Due to its geography and history, Kazakhstan remains closely linked to Russia through the Eurasian Economic Union, the Community of Independent States (CIS) and the Collective Security Treaty Organisation (CSTO).

3. China ranks among Kazakhstan's top five investment partners. The bilateral trade between Kazakhstan and China reached USD 43.8 billion with a growth of 9 per cent in 2024. Some 62 joint projects worth USD 8.7 billion have been completed. An additional 55 projects worth USD 13.5 billion are under development, and plans for 222 projects exceed USD 60.5 billion.

Carnegie launched research on Chinese engagement strategies in seven regions of the world – Africa, Central Asia, Latin America, the Middle East and North Africa, the Pacific, South Asia, and Southeast Asia. The research made, inter alia, the following observations with respect to Kazakhstan:

> *"China's growing presence in Central Asia – and Kazakhstan especially – has been accompanied by steady anti-Chinese sentiment. Beijing's reputation has suffered amid protests and controversies surrounding investment projects, the treatment of local workers, and close relationships between local elites and Chinese players.*
>
> *In the past, Beijing and its proxies often ignored societal views on Chinese presence in Kazakhstan, relying instead on ties of trust with elites. But in recent years, especially after massive protests in January 2022, Beijing has adapted by starting to intensify its soft-power efforts, developing language courses, education, and people-to-people connections aimed at reaching more deeply into Kazakhstani society, beyond the tight elite circle on which Beijing long relied. Today, we see considerable evidence of China's adaptability in the face of changing power-to-people dynamics in Kazakhstan and in Kazakhstani policymaking.*
>
> *Despite the significant increase in China's economic power in Kazakhstan, anti-Chinese sentiments – deeply rooted in history – have not declined significantly. According to the Central Asian Barometer survey conducted in 2022 and 2023, about 70.5 percent of respondents had an unfavourable opinion of China (with 35.2 percent reporting 'somewhat unfavourable' and 35.3 reporting 'very unfavourable'.*

4. The European Union (EU) remains Kazakhstan's largest trading partner and top foreign investor. Bilateral trade reached USD 49.7 billion in 2024, with the majority comprising energy exports from Kazakhstan, highlighting its role as a key supplier to European markets. The EU collectively accounts for a significant share of Kazakhstan's FDI representing approximately 50–55 per cent of Kazakhstan's total FDI.

The Enhanced Partnership and Cooperation Agreement (EPCA), in effect since 2020, underpins the EU-Kazakhstan bilateral relationship, providing a legal framework for cooperation across 29 sectors. Kazakhstan, with its mineral wealth and renewable energy potential, is well-positioned to contribute to Europe's supply chain resilience in clean technologies. The Trans-Caspian International Transport Route, or 'Middle Corridor,' is increasingly viewed as a viable overland route connecting China to Europe via Kazakhstan. The EU's Global Gateway strategy includes a € 12 billion commitment to infrastructure in Central Asia, covering transport, energy, and digital initiatives.

5. According to the US Trade Representative, in 2024, total trade between the two countries was estimated at USD 3.4 billion. US exports totalled approximately USD 1.1 billion, representing a 7.2 percent decrease from 2023. On the other hand, imports worth USD 2.3 billion registered a 4.5 percent increase, resulting in a 17.2 percent growth in trade deficit compared to 2023. Approximately 600 US companies currently operate in Kazakhstan, with the USA's total foreign direct investment (FDI) exceeding US$65 billion by the end of 2024. Main exports from Kazakhstan to the USA include crude petroleum, uranium, silver, and other rare earth metals. However, according to the Kazakh Ministry of Trade, in 2024, trade between the two countries totalled approximately USD 4.2 billion, with Kazakhstan importing goods worth USD 2.2 billion and exporting roughly USD 2 billion to the USA. Oil remains Kazakh's primary export to the USA, accounting for approximately 56 per cent of the total in 2024, uranium followed with a 16 per cent share, silver at 12 per cent, and ferro alloys at 9.5 per cent. The conflicting data presented by both countries for 2024 has created some confusion.

6. India has a very small trade with Kazakhstan. The total bilateral trade between the two countries in 2024 was 974.9 million which was 5.3 per cent less as compared to 2023. The export from India to Kazakhstan was 510.7 million in 2024 which was 12 per cent less as compared to 2023 whereas India's import from Kazakhstan in 2024 was 462.2 million which was 3.3 per cent more as compared to 2023. The total volume of investments from India to Kazakhstan over the past 20 years exceeded USD 45 million. Today, more than

600 Indian companies operate in Kazakhstan in pharmaceuticals, mining and food production.

During the current year, bilateral trade is decreasing. In July, 2025, Kazakhstan exported only USD 634,000 and imported only USD 8.67 million from India. The top exports of Kazakhstan to India were other crude minerals, inorganic chemicals and finished leather while the main imports of Kazakhstan from India were drug formulations, biologicals, tea and Ayush and herbal products.

Kazakhstan and SCO

Kazakhstan fully supports the key objectives of the SCO: an equitable multipolar world order, security and stability, non-interference in the internal affairs of states and recognition of their right to sovereign development, fair international trade, and mutually beneficial investment cooperation.

During the SCO summit in August 2025, Kazakhstan and China signed 70 agreements worth nearly USD 15 billion. China offers Kazakhstan considerable opportunities in terms of technology transfer and the establishment of joint ventures that could help Kazakhstan move up the value chain. However, there is another side to the coin. In particular, adopting Chinese-designed smart city technologies and surveillance systems would raise questions of data security and privacy. This underscores the dual challenge for Kazakhstan: to benefit from Chinese technological expertise and investment while ensuring safeguards that protect national interests and maintain citizens' trust.

China's growing role in the region, especially as Russia's influence has contracted since the start of its war in Ukraine, narrows Kazakhstan's room for alternative choices. The nuclear power plant projects are a telling example: two of the three planned plants will be built by Chinese firms, underscoring both the scale of Chinese involvement and Kazakhstan's potential future dependence on Chinese technology and capital in critical infrastructure. The challenge for Kazakhstan is, therefore, less about resisting China outright and more about embedding its own priorities into Chinese-led initiatives. Its success will depend on how effectively it leverages alternative partnerships and regional institutions to maintain agency.

Foreign Direct Investment in Kazakhstan

Amid global economic volatility and intense competition for capital, Kazakhstan has maintained a stable inflow of foreign direct investment, reaffirming its position as one of the leading investment destinations in the Central Eurasian region.

According to 'FDI Markets,' gross FDI inflow for January–October 2024 amounted to $16.3 billion, with 49 investment projects implemented, resulting in the creation of 17,828 new jobs.

In April 2025, EY has presented its annual report on Kazakhstan's investment attractiveness. As per the Report, the main investment areas remain unchanged: energy ($6.5 billion), transport and warehousing ($5.9 billion), metallurgy ($2.1 billion). There is also sustained interest in projects in renewable energy, food production, business services, and R&D.

Among the largest investors are Qatar ($11 billion), China, Turkey, Australia, and Germany. These countries are implementing both infrastructure and technological projects, including the construction of gas processing plants, logistics hubs, and rare earth metals production facilities. The most important factors in choosing an investment jurisdiction, according to respondents, include: the qualifications and availability of the workforce, transparency and stability of the legal and tax environment, political stability and regulatory predictability, developed infrastructure and market access.

According to the latest report from the International Institute for Management Development (IMD) issued in September 2025, Kazakhstan has secured the 34th position in the global competitiveness ranking among 69 countries. The country's economy reached $288.4 billion in GDP in 2024, with a growth of 4.8 per cent and per capita income of $41,675 (PPP). Strengths include a favourable tax policy (7th globally) and strong management practices (16th globally).

The report highlights several priorities for Kazakhstan in the year ahead: establishing a stable fiscal policy to support quality growth and business responsibility, modernising the energy and public utility sectors, expanding the skilled blue-collar workforce, integrating artificial intelligence into e-government systems and enhancing the investment climate and business environment.

The Trade Policy Review published by the World Trade Organisation (WTO) on its website reveals that since its accession to the WTO in November 2015, Kazakhstan has taken steps to further liberalise its trade regime. This is consistent with some of its key development strategies aimed at diversifying an economic base that remains concentrated in the oil and gas sector, and at creating favourable conditions to promote trade.

Because Kazakhstan is a landlocked country, its trade with the world is dependent on cross-border transport, which highlights the vital importance of both its domestic transport network, which is the most developed in the region, and that of neighbouring countries. Furthermore, the authorities have been prioritising infrastructure upgrades on the Trans-Caspian International Transport Route, which links China, Kazakhstan, and Europe, as an addition to the Northern Corridor (via the Russian Federation) through which more than 80 per cent of Kazakhstan's oil is currently exported.

Over the last few years, Kazakhstan has taken steps to align its IPR regime more closely with EAEU agreements and international practice by amending the Copyright Law, the Patent Law, and the Trademarks Law and introducing additional protection for geographical indications and short-term protection for unregistered industrial designs.

The extractive industries attracted roughly half of total FDI inflows; specifically, FDI into the production of crude oil and natural gas. An increase in investments in non-extractive activities was also observed during the period under review 2017-2023. As part of the national policy aimed at economic diversification, the implementation of investment attraction initiatives along with Kazakhstan's widespread WTO accession commitments in key services sectors contributed to increased FDI into the non-extractive sectors of the economy. FDI into wholesale and retail trade and car repair recorded the largest percentage of total gross FDI increase during the review period.

In addition, the manufacturing sector, especially the manufacturing of basic metals and fabricated metal products, was also a major recipient of FDI during the same period. In terms of gross outflows of FDI, financial and insurance activities, transportation and storage, and manufacturing were the largest drivers during the period under review.

What Makes Kazakhstan more Attractive for India to Invest in?

Kazakhstan has expanded its trade infrastructure; upgraded the technical regulation and metrology system to enhance the safety and quality of goods and services; strengthened the consumer protection system; developed the legal and policy framework for e-commerce; facilitated trade through simplification and digitalisation of export-import and domestic trade-related procedures; and strengthened its participation in the multilateral trading system. Kazakhstan's economic diversification away from oil and gas is also underway, underpinned by investment incentives in the manufacturing and services sectors.

Kazakhstan is diversifying and further enhancing its investment climate by liberalising its economy to promote industrial growth, reduce its reliance on Russia, and counter-balance China's growing influence in Central Asia. It is worthwhile to know more about developments in the related fields in Kazakhstan.

Mining Prospects, including Rare Earth Elements

Kazakhstan has all the capabilities to firmly integrate into global production and trade chains, rare earth metals comprising a group of 17 elements including scandium, yttrium, and the lanthanides, that are essential for manufacturing electronics, batteries, renewable energy equipment, and defence technologies.

Beijing controls nearly 60 percent of the world's rare earth mining and accounts for over 85 percent of the global processing capacity. In this context, Central Asia is increasingly viewed as a potential challenger to China's monopoly, owing to its abundant reserves of rare earth elements. Kazakhstan alone has over 5,000 rare earth deposits valued at more than US$ 46 trillion.

Over the past five years, the Kazakh government has ramped up rare earth mineral mining, nearly quintupling its exports in 2024. However, between 2023 and 2024, the bulk of these exports went almost exclusively to China rather than to the USA or the EU. Amid the intensifying global competition for rare earth metals among major world powers, Beijing is taking bold steps to increase its influence in Central Asia by expanding its 'circle of friends.' Given this context, the imposition of unilateral US tariffs on Kazakh exports inadvertently accelerates Kazakhstan's pivot towards China.

Kazakhstan affirms its openness to foreign investment and emphasised the country's intention to become a key player in the supply of strategic raw materials. Kazakhstan's efforts to harness its lithium reserves in East Kazakhstan are expected to boost the country's role in the global energy transition and significantly enhance investment opportunities in the region.

Despite holding substantial reserves, Kazakhstan has traditionally exported rare earth metals in raw form though Kazakhstan is building partnerships with the EU, USA, Japan, South Korea, and China to advance these sectors. For example, two new industrial facilities dedicated to the mining and processing of lithium are set to be established in the Ulan district of East Kazakhstan Region by 2029 with a German mining company that plans to invest $500 million in the development of a lithium deposit. The initiative will include both the extraction of raw materials and the production of lithium oxide concentrate, a product in high demand across the global high-tech sector. India can get involved in the rare earth metal processing industry by entering into technical and financial collaborations.

Transport Sector

The International North-South Transport Corridor (INSTC) is designed to connect Russian ports on the Baltic and Arctic seas with the Persian Gulf and the Indian Ocean. It provides a critical rail and maritime link between Russia's Murmansk Port and Iran's Bandar Abbas Port.

Since India is one of the founding members of the INSTC plan, it should make all the efforts to ensure early completion of the project as it would facilitate smoother trade and transit across the region. This move can help India overcome landlocked challenges and expand economic horizons.

Digital Transformation

On September 8, 2025, President Kassym-Jomart Tokayev outlined key initiatives in forming a new institutional framework for the country's digital transformation. These steps signify a qualitative shift from fragmented digital solutions to a more systemic approach to artificial intelligence and advanced technologies.

The Ministry of Artificial Intelligence, to be established by presidential order, will become a specialised government body responsible for developing, implementing and monitoring AI policy. A Digital Code, to be adopted, will serve as the primary legal instrument in the digital sphere. The State Digital Asset Fund under the National Bank is being established to build a crypto reserve and finance key digital infrastructure projects. The Regulatory Intelligence Centre, also announced in the address, will act as a 'policy lab' for testing new regulatory models within the digital economy. The use of the digital tenge, the National Bank's digital currency, also deserves attention. It is already being used to fund projects through the National Fund.

The town of Alatau, envisioned as a national hub of innovation and business activity, is set to become the first fully digital city in the region, combining advanced Smart City technologies with a highly liveable urban environment. Drawing inspiration from global examples such as Shenzhen, the project will involve a leading Chinese company that participated in building that renowned Technopolis.

The development of Kaz LLM, the first Kazakh-language large language model, introduced in 2024, marked a symbolic milestone. Kazakhstan is not merely adopting foreign technologies; it is creating its own. In 2025, updated versions of Sherkala (8B) and Sherkala-Chat (8B) were released, multilingual LLMs based on LLaMA 3.1, specifically fine-tuned for the Kazakh language. The launch of Alem.AI, an international artificial intelligence centre, further reinforced Kazakhstan's ambitions. As part of the Tech Orda programme, almost 10,000 IT professionals have received free education in the field of information technology.

A standout initiative is Kazakhstan's effort to attract digital nomads. In 2024, the country introduced the Neo Nomad Visa, allowing remote workers with a verified income of $3,000/month to live and work in Kazakhstan. In 2025, the government launched a new B9 residence permit option for long-term stays.

All these initiatives are integrated into the national programme, Digital Kazakhstan, the update and redesign of which has been assigned to the government. These steps create a system-wide architecture for integrating AI into the economy, education, governance, and infrastructure.

India should explore active participation of its tech companies in these efforts of the Kazakhstan Government to digitalise its economy. Indian companies have shown extremely good performance in digitalisation of its economic and financial services sector in India. India has a pool of talented and experienced personnel for the jobs, which can be a good credential to secure business in this field in Kazakhstan.

Medical Tourism

Kazakhstan has taken the lead in terms of the rapid development of medical tourism. In 2022, just 1,280 medical tourists were recorded. By 2023, that figure had jumped to 8,000 and by 2024, it reached 80,000. Around 90 per cent of foreign patients come from neighbouring countries: Kyrgyzstan, Russia, Uzbekistan, plus nearby Tajikistan. The remaining 10 per cent hail from countries such as the USA, Germany, Israel, Austria and Switzerland.

The most in-demand services include reproductive medicine, dentistry, and aesthetic procedures. Kazakhstan offers these treatments at lower costs while maintaining acceptable standards of quality. Despite its rapid development, the sector still faces significant legal challenges. Krivets pointed out that medical tourism is not yet defined in Kazakh legislation.

Kazakhstan would require a large number of medical doctors, medical support staff, nursing staff and lab technicians to achieve this target of establishing itself as a desired medical tourism centre which India can easily provide. Indian hospital chains should be encouraged to invest in this segment. There would be scope for backward and forward integration in this for setting up medical colleges, pharmacies and medicine manufacturing units.

Conclusion

Kazakhstan aims to double its economy by 2030 from 2023 levels, focusing on accelerating growth. To achieve this, the country must reduce state intervention, foster competition, invest in infrastructure and human capital, and advance decarbonisation efforts. These measures are essential to enhance competitiveness and address the long-term challenges posed by global decarbonisation efforts.

Kazakhstan is currently the 20th largest emitter worldwide of greenhouse gases (GHG) on a per capita basis, with electricity and heating accounting for 84 percent of overall emissions.

Kazakhstan is among the top ten most energy-intensive economies, using three times as much energy per unit of output compared to the OECD average. Therefore, decarbonising the economy is an urgent priority.

While oil production is set to grow, oil-related revenues are expected to remain constrained amid forecasts of stable yet modest oil prices through 2027. Non-oil revenues will likely benefit from improving administration efforts and ongoing digitalisation efforts, but expenditure growth is projected to outpace revenue gains, widening the fiscal deficit to 3.1 percent in 2025 before easing slightly to 2.7 percent in 2026.

India has been looking for economical and consistent suppliers of rare earth metals for its renewable (EV, solar) energy, electronic and semiconductors industries. India is also scouting for buyers for its unique digital assets, Ayurvedic and Ayush products and soft powers such Yoga and meditation techniques. All these expectations of India can be fulfilled by enhancing business relationships with Kazakhstan. More and more Indian industry has to invest in Kazakhstan and set up joint ventures with Kazakhstan industries.

References

1. India-Kazakhstan Business Ties – bilateral brief, June 2024.pdf
2. India invested over $450min Kazakhstan in 20 years – www.awaz.the.voice.in.opinion.
3. Why Kazakhstan is a perfect destination for India's diversified exports – Kazinform International News Agency.
4. WTO – Trade Policy Review.
5. Kazakhstan and Russia Push Toward $30 Billion Trade Goal, Eye Key Transit Routes – *Caspian News.*
6. Kazakhstan-Russia bilateral trade hits $30bn.

7. Kazakhstan-European Commission. 11.C_2024_9253_F1_ANNEX_EN_V3_P1_3718875.PDF
8. Bilateral Trade Turnover Between Kazakhstan and China Reaches $43.8 billion – *The Astana Times.*
9. How Local Realities Compelled China to Adapt Its Soft-Power Strategy in Kazakhstan – Carnegie Endowment for International Peace.
10. EU-Kazakhstan Relations/Strategic Cooperation Amid Geopolitical Shifts – *The Times of Central Asia.*
11. United States Tariff Increase/ What Awaits Kazakhstan's Exports? – *The Astana Times.*
12. www.indiaastana.gov.in Bilateral Trade.
13. OEC-Kazakhstan India Trade – Latest Trends.
14. Key Takeaways from SCO's Largest Ever Summit in Tianjin – *The Astana Times.*
15. Kazakhstan's Investment Attractiveness in 2024/ steady interest from investors, EY in Kazakhstan, Kazakhstan Gains in Global Competitiveness, Surpasses Japan and Spain – *The Astana Times.*
16. Ibid.
17. Trump's Tariffs on Kazakhstan Strengthen China in Central Asia.
18. Kazakhstan to Launch Internationally Accredited Rare Earth Laboratory – *The Times of Central Asia.*
19. Ibid.
20. Opinion/ Kazakhstan in the Digital Era/ Human Capital and Al as Foundations for Regional Leadership – *The Times of Central Asia.*
21. Kazakhstan Emerges as Regional Leader in Medical Tourism – *The Times of Central Asia.*
22. Kazakhstan Overview/ Development news, research, datal World Bank.
23. Kazakhstan/ Inclusive and Sustainable Economic Growth Development Policy Operation.
24. https/documents1.worldbank.org/curated/en/.

SECTION IV

Energy, Nuclear Issues and Strategic Security Cooperation

13

Investing in Future Trajectories: Indo-Kazakh Cooperation in Civil Nuclear Energy and Critical Minerals

Dr. Cauvery Ganapathy

ABSTRACT

There is a Eurasia moment gathering pace. It is no longer a region satisfied with a passive responder status, where international geopolitics and geo-economics is concerned. Countries like Kazakhstan are now emerging as players who know the value they bring through their resources and their geostrategic location to any partnership. More significantly, perhaps, they are now players who appear willing to leverage this value. Kazakhstan's declared multi-vector foreign policy is indicative of the need the country feels to hedge its bets as it navigates an increasingly complex matrix of international politics where zero-sum games may have become passé. It is one that is actively seeking diversification in its foreign engagements. It would be a lost opportunity for India not to re-imagine the contours of its engagement with the region more expeditiously at this time.

This chapter makes the case for India-Kazakhstan ties to be consolidated through more deliberate and ambitious frameworks of cooperation in the domains of civilian nuclear energy and critical minerals. Enhancing coordination in these two sectors which are intrinsically tied to the future growth trajectories that India and Kazakhstan hope to chart for themselves, would be to the immediate as well as long-term mutual benefit of both. The two sectors and enhanced cooperative frameworks in them could underwrite a broader partnership across clean energy verticals between the two countries as interests and compulsions expand investments in the associated domains within both.

The most recent variation – and, arguably, the most compelling one in the last four decades- of a nuclear renaissance that appears to be underway and the integration of critical minerals into the global economic value-chain, have in many ways effected a change in the value proposition of Kazakhstan, a nation with a rich resource base on both these counts. While the country has for long been the largest natural uranium producer of the world with 14 per cent of the global uranium reserve, and nearly 40 per cent of the mined uranium, its most recent discovery in the Karangandy region of potentially large deposits of Rare Earth Elements, accords the country a new relevance in the global economy. It is a change that carries the potential to also redraw the nature of the India-Kazakhstan bilateral by capitalising on Kazakhstan's resources and India's innovation and technical prowess to transform the relationship into a more forward-looking one.

Existing trends in the partnership

The bilateral partnership between the two countries has over the years spanned cooperation in sectors such as energy, agriculture, medicine, pharmaceuticals, education, space, information technology, counter-terrorism and military exercises.

The India-KZ Intergovernmental Commission (est.1993) has been the primary institutional mechanism helping forge economic and trade cooperation between the two sides. Trade in crude and pharmaceuticals has been the mainstay of this relationship. Despite the consistency in the bilateral engagement through these sectors, given the size of the Indian market with a growth rate of 7-8 per cent and a resource base as rich as the one that Kazakhstan has, the status of the bilateral trade has been disappointing. While the numbers stood at $2.5bn in 2023-24, it has now come down to a meagre $900mn. This drop is largely attributable to the dramatic changes in the spot price of crude oil in the aftermath of the Russia-Ukraine war. Significantly, however, despite the marginal decrease in the main component of trade between the two and the continuing complications due to the absence of direct land corridors, bilateral trade between India and Kazakhstan has been uninterrupted.

These numbers, though, reveal a more fundamental issue of concern. First, that there is an oversized role that one commodity alone plays in the bilateral trade between the two countries, something that is a poor economic metric in any bilateral partnership that hopes to sustain and flourish in the future. Second, relatedly, that the two countries have not been able to affect any meaningful diversification in their dealings with each other, despite the existence of a formal Strategic Partnership between the two sides. This has been despite the fact that both countries have national priorities that hope to expand the role of manufacturing and attendant export promotion as part of their economic visions; ambitions that would ideally be complementary if the bilateral had been able to explore more avenues of cooperation.

The equation between the two countries has definitely been propelled further to being more consequential since the signing of the Strategic Partnership in 2009 and the pursuit of India's Connect Central Asia Strategy of 2015. Notably, India and KZ have also been supportive of each other's positions in multilateral forums such as the UN, CICA and the SCO. Yet, New Delhi's interests and stakes in Central Asia have been enduring, built on strategic and security considerations as much as on the quest for energy resources; it is a bilateral dynamic that is relatively muted in comparison to other regional actors such as Russia and China.

Focusing on Nuclear and Rare Earth

There are, however, two priority areas in which the India-KZ partnership could actualise the potential of a strategic partnership more meaningfully. A concerted focus on expanding cooperation in the field of nuclear energy and rare earths offers such an opportunity. Notably, these are both areas in which KZ already has developed substantial linkages with Russia and China on the one hand and the USA and EU on the other. It would therefore be a mark of deft resource diplomacy on the part of New Delhi to present itself as a partner of value in both the sectors.

Establishing a mutually beneficial partnership must begin with the identification of the specific needs or ambitions of both. In the Indian case, a reliable uranium supply is non-negotiable given the government's commitment to mission-mode development of nuclear reactors in fleet mode, and the expectation that 100GW of nuclear power would be part of the country's energy mix by 2047. Similarly, critical minerals are central to the country's ambitions across multiple domains, including defence, aerospace, energy transitions, including electrification of industry and automobiles. The volatility in the supply chains of both these inputs, especially in that of critical minerals, can directly impinge upon India's ambitious growth targets.

In the case of Kazakhstan, in addition to earning from its massive deposits of uranium and critical minerals, there could be no better time for the Central Asian Republic to leverage its resource abundance in a manner that would help transition its domestic economy to higher parts of the global value chain. Using this access to sizeable deposits of two kinds of minerals that sit at the nub of technological advances that span not just the present but the next-generation as well, could enable a dramatic transformation of the country's own economic and, by extension, global profile. By working with the right partners who are willing to share technology and innovation and do so in a manner that will not demand any compromising of national sovereignty or strategic agency, Astana would be able to usher in changes that would enable the country to partake in the more lucrative downstream sectors related to these minerals, too.

Nuclear Energy

Trade in nuclear energy offers the kind of multi-decadal partnerships that few other domains can forge. This is because the life-cycle of a nuclear plant ranges between 40 and 60 years. It is ideal not to keep changing the profile of the fuel used in each reactor's processing. As such, establishing a reliable fuel source is a necessary pre-requisite to a stable nuclear enterprise in a country. Consolidating partnerships in the field, therefore, could prove to be an effective anchor in Indo-Kazakh relations as well. Simultaneously, and importantly, it is also an arena in which the future growth ambitions of both countries could find long-term coincidence.

Kazakhstan today is an important actor in the global nuclear order, both on issues of nuclear security as well as on those of deployment. In addition to being the IAEA's chosen partner for storing of the Low-enriched Uranium Bank, it also holds the presidency of the World Nuclear Association. India, on the other hand, has been a responsible figure in the field of global civilian nuclear energy despite the moratoriums imposed on it until US-India Civil Nuclear Agreement. It is also a country that is poised to become the third-largest economy in the world over the next decade, and is committed to harnessing nearly 40 per cent of its power from nuclear energy on the path to this economic growth. A concerted partnership between the two countries in the field seems a natural synergy of abilities and ambitions.

Now, India does have a long-standing uranium supply agreement with Kazakhstan. India's Department of Atomic Energy and the Nuclear Power Corporation of India signed these long-term agreements with Kazakhstan's state-owned enterprise, KazAtomprom, in 2015. It has been a mainstay in the bilateral partnership, and one that has not been affected by changes in the geopolitical equations of either partner with a third party. While Kazakhstan's share of uranium export to both Russia and China have increased over the past decade, Astana has also actively sought to position itself as a reliable supplier of uranium to the European Union and to countries in the Middle East. None of this diversification, notably, has until now diluted the commitments that Kazakhstan has made towards India through the agreement of 2015.

However, in the wake of the apparent nuclear renaissance that appears to be on the anvil, uranium as a resource is likely to be leveraged differently by those who own it. For instance, KazAtomprom reported a 6 per cent drop in its sales for the financial year 2024-25. Significantly, this drop in sales is not attributed to a concurrent fall in demand, but to an organisational call to withhold sales. This, by all accounts, counts as an individual company's decision based on its own fiduciary considerations and ambitions. A fact that should, however, raise the profile of this seeming company policy to a point of international consideration is that Kazakhstan's share of the global uranium market is larger than OPEC's share of the international market for crude oil. Furthermore, KazAtomprom's share of Kazakhstan's total uranium is close to more than 56 per cent, and it produces nearly 22 per cent of the global primary uranium production. This outsized share of one company over global uranium resources translates directly into a severe tightening of uranium supplies in the event of any recalibration of strategy in terms of access or privileges offered to one customer over another.

This, expectedly then, will make the mineral – so crucial to India's plans for developing its domestic nuclear programme at the scale it hopes to – expensive, given the global demand spurt in the wake of the nuclear renaissance. At a time when a 28 per cent surge in uranium demand is expected off the back of the anticipated growth in the nuclear deployment in general and SMR development in particular worldwide, the possibility that the world's largest uranium producer may decide to hold back on bringing supplies to the market in anticipation of price rises does not fall in the remit of the unusual.

Given this, it is imperative that India develop the best possible relationship with KazAtomprom and the Kazakh government as a whole. This relationship should be based ideally on an offering that India can harbour some exclusivity over, so as to ensure that this is a mutually beneficial partnership. New Delhi would do well to identify points of further consolidation of the partnership with the world's largest uranium producer before Astana pledges its resources to other actors. It is essential to lock in deals and off-take agreements similar to the ones the country makes in overseas crude and gas in the case of uranium too with Kazakhstan. While there may be the fiscal consideration that these commitments require substantial buy-in of resources that may already be overleveraged, it is a financial choice that India will have to make if it wishes to secure its uranium supply.

Other potential offerings from the Indian side could focus on bringing its own expertise to assist in the delivery of public goods and utilities within the Central Asian giant. Kazakhstan, notably, suffers from problems of electricity scarcity. This has led to the country having to import sizeable amounts of electricity from Russia. It seems almost counter-intuitive that the country with the largest reserves of natural uranium in the world has not yet developed a national civilian nuclear enterprise to generate electricity and become more self-sufficient in this domain, in the manner France, for example, has on the back of massive imports of uranium from outside. Civilian nuclear energy is an area in which India has developed commendable expertise. Notably, it has done so through the adoption of a frugality-based innovative approach. There are lessons and learning curves inherent in the Indian experience that could suit the Kazakh case. While Kazakhstan's first and second nuclear reactors are going to be built by Rosatom (Russia) and China National Nuclear Power Corporation (CNNC) – both understandable choices given the highly rare and prized construction and last-mile delivery expertise both countries have – India could leverage its own nuclear facilities and management expertise, as it has done with the UAE.

It is not ideal that despite these close linkages between the two countries, India could not present itself as the partner of choice when Kazakhstan began looking outward for expertise on radioactive waste management and decommissioning. The bid for collaborating and providing consulting on the subject has instead been won by Nukem Technologies Engineering Services from Germany. Such collaborations have a long-term aspect to them and lead to offshoots in ancillary/tertiary arrangements between countries. It is vital that New Delhi consciously seek out discussions with its Kazakh partners to identify the needs of industries in a domain-specific manner. Many small misses may, otherwise, compound into a larger pattern of strategic losses akin to the one that India's international energy companies were suffering from at the peak of their competition with the Chinese decades ago.

Critical Minerals

The second area of cooperation that India and Kazakhstan could focus on to further consolidate the bilateral in pathways that are relevant for the future is in the field of critical minerals exploitation, processing and development of downstream production. Uninterrupted and reliable access to critical minerals (including rare earths) is integral to India's economic and national security. While cooperating in this sector can directly feed into the energy transition that India is committed to, and one that has been assessed as being essential for the country's high-tech ambitions, including defence indigenisation, a well-crafted coordination policy could also prove valuable for the economic diversification strategy that Astana wishes to pursue. Nearly 12.1 per cent of Kazakhstan's GDP comes from mining, a figure that accounted for nearly 16tn KZT in 2024.

By some estimates, the harnessing of these reserves could position the contribution of critical minerals to the national economy to be close to the 7 per cent mark that oil and gas resources now stand at.

On the back of its latest discoveries in Kuyirektykol in the Karagandy region of the country, Kazakhstan is poised to develop another vertical of incredibly profitable resource wealth. The Zhana (New) Kazakhstan deposit once confirmed by the US Geological Survey (standard metric for official global recognition of such resource strengths) with its expected reserves of 20mn tonnes (notably constituting neodymium, lanthanum, cerium and yttrium) could prove to be the third largest deposit of rare earths in the world, behind only China and Brazil.

Table 1. Critical Minerals Confirmed in Kazakhstan

Beryllium
Tantalum
Titanium
Rhenium
Osmium
Cerium
Lanthanum
Yttrium
Neodymium

Byproducts from the extraction of these have also led to access of elements such as bismuth, selenium, tellurium and antimony. Significantly, every single one of these minerals is part of the Critical Minerals list that the Indian Ministry of Mines officially declared as critical in 2023. Notably, about 18 of the 34 minerals identified as critical by the EU are also available in Kazakhstan.

Table 2. Kazakhstan's Mineral Potential

Gold	**Share of world reserves - 3.59%** **Share of world production -3.94%** 1. Altyntau Kokshetau (438 thousand ounces) Glencore 2. Kyzyl Project (345 thousand ounces) Polymetal Int. 3. Varvara Mine (204 thousand ounces) Polymetal Int. 4. Bozshakol Mine (117 thousand ounces) KAZ Minerals 5. Pustynnoe Mine (103 thousand ounces) AK Altynalmas
Copper	**Share of world reserves -2.04%** **Share of world production -3.22%** 1. Aktogay Mine (230 thousand tonnes) KAZ Minerals 2. Zhezkazgan Mine (171 thousand tonnes) Kazakhmys 3. Bozshakol Mine (105 thousand tonnes) KAZ Minerals 4. 50 Let Oktyabrya Mine (38 thousand tonnes) Russian Copper Co. 5. Nurkazgan Mine (25 thousand tonnes) Kazakhmys Astana International Financial Centre

Zinc	**Share of world reserves - 3.30%** **Share of world production -3. 08%** 1. Zhairemsky Mine (81 thousand tonnes) Glencore 2. Akzhal Zinc Lead Mine (38 thousand tonnes) Chelyabinsk Zinc Plant 3. Maleevsky Mine (34 thousand tonnes) Glencore 4. Shaimerden Mine (27 thousand tonnes) Glencore 5. Orlovsky Mine (22 thousand tonnes)
Silver	**Share of world deposits- 2.7%** 1. Zhezkazgan Mine (8.4 million ounces) Kazakhmys 2. Aktogay Project (1.2 million ounces) KAZ Minerals 3. Zhairemsky Mine (1.1 million ounces) Glencore 4. Maleevsky Mine (0.9 million ounces) Glencore 5. Artemyevsky Mine (0.9 million ounces) KAZ Minerals
Bauxite (Aluminium)	**Share of world deposits - 1.09%** **Share of world production - 0.97%** 1. Krasno Oktyabrskoye 2. Turgai Bauxite METALS AND MINING 2025/37 Source: mining-technology.com
Uranium	**Share of world deposits - 13.74%** **Share of world production in percentage- 38.95%** 1. Inkai, sites 1-3 (3,201 tonnes U) 2. Karatau (Budenovskoye 2) (2,560 tonnes U) 3. South Inkai 4 (1,600 tonnes U)

Source: Astana Financial Centre's report on 'Kazakhstan as a minerals investment hub: Unlocking Potential through the AIFC,' 2025.

While local industrial estimates anticipate a period of close to 10-12 years before extraction of ores may take place profitably from within these mines, it is important to highlight the upfront investments that interested parties must make if they wish to gain access to these elements. Significantly, Kazakhstan's marginal domestic demand and utilisation capabilities presently mean that the bulk of these resources, many of them available in the form of ready-to-use-metals, will be earmarked for exports. Given this, the proposal of bearing upfront costs through FDI in the finance-heavy minerals exploration and extraction sector in the country, must be treated as sunk costs if countries wish to gain access to these highly limited resources. It is an opportune moment for India to commit financial investments towards the development of greenfield mining projects in Kazakhstan.

The Government of India's KAABIL initiative is a timely step in the domain, and it is one that must be adapted to seek out the kind of investment opportunities that are present in Zhana Kazakhstan. Whether by way of participating in feasibility assessments or by considering how India may contribute by way of appropriate expertise in geological mapping and mining technology, the bilateral could strengthen its cooperation in the domain of critical minerals. The joint venture between the two countries – IREUK Titanium Limited which was built to process Odisha's Ilmenite reserves into high-grade Titanium feedstock – is a good example of how the two countries may be able to synergise their strengths and mitigate gaps in their individual capacities.

Kazakhstan, by many local industrial estimates, lacks processing capabilities where rare earth elements are concerned. This explains the partnership patterns it has with China where it sends the bulk of its REE as raw materials for processing and use in downstream industries such as batteries and energy transition hardware. While China's importance to the Kazakh rare earths industry can be explained by the investments that Beijing has been making in the sector in Central Asia for a while, and the fact of China being the largest producer and consumer of REEs globally, it must be taken as a matter of introspection as to why the Kazakhs appear to be establishing better agreements with the Europeans as the second-most important partner in this sector instead of India.

The movement eastwards to Europe needs the adequate development of the Middle Corridor – something that has been a challenge in terms of contested logistics and financial risk undertaking. It may be valuable at this time to make the case for the revival and development of a parallel route of value between India and Kazakhstan. The lack of a direct overland route through uncontested geographic spaces and the recurrent threat of sanctions associated with the Chabahar port complicates India's access points into the CARs. While India and Kazakhstan could invest greater focus on the International North-South Transport Corridor (INSTC) at the same time so as to offer an alternative avenue for Kazakhstan's mineral wealth, it is important to underline that the sheer scale of the financing and logistics involved in the more than 7,000-km meant to connect St. Petersburg to Mumbai via Iran is further compounded by the inherent security concerns along the entire route.

The Path Ahead

The India-Central Asia Foreign Ministers Forum that took place in early 2025 is a good initiative which recognises the value and import of the India-Kazakhstan partnership. It is important that it translate into structural coordinating mechanisms. The inclusion of bodies such as the FICCI is an encouraging step in the right direction. Some of the additional steps could be based on the following considerations:

- While 65 per cent of Kazakhstan's estimated reserves remain geographically unexplored, only 17 per cent of the FDI is indicated to have been directed at the sector in 2024. What the gap indicates is a substantial potential for investment in the domain for actors such as India. Or, even India in partnership.
- Off-take agreements must be pursued systematically and deliberately. While allowing the Kazakhs fiscal room, this would also help Indians establish a clear pathway for resource development.
- Establishment of task forces directly coordinating work on industrial and financial cooperation templates in the fields of critical minerals and nuclear cooperation, could help facilitate this partnership more effectively.

Countries like Russia, China and France have been made partners of choice in many of the renewable energy projects that the Central Asian nation has been developing. India, however, despite having deployed an impressive domestic solar and wind energy programme, has not featured among the preferred partners in the sector for Astana. Advocating for Indian technical expertise in the sector, where costs have been kept at a minimum too, must be made part of the broader approach of New Delhi to Kazakhstan.

India and Kazakhstan could consider a specific collaboration focused on developing and honing their recycling processes aimed at recovery of rare earth elements from mining and industrial waste.

While FDI is a necessary input for furthering growth, it has also had to navigate a complicated domestic matrix where resource nationalism has been growing in resource-rich states. The degree of risk involved, then, becomes substantial. Given this, it would serve both countries well if investment in these two identified strategic sectors could be made part of a bilateral approach of international financial organisations that may underwrite part of the expenses and the attendant risks.

The Democratic Republic of Congo (DRC) is an example of a country that has come to gradually learn the value of leveraging its natural wealth in a manner that would bring it greater participation in the value chain of these raw materials. As part of this, the Government of the DRC called for a renegotiation of the terms of trade it had signed with China in the field of exploration and mining of these minerals. Simultaneously, when the second Trump Administration raised the demands for access to Greenland and Ukraine's critical minerals, the DRC used the opportunity to offer parts of its own reserves to meet American needs. This is an example of a resource-rich country that begins positioning itself in a manner that would allow it to better leverage its resource wealth. As the global nuclear renaissance takes hold, Kazakhstan could be expected to follow this trajectory, and recalibrate how it utilises its abundant natural resources. It would be prudent on India's part to plan ahead to meet such a recalibration on Astana's part. Re-negotiating to acquire sizeable and reliable off take commitments with Astana, for both uranium as well as critical minerals, should be among the foremost deliverables for energy/ resource diplomacy in the CARs presently. Such agreements may require a substantial capital lock-in presently, but it would prove to be a reliable and lucrative asset in the future.

Conclusion

Energy may be the mainstay of this bilateral, but it cannot be a linear pursuit. The rest of the strategic relationship has to be developed to ensconce this energy relation properly. In so far as this is true, it may also be pertinent to consider if India's road to Kazakhstan may lie through Russia, given the relations Moscow has with both New Delhi and Astana in the fields of civilian nuclear cooperation in particular and resource trade in general.

Simultaneously, however, India may also be a valuable partner for Washington in the region, given the USA's own efforts to regain currency in Eurasia while gaining access to the vast mineral wealth of countries like Kazakhstan. Despite the seeming rupture in the Indo-US ties presently, it may be useful to consider if Washington would not in fact prefer a greater Indian proximity and presence in Kazakhstan's resource industry than that of China or Russia. It may, then, not be unrealistic to consider if the USA could coordinate with India to help underwrite some of the expensive, but necessary buy-ins required particularly in the greenfield projects Kazakhstan is presently looking at.

Global politics today reflects a conscious security-centred approach to resource ownership, management, trade, and acquisition. Issues of resource nationalism, in addition to concerns of securitisation, further compound an already complex matrix of interest-based geopolitical calculations. What this has very effectively done is made it increasingly difficult for countries to invest where returns may not be immediate or sizeable. As a result, historical ties and cultural affinities do not argue the case for partners as well today as they did earlier, should they not translate into immediate strategic or economic benefits.

Sustaining meaningful and consequential partnerships between countries demands that they be built as much on the needs of the future as it benefits from the moorings of the past. Actualizing a partnership between India and Kazakhstan based on two domains that have particular resonance to each of their future trajectories carries within itself the possibility of consolidating the inherent value of the bilateral long-term in a manner few other avenues may beget.

References

1. https://world-nuclear.org/information-library/country-profiles/countries-g-n/kazakhstan.
2. World-nuclear.org.. 'Uranium and Nuclear Power in Kazakhstan', World Nuclear Association, 19 June 2025, https://world-nuclear.org/information-library/country-profiles/countries-g-n/kazakhstan#:~:text=Kazakhstan%20has%2014%25%20of%20the,generating%20electricity%20and%20desalinating%20water.
3. Galiya Khassenkhanova. 'Kazakhstan discovers rare earths reserve said to be third-largest in the world'. 10/04/2025, https://www.euronews.com/2025/04/10/kazakhstan-discovers-rare-earths-reserve-said-to-be-third-largest-in-the-world.
4. https://www.cnbc.com/2025/08/29/indias-economy-grows-faster-than-expected-at-7point8percent-in-the-june-quarter.html.
5. https://www.pib.gov.in/PressReleasePage.aspx?PRID=2124961.
6. https://world-nuclear.org/information-library/nuclear-fuel-cycle/nuclear-waste/decommissioning-nuclear-facilities.
7. https://www-pub.iaea.org/MTCD/publications/PDF/te_1345_web/t1345_part1.pdf.
8. https://www.iaea.org/newscenter/news/iaea-and-kazakhstan-sign-agreement-establish-low-enriched-uranium-bank.
9. https://www.pib.gov.in/PressReleasePage.aspx?PRID=1596202.
10. https://www.kazatomprom.kz/en/media/view/1h2025_financial_results.
11. https://www.eia.gov/finance/markets/crudeoil/supply-opec.php.
12. https://www.enerdata.net/publications/daily-energy-news/uranium-production-rising.html.
13. https://www.reuters.com/business/energy/uranium-demand-set-surge-28-by-2030-nuclear-power-gains-momentum-wna-says-2025-09-05/.
14. Kazatomprom is Kazakhstan's national nuclear company and the world's largest producer of natural uranium, with priority access to one of the world's largest resource bases. The Samruk-Kazyna sovereign wealth fund owns 75 percent of Kazatomprom's total issued shares, while 25 percent are publicly traded on the Astana International Exchange and the London Stock Exchange.
15. https://astanatimes.com/2025/08/kazakhstan-holds-negotiations-with-china-on-nuclear-power-plant-construction/.
16. https://www.indianeconomicobserver.com/news/india-to-collaborate-with-central-asian-countries-for-exploration-of-rare-earth-critical-minerals20250609144645/.
17. https://www.reuters.com/markets/commodities/kazakhstan-says-it-has-discovered-20-million-ton-rare-earth-metals-deposit-2025-04-02/.
18. Ibid.
19. https://www.euronews.com/2025/04/10/kazakhstan-discovers-rare-earths-reserve-said-to-be-third-largest-in-the-world.
20. https://astanatimes.com/2025/10/kazakhstan-france-china-advance-nations-largest-renewable-energy-project/.

14

India's and Kazakhstan's Approaches to Energy Security

Dr. Zhulduz Baizakova

Introduction

Global energy demand continues to rise each year, primarily driven by the expanding economies and population growth. This increasing demand has made energy production one of the largest contributors to greenhouse gas emissions, with current emission levels surpassing 53.2 Gt CO_2-equivalent, placing the world off-track from the 1.5°C climate target.

India and Kazakhstan have a growing partnership in the energy sector, driven by mutual interests in diversifying energy sources and ensuring energy security. Each country is currently struggling with its own set of issues related to energy security. As the world navigates geopolitical realignments and the urgent imperative of climate transition, Kazakhstan faces the dual challenge of maximising its resource wealth for economic development while strategically diversifying its energy mix and export routes to ensure long-term stability and resilience.

Geopolitical factors continue to exert a profound impact on both India's and Kazakhstan's energy security. The ongoing Russia-Ukraine conflict, for instance, has demonstrated the vulnerability of global energy markets to geopolitical tensions, leading to price volatility and supply chain disruptions. The growing influence of China and Russia in Central Asia poses challenges for India as it seeks to strengthen its position in the region and cultivate strategic relationships.

India's pragmatic approach of increasing imports of discounted Russian oil, while navigating its relationships with Western countries, highlights the complex diplomatic balancing act required to secure its energy interests. Furthermore, tensions in the Middle East and maritime commercial traffic disruptions in the Indian Ocean region also pose potential threats to oil shipments.

Kazakhstan, on the other hand, as Central Asia's largest economy and a pivotal player in global energy markets, finds its current energy security defined by a complex interplay of vast hydrocarbon and uranium reserves, entrenched export dependencies, and a burgeoning commitment to a greener future. This paper will explore the energy security strategies of India and Kazakhstan, while also examining key bilateral projects, initiatives, and future perspectives.

India's Perspectives

For a country like India, which is home to one-sixth of the world's population, ensuring a stable and sustainable energy supply is not merely an economic imperative but a matter of national security. India is the world's fourth-largest importer of crude oil, primarily from Middle Eastern nations such as Saudi Arabia, Iraq, Iran (though limited due to sanctions), and the United Arab Emirates. It ranks as the second-highest energy consumer and the third-largest energy producer globally, following China.

The demand for electricity has been increasing consistently, driven by growing industrial activity, urban expansion, and broader access to energy in rural areas. Forecasts suggest that demand will continue to rise, with major cities and agricultural zones showing the highest consumption growth. At the same time, India's energy sector is undergoing rapid transformation in response to rising consumption patterns. As the economy expands, electricity demand has surged, with the peak power requirement in 2025 reaching approximately 273 gigawatts (GW). This marks a significant annual growth rate of 6 to 9 per cent, higher than the historical average of around 5 per cent.

India's journey towards achieving energy security is marked by a strategic blend of traditional and renewable resources. Under the leadership of Prime Minister Narendra Modi, India's energy policies have evolved significantly, aiming to balance economic growth with environmental sustainability.

India's current energy landscape is characterised by a continued reliance on traditional fossil fuels, predominantly coal, while simultaneously witnessing a robust expansion in renewable energy. As of January 2025, coal accounts for nearly 47.29 per cent of India's total installed power capacity, underscoring its foundational role in meeting the nation's vast energy requirements. Oil and natural gas contribute significantly as well, making up approximately 28 and 8 per cent of the energy mix, respectively. This heavy dependence on fossil fuels, particularly oil, translates into substantial import dependency.

In 2025, India's crude oil import dependency reached a record high of 89.1 per cent, an increase from 88.6 per cent in the previous year, with natural gas import dependency also rising to 8 per cent. This makes India highly susceptible to global price volatility and supply disruptions. The International Energy Agency (IEA) projects that by 2030, India will become the primary driver of global oil demand growth, in contrast to China, where fuel demand may have already peaked. Analysts from FGE anticipate that petrol and diesel consumption in India will grow at an average annual rate of approximately 4 and 2 per cent, respectively, over the coming decade. Such market volatility renders business diversification towards the domestic market a prudent and strategic move for private companies.

Recognising these vulnerabilities, the Indian government has intensified its efforts to enhance energy security through a multi-pronged strategy. Diversification of import sources has become a key focus, with India strategically increasing its oil and gas imports from various countries, including the USA and Russia, to mitigate risks associated with over-reliance on any single region. Furthermore, there is a concerted push to boost domestic oil and gas production through policy reforms like the Hydrocarbon Exploration and Licensing Policy. Strategic Petroleum Reserves (SPR) are being expanded and commercialised to provide a crucial buffer against unforeseen supply shocks and price fluctuations.

However, the most transformative aspect of India's energy security strategy in 2024-2025 is its aggressive pursuit of renewable energy. For example, India has set an ambitious target of achieving 500 GW of non-fossil fuel-based energy capacity by 2030. Achieving this necessitates the rapid reduction of fossil fuel dependence and a transition towards sustainable energy alternatives.

The country is undergoing a significant transformation in its energy sector, driven by the urgent need to transition to cleaner, more sustainable sources of power. India has recognised the importance of renewable energy in addressing environmental challenges, reducing dependence on fossil fuels, and meeting the growing energy demands of a rapidly developing economy. As part of its broader energy strategy, India is making substantial investments in solar, wind, bioenergy, and hydropower.

Currently, renewable sources account for approximately 43 per cent of India's electricity generation, representing 426.72 GW (excluding nuclear energy), and this share continues to grow steadily. The progress in 2024-2025 has been remarkable, with total installed renewable energy capacity reaching 220.10 GW as of March 31, 2025. Solar energy has been the primary driver of this growth, with a record addition of 23.83 GW in 2024-25, bringing the total installed solar capacity to over 105 GW. Wind energy also saw substantial growth, crossing the 50 GW milestone. The government is also investing in manufacturing capabilities for solar PV and wind turbines to reduce import dependence in the renewable sector.

In recent years, pilot projects and the establishment of regulatory frameworks have been actively underway. The long-term vision is to position India as a global hub for green hydrogen production and export, significantly reducing reliance on fossil fuels in hard-to-abate sectors like fertilizers, refining, and steel. This also has the potential to decarbonise heavy transport and act as a large-scale energy storage medium, further buttressing grid stability.

Furthermore, the socio-economic dimension of India's energy transition is gaining increasing prominence. Ensuring stable energy access and affordability for all remains a foundational principle. While rural electrification has made significant strides, the quality and reliability of supply, particularly in remote areas, need continuous improvement. The transition away from coal also raises concerns about a 'just transition' for coal-dependent regions and their workforces. This involves planning for reskilling programmes, creating alternative livelihoods, and investing in new economic activities in these areas to prevent socio-economic disruption.

However, the rapid influx of renewable energy necessitates a robust and smart grid infrastructure. In 2024-2025, significant investments are being channelled into modernising India's transmission and distribution networks. This includes upgrading existing lines, establishing green energy corridors, and deploying smart grid technologies such as advanced metering infrastructure, demand-side management systems, and battery energy storage systems. These investments are crucial to manage the intermittency of renewables, ensure seamless power flow, and minimise transmission losses. Without these upgrades, the full potential of renewable capacity additions cannot be realised.

This aims to reduce reliance on imports, particularly from China, thereby enhancing self-reliance and insulating the domestic industry from global supply chain shocks. Similarly, efforts are underway to foster domestic manufacturing capabilities for wind turbine components and battery storage systems, crucial for grid stability in a high-renewable scenario.

Nearly half of the country's energy supply is derived from coal. The continued reliance on conventional, non-renewable energy sources has led to a significant increase in CO_2 emissions, which rose by 8.2 per cent in 2023.In a developing country like India, where coal remains the dominant energy source, the burning of fossil fuels plays a significant role in contributing to CO_2 emissions. As one of the world's fastest-growing economies, India faces a dual challenge: sustaining economic development while ensuring environmental protection. For instance, the Green Revolution significantly improved agricultural productivity, but it also led to the overuse of groundwater resources and a rise in greenhouse gas (GHG) emissions. Additionally, India's per capita CO_2 emissions rose sharply from 36 kg in the 1970s to 1,590 kg by 2014, though this figure still remains lower than that of most developed countries. Despite this, the rate of increase in per capita emissions is deeply concerning, as it may worsen the adverse effects of climate change, particularly those associated with air pollution.

In 2018, India's Integrated Energy Policy (IEP) was launched, providing a comprehensive framework for the energy sector. The policy emphasises clean energy, energy efficiency, and the integration of renewables into the grid while also addressing traditional challenges such as coal-based power generation. It aims to create a sustainable future through a balanced approach that includes both conventional and renewable sources. The IEP was first formulated in 2006 by the Planning Commission of India to address the country's growing energy challenges in a coordinated manner. The policy seeks to ensure energy security, provide affordable access to energy for all, and promote sustainable development, while supporting economic growth.

Launched at the 2015 United Nations Climate Change Conference (COP21) in Paris, the International Solar Alliance (ISA) is a multilateral platform initiated by India and France to promote the adoption of solar energy globally, especially in sun-rich developing countries located between the Tropics of Cancer and Capricorn. Located in Gurugram, India, the ISA is the first international organisation with its headquarters in India, reflecting the country's commitment to climate leadership. The ISA aims to mobilise $1 trillion in solar investments by 2030, reduce the cost of solar technologies, and facilitate and promote solar project financing and their applications in agriculture, health, and rural electrification. Kazakhstan has shown strong interest in joining the ISA; when India's Prime Minister Narendra Modi invited Kazakhstan's president during an SCO summit to join the ISA, Kazakh authorities responded positively.

Another ambitious initiative in this direction is the National Solar Mission, which aims to significantly expand India's solar energy capacity as part of the country's broader goal of achieving 450 gigawatts (GW) of renewable energy capacity by 2030, including around 280 GW from solar power. This initiative represents a major push towards harnessing India's abundant solar potential. A significant portion of this target is expected to come from the rooftop solar installations, which offer a decentralised approach to power generation. This not only reduces the load on the national grid but also empowers households and businesses to become self-reliant in their energy needs.

In addition to solar energy, wind power represents another vital pillar of India's renewable energy strategy. The country possesses vast wind energy resources, particularly in coastal states and high-altitude regions. To tap into this potential, the government has implemented favourable policies and auction mechanisms to attract private investment and accelerate the installation of wind farms. These initiatives are instrumental in diversifying the renewable energy mix and ensuring a more balanced and stable power supply.

Bioenergy also plays a crucial role in India's renewable agenda, particularly in rural and agricultural regions. By promoting the use of agricultural waste to produce biogas and biofuels, the government is addressing multiple challenges simultaneously: managing waste, providing cleaner cooking and transportation fuels, and supporting rural livelihoods. This sustainable approach helps reduce carbon emissions while creating economic opportunities in the agricultural sector.

Hydropower continues to be an integral part of India's renewable energy landscape. Large-scale hydroelectric projects are being developed to provide a steady and reliable source of clean energy. At the same time, small decentralised hydropower plants are being promoted in remote and hilly areas, where extending the conventional grid is difficult. These small-scale projects are particularly valuable for rural electrification and community development.

India's nuclear energy policy has evolved significantly in response to growing energy demands, climate change commitments, and geopolitical considerations. The Revised Nuclear Power Policy reflects a strategic realignment aimed at expanding the role of nuclear energy in the national energy mix, enhancing energy security, and meeting the country's climate goals under the

Paris Agreement. India is aiming to increase its nuclear capacity significantly, with plans to add around 63 GW by 2030 through new reactors and expansion of existing facilities.

India has also committed to constructing 12 new nuclear reactors with a combined capacity of 9,000 MW, using indigenously developed Pressurised Heavy Water Reactors (PHWRs). These efforts are in line with the 'Make in India' initiative and aim to strengthen domestic technological capabilities. These policy initiatives reflect India's commitment to reducing its carbon footprint, enhancing energy security, and ensuring sustainable development. By diversifying energy sources and promoting efficient usage, Prime Minister Modi's policies aim to create a more resilient and green energy ecosystem in the country.

Despite this impressive progress, several challenges persist. Grid integration of intermittent renewable sources, the need for large-scale energy storage solutions, and significant financial investment remain critical hurdles. While renewable energy targets are ambitious, the sheer scale of India's energy demand means that coal will continue to play a vital role in its energy mix for the foreseeable future. Balancing this reliance on coal with environmental commitments and the rapid expansion of renewables is a delicate act. Challenges also extend beyond technical integration to include land acquisition and financing. Large-scale solar and wind projects require vast tracts of land, often leading to complexities in acquisition and potential social displacement. Streamlining these processes while ensuring fair compensation and environmental safeguards remains an ongoing challenge.

Kazakhstan's Perspectives

Kazakhstan, as Central Asia's largest economy and a significant global energy player, faces a complex and evolving set of dynamics concerning its energy security in 2025. As a major producer and exporter of oil, natural gas, and uranium, the nation's energy security is intrinsically linked to its economic stability and geopolitical standing. However, internal challenges, global energy transitions, and regional geopolitical shifts necessitate a proactive and diversified approach to maintaining a secure, affordable, and sustainable energy supply.

Kazakhstan's energy sector is a significant part of its economy, contributing substantially to both domestic consumption and international trade. The energy landscape today is shaped by export diversification, green transition commitments, and international energy partnerships. Kazakhstan's energy security is anchored in its immense hydrocarbon reserves; it holds the 12th largest proven oil reserves globally and significant natural gas resources, making it a pivotal supplier to international markets. The country is also the world's leading uranium producer, accounting for over 40 per cent of global output in 2024, with plans to increase production in 2025.

Generally, oil exports, primarily through the Caspian Pipeline Consortium (CPC) to the Black Sea, remain the cornerstone of its foreign exchange earnings. Natural gas production largely serves domestic consumption and limited exports to neighbouring countries and Russia. Simultaneously, Kazakhstan is the world's leading uranium producer, providing a vital input for global nuclear energy, and by extension, a strategic energy security asset. Domestically, coal continues to dominate the power generation mix, accounting for over 70 per cent of electricity production, supplemented by hydropower and a nascent but growing renewable energy sector.

Its oil and gas sectors are robust, driven by large-scale projects like Tengiz, Kashagan, and Karachaganak. In 2024, oil production reached 87.7 million tonnes, with a planned increase to 96.2 million tonnes in 2025, largely due to the Future Growth Project (FGP) at Tengiz. Gas production stood at 59 billion cubic metres in 2024, projected to rise to 62.8 billion cubic metres in 2025.

Kazakhstan is among the top 15 global oil exporters, with over 80 million tons of crude oil produced annually and approximately 75 per cent exported, primarily through pipelines to China and via Caspian Sea routes to Europe. However, many key oil fields in Kazakhstan have reached or are nearing the end of their productive life. While a major revenue source, the economy's heavy dependence on oil exposes it to the inherent volatility of global oil markets. Given the significant contribution of hydrocarbon exports to the national budget, Kazakhstan's economic stability is highly sensitive to global oil and gas price fluctuations. This necessitates continued efforts towards economic diversification.

Kazakhstan, a leading energy exporter in Central Asia, remains heavily dependent on hydrocarbons while cautiously transitioning towards renewable energy. Despite ambitious renewable energy targets, Kazakhstan's domestic energy mix remains heavily dominated by fossil fuels. Coal, in particular, continues to be the primary source for electricity generation, making up approximately 55 per cent of the total in 2024, followed by natural gas (28 per cent). While the share of renewables has steadily increased, reaching 6.43 per cent of total electricity generation in 2024 (up from 3 per cent in 2020), it experienced a slight dip in Q1 2025 to 5.93 per cent due to a broader increase in total electricity generation and the commissioning of new conventional power capacities.

Despite increased renewable energy capacity and ambitious targets (15 per cent by 2030 and 50 per cent by 2050), the foundational role of coal means that a full transition will be complex and gradual. Managing the socio-economic impacts of decarbonisation in coal-dependent regions also remains a significant challenge.

Kazakhstan has revised its renewable energy target upward to 15 per cent of its energy mix by 2030, supported by competitive auctions for new projects and long-term agreements for large-scale developments. International collaborations, such as the $1.4 billion wind power station spearheaded by UAE's Masdar and commitments from Total Energies, underscore global confidence in Kazakhstan's green energy potential.

In 2025, there is a visible acceleration in solar and wind power projects, driven by attractive investment incentives, auctions for renewable energy capacities, and the establishment of a robust regulatory framework. The country's vast steppes offer immense potential for large-scale wind and solar farms.

Discussions and feasibility studies for constructing a nuclear power plant are ongoing, with a potential site near Lake Balkhash being considered while a long-term project, moving forward with nuclear energy, would significantly diversify the domestic energy mix, reduce reliance on coal, and provide a stable, baseload power source, bolstering energy independence.

Despite its vast resource wealth, Kazakhstan faces several critical energy security challenges. Foremost among these is the aging energy infrastructure. Many power plants, transmission lines, and pipelines date back to the Soviet era, leading to inefficiencies, frequent breakdowns, and high energy losses. Rapid economic growth fuels increased domestic energy consumption, putting pressure on balancing export commitments with ensuring sufficient and affordable energy for its own population. A significant portion of Kazakhstan's energy infrastructure, particularly in power generation and transmission, is aging. By the end of 2024, some power plants showed 70–90 per cent wear and tear, leading to increased technical violations and electricity losses. Modernisation efforts with substantial investments (estimated at US$25.5 billion for energy and utilities by 2029) are underway to address these issues.

Modernisation and upgrades require substantial investment, a challenge particularly relevant in 2025 as the country seeks to attract foreign capital amidst global economic uncertainties. Furthermore, the heavy reliance on fossil fuels for domestic power generation contributes to significant environmental pollution and presents a long-term vulnerability in the face of climate change commitments and the global push for decarbonisation.

Internally, growing domestic energy demand driven by population growth, industrial development, and urbanisation presents a challenge to energy security. Ensuring sufficient and reliable electricity supply for its citizens and industries, particularly during peak winter months, is a recurring concern, occasionally leading to power shortages in certain regions. The government's push for energy efficiency measures, while vital, requires widespread adoption and investment in energy-saving technologies across all sectors.

As a landlocked country, secure and diversified export routes are paramount. This involves navigating complex geopolitical dynamics with neighbouring transit countries. The primary export route for Kazakh oil is the Caspian Pipeline Consortium (CPC), which transports over 80 per cent of its crude to the Black Sea port of Novorossiysk. While crucial, this reliance on Russian territory introduces geopolitical risks, as evidenced by past disruptions. Regional and global geopolitical events, such as the Russian-Ukrainian conflict, directly impact transit routes and market stability. While Kazakhstan has strategically navigated these tensions, actively exploring alternative routes, the risk of secondary sanctions or supply disruptions remains.

While efforts have been made to diversify export routes, including increasing shipments across the Caspian Sea and through China, the reliance on a single primary pipeline route exposes Kazakhstan to geopolitical risks and transit fee negotiations. In 2022–2025, the ongoing geopolitical tensions, particularly those related to the Russia-Ukraine conflict, continue to underscore the urgency of developing alternative corridors and strengthening east-west energy links.

Bilateral Cooperation

By 2025, India and Kazakhstan's energy cooperation is poised to expand significantly, driven by shared goals of diversifying energy sources, enhancing infrastructure, promoting innovation, and ensuring long-term energy security for both nations. Both countries share a mutual interest in diversifying energy sources and enhancing energy security through strategic partnerships.

The two countries cooperate within several frameworks like the India-Central Asia Summit (2022–2024), the Shanghai Cooperation Organisation (SCO) Energy Dialogue, and the Joint Working Group on Hydrocarbons (revived in 2024).

India continues to strengthen its energy ties with Kazakhstan in 2025, particularly in the hydrocarbon sector. Kazakhstan, endowed with rich reserves of oil and natural gas, is a significant player in India's energy diversification strategy, especially as India seeks to reduce dependence on Middle Eastern oil. A significant portion of India's crude oil imports (over 60 per cent) comes from the Middle East, especially from countries like Iraq, Saudi Arabia, and the UAE. Any regional instability (e.g., wars, sanctions, or internal unrest) can threaten India's energy supply. Conflicts involving Iran, Yemen, and broader US-Iran tensions increase the unpredictability of Middle Eastern oil supply. India has ramped up purchases from countries like the USA, Brazil, Nigeria, and more recently, Russia. Since 2022, Russia has been steadily increasing its supplies of discounted crude oil to Delhi due to the ongoing sanctions and other limitations. India is also preoccupied with achieving strategic autonomy and does not want to be caught in the middle of regional or global rivalries.

The trade relationship is predominantly focused on crude oil and liquefied natural gas (LNG) exports from Kazakhstan to India. In 2025, hydrocarbon exports from Kazakhstan to India have seen consistent activity, with Indian public sector and private firms increasingly engaging in long-term contracts and spot market transactions. Today, the bilateral trade is estimated at around 2.1–2.5 billion USD.

Hydrocarbons have historically constituted the dominant share of India's imports from Kazakhstan, accounting for roughly 85–90 per cent of the total trade volume during peak periods of engagement. The Ministry of External Affairs Bilateral Brief underscores this dependency, highlighting that India primarily imports crude oil and various petroleum products from Kazakhstan. In recent years, these energy commodities have consistently represented the vast majority of the import value, solidifying energy security as the cornerstone of the bilateral economic relationship.

According to data from the World Bank's World Integrated Trade Solution (WITS), Kazakhstan currently exports the majority of its fuels to European and East Asian markets, specifically Italy, China, and the Netherlands. However, geopolitical shifts have prompted a strategic pivot. In 2025, Kazakhstan expanded its market diversification strategy to reduce reliance on traditional western routes, placing a renewed focus on high-growth markets in India and Southeast Asia.

This strategic realignment is corroborated by recent trade metrics. The May 2025 trade bulletin released by the Press Information Bureau (PIB) of India notes an overall increase in oil and gas imports during the fiscal period. This upward trend signals a strengthening of energy ties with Central Asian producers, suggesting that Kazakhstan's efforts to diversify its export destinations are beginning to materialise in the Indian market.

Two key routes are being used for transportation: the Caspian Sea–Russia–India route and the International North-South Transport Corridor or INSTC (via Iran). The INSTC itself is a 7,200-kilometre multimodal transportation network connecting India, Iran, Russia, and Central Asia, with further extensions towards Northern Europe. The corridor was established following an Intergovernmental Agreement signed by the founding members: India, Iran and Russia in St. Petersburg in September 2000, which was then formally ratified in 2002. The primary objective of the INSTC is to reduce transit time and logistics costs for trade between South Asia, the Persian Gulf, Central Asia, and Europe. Studies indicate the route is 30 per cent cheaper and 40 per cent shorter than the traditional Suez Canal route. In the current geopolitical landscape, defined by the Russia-Ukraine war and subsequent Western sanctions on Russia, the INSTC has acquired renewed strategic importance. As Russia seeks alternative trade avenues and India balances its relationships between Western partners and Eurasian powers, the corridor serves as a vital economic artery, bypassing traditional choke points and facilitating direct commerce across the Eurasian heartland.

The INSTC serves as India's strategic response to China's Belt and Road Initiative (BRI), particularly the China-Pakistan Economic Corridor (CPEC), which passes through Pakistan-occupied Kashmir, a region India claims as its own. By developing an alternative Eurasian trade route that bypasses Pakistan, India strengthens its regional influence and reduces dependency on Chinese-dominated supply chains. Despite Western sanctions on Russia following its invasion of Ukraine, India has maintained robust economic ties with Moscow, particularly in energy trade. The INSTC provides a reliable overland route for India to import Russian oil, fertilizers, and defence equipment while exporting pharmaceuticals, textiles, and machinery. Additionally, it enhances India's Connect Central Asia Policy by improving access to resource-rich Kazakhstan, Uzbekistan, and Turkmenistan.

While the International North-South Transport Corridor (INSTC) remains India's primary connectivity framework in Eurasia, the Trans-Caspian International Transport Route (TITR), often referred to as the 'Middle Corridor', has emerged as a critical complementary branch. Unlike the INSTC, which focuses on the North-South axis (Russia–Iran–India), the TITR runs East-West, connecting Southeast Asia and China to Europe via Kazakhstan, the Caspian Sea, Azerbaijan, and Georgia. Although India is not a direct signatory to the TITR association, the route has gained strategic prominence in New Delhi's calculus as a viable alternative to the Northern Corridor (via Russia), which has been heavily impacted by Western sanctions and the war in Ukraine. Recent data highlights the corridor's growing relevance: the 2024-2025 fiscal period indicates a substantial reconfiguration of trans-Eurasian logistics, with freight volumes along the TITR registering a year-on-year expansion exceeding 60 per cent. This surge is primarily attributable to the strategic diversion of trade flows away from the Northern Corridor, following the imposition of sanctions and the resultant operational constraints on Russian transit routes.

From New Delhi's strategic vantage point, the TITR provides a dual imperative for enhancing economic resilience. First, it facilitates the diversification of supply chains, thereby mitigating the systemic risks associated with maritime bottlenecks in the Suez Canal and the prevailing geopolitical instability affecting the Northern route. Second, it advances India's objective of strategic autonomy by sustaining commercial connectivity with Central Asia through infrastructure independent of the Chinese-led Belt and Road Initiative (BRI).

Nuclear Cooperation

Kazakhstan's civil nuclear deal with India represents a significant partnership in the field of nuclear energy, reflecting the growing interest of both nations in cooperation in the energy sector. Kazakhstan is rich in uranium reserves, being the world's largest producer of uranium. Following the breakup of the Soviet Union, it inherited extensive nuclear knowledge and facilities, including a nuclear testing site at Semipalatinsk. In the post-Soviet era, Kazakhstan has sought to leverage its nuclear resources for peaceful purposes, focusing on developing a strong energy sector while promoting international non-proliferation efforts.

India, on the other hand, has been aiming to secure reliable nuclear fuel sources to support its ambitious energy needs and growing economy. Post the Indo-US Civil Nuclear Agreement, India has been actively seeking to diversify its nuclear fuel supply sources. The formal economic and nuclear cooperation was initiated with the signing of the Nuclear Cooperation Agreement in 2011. This agreement allows for the supply of uranium and enhances collaboration in various modalities of nuclear technology for peaceful purposes. It sets the framework for joint research, development, and personnel training in nuclear technology and provides a legal structure for the supply of nuclear fuel. Under this agreement, Kazakhstan has committed to supply India with uranium, which is critical for fuelling India's nuclear power plants. The deal facilitates the supply of physical uranium and has involved significant quantities, such as the contract of 5,000 metric tons of uranium agreed upon in 2015, aimed at addressing India's energy demands. Both nations have emphasised that their nuclear cooperation is strictly focused on peaceful uses of nuclear energy, aligned with respective international obligations. This aspect is crucial for Kazakhstan, which has actively promoted a non-proliferation agenda while engaging with various international nuclear frameworks.

TAPI Pipeline

Kazakhstan is one of the world's largest producers of natural gas, with significant reserves in the Kashagan field and other regions. Natural gas is primarily exported via pipelines to China, Turkey, and Europe. The TAPI pipeline project remains a strategic goal for diversifying export routes. The Turkmenistan-Afghanistan-Pakistan-India (TAPI) pipeline is an important infrastructure project aimed at transporting natural gas from Turkmenistan through Afghanistan and Pakistan to India. The pipeline runs approximately 1,814 kilometres from the Galkynysh gas field in Turkmenistan, through southern Afghanistan, to the city of Quetta in Pakistan and then onto India. The pipeline is intended to carry about 33 billion cubic metres of natural gas annually. The primary objective is to reduce India's dependence on traditional sources of energy and provide a stable supply of natural gas to fuel its fast-growing economy.

Construction on the Turkmen section (214 km) was completed in 2020, and the Afghan segment (735 km) saw partial progress before the Taliban's 2021 takeover. However, work in Afghanistan and Pakistan has stalled due to security concerns and funding shortages. The Taliban's assurances of pipeline security have not convinced investors. While the group has pledged to protect TAPI as a 'national priority,' attacks on infrastructure by ISIS-K and other militants persist. No significant construction has occurred in Afghanistan since 2021, and international firms remain hesitant to engage.

As of 2024, significant portions of the pipeline have seen construction advancements in Turkmenistan, with ongoing discussions regarding construction phases in Afghanistan and Pakistan. Regular meetings among stakeholders continue to address logistical and technical contributions to the pipeline's ongoing progress. The resurgence of the Taliban and the resultant uncertainty about the political and security environment in Afghanistan create risks for the project.

Additionally, India's historically strained relations with Pakistan raise concerns about whether gas supplies would be reliable amid potential geopolitical tensions. Securing investments for the TAPI has always proved rather challenging, with stakeholders needing assurances of profitability and stability.

As of 2025, TAPI's progress remains uncertain, with Afghanistan's Taliban administration, Pakistan's economic crisis, and India's shifting energy priorities complicating its realisation. While Turkmenistan and Pakistan still advocate for the project, Afghanistan's instability and India's declining interest diminish its feasibility. Unless a consortium of international investors steps in and the Taliban provides enforceable security assurances, TAPI risks becoming another unrealised vision of regional connectivity.

India, initially a key stakeholder, has reduced its reliance on TAPI due to: increased LNG imports from Qatar, the USA and Australia; domestic renewable energy expansion (500 GW target by 2030); strategic gas deals with Russia and Iran.

While India has not officially withdrawn, its participation appears increasingly unlikely. At the same time, Kazakhstan managed to express an interest in participating in the TAPI project, which represents a significant development in Central Asian energy cooperation. By participating in TAPI, Kazakhstan can enhance its strategic economic ties with South Asia. This aligns with Kazakhstan's geopolitical strategy to diversify its energy export routes. Kazakhstan's interest in the TAPI pipeline reflects a broader strategy of enhancing regional cooperation, diversifying energy routes, and promoting energy security in Central Asia and South Asia. The successful integration of Kazakhstan's gas resources into the TAPI framework could have positive implications for broader geopolitical dynamics, allowing for increased connectivity and energy partnership among nations in the region.

Conclusion

India's energy geopolitics involves a balance between domestic production, international trade, policy frameworks, and strategic partnerships. The country continues to invest heavily in renewables while maintaining its reliance on traditional sources like coal and natural gas to ensure energy security and reduce carbon emissions. Bilateral energy dialogues with major energy producers (e.g., Saudi Arabia, UAE, Russia, USA) and consumers (e.g., Japan, South Korea) are critical for securing long-term supply contracts and attracting investments in its energy sector. The diversification of oil imports, including increasing volumes from non-traditional suppliers, signifies a pragmatic foreign policy approach prioritising national energy security. In recent years, India's approach is evolving towards a more balanced and sustainable mix of traditional and renewable sources. The government's ambitious targets under the International Solar Alliance and the National Action Plan on Climate Change are part of this transition. Geopolitically, India's energy security narrative today is increasingly shaped by its role in international energy governance. As a founding member of the International Solar Alliance (ISA), India leverages this platform to promote solar energy deployment globally, foster technology transfer, and establish common standards. Its engagement with the Quad (Quadrilateral Security Dialogue) also includes discussions on energy security, critical minerals, and supply chain resilience.

As with many other nations, both Kazakhstan and India continue to face several challenges in terms of the transition. They include ongoing reliance on coal and imported crude oil, slow adoption of clean technologies in some sectors, infrastructural gaps in rural areas, and balancing energy demand with environmental sustainability. There are differences and commonalities in India and Kazakhstan's approaches to energy security. While India finds itself preoccupied with regional geopolitics and heavy reliance on tumultuous energy prices, Kazakhstan's current energy sector is robust but faces challenges that require strategic partnerships, technological advancements, and sustained investment. The growing cooperation with India could significantly enhance the energy security and diversification efforts of both countries.

References

1. Joint Research Centre. (2025, September 9). World emissions hit record high, but the EU leads trend reversal. [https://joint-research-centre.ec.europa.eu/jrc-news-and-updates/world-emissions-hit-record-high-eu-leads-trend-reversal-2025-09-09_en].
2. TOI Business Desk. (2025, May 16). 'US overtakes UAE to become India's 4th largest crude oil supplier; Russia still tops the chart.' *TheTimes of India*. https://timesofindia.india

times.com/business/india-business/us-overtakes-uae-to-become-indias-4th-largest-crude-oil-supplier-russia-still-tops-the-chart/articleshow/121204301.cms.

3. Anand, S. (2025, March 19). 'India's electricity demand to touch 273 GW in 2025 – Can the grid handle the surge? '*ETEnergyWorld*. [https://energy.economictimes.indiatimes.com/news/power/indias-electricity-demand-to-touch-273-gw-in-2025-can-the-grid-handle-the-surge/119189112].
4. Central Electricity Authority. (2025). All India installed capacity report. Ministry of Power, Government of India.
5. Gupta, S. (n.d.). India's oil import dependency reaches record high. Study IQ. https://www.studyiq.com/articles/indias-oil-import/.
6. Shankar, A., Saxena, A. K., & Idnani, T. (2022). Roadmap to India's 2030 decarbonization target [Discussion paper]. The Energy and Resources Institute. https://www.energy-transitions.org/wp-content/uploads/2022/08/Roadmap-to-India-2030-Decarbonization-Target.pdf
7. Ministry of Environment, Forest and Climate Change. (2023). India's third biennial update report to the UNFCCC. Government of India. https://moef.gov.in.
8. Planning Commission of India. (2006). Integrated energy policy: Report of the expert committee. Government of India. https://niti.gov.in/planningcommission.gov.in/docs/reports/genrep/rep_intengy.pdf.
9. Mishra, B.K. et al. (2024). A review of India's renewable energy transition: Policies, achievements, and integration challenges. In 2024 10th International Conference on Electrical Energy Systems (ICEES) (pp. 1–7). Chennai, India: IEEE. https://doi.org/10.1109/ICEES61253.2024.10776919.
10. *Business Standard*. (2018, June 10). PM Modi invites Kazakhstan to join ISA. *Business Standard*. https://www.business-standard.com/article/news-ani/pm-modi-invites-kazakhstan-to-join-isa-118061000389_1.htm.
11. Energy Transitions Commission. (2020). Renewable power pathways: Modelling the integration of wind and solar in India by 2030. [https://www.energy-transitions.org/publications/renewable-power-pathways/].
12. Grover, R. B. (2024). Nurturing nuclear power in India. Retrieved from https://www.researchgate.net/profile/Ravi-Grover-2/publication/389767070_Nurturing_nuclear_power_in_India/links/67fb68a9bfbe974b23a973b9/Nurturing-nuclear-power-in-India.pdf.
13. International Energy Agency. (2024). World Energy Outlook2024. [https://www.iea.org/reports/world-energy-outlook-2024].
14. Office of the Prime Minister of the Republic of Kazakhstan. (2025, March 3). Ministry of Energy of Kazakhstan: 2024 results and strategic plans for 2025. [https://primeminister.kz/en/news/reviews/ministry-of-energy-of-kazakhstan-2024-results-and-strategic-plans-for-2025-29771].
15. International Energy Agency. (2025). World Energy Outlook 2025. [https://www.iea.org/reports/world-energy-outlook-2025].
16. International Energy Monitor. (2025, May 12). 'Kazakhstan approves $1.4bn wind energy agreement with UAE.' *Energy Monitor*. [https://www.energymonitor.ai/news/kazakhstan-approves-wind-energy/].
17. Abuova, N. (2025, January 22). 'Kazakhstan's energy sector modernization: Challenges and national plan.' *The Astana Times*. [https://astanatimes.com/2025/01/kazakhstans-energy-sector-modernization-challenges-and-national-plan/].
18. Daly, J.C.K. (2025, May 15). 'Kazakhstan faces oil export challenges amid Russia's war against Ukraine.' *Jamestown Eurasia Daily Monitor*. [https://jamestown.org/kazakhstan-faces-oil-export-challenges-amid-russias-war-against-ukraine/].

19. Chaudhury, D.R. (2021, November 25). 'Kazakhstan aspires to India's hub for regional investments.' *The Economic Times*. [https://economictimes.indiatimes.com/news/india/kazakhstan-aspires-to-indias-hub-for-regional-investments/articleshow/87905044.cms].
20. Ministry of External Affairs. (2025). India-Kazakhstan bilateral relations. Government of India. [https://www.mea.gov.in/].
21. World Bank. (2025). Kazakhstan trade summary: World Integrated Trade Solution (WITS). [https://wits.worldbank.org/].
22. Ministry of Commerce & Industry. (2025, May 15). PIB release: India's foreign trade April 2025 [Press release]. Government of India. [https://www.commerce.gov.in/wp-content/uploads/2025/05/PIB-Release-April-2025-final-revised-1.pdf].
23. Agreement on the International North-South Transport Corridor (INSTC). (2000). Ministry of Commerce & Industry, Government of India.
24. Railways of Kazakhstan (KTZ). (2025). Trans-Caspian International Transport Route (TITR) and North-South Corridor reports.
25. Observer Research Foundation. (2025). India's strategic pivot: Navigating the Middle Corridor.
26. Trans-Caspian International Transport Route Association. (2025). Annual volume and logistics report 2024–2025.
27. Ministry of External Affairs (MEA). (2011). Agreement between the Government of the Republic of India and the Government of the Republic of Kazakhstan for cooperation in the peaceful uses of nuclear energy. Government of India.
28. World Nuclear Association. (2025). Uranium and nuclear power in Kazakhstan. [https://world-nuclear.org/information-library/country-profiles/countries-g-n/Kazakhstan.
29. Asian Development Bank. (2025). Environmental and social impact assessment: TAPI Gas Pipeline Project, Phase 1 (ESIA Report – Project No. 52167-001). [https://www.adb.org/sites/default/files/project-documents/52167/52167-001-esia-en_52.pdf]
30. Ibid.

15

India and Kazakhstan's Approaches to Nuclear Non-Proliferation Issues

Prof. Kuralay Baizakova

Introduction

The international community remains concerned about a range of issues related to nuclear non-proliferation. The current comprehensive UN strategy for preventing the spread of nuclear weapons is still being developed.

The nuclear non-proliferation regime is under threat due to non-compliance with commitments, withdrawals or threats to withdraw from the Nuclear Non-Proliferation Treaty (NPT) in order to evade obligations, changes in the international security environment, and the proliferation of technology. One of the concerns of the UN is that, in the long term, the entire NPT regime could become undermined or even collapse. At the same time, the accumulated vast arsenal of nuclear weapons does not protect against real threats – such as the proliferation of nuclear weapons worldwide or the potential for a missile strike.

According to UN experts, multi-vector activity is now necessary. First and foremost, it is noted that "the primary vector of an effective strategy to prevent the proliferation of nuclear, radiological, chemical, and biological weapons should be focused on global mechanisms that reduce the demand for these types of weapons." The next vector "should be aimed at global mechanisms regulating supply, so that both states and non-state actors have fewer opportunities to acquire weapons, as well as the materials and knowledge necessary for their production..."

The purpose of this section is to examine Kazakhstan's and India's approaches to nuclear non-proliferation issues and the possibilities for further cooperation between the two countries. The section has been prepared as part of scientific project AR26100515 'Risk management strategies and strengthening Kazakhstan's foreign policy in the context of geopolitical challenges and regional instability'.

Kazakhstan's Initiatives to Strengthen the Nuclear Non-Proliferation Regime

Kazakhstan joined the United Nations not just as a new member of the global community, but as a state actively engaged in addressing the most pressing international issues of our time. Its position within the UN is shaped by considering Kazakhstan's interests across the full spectrum of issues examined by the Organisation. A particular area of analysis is Kazakhstan's foreign policy focus on the role in strengthening the nuclear non-proliferation regime.

Although Kazakhstan's contribution to ending nuclear testing is widely recognised, the country's leadership does not consider its mission complete. On August 29, 1991, the first President of the Republic of Kazakhstan, Nursultan Nazarbayev, ordered the closure of the Semipalatinsk nuclear test site. This was one of the largest test sites during the Soviet Union era. Since 1949, at least 468 tests were conducted there, during which 616 nuclear devices were detonated underground, on the ground, and in the air. The last detonation occurred on August 19, 1989. That same year, the unique movement 'Nevada-Semipalatinsk' was established, uniting victims of nuclear tests worldwide.

Nuclear tests at the Semipalatinsk site caused irreparable damage to human health and the environment. They led to high rates of illness and mortality among the population and resulted in intense radioactive contamination of surrounding areas. Around the 300,000-square-kilometre test zone, approximately one and a half million people lived. According to experts, over 500,000 individuals were directly exposed to radiation.

In October 1993, Nazarbayev announced the signing of the Nuclear Non-Proliferation Treaty and began transferring nuclear warheads from the country to Russia for destruction. In May 1995, Kazakhstan dismantled and destroyed all nuclear warheads on its territory.

Kazakhstan was one of the first signatories of the Comprehensive Nuclear-Test-Ban Treaty in 1996 and subsequently ratified it in 2001. By around 1997, Kazakhstan had practically eliminated its nuclear weapons and nuclear facilities on its territory.

The abolition of nuclear weapons in Kazakhstan is an important step forward in international security and lays a solid foundation for global peace and stability. This historic decision not only reflects Kazakhstan's courage and wisdom but also demonstrates the shared understanding and resistance to the threat of nuclear weapons by the international community.

Since 2004, projects involving Kazakhstan, Russia, and the USA have been implemented to eliminate the consequences of past nuclear tests and strengthen physical facilities at the former Semipalatinsk test site.

Although Kazakhstan's contribution to ending nuclear testing is widely recognised, the country's leadership does not consider its mission complete. Kazakhstan continues to advocate for strengthening global nuclear security and is committed to the idea of complete and universal nuclear disarmament, which is the only guarantee of nuclear safety.

In 2009, Kazakhstan and four regional partners signed the Semipalatinsk Treaty on a nuclear-weapon-free zone in Central Asia and called on all parties to establish a similar zone in the Middle East. In the same year, the UN General Assembly unanimously adopted a Kazakhstani resolution declaring August 29, the date of the decree closing the Semipalatinsk test site, as the 'International Day of Action for the Prohibition of Nuclear Tests.'

As noted by the President of Kazakhstan, K. Tokayev, "The International Day of Action against Nuclear Tests holds great significance for humanity. Atomic explosions have caused colossal damage to the Kazakh land. This tragedy must not be repeated. Our country will always stand firmly on the principles of nuclear safety".

Within the framework of the UN, Kazakhstan has put forward various initiatives over the years, which have been implemented or are in the process of being realised. One of the important initiatives was the declaration of August 29 as the International Day of Action against Nuclear Tests.

In 2012, Kazakhstan launched the ATOM project ('Say No to Testing'). This international educational and advocacy activity aims to help the global community raise awareness about resistance to nuclear weapon testing and ultimately achieve the goal of nuclear disarmament.

Kazakhstan's initiatives in the field of nuclear security have strengthened the country's position in the international community. One of the key initiatives in this area is the continued promotion of nuclear disarmament as the main goal of the 21st century. The leadership of Kazakhstan proposed achieving a nuclear-free world by the 100th anniversary of the Organisation. The international community supported this idea, and on December 7, 2015, during a UN General Assembly session, a resolution on the Universal Declaration for a world free of nuclear weapons was adopted, initiated by Kazakhstan.

In 2015, Kazakhstan signed an agreement with the International Atomic Energy Agency to establish a low-enriched uranium bank in Kazakhstan. This type of bank is the first of its kind in the world. It ensures guaranteed supplies of low-enriched uranium for civilian use and makes an important contribution to strengthening the nuclear non-proliferation regime.

Considering its contribution to enhancing international security and the nuclear non-proliferation regime, as well as active engagement in the UN, Kazakhstan was elected as a non-permanent member of the UN Security Council for 2017-2018.

Kazakhstan set the goal of promoting initiatives in the UN Security Council in the field of nuclear non-proliferation. One of the key initiatives in nuclear security was further advancing the idea of nuclear disarmament as the main goal of the 21st century, based on the Universal Declaration of Building a World Free of Nuclear Weapons.

In his address 'Kazakhstan's Conceptual Vision for Strengthening Global Partnership to Build a Safe, Just, and Prosperous World,' President N. Nazarbayev presented Kazakhstan's vision of its mission as a non-permanent member of the UN Security Council, including the goal of "moving towards a world without nuclear weapons".

The main event of Kazakhstan's presidency at the UN Security Council was the high-level thematic briefing held on January 18, 2018, on the topic 'Non-Proliferation of Weapons of Mass Destruction: Confidence-Building Measures.' Kazakhstan presented a substantive and comprehensive programme to the global community, focusing on current issues of non-proliferation through confidence-building measures. "The meeting demonstrated that confidence-building measures, as well as strengthening preventive diplomacy tools, can serve as a starting point for making progress on many critical issues that remain unresolved due to political considerations in the relations among major powers," noted Kazakh diplomats.

Kazakhstan is a participant in the Nuclear Non-Proliferation Treaty (NPT) and the Comprehensive Nuclear-Test-Ban Treaty (CTBT). In 2019, Kazakhstan ratified the Treaty on the Prohibition of Nuclear Weapons – the first legally binding multilateral agreement banning the development, testing, stockpiling, and use of nuclear weapons. Kazakhstan is the only country in the post-Soviet region to have signed the NPT and the only country in Central Asia to have ratified the Convention on Nuclear Safety.

In recent years, Kazakhstan has put forward a package of new proposals to strengthen the nuclear non-proliferation regime. Firstly, Kazakhstan proposed developing and signing new international agreements in the field of nuclear disarmament. Secondly, Kazakhstan advocated for enhanced international control over nuclear energy programmes. Thirdly, Kazakhstan called for the creation of new nuclear-weapon-free zones, including in the Middle East. These proposals received high praise from leaders of the world's leading countries.

As a means to strengthen trust in the non-proliferation sphere, Kazakhstan also proposes making exit from the NPT more difficult, including sanctions and coercive measures for countries that violate the Treaty.

It seems appropriate to agree with the opinion of several experts who believe that renouncing nuclear deterrence is only possible if global security is built on other principles, where small states no longer fear larger ones and do not attempt to balance power through the 'nuclear stick.'

Kazakhstan supports the idea of developing a multi-vector strategy for preventing the proliferation of nuclear, radiological, chemical, and biological weapons and believes that real progress in this area can only be achieved if all member-states fulfil their commitments regarding nuclear disarmament, as well as vertical and horizontal non-proliferation of WMDs.

"We advocate for the resumption of high-level dialogue between nuclear-weapon states and for the revitalisation of multilateral actions aimed at significantly reducing the threat of nuclear weapons use," said the President of Kazakhstan, K.K. Tokayev, at the United Nations General Assembly in 2025.

Today, Kazakhstan is firmly committed to the main principles of non-proliferation, control, and reduction of all types of armaments, and is a full participant in all major disarmament and international security treaties. The active role of Kazakhstan in disarmament and strengthening the non-proliferation regime of nuclear weapons is widely recognised within the UN, along with our country's commitment to all international agreements in this field.

India's Approaches to Nuclear Non-Proliferation Issues

To understand India's contemporary approaches to nuclear non-proliferation, let us briefly review the history of its nuclear weapons development. Indian nuclear ambitions have a long-standing history: the country began implementing its nuclear programme immediately after gaining independence.

After independence and with increasing economic capabilities, India's first Prime Minister, Jawaharlal Nehru, laid the foundations of the country's nuclear policy. For the leaders at that time, possessing atomic energy became a symbol of national pride and technological self-sufficiency.

Indian scientific research in nuclear science and technology started during World War II, and on April 6, 1948, the government, led by Nehru, adopted the Atomic Energy Act. Accordingly, the Indian Atomic Energy Commission was established, headed by H.D. Bhabha, who became the founder of the country's nuclear programme. At the same time, in March 1949, Nehru stated in Parliament: "We do not contemplate the creation of an atomic bomb." However, he also acknowledged that "in case of necessity, there must always be an inherent advantage in defence capability," understanding this as nuclear weapons. Experts note that these two different approaches set the tone for India's future military policy and its nuclear component.

The term 'nuclear energy' became widely known in India only after 1956, when the country's first nuclear reactor, 'Apsara,' was commissioned. This reactor, located in Bombay, also became the first nuclear reactor in Asia. Its creation marked a milestone in India's nuclear programme. Dr. Homi Bhabha, known as the 'Father of India's nuclear programme,' developed the reactor concept. Prime Minister Nehru named the reactor 'Apsara,' which means 'divine and heavenly beauty'.

Regarding the NPT, India refused to sign it, considering it discriminatory, and developed its own nuclear arsenal. On September 7, 1970, amid tensions with Pakistan, Indira Gandhi authorised the creation and testing of a nuclear explosive device (NED).

Preparation for the test of the nuclear device was carried out in complete secrecy. No one in the world expected it. On May 18, 1974, India conducted its first nuclear test – 'for peaceful purposes', as declared by Indira Gandhi. At the same time, a comprehensive programme to develop guided missile weapons of various categories was initiated, enabling India today to expand its nuclear and conventional arsenals.

India received assistance from several countries such as the USA, Canada, and Russia to develop its nuclear technologies. Agreements were signed to ensure the peaceful use of nuclear energy. However, after India's first nuclear test in 1974, known as the 'Smiling Buddha,' international aid was significantly reduced.

The 1974 nuclear test demonstrated India's scientific capabilities and placed it among the countries possessing nuclear weapons outside the permanent members of the UN Security Council. The nuclear tests ('Smiling Buddha,' 1974) became a kind of challenge to the international order, where nuclear weapons remained a privilege of a select few. India claimed that the test was purely peaceful in nature, but it also marked a step towards the escalation of its nuclear programme.

After the first test, India pursued a policy of restraint in developing military nuclear technology. However, in early May 1979, India began revising its nuclear policy in response to reports from various sources indicating that Pakistan was pursuing nuclear weapons. This led to increased technological efforts in India to develop nuclear weapons, although the government did not make a decision to conduct a test, only issuing instructions to create the appropriate weapon components.

The international situation and the military-political environment in South Asia began to change fundamentally from the early 1990s, which influenced India's stance on nuclear issues.

India, which held a firm position on the necessity of establishing a multipolar world to replace the previous bipolar global system, believed that it might soon become one of the main players on the world stage alongside the USA, China, Japan, the European Union, and Russia. In this context, India continued to develop its nuclear weapons programme. This enabled it, on May 18, 1994, to conduct a test of a bomb without a nuclear charge, to adopt the 'Prithvi-1' missile into service, and subsequently to begin work on the 'Agni-1' missile. At the same time, India sought to acquire advanced nuclear technologies, and in 1995, it refused to renew the NPT, which had expired after 25 years, as it was now considered indefinite. The Indian leadership reaffirmed its previous stance that the treaty was "unequal, unjust, and discriminatory."

In 1998, India conducted a series of five nuclear tests in Pokhran. This was the country's second major test, involving one thermonuclear explosion and four fission-based explosions. These tests drew international condemnation, including sanctions from the USA and Japan.

After 1998, India declared its policy of 'no first use' of nuclear weapons and committed to using nuclear technology solely for peaceful purposes. Jawaharlal Nehru emphasised that India should develop atomic energy for its progress, not for military purposes.

The emergence of the Indian economy at the end of the 20th and the beginning of the 21st century on the global stage has increasingly highlighted the need to improve its defence capabilities, of which the nuclear arsenal is a crucial component. At the same time, the country's leadership viewed nuclear weapons not primarily as a means of warfare but rather as a necessary political attribute for deterrence against neighbouring nuclear states – China and Pakistan.

Given the tense international situation, India's leadership adopted a forward-looking defence budget plan for 2001–2015 in 2000, allocating 20 per cent of the budget to the development of nuclear forces. To this end, a special agency called the Nuclear Command Authority was established in January 2003.

India's nuclear embargo lasted for about thirty years and was broken by the GYAP decision of September 6, 2008, which lifted the export ban to the country. This was made possible through a nuclear deal signed between Washington and Delhi in July 2005. According to the agreement signed by President George W. Bush and Prime Minister Manmohan Singh, Washington agreed to lift restrictions on the supply of materials and technologies to India in exchange for certain concessions from India. These included the separation of civilian and military nuclear facilities and placing the former under IAEA safeguards.

However, the Nuclear Damage Liability Act passed by the Indian Parliament in 2010 effectively halted the efforts of Prime Minister Singh's government to open access to foreign nuclear technologies.

India is actively developing its nuclear energy sector, including in cooperation with Kazakhstan. The first Indian nuclear power plant was installed in 1969 in Tarapur, Maharashtra. Currently, the country operates 21 nuclear power plants. It is planned that by 2025, India will generate 25 per cent of its electricity from nuclear sources. India continues to develop its scientific and technological capabilities, aiming to strengthen its defence and energy positions while maintaining peaceful intentions regarding nuclear energy.

India has unilaterally established an effective national export control mechanism, whereas Pakistan, on the other hand, has become a primary source of illegal shipments of nuclear materials and technologies.

Researchers note that at the beginning of his tenure as Prime Minister, Narendra Modi promised to ensure that every Indian household has at least one electric light bulb. To achieve this goal, the Indian Ministry of Atomic Energy has planned to increase the installed capacity of nuclear power plants. To this end, agreements on cooperation in the nuclear field have been initiated with several countries, including the USA, Australia, and others.

The crisis of the nuclear non-proliferation regime, which has become one of the acute issues of recent international security, is fully manifested in South Asia. For several decades, there has been, in one case openly, in another covertly, a missile-nuclear confrontation between India and Pakistan, and especially with nuclear China. Taking this into account, the Indian government led by Narendra Modi is pursuing an appropriate policy. "India must be prepared for a two-front war, and must create deterrent forces that will ensure opponents understand the futility of conflict," stated A.K. Doval, currently India's National Security Adviser. "India has two neighbours, both possessing nuclear weapons, maintaining good relations with each other, and harbouring hostile attitudes towards India." At the same time, Delhi considers nuclear weapons to be a central element of its national security policy, foreign policy strategy, and state-building efforts for the future. Therefore, in the medium and long term, Delhi will implement a doctrine of minimal nuclear deterrence.

According to Delhi, India's future nuclear forces should be effective, flexible, and responsive to emerging operational needs, in accordance with the concept of a reliable minimum deterrent. These forces should have a three-component structure, including a "set of potentials based on land, air, and sea." It is expected that by 2030, Indian nuclear forces will have at least 300 land, air, and sea-based delivery systems and over 400 nuclear warheads on them.

India is a consistent critic of the NPT and remains outside its framework to this day. Currently, efforts are underway to separate the country's nuclear programme into civilian and military components.

At present, the international community has essentially accepted India's and Pakistan's nuclear status. Sanctions imposed by several countries after their nuclear tests in 1997 have largely been lifted. The focus is on ensuring that Delhi and Islamabad do not become sources of proliferation of nuclear materials and technologies.

Today, India's strategic nuclear triad consists of land- and sea-based ballistic missiles with nuclear warheads, as well as air-dropped bombs deployed on combat aircraft. India's nuclear arsenal is primarily intended for deterrence against strategic threats from Pakistan and China. According to various estimates, by early 2025, India possessed approximately 160–170 nuclear warheads. India's nuclear forces are built around the concepts of 'minimum credible deterrence' and 'no first use.'

India's approaches to nuclear weapons, as noted by experts, are political rather than military in nature. Under this approach, nuclear weapons are viewed as a political tool, unsuitable for use in any purpose other than deterrence. This perspective is completely opposite to an operational approach, where nuclear weapons are considered as a supplement to conventional armed forces. The concept of nuclear war is not popular even among military leadership. Overall security strategy and nuclear strategy in particular are fully under civilian control.

India's traditional view is that nuclear weapons are necessary for achieving the status of a great power. Delhi believes that this status will enable India to secure a seat on the UN Security Council. For this reason, India has for many decades refused to heed calls to abandon the 'nuclear option.' India understands well that acquiring its own nuclear arsenal, despite some costs, will compel other powers to listen to its opinions.

At the current stage, India adopts a strategic approach to nuclear weapons, based on principles of deterrence and national security. The main aspects of its policy include the following components:

- *'Indirect' deterrence strategy:* India considers nuclear weapons as a means to prevent possible aggression from its neighbours, especially Pakistan and China. Accordingly, it adheres to a policy of 'no first use' of nuclear weapons, meaning that nuclear weapons may be used in response to a nuclear or large-scale conventional attack.
- *Ensuring National Security:* India is developing its nuclear arsenal within the framework of the 'strategic deterrence' concept to safeguard its security and sovereignty amid regional threats.
- *Development of Nuclear Technologies and Infrastructure:* India is actively working on modernising its nuclear forces, expanding nuclear fuel production, and improving delivery systems (ballistic missiles, cruise missiles, and other means).
- *International Commitments and Policy:* Unlike some nuclear powers, India has not signed the NPT, which allows it to maintain autonomy in developing its nuclear programme. However, it declares its intention to use nuclear weapons solely for national defence purposes.
- *Strategic Initiatives:* In recent years, India has intensified efforts to develop its strategic forces, including the creation of submarines

equipped with nuclear missiles, enhancing its capabilities for nuclear deterrence.

- *Regional Context:* Amid tensions with Pakistan and China, India continues to develop its nuclear strategy aimed at maintaining a balance of power and preventing potential conflicts.

Overall, India's modern nuclear policy is characterised by pragmatism, a focus on national security, and the preservation of strategic autonomy. At the same time, it adheres to policies minimising the risk of nuclear escalation and emphasises responsibility in the use of nuclear weapons.

Thus, India follows a policy of 'no first use' of nuclear weapons and strives to establish a reliable deterrence system that promotes stability and security in the region.

Cooperation between Kazakhstan and India in the Field of Nuclear Energy

India's key long-term strategic interests in Central Asia include access to energy resources, expanding India's economic influence, and deepening regional integration.

During the visit of Kazakhstan's first President N. Nazarbayev to India in 2009, an Agreement was signed with the Indian side on joint work in the field of nuclear energy. Thus, Kazakhstan became the fourth country to sign such an agreement with India, which signified close mutual cooperation between the two countries. Currently, there are four bilateral agreements on mutual cooperation in the field of nuclear energy between India and other countries: with the USA, France, and Russia.

According to Kazakhstani diplomats, uranium supplies are important for both sides and became possible after the announcement on September 6, 2009, of the end of India's nuclear apartheid, which lasted for 30 years. However, the nuclear cooperation between the two countries is not limited to uranium supplies. Joint research in nuclear fuel production and the construction of nuclear power plants are also possible.

India's main objectives in the region were outlined in the 2012 Indian policy document: 'Connect Central Asia.' In recent years, India's efforts to participate in the region have become increasingly relevant amid the growing economic influence of China in the area. Among India's key interests are the following:

India aims to gain access to supplies of uranium, natural gas, oil, and coal from Central Asia as part of its national energy security strategy· The goal of

India's energy security policy is to reduce its excessive dependence on crude oil from the unstable Persian Gulf region by diversifying its sources of crude oil through new procurement from Africa, the USA, and other sources. In this context, India considers access to Central Asian natural gas resources an important element of its energy security strategy. Similarly, access to uranium supplies from Kazakhstan is of utmost importance for India's civilian nuclear programme.

Kazakhstan and India regularly discuss further prospects for mutually beneficial cooperation in the field of nuclear energy. For example, during a meeting in February 2025 between M. Yusupov, Chairman of Kazatomprom, and the Indian ambassador to Kazakhstan, Nagendra Prasad, various aspects of cooperation in the nuclear industry were discussed. They noted the "successful long-term partnership between Kazakhstan and India in previous years, particularly in the supply of Kazakh natural uranium for India's nuclear energy needs."

In 2023, during a meeting between the Ambassador of the Republic of Kazakhstan, Nurlan Zhalgasbayev, and the Secretary of the Department of Atomic Energy of India, Ajit Kumar Mohanty, the issues of cooperation between the two countries in the energy sector were discussed in detail. They emphasised the successful collaboration in civil nuclear energy since 2009 and agreed to continue supporting exchanges and training courses to enhance experience in joint scientific research and professional development. They also discussed prospects for the use of radioisotopes in the pharmaceutical field.

Thus, India's main strategic interest lies in gaining access to Kazakhstan's uranium deposits to support India's national nuclear energy security strategy. Kazakhstan is the world's largest producer of uranium, accounting for approximately 15 percent of global uranium extraction. However, in the short term, India's ability to achieve these goals is limited by three complicating factors: Iran's conflict with the USA, the deepening of Iran's economic relations with China, and the future role of the Taliban in Afghanistan.

Kazakhstan diplomatically supported India's efforts to obtain an exemption that allows for civil nuclear cooperation with the Nuclear Suppliers Group (even though India has not signed the Non-Proliferation Treaty) and endorses the idea of India gaining membership in the group. With the support of the Kazakhstan-India Business Council, a contract for uranium supplies from 2020 to 2024 was signed, and agreements were reached to expand cooperation in the fields of oil, gas, and renewable energy.

Thus, it can be concluded that despite differences in the approaches of Kazakhstan and India to the development of nuclear energy, both countries are committed to maintaining peace and preventing the use of nuclear weapons for military purposes.

References

1. Report of the High-level Panel on Threats, Challenges and Change:' A Safer World: Our Shared Responsibility'. – URL: http://docs.pravo.ru/document/view/26514201
2. Ibid.
3. Kazakhstan will always stand firmly on the principles of nuclear safety (Казахстанвсегдабудеттвердостоятьнапринципахядернойбезопасности). – URL: https://kazpravda.kz/n/kazahstan-vsegda-budet-tverdo-stoyat-na-printsipah-yadernoy-bezopasnosti-tokaev/
4. Universal Declaration on a Nuclear-Weapon-Free World. URL: http://tarih-begalinka.kz/ru/history/independent/history/page3584/
5. Nazarbaycv N. 'Kazakhstan's conceptual vision of strengthening global partnership for building a safe, fair and prosperous world' (Казахстанскоеконцептуальноевидениеупроченияглобальногопартнёрствадляпостроениябезопасного, справедливогоипроцветающегомира). URL: http://www.m.kazpravda.kz/news/view/104448/
6. Foreign Ministry summed up the results of Kazakhstan's chairmanship in the UN Security Council.
URL: https://bnews.kz/ru/news/mid_podvel_itogi_predsedatelstva_kazahstana_v_sb_oon
7. Address by President of the Republic of Kazakhstan N. Nazarbayev at a meeting of the UN Security Council.' Non-proliferation of WMD: confidence-building measures'. URL: http://www.mfa.kz/ru/kabul/content-view/vystuplenie-prezidenta-respubliki-kazahstan-nursultana-nazarbaeva-na-zasedanii-soveta-bezopasnosti-oon.
8. Kazakhstan is ready to accept a dialogue on nuclear disarmament (Казахстанготовпринятьдиалогпоядерномуразоружению). URL: https://ria.ru/20250923/kazahstan-2043861003.html
9. Paskhalny P.I. 'India's Nuclear Policy at the Present Stage'. (ЯдернаяполитикаИндиинасовременномэтапе). URL: https://nvo.ng.ru/concepts/ 2018-06-01/1_998_india.html
10. India's nuclear program. URL: https://dzen.ru/a/Z3jBPLVB1DUQ-qI4
11. Rajesh Basroor. 'On India's Nuclear Doctrine.' URL: https://www.perspektivy.info/book/k_voprosu_o_jadernoj_doktrine_indii_2007-01-01.htm
12. India's nuclear program. URL: https://dzen.ru/a/Z3jBPLVB1DUQ-qI4
13. Ibid.
14. Shikin V. 'Narendra Modi's Nuclear Triumph and the Nonproliferation Regime's "Half-Life".' (ЯдерныйтриумфНарендрыМодии «полураспад» режиманераспространения). URL: https://russiancouncil.ru/analytics-and-comments/analytics/yadernyy-triumf-narendry-modi-i-poluraspad-rezhima-neraspros/
15. India's nuclear program. URL: https://dzen.ru/a/Z3jBPLVB1DUQ-qI4
16. Shikin V. 'Narendra Modi's Nuclear Triumph. URL:https://russiancouncil.ru/en/analytics-and-comments/analytics/narendra-modi-s-nuclear-triumph-and-the-semi-decay-of-the-no/
17. India's nuclear policy at the present stage. URL: https://nvo.ng.ru/concepts/2018-06-01/1_998_india.html
18. India's military nuclear program. URL: https://pircenter.org/2022/08/08/voennaja-jadernaja-programma-indii/
19. Pikaev A.A. 'International Nuclear Non-Proliferation Regime' (Международный режимнераспространенияядерногооружия). URL: https://www.perspektivy.info/print.php?ID=36218

20. Averin A. 'India's Nuclear Arsenal: A Medium-Range Strategic Triad'. (Ядерныйарсенал Индии: стратегическаятриадасреднейдальности). URL: https://amalantra.ru/yadernyy-arsenal-indii/
21. On signing the Agreement between the Government of the Republic of Kazakhstan and the Government of the Republic of India on cooperation in the peaceful use of atomic energy. Resolution of the Government of the Republic of Kazakhstan dated April 6, 2011 (О подписании Соглашения между Правительством Республики Казахстан и Правительством Республики Индия о сотрудничестве в области мирного использования атомной энергии). URL: https://adilet.zan.kz/rus/docs/P1100000381
22. Nuclear cooperation between Kazakhstan and India (ЯдерноесотрудничествоКазахстана и Индии). URL: https://www.inform.kz/ru/yadernoe-sotrudnichestvo-kazahstana-i-indii_a225109
23. India's Interests in Central Asia (ИнтересыИндии в ЦентральнойАзии). URL:http://berlek-nkp.com/tadzhikistan/9569-interesy-indii-v-centralnoy-azii.html
24. Kazakhstan and India explore opportunities for mutually beneficial cooperation in the field of nuclear energy (Казахстан и Индияизучаютвозможностивзаимовыгодногосотрудничества в областиатомнойэнергетики). URL: trend.az.
25. Индия и Казахстан укрепляют отношения в сфере атомной энергетики. URL: https://optimism.kz/2023/09/16/indiya-i-kazahstan-ukreplyayut-otnosheniya-v-sfere-atomnoj-energetiki/
26. Интересы Индии в Центральной Азии. URL: http://berlek-nkp.com/tadzhikistan/9569-interesy-indii-v-centralnoy-azii.html

16

Opportunities for Cooperation between India and Kazakhstan in Combating International Terrorism

Prof. Kuralay Baizakova

Introduction

Currently, the issue of religious radicalisation is becoming increasingly urgent in many countries around the world, as more and more terrorist organisations involve youth in their influence sphere and attract them to their activities, turning them into the foundation of their social base.

The growth of societal and socio-political radicalisation is a common feature of the current period. The global community faces this problem everywhere. Additionally, recent events in the Middle East have significantly altered the ideology and forms of radical extremism and terrorism worldwide. They have evolved and modernised. The intensification of activities by various extremist and terrorist groups in the Middle East, Afghanistan, and Pakistan creates a new threat to Kazakhstan's security system.

In the context of globalisation, terrorism has become the most dangerous phenomenon. Therefore, it is critically important to develop theories and practices, methods and methodologies for countering it, as well as socio-political and cultural-ideological measures for prevention, overcoming, and eradication of terrorism in Kazakhstan and among its partners, such as India.

Considering the current trend of increasing transnational and domestic radicalism, extremism, and terrorism, combating these phenomena – including

India–Kazakhstan Partnership in a Changing Geopolitical Order their ideologies and organisational structures – has become a top political priority for governments worldwide. *The section has been prepared as part of scientific project AR26100515 'Risk management strategies and strengthening Kazakhstan's foreign policy in the context of geopolitical challenges and regional instability'.*

Features of Countering Terrorism in the Republic of Kazakhstan

In this context, the issue of identifying the dimensions of this phenomenon that can explain the mechanisms of youth radicalisation and contribute to the adoption of adequate and effective measures by the state and society for de-radicalisation becomes relevant for the Republic of Kazakhstan. President of the Republic of Kazakhstan Kassym-Jomart Tokayev, characterising extremism and terrorism as an attack on peace and stability in the country, noted: "The main goal is to prevent the propaganda of extremist ideas and the recruitment of youth into terrorist organisations". In this regard, it is important for Kazakhstan to create conditions that foster immunity against the propaganda of religious extremist organisations.

Among the various threats in Central Asia, threats of terrorism and religious extremism, which are systemic in nature, have become particularly relevant in the light of the January 2022 events in Kazakhstan. The threats of extremism and terrorism, as well as the main areas of cooperation between the Republic of Kazakhstan and international organisations in combating them, have been analysed by Kazakhstani experts: E. Karin, M.T. Laumulin, B.K. Sultanov, K.I. Baizakova, F.T. Kukeva, Zh. Baizakova, A. Chebotarevand others.

One of the serious works dedicated to the history of the infiltration of extremist groups, 'Soldiers of the Caliphate' into Kazakhstan is E. Karina's book, which presents an interesting study highlighting the role of youth in major terrorist organisations·

Thus, a review of scientific literature showed that, despite the fact that the phenomenon of terrorism and extremism is constantly evolving in modern conditions, acquiring new forms and methods, there is a lack of specialised research in the scientific literature that comprehensively examines new trends in the theory and practice of combating religious extremism and terrorism, as well as studies on the causes of youth radicalisation in Kazakhstan.

It should be noted that the overwhelming majority of researchers study the definition of 'terrorism,' and accordingly, extremism and radicalism are considered as varieties of terrorism. According to legal experts, the definition of terrorism in international acts as the most radical manifestation of extremism indicates an emerging trend in international law to develop measures against extremism through the lens of counter-terrorism. The general concept of extremism is defined in the Shanghai Convention on Combating Terrorism, Separatism, and Extremism of June 15, 2001.

There are two models of modern terrorism and extremism: the 'Western' and the 'Eastern.' The 'Western' model of terrorism and radicalism is characteristic of the Euro-Atlantic civilisation. The 'Eastern' model of terrorism and extremism, which pertains to the extensive Asian-North African region, has both intra-civilisational and inter-civilisational features. It represents a confrontation of terrorists against individual states, entire regional countries, as well as leading world powers (the USA, Russia).

The identification of the spiritual and ideological foundations of the 'Eastern,' primarily Islamic, terrorism and extremism become particularly relevant because, at the beginning of the 21st century, political Islam is viewed as bearing primary responsibility for the spread of terrorism and political extremism worldwide. The 'Eastern' model of terrorism is rooted more in religious than in ideological or political motives.

Modern Islamic radicalism is gaining strength by cultivating the image of the main enemy as foreign states, which, by promoting their foreign policy interests in the region of Islamic proliferation, undermine, from the radicals' perspective, traditional values.

Islamic terrorism/extremism is carried out under religious slogans and presents itself as a continuation of the Islamic religious doctrine, which, in essence, does not correspond to reality. It is based on distortion and significant misrepresentation of Islamic teachings. There is a fundamental difference between the genuine spiritual potential of true Islam and the ideological content of Eastern extremism, which differs from it. Without understanding this difference, it is impossible to effectively combat Islamic radicalism. The issue of religious terrorism, which is primarily associated with Islam in scholarly literature, overlooks the fact that tendencies towards radicalisation exist in any religion and ideology.

Specifically, in Kazakhstan, Islamism has a Salafist-Wahhabist orientation. This branch of Islam is characterised by particular intolerance, promotes isolationism, and calls for violent actions. The nature of terrorist attacks in Kazakhstan is mainly anti-government in character, as seen in 2011 and 2016.

Analysing the factors that generate terrorism in the context of globalisation is of particular importance. It should be noted that the essence of modern terrorism cannot be explained solely based on factors from past eras.

The analysis of the causes of radicalisation among youth in Kazakhstan and Central Asian countries reveals the presence of a number of internal and external factors contributing to radicalisation. Internal factors primarily determine the dynamics of radicalisation within these countries and include social and economic stability, the level of education among young people, their involvement in social processes, and timely policy measures.

One of the increasingly significant factors is the growing trend of politicisation of Islam. The political aspect can also explain youth radicalisation through disillusionment and the inability to meet basic needs, such as obtaining education and employment opportunities, political instability, and other related issues.

In recent decades, there has been a trend of increasing interaction between organised criminal groups and Islamist radical organisations. In Kazakhstan, the intertwining of criminality and radical extremist groups is partly due to prison radicalisation.

Geopolitical trends are key factors influencing the development of radicalism and terrorism in Central Asia. Existing geopolitical contradictions across the vast Eurasian continent directly or indirectly impact the processes of youth radicalisation.

Analysis of external factors allows us to conclude that:

Firstly, certain threats to the national security of the Republic of Kazakhstan in the medium and long term are associated with the growth of religiosity among the younger generation and a shift towards radical or extremist interpretations of faith.

Secondly, the public threat is posed by citizens who participated in 'hot spots' on the side of illegal armed formations, as well as their family members, who have been subjected to propaganda and ideological manipulation.

Thus, the main causes of the emergence of the threat of religious extremism are the results of various factors of psychological, economic, political, religious, and sociological nature. The reasons for youth radicalisation in Kazakhstan and Central Asian countries are complex.

An analysis of manifestations of religious extremism in the territory of the Republic of Kazakhstan shows the need for religious enlightenment and education among the population. It is necessary to clearly distinguish between 'religiosity' and radical or violent extremist ideologies and to raise awareness among the general public about this distinction. Strengthening cooperation between government agencies and civil society organisations in countering religious extremism and terrorism is essential. The Spiritual Administration of Muslims of Kazakhstan should conduct extensive explanatory work among believers by promoting traditional Islam in Kazakhstan. Educational institutions, youth, the public and scientific organisations, and NGOs should play a significant role in the prevention of this phenomenon. More active measures should be taken to prevent radicalisation within penitentiary institutions.

The accumulated experience of Kazakhstan in preventing various conflicts can be useful for other countries in developing concepts of humanitarian and informational security. Another positive example from Kazakhstan is the measures taken to rehabilitate individuals convicted of radical extremism.

Kazakhstan's legislation in the field of counter-terrorism and extremism is regularly updated and amended, with changes and additions being made. It can be said that Kazakhstan's legislation in the fight against terrorism is the most advanced among Central Asian countries. The country focuses on preventing radicalisation, especially among youth. Various social and youth programmes, as well as economic projects, are in place. Additionally, NGOs work in the areas of rehabilitation and reintegration of convicted individuals for terrorism and extremism, including their relatives. The main laws of the Republic of Kazakhstan concerning counter-terrorism and extremism are the laws 'On Counteracting Extremism' dated February 18, 2005, and 'On Counteracting Terrorism' dated July 13, 1999. Kazakhstan has ratified 15 out of 19 UN resolutions and other documents related to the fight against terrorism.

In the State Programme for Counteracting Religious Extremism and Terrorism in the Republic of Kazakhstan, among the objectives are such measures as improving the prevention of religious extremism and terrorism; reducing the influence of external factors on the radicalisation of the population; increasing the effectiveness of identifying and preventing cases of religious extremism and terrorism; and enhancing the system for responding to acts of religious extremism and terrorism, as well as minimising and (or) eliminating their consequences.

Kazakhstan's security policy has incorporated the most successful examples from other countries in the fight against terrorism and extremist activities. The main goal of Kazakhstan's domestic policy has been and remains the strengthening of inter-ethnic and inter-religious harmony, as well as the prevention of social, religious, and other conflicts. The implementation of such a policy should continue to foster a tolerant environment in the fields of inter-ethnic, inter-cultural, and inter-faith relations, promote a culture of inter-cultural communication, and contribute to the prevention of manifestations of political or religious extremism within the country, region, and globally.

Since the activities of extremist and other destructive organisations in Central Asia are predominantly transboundary in nature and involve active participation from international extremist groups, it is essential to prioritise cooperation within multilateral mechanisms to address issues related to international terrorism and religious extremism. For example, within the system of the Committee of the Penal System of the Ministry of Internal Affairs of Kazakhstan (CPS), a Theological Rehabilitation Service was established within the educational units. Today, KUIS, in cooperation with the UN Office on Drugs and Crime (UNODC), is implementing a three-year plan to prevent terrorism and extremism, as well as to rehabilitate prisoners during incarceration and after their release.

It is also worth noting that during its chairmanship of the UN Security Council, Kazakhstan paid special attention to mechanisms ensuring humanitarian cooperation at the global and regional levels. In January 2018, at the UN platform, Kazakhstan held a high-level special event to launch the Code of Conduct project aimed at achieving a terrorism-free peace. The main goal of this document is to attain a terrorism-free peace by 2045 and to build a broad international coalition of partner countries.

To ensure security and promote military-political cooperation, deepen humanitarian engagement, and enhance the level of coordination within the global community in the face of threats posed by radicalism and extremism, one of Kazakhstan's areas of cooperation with the UN as a whole and UNESCO in particular in the field of humanitarian security could be the implementation of measures to counter extremism through systematic efforts as part of comprehensive initiatives to prevent terrorism, curb the spread of extremist ideas, and organise effective counter-propaganda.

Kazakhstan's experience of cooperation with other international organisations demonstrates the need to establish comprehensive contacts – not only military-political but also humanitarian – to prevent the spread of radicalism. The country's collaboration with international organisations can contribute to the development of effective mechanisms for the comprehensive protection of national security.

The cooperation of the Republic of Kazakhstan with other states demonstrates the need to establish comprehensive contacts, not only military-political but also humanitarian, in order to prevent the spread of radicalism. Unlike European countries, Kazakhstan adopts a more holistic approach – in addition to prohibitions, threats of imprisonment, and other coercive measures, regional states have also proposed alternative options: amnesty, as well as the possibility of reintegration into normal life after a rehabilitation period, including the safe return of children and widows of militants to their homeland, as implemented through the 'Jusan' operation conducted by the Kazakh security agencies.

Successful strategies for Kazakhstan also include: engaging with the global community, adhering to international conventions and human rights standards; controlling migration flows within the country; preventing the infiltration of extremist preachers; deepening regional integration processes by involving partner countries in joint measures to prevent and combat religious extremism;, and involving youth in extremist organisations, as well as strengthening the authority of local spiritual leaders.

Features of Combating International Terrorism in India

Since gaining independence from Britain in 1947, India has faced several internal threats. The increasing radicalisation of a small but significant segment of the Muslim community in the country has become one of the most serious security challenges for India.

India has played a significant role in strengthening the international consensus on combating terrorism within the United Nations, the Non-Aligned Movement, and the South Asian Association for Regional Cooperation. India has signed key international conventions against terrorism and incorporated them into its domestic legislation: Researchers have repeatcdly noted that "India has also played a major role in creating consensus on terrorism within the Non-Aligned Movement. The Non-Aligned Movement has unequivocally stated that criminal acts aimed at sowing fear among the population, groups, or individual citizens, regardless of the reasons, are unjustifiable". Furthermore, there is an ongoing call in India to adopt and implement the comprehensive convention on international terrorism.

The nature of jihadist terrorism in India has undergone significant changes over the past two decades. Initially supported by Pakistan and limited to specific areas of Indian Kashmir, it has now become more dispersed without a defined territory. In recent years, targets of terrorist attacks have included cities such as Mumbai, Bengaluru, Hyderabad, and New Delhi. This makes resolving the issue and prosecuting jihadist terrorists much more complex than before.

Indian Prime Minister Narendra Modi, during a joint session of the US Congress Security Council, emphasized: "Our country faced the horrors of terrorism long before the world took serious notice of it. For decades, terrorism in various names and forms has tried to harm India. We have lost thousands of precious lives, but we have fought terrorism bravely".

One government initiative after another, India has worked to formulate an adequate response to this challenge, which adds to the burden on India's security system, particularly its police and intelligence agencies. The Indian government leadership has always maintained an uncompromising stance against any manifestations of terrorism. For example, Foreign Minister S. Jaishankar in Bhopal stated in his speech: "Regardless of where and for what reason terrorism occurs, and in whatever form it manifests, it is against humanity. In such circumstances, we will always have to be extremely strict regarding terrorism".

Policing efforts to combat terrorism in India are fraught with numerous difficulties. The legal framework inherited from the colonial past struggles to meet the demands placed upon it. The Indian Ministry of Home Affairs oversees the national police, local intelligence agencies, and paramilitary formations. The main legal instrument regulating the fight against terrorism is the Prevention of Unlawful Activities Act. Some Indian states, such as Maharashtra and Karnataka, use their own laws to file charges against suspected terrorists. The Terrorist and Subversive Activities (Prevention) Act (TADA), the first anti-terrorism law designed to define and combat terrorist activities, was enacted in 1995. When allegations of misuse of this new anti-terrorism law emerged in 2004, it was decided to repeal it. Subsequently, several similar laws were enacted.

After 9/11, the USA established the Department of Homeland Security. In India, the need to create a separate Ministry of Home Affairs had been felt for a long time, but proposals for its creation were repeatedly postponed. The police are the first responders in the event of a terrorist attack. They also form the backbone of Indian intelligence agencies, investigative bodies, and anti-corruption agencies. To ensure the safety of ordinary citizens and to combat the threats faced by the country, India required reformed and restructured police forces.

Over time and with technological advancements, the operational methods of terrorists have evolved. Two critically important aspects require special attention. Firstly, Jammu and Kashmir predominantly faces terrorism directed or influenced by Pakistani security agencies, either directly or indirectly, through anti-Indian terrorist organisations such as Lashkar-e-Taiba, Jaish-e-Mohammed, and Indian Mujahideen. The terrorists' firepower has also significantly increased, partly due to the increased influx of resources from abroad.

Secondly, jihadist terrorism in India is on the verge of gaining a global projection, as radicalisation and recruitment have become more sophisticated thanks to social media and the Internet. According to an expert, this signifies a complete departure from the past when jihadist terrorism was almost synonymous with the conflict in Kashmir.

After the sudden attack by Pakistan in Kargil in 1999, the Indian government carried out a comprehensive review and reform of the Indian intelligence apparatus in particular, and the national security system as a whole. The main distinguishing feature of the new mechanism was the creation of the National Security Council (NSC) chaired by the Prime Minister and comprising a small number of cabinet members who discuss issues of national security.

The nature of jihadist terrorism in India is changing as methods of radicalisation and recruitment become more sophisticated. There are concerns that India could become a soft target for global jihadist plans by al-Qaeda, which not only incites violence through sleeper cells but also attracts educated young Muslims via the Internet to expand its terrorist activities, leveraging local issues.

An Indian expert points to two mechanisms of counter-terrorism activity: counter-terrorism within the framework of criminal law, which deals with acts of terrorism as part of law enforcement, and military counter-terrorism, which considers terrorism a threat to national security that should be countered with military force. In its counter-terrorism efforts, India relies on a combination of these two approaches.

Due to the size of India and its heterogeneous nature, the Indian Constitution includes the distribution of power between the central government and the state governments; maintaining law and order is the responsibility of the states. However, experts believe that the federal nature of the state structure complicates the mechanisms necessary to combat terrorism. Considering these issues, India's performance in police efforts against terrorism has been mixed.

Despite constitutional provisions, the central government has organised seven Central Armed Police Forces (CAPF), which are regularly deployed to perform law enforcement tasks alongside the police forces of the respective states. The most important of these seven are the Central Reserve Police Force (CRPF), which carries out a wide range of tasks, including maintaining law and order, combating insurgents, and fighting terrorism across India. Structures designed to secure borders play a crucial role in operations against insurgents and terrorism in three critical conflict zones: the Northeast, Maoist-affected areas, and Kashmir. The R&AW (Research and Analysis Wing) is considered a key counter-terrorism agency and works closely with the federal police and central armed police forces on counter-terrorism intelligence matters.

Considering the complexity of Indian national security architecture, experts believe that improving coordination between various federal and state agencies involved in security is crucial. After the Mumbai terrorist attacks, the first step in this direction was strengthening the existing Inter-Agency Centre (IAC), a 'data-sharing' hub for intelligence exchange established by R&AW in 2002 following the Kargil conflict of 1999. The National IAC coordinates among two dozen representatives from different intelligence agencies within the ministries of Home Affairs, Finance, and Defence.

The incapacity of the police was revealed by the Mumbai attacks in 2008 and the attack on the Pathankot air base in 2016, exposing critical vulnerabilities in India's counter-terrorism defensce. These incidents reflect not only the high level of sophistication among some jihadist planners but also demonstrate that India's police system is lamentably inadequate to handle suicide bombings and terrorist assaults.

Ajai Sahni, Executive Director of the Institute for Conflict Management, stated that Indians "cannot have first-class counter-terrorism in a third-class police system." Pravir Swami, one of India's leading journalists with extensive knowledge of terrorism, confirmed Sahni's words, noting that "policing is the frontline of counter-terrorism; India's frontline has fallen apart".

The attack on the Pathankot airbase in January 2016, which revealed critical vulnerabilities in India's defence against terrorism, is the latest example of the ongoing weaknesses in India's decision-making process regarding national security, border permeability, limited law enforcement capabilities, and the influence of political considerations. Similarly, the terrorist assault on the headquarters of the Indian Army's Rashtriya Rifles in the border town of Uri in Jammu and Kashmir in September 2016 once again highlighted the threat

India faces from cross-border terrorism. The attack, which resulted in the deaths of 19 Indian soldiers, was one of the most significant psychological and strategic blows to Indian security forces in Jammu and Kashmir.

The Indian state of Punjab experienced two terrorist attacks within six months, the first in Dinanagar, Gurdaspur district, in July 2015, followed by the Pathankot attack in January 2016. In addition to the threats posed by Pakistan-based jihadist groups, there are numerous young Indian Muslims believed to be fighting for ISIS in Iraq and Syria.

The investigation into the March 2017 explosion on the Bhopal-Ujjain passenger train, which was declared the first major operation by ISIS in India, provided intelligence agencies with new grounds to identify sympathisers of this global extremist organisation and to track down Indian Muslims who fought in Iraq and Syria.

Prime Minister Narendra Modi has repeatedly spoken from the podiums of multilateral forums condemning terrorism in all its forms. For example, at the 9th G20 Parliamentary Speakers' Summit in New Delhi in 2023, he stated: "We condemn terrorism in all its forms and manifestations, including acts based on xenophobia, racism, or intolerance, as well as those committed in the name of religion or faith. This recognition applies to all religions that promote peace, emphasising that terrorism is one of the most serious threats to international peace and security."

One of the latest dramatic terrorist attacks in India occurred on April 22, 2025, when armed individuals carried out an attack in the popular tourist city of Pahalgam (in the Union Territory of Jammu and Kashmir). The assailants, dressed in khaki, opened fire with automatic weapons. Twenty-six civilians were killed, and many others were injured. The attackers managed to escape. Responsibility for the bloody attack was claimed by a group calling itself 'Kashmir Resistance,' which, according to Indian authorities, is also known as the 'Resistance Front' and is linked to the Lashkar-e-Taiba (LeT) – an organisation recognised as terrorist by the UN. New Delhi accused Islamabad of supporting the massacre, while Pakistan denied any involvement. Indian intelligence agencies found evidence of the Pakistani Inter-Services Intelligence (ISI)'s involvement in the attack carried out by LeT militants in Pahalgam. The crisis triggered by this attack soon escalated into a major military conflict between the two arch-rivals, both possessing nuclear weapons.

The Indian Ministry of Defence announced the launch of 'Operation Sindoor,' during which strikes were carried out against nine targets of 'terrorist infrastructure' in Pakistan. The operation was a 'surgical' response by India to the April attack in Pahalgam.

Prime Minister Modi stated that the Indian Air Force, Army, Navy, Border Security Force, security services, and paramilitary formations are constantly on high alert. "After the surgical strike and airstrike, Operation Sindoor has become India's policy against terrorism. The operation set a new standard in our fight against terrorism, a new benchmark and a new norm," he emphasised. Narendra Modi also declared that "India will not differentiate between the government sponsoring terrorism and the instigators of terrorism. First, if India is subjected to a terrorist attack, a worthy response will be given. We will respond appropriately only on our terms. We will act decisively wherever the roots of terrorism take hold. Second, India will not tolerate any nuclear blackmail. India will deliver a precise and decisive strike against terrorist hideouts operating under the cover of nuclear blackmail."

India has also suspended the long-standing Indus Waters Treaty, and Pakistan announced that it has nearly completely cut off water flow across the border via the Chenab River, which is crucial for irrigating agricultural lands, according to Bloomberg. Tensions between India and Pakistan are centred around the Kashmir border region – territory in the Himalayas claimed by both countries, with parts administered by each. New Delhi believes that the Pakistani military supports terrorist groups that carry out attacks within India.

India's response to terrorism generally differs by adhering to an ad-hoc principle ('here and now'), which often leads to the creation of new agencies, meta-institutional innovations, and excessive centralisation, as well as the illusion of power created by technological acquisitions and the abdication of states from their responsibilities for law enforcement. Political influence often further complicates the problem. State authorities are too preoccupied with their own survival in power, hindering their ability to consider long-term issues. The internal security system is fragmented and poorly coordinated, as numerous investigative and law enforcement agencies operate at both the central and state levels. State police have their own counter-terrorism and intelligence units, which are often small and work in isolation.

One of the main shortcomings of the Indian institutional approach to counter-terrorism is the significant divide between how the central government and the state governments view counter-terrorism efforts. As Indian experts have noted, "To combat the rapidly evolving threat of jihadist terrorism, India needs a comprehensive and innovative approach based on a framework of long-term strategic planning and coordination of capabilities for intelligence activities, physical security, investigations, and crisis management".

Cooperation between Kazakhstan and India in the Fight against International Terrorism

The cooperation between Kazakhstan and India takes place both bilaterally and within multilateral forums such as the Shanghai Cooperation Organisation (SCO) and the CICA.

The issue of terrorism is regularly discussed at meetings of the India-Kazakhstan Working Group on Counter-terrorism. For example, at the fifth meeting of this group in Astana on April 8, 2024, both sides assessed "the challenges of combating terrorism, including the use of new technologies by terrorists, the misuse of the Internet for terrorist purposes, radicalisation, and the financing of terrorism. During the negotiations, both parties emphasised the importance of strengthening cooperation in the fight against terrorism through information exchange, exploring new opportunities, educational programmes, and collaboration within multilateral forums such as the UN, Eurasian Group on Combating Money Laundering and Financing of Terrorism and SCO.

In 2023, an Indian Army and Indian Air Force contingent, including 120 personnel, participated for the first time in Kazakhstan in the seventh military exercise 'KAZIND-2023,' held in Otara. The main objective of this exercise was for both sides to practice counter-terrorism operations. As part of the exercise, contingents jointly carried out various tactical tasks, including raids, search-and-destroy operations, insertion and extraction of small teams. In the light of modern challenges, the scope of the exercise also included operations to counter unmanned aerial systems.

The Department of Revenue (DoR), in collaboration with the Ministry of External Affairs (MEA) and the National Security Council Secretariat (NSCS), successfully organised the first-ever Capacity Building Programme for the Central Asian Republics (CAR) on the topic of 'Countering Terrorist Financing (CTF) through Cryptocurrency, Crowd funding, and Non-Governmental Organisations'. The two-day programme took place on April 21-22, 2025. The programme, which involved leading experts from five Central Asian countries – Uzbekistan, Turkmenistan, Kazakhstan, Tajikistan, and Kyrgyzstan – served as a platform for knowledge exchange and regional cooperation in the fight against terrorist financing.

Designed to address the specific needs of the Central Asian region, the programme aimed to strengthen technical capabilities and deepen understanding of emerging terrorist financing risks, contributing to the development of a joint approach to key challenges. As noted by experts, this initiative marks a significant step forward in enhancing regional cooperation and counter-terrorism efforts, reflecting India's commitment to global efforts in combating terrorism.

An important mechanism for regional cooperation and security in the fight against international terrorism, separatism, and extremism for Kazakhstan and India remains the SCO. Cooperation in combating terrorism and extremism is a key area of activity for the SCO and even a system-forming element of this international organisation. SCO member-states have concluded a number of agreements aimed at enhancing the effectiveness of cooperation against terrorism and extremism. In its strategy until 2025, the SCO has prioritised the fight against the activities of international terrorist organisations aimed at recruiting citizens of member-states, including cooperation with international and regional structures to identify and block channels of movement for potential extremists and terrorists.

The activities of the SCO Regional Anti-Terrorist Structure (RATS), which collaborates with law enforcement agencies of Belarus, Afghanistan, Mongolia, and others, serve as one of the successful examples of utilising the possibilities of geopolitical pluralism in the region. The SCO security strategy for developing joint measures to counter terrorism and extremism is more focused on solving informational, analytical, and coordination tasks. In the near future, it would be advisable for the SCO to address practical issues related to Afghan settlement.

According to the Deputy Chairman of the SCO, Sabyr Imandosov, in a world where terrorism has become a transnational evil without nationality, active participation by major players such as India in combating this issue will positively impact the overall work of the SCO in this direction. "I am confident that India's and Pakistan's extensive experience in fighting terrorism will enhance the effectiveness of our joint efforts. Terrorism has long become a transnational evil that does not have a specific country or national affiliation", emphasised the SCO Deputy Secretary-General.

During the 2024 SCO Astana Summit, in a message from Indian Prime Minister Narendra Modi, it was stated that the fight against terrorism should be a priority for the Shanghai Cooperation Organisation: "International terrorism requires a decisive response, and we must resolutely oppose the financing of terrorism and its recruitment. We should also take active steps to prevent the spread of radicalisation among our youth".

The fight against terrorism in all its forms and manifestations is also one of the tasks of the CSTO. The CSTO's initiatives against terrorism and religious extremism should also include cooperation between law enforcement agencies; strengthening efforts to combat poverty.

Conclusion

Among the areas of international cooperation, increasingly involving other countries, are the conduct of joint operational activities; the exchange of technologies and experience in the production and application of technical and combat means to counter radical elements; the development of legal norms regulating the possibility of using assistance from other states for anti-terrorist operations; and the definition of the role and place of mass media in shaping global public opinion regarding intolerance towards radical extremism and terrorism, as well as providing balanced coverage of related issues.

Further stabilisation of the socio-economic situation in Central and South Asian countries, and consequently the victory in the fight against radical extremism and terrorism, is unthinkable without improving the quality of life of their populations, ensuring employment, and providing a decent standard of living.

When formulating medium-term measures to prevent threats to regional security posed by radical extremism, it is advisable to primarily focus on identifying and eliminating the causes and conditions that foster the growth of radical sentiments. All leverage for preventive impact on the actual situation should be employed: political, social, economic, legal, educational, informational, propaganda, and others.

At the same time, researchers believe that there are significant short-comings and omissions in the development of a comprehensive policy to counter extremism and terrorism. Another weakness is the narrow focus of efforts to prevent radicalisation and violent extremism, which primarily centres on increasing control over religious ideology and materials.

In modern conditions, there is a pressing need to consolidate efforts with geopolitical partners to counter manifestations of motivated violence, inter-ethnic discord, and the increasing involvement of young people in informal youth groups of extremist orientation. Changes in the geopolitical status quo could fundamentally exacerbate contradictions among superpowers and regional leaders, potentially leading to the outbreak of hybrid wars in the region – either directly or indirectly – through the strengthening of the combat capabilities of various extremist and terrorist organisations and movements.

Therefore, based on the above, we conclude that the main directions for countering terrorism at the present stage are:

- Establishing an international legal framework as a crucial condition for implementing coordinated and effective anti-terrorist actions;
- Creating international anti-terrorist centres to combat extremism;
- Intensifying efforts to prevent citizens from joining militant groups;
- Opening new expert platforms for the implementation of advanced criminal and procedural standards within the anti-terrorist justice systems of countries with high terrorist activity;
- Continuing joint efforts to enhance mutual trust, consolidate political will, and overcome bureaucratic and technical barriers that hinder effective international cooperation among judges and prosecutors in investigating terrorist crimes;
- Suppressing manifestations of extremism in the information sphere: counter-propaganda against Islamism, blocking internet resources used for recruitment;
- Improving the socio-economic situation in countries and regions that are primary sources of armed conflicts.

Recognising the global danger of terrorism requires a revision, first and foremost, of the existing paradigm for ensuring international security and strategic stability, as well as uniting the efforts of all countries in the face of this new real threat.

References

1. Tokayev called on the international community to move to a comprehensive strategy for the eradication of terrorism (Токаевпризвалмеждународноесообществоперейтиквсеобъемлющейстратегиииискоренениятерроризма). URL: https://www.kt.kz/rus/politics/1153636779.html
2. Karin E. 'Terrorism in Kazakhstan: from virtual to real?' (Терроризм в Казахстане: от виртуального к реальному?) URL: https://www.kursiv.kz/dopolnitelnye-razdely/tendencii-weekly/
3. Laumulin M. *The Geopolitics of XXI Century in Central Asia*, Almaty: KazISS, 2007, p. 281.
4. Sultanov B. 'Current security issues in Central Asia (Актуальныепроблемыобеспечениябезопасностив ЦентральнойАзии) // *Central Asia: the state and prospects of regional interaction*. Almaty: KISI, 2008, pp. 52–64.
5. Baizakova, K.I., Kukeyeva, F.T. et al. Crispes et crisparation internationals a l'ere du terrorisme au XXI siecle. Bruxelles, 2011. p. 480; Baizakova, K.I. Les conséquencesgéo politiques du printemps Arabe pour les pays de l'Asie Centrale // *Politiques et cooperation dans l'espace euro-mediterraneen*. Banska Bystrica: l'Harmattan, 2014, pp. 155–165.

6. Baizakova, K.I. 'Economic cooperation as a form of prevention of the fight against terrorism and extremism (Экономическоесотрудничествокакформапрофилактикиборьбыстерро ризмомиэкстремизмом) // BRI in the context of regional security. Almaty, 2017. pp. 106–116; Challenges and threats of religious extremism and terrorism in Central Asia: factors and methods of struggle (Вызовыиугрозырелигиозногоэкстремизмаитерроризмав ЦентральнойАзии: факторыиметодыборьбы) // Reasons for the spread of the ideas of terrorism and religious extremism among the youth of the CA countries. Almaty, 2017. pp. 10–20.
7. Kukeyeva, F.T. 'Democracy as a strategy of anti-terrorism'. (Демократиякакстратегияан титерроризма). URL: https: //articlekz.com/article/11779; Kukeyeva, F.T. 'The threat of extremism and terrorism to the stability of the political regimes of the countries of Central Asia' (УгрозаэкстремизмаитерроризмадлястабильностиполитическихрежимовстранЦентр альнойАзии) // *BRI and topical issues of security and cooperation in Central Asia*. Almaty, 2016, pp. 33–42.
8. BaizakovaZh. 'New Antiterrorist Legislation: Following The Reality' // *Asya-Avrupa journal*. 2016. № 9-10 (September-October), pp.20–28; BaizakovaZh. & Terpstra N. 'Central Asian Security Challenges: Religious Extremism and Uncertainty in the Afghan Borderlands. URL: https://securing-europe.wp.hum.uu.nl/central-asian-security-challenges
9. Chebotarev A. 'Extremism in Kazakhstan: current state and counter-measures (ЭкстремизмвКазахстане: современноесостояниеивопросыпротиводействия). URL: http://www.ca-portal.ru/article:27203
10. Karin, E.T. '*Soldiers of the Caliphate: Myths and Reality* (СолдатыХалифата: Мифыиреальность). Almaty, 2014, p. 173.
11. Shanghai Convention against Terrorism, Separatism and Extremism of June 15, 2001- URL: https://online.zakon.kz/document/?doc_id=1027029.
12. Beisembaev S. 'Religious extremism in Kazakhstan: between crime and jihad (РелигиозныйэкстремизмвКазахстане: междукриминаломиджихадом). URL: http://www.ofstrategy.kz/index.php/ru/research/socialresearch/item/485-religioznyj-ekstremizm-v-kazakhstane-mezhdu-kriminalom-i-dzhikhadom
13. Approval of the State Programme on Countering Religious Extremism and Terrorism in the Republic of Kazakhstan for 2018-2022 (ОбутвержденииГосударственнойпрограм мыпопротиводействиюрелигиозномуэкстремизмуитерроризмувРеспубликеКазахста нна 2018–2022 годы). URL: http://knb.gov.kz/ru/article/ob-utverzdenii-gosudarstvennoi-programmy-po-protivodeistviu-religioznomu-ekstremizmu-i
14. Results of Kazakhstan's chairmanship in the UN Security Council: success of the initiatives of the Head of State on a regional and global scale (Итогипредседательства Казахстанав СоветеБезопасностиООН: успехинициатив Главыгосударстваврегиональномигло бальноммасштабе). - URL: http://mfa.gov.kz/ru/roma/content-view/itogi-predsedatelstva-kazahstana-v-sovete-bezopasnosti-oon.
15. Yakovlev A.Yu. 'Indian experience in countering terrorism'. (Индийскийопытпротиводействиятерроризму). – URL: https://cyberleninka.ru/article/n/indiyskiy-opyt-protivodeystviya-terrorizmu/viewer
16. 'Terrorism is the enemy of humanity': India's stance remains consistent and ambiguous'. («Терроризм - врагчеловечества»: позицияИндииостаетсяпоследовательнойинеод нозначной). – URL: https://www.indianewsnetwork.com/ru/20231101/terrorism-is-an-enemy-of-humanity-india-s-stand-has-been-consistent-unambiguous
17. Ibid.
18. Vinay Kaura. 'India's Anti-Jihadist Terror Policy: Challenges and Prospects.' // *Connections: The Quarterly Journal, Connections QJ* 16, № 4 (2017): 57–76. URL: https://doi.org/10.11610/Connections.rus.16.4.03
19. Ibid.

20. Ibid.
21. Praveen Swami 'A Decade After 9/11, Indian Jihad Still Thrives.' *The Hindu*, September 9, 2011. URL: https://www.thehindu.com/opinion/lead/a-decade-after-911-indian-jihad-still-thrives/article2439813.ece
22. Punya Priya Mitra. 'ISIS Module Behind Blast in Bhopal-Ujjain Passenger Train in Madhya Pradesh, Police Say.' URL: https://www.hindustantimes.com/india-news/isis-module-behind-blast-in-bhopal-ujjain-passenger-train-in-madhya-pradesh-police-sa
23. How the Kashmir conflict is affecting Indian and Pakistani politics (КакконфликтвКашмиревлияетнаполитикуИндииПакистана). URL: https://www.dw.com/ru/kak-konflikt-v-kasmire-vliaet-na-politiku-indii-i-pakistana/a-72531506
24. India intends to continue the fight against terrorism until its eradication. (ВИндиинамереныпродолжитьборьбустерроризмомдоегоискоренения). URL: https://tass.ru/mezhdunarodnaya-panorama/23835867
25. India strikes nine 'terrorist camps' in Pakistan (Индиянанеслаударподевяти «лагерямтеррористов» вПакистане). URL: https://www.forbes.ru/society/536810-india-nanesla-udar-po-devati-lageram-terroristov-v-pakistane
26. 'Narendra Modi: Operation "Sindoor" is India's policy against terrorism and a new standard.' URL: https://kaktus.media/doc/523730_narendra_modi:_operaciia_sindyr_eto_politika_indii_protiv_terrorizma_i_novyy_standart.html
27. Ibid.
28. India and Kazakhstan discuss challenges in the field of combating terrorism in the region, consider issues of strengthening cooperation. (Индияи Казахстанобсуждаютвызовы вобластиборьбыстерроризмомврегионе, рассматриваютвопросыукреплениясотрудничества). URL: https://www.indianewsnetwork.com/ru/20240409/india-kazakhstan-discuss-counter-terrorism-challenges-in-the-region-look-at-closer-cooperation
29. Ibid.
30. India for the first time adopts Capacity Building Program to Combat Terrorist Financing for Central Asian Republics. (Индиявпервыепринимает Программупонаращиванию потенциалапоборьбесфинансированиемтерроризмадляреспубликЦентральнойАзии). URL: https://eurasiangroup.org/ru/india-hosts-inaugural-capacity-building-programme-for-central-asian-republics-on-combating-terrorism-financing
31. Ibid.
32. Opinion: India and Pakistan's experience will help the SCO in the fight against terrorism. (Мнение: опытИндииПакистанапоможетШОСвборьбестерроризмом). URL: https://www.ritmeurasia.ru/news--2017-11-02--mnenie-opyt-indii-i-pakistana-pomozhet-shos-v-borbe-s-terrorizmom-33278
33. Indian Prime Minister called the fight against terrorism a priority of the SCO. URL: https://internationalaffairsreview.com/ru/2024/07/04/

SECTION V

Civilisational Linkages, Societal Interfaces and Future Outlook

17

Tracing Civilisational Ties between India-Kazakhstan and Future Prospects

Yashvi Bhat

"The farther backward you can look, the farther forward you are likely to see."

– Winston Churchill

Historical continuities, rather than geographical adjacency, have shaped the trajectory of Indo-Kazakh relations.

When we look at the modern diplomatic maps connecting New Delhi to Astana, we are not looking at a new architecture, but into a civilisational history. The re-emergence of Kazakhstan in India's foreign policy since the end of the Cold War is often described as a strategic pivot, but this description of the two Asian nations is not exhaustive. India and Kazakhstan share a history spanning more than 2,000 years, going beyond the geopolitical ripples of 1991 and the fallout of the Soviet collapse. Underneath the post-Cold War developments, lies a deeper pulse and shared rhythmic beat that has connected the Indian subcontinent to the Eurasian heartland for thousands of years. To study this relationship today, one has to wipe away the dust of the last century to find a reflection that has been staring back at us since antiquity.

We have to recognise that today's strategic partnership is the modern flowering of a seed planted in a shared past. India's geography has long positioned it as both a maritime and terrestrial gateway of the Global South. Historically, it functioned as a subcontinental core: its river-fed plains sustained powerful, sedentary polities whose capacity for absorption and continuity contrasted sharply with the mobility of the Eurasian steppe. While Central Asia enabled movement, India often functioned as a destination – drawing merchants, monks, and conquerors into a civilisational space capable of integrating external influences without rupture. Within this broader Eurasian ecology, the territory of present-day Kazakhstan occupied a pivotal position. Located in the eastern steppe zone, it once formed one of the world's most vital arteries of transcontinental interaction. Long before the emergence of fixed borders, Kazakhstan functioned as a grand corridor of movement, marked by the heavy tread of trade caravans, the wandering paths of nomadic pastoralists, and the quiet chants of monks moving alongside the busy workshops of artisans. Kazakhstan's position at the heart of the steppe made it the ultimate intermediary, where cultures met and at times were irrevocably transformed by their friction with one another. In this context, the Steppe appears not as a barrier, but as a connective tissue. It was a living geography of circulation and synthesis. While the mountains and seas often isolated other regions, the open horizon of the steppe forced an outward-looking perspective. It produced societies that were comfortable with plurality and adept at negotiating difference. This is where the interaction of the Indian subcontinent with Central Asia becomes pivotal. India-Kazakhstan ties can be better understood as an alliance built on exchange rather than conquest, and on the steady, quiet rhythm of continuity rather than the sudden shock of rupture.

I. The Genetic and Spiritual Bedrock of Eurasian Connectivity

In the second millennium BCE, the Kazakh region was a vibrant centre of gravity. It was here that the late Bronze Age 'Andronovo complex' flourished, characterised by a sophisticated network of mobile pastoralists who were masters of advanced metallurgy, chariot-making, and horse domestication. They created a shared ecological and cultural bridge that stretched from the heart of Central Asia towards the Iranian plateau and the north-western reaches of the Indian subcontinent. The archaeological record acts as a reflection of this ancient mobility. In the ruins of fortified settlements, metallurgical workshops, and burial mounds, we find physical proof of a society built for the long haul. This was a world where technological prowess allowed cultural practices and linguistic forms to diffuse across the open plains of Eurasia. Scholars today see these societies as the likely ancestors of the early Indo-Iranian-speaking populations, whose wandering paths laid the very foundations of the Asian demographic map.

The parallels between Vedic Sanskrit and Old Iranian preserved in the sacred verses of the *Rig Veda* and the *Avesta,* respectively, reveal shared ideas of culture and society. This encompasses a common vocabulary of the soul: ideas of cosmology, the sanctity of ritual sacrifice, and the structures of divine hierarchy. These were not the result of sudden, violent shocks of migration, but rather a slow process of '*cultural osmosis*'. They point to a sustained interaction where ideas were polished like stones in a river, gradually differentiating only after centuries of shared Eurasian life. The Kazakh ideal of '*Beybitshilik*' – a peace defined by balance and coexistence in a mobile world – finds its perfect counterpart in the Indic notion of '*Śānti*', or the pursuit of cosmic and inner harmony. Though they speak in different tongues, both concepts are rooted in the same civilisational wisdom; in a world defined by movement and plurality, peace is not a static border, but a constant negotiation. They are parallel aspirations born from societies that valued the open path over the rigid fence, and interdependence over isolation.

II. Sakas, Kushans, and the Political Flow of the Steppe

Between the ancient Bronze Age foundations and the later spiritual blossoming of the Buddhist era, there exists a pivotal, transitional period – the era of the Saka and Kushan invasion and settlement in the Indian subcontinent beginning from the first century BCE. The Sakas were nomadic tribes who originated from the Central Asian region, including areas that today are in Kazakhstan, Uzbekistan, and their neighbouring countries. Their interaction with Indian society led to cultural syncretism across polity, art, religion, language, and social structure.

The Sakas brought strong Central Asian influences into India, enriching its cultural diversity. They introduced the satrap administrative system, promoted cavalry warfare, and contributed to feudal tendencies. Their patronage helped develop Gandhara art with Greco-Roman features in Buddhist imagery. They encouraged religious coexistence and were great patrons of Buddhism. The Sakas, apart from leaving Central Asian blueprints on the Indian subcontinent, were gradually absorbed into the Indian social order. Through control of trade routes, bilingual coinage, and steppe-style motifs, they strengthened India's links with Central Asia and enhanced economic and cultural exchange. By the 4th century CE, their impact waned, making way for the Kushanas.

The Kushanas emerged from the Yuezhi confederation in Central Asia. They forged a colossal polity that linked the Oxus basin to the Gangetic plains. In the reflection of rulers like Kanishka, we see a state that functioned as the world's first truly globalised hub. The Kushans curated connectivity, standardised coinage across vast distances, and patronised a breathtaking array of faiths – from Buddhism to Zoroastrianism. The true genius of the Kushan moment was its 'political ecology.' Rather than enforcing a rigid homogeneity, the Kushans governed through movement. They secured the caravan routes, fortified the mountain passes, and breathed life into urban centres that functioned as massive organs of exchange. In this mirror, the steppe is no longer a void to be crossed; it is a vital organ of participation.

III. Buddhism as a Civilisational Bridge

The exchange of religious thoughts and intellectual rigour represents perhaps the most resilient part in the long history of India's engagement with Central Asia. Among these multifaceted processes, the northward flow of Buddhism along the arteries of the Silk Route stands as a transformative civilisational bridge. This was far more than the simple migration of a faith; it was the birth of a transregional moral and intellectual ecumene. In this spiritual reflection, we see the Indian subcontinent reaching out to the Kazakh area, China, and the horizons beyond, creating a community of shared values that transcended the barriers of language and geography.

From the height of the Kushan era, a steady stream of Buddhist monks from India, with meticulous translators, scholars and pilgrims, ventured northwards from the Gangetic heartland. They carried with them a precious cargo of palm-leaf scriptures, sophisticated philosophical debates, and intricate ritual practices. These gruelling journeys were made possible by the established trade routes, where merchant patronage funded the construction of monastic sanctuaries. These monasteries, emerging like beacons along the dust-choked caravan corridors, served a dual purpose: they were both sacred retreats and bustling centres of hospitality and translation. They provided sanctuary to travellers, preserved the collective memory of the faith in vast libraries, and functioned as vital nodes in an ever-expanding web of cultural connectivity.

The detailed chronicles of the seventh-century Chinese pilgrim, Xuanzang, offer an intimate reflection of this Buddhist world. Xuanzang meticulously recorded the existence of flourishing monastic communities across Central Asia, specifically pinpointing the Zhetysu (Seven Rivers) region of modern-day Kazakhstan. His accounts describe local Turkic rulers who actively patronised Buddhist institutions. The physical reflection of this era is etched into the very stones of the Kazakh landscape. At sites such as Tamgaly-Tas, the rock-face carvings and inscriptions offer a silent, stony testimony to centuries of Buddhist devotion. While many of these icons were carved or renewed in later periods, their spiritual DNA is undeniably Indian. The iconography, featuring the serene faces of Bodhisattvas and the rhythmic flow of Sanskrit mantras, represents artistic traditions that travelled thousands of miles from the Indian heartland. The shadow of Gandhara is visible here; the sculptural forms and iconographic conventions reveal a stylistic mirror where the aesthetics of the Indian plains were beautifully localised and adapted to the rugged environment of the region.

Ultimately, the spread of Buddhism through Central Asia provides a unique civilisational context; it illustrates an influence built not on the sword, but on the sutra. It was a conquest of the mind, achieved through ethical persuasion and the profound appeal of intellectual inquiry. This was an early, potent form of cultural diplomacy that bound distant societies together through a shared moral vocabulary. Even today, Buddhism remains one of the most durable and evocative historical linkages between the people of India and the vast territories that now form the Republic of Kazakhstan.

IV. Otrar, Taraz, and the Commerce of Trust

If the spread of Buddhism provided the spiritual nervous system of Eurasia, then commerce provided its lifeblood. As Indian ideas travelled northward, commercial exchange followed in a parallel, rhythmic flow. The Silk Route was a sophisticated and dense labyrinth of land and riverine corridors that functioned as the world's first global economy. Within this vast network, the urban citadels of Otrar and Taraz, standing in the heart of modern-day Kazakhstan, rose as great centres of economic and cultural interaction, reflecting the wealth and ingenuity of the Indian subcontinent back into the Eurasian interior.

Otrar, perched strategically at the confluence where the wild grassland meets the fertile oasis of the Syr Darya, was a reflection of the 'Citadel-Market' ideal. From antiquity deep into the medieval era, it was a massive commercial engine. Modern archaeological excavations offer a clear reflection of this prosperity and uncover an expansive urban infrastructure of fortified walls, bustling marketplaces, and the skeletal remains of great caravanserais. These stones tell a story of sustained engagement with the markets of India. Remnants found in the soil suggest that high-value textiles, rare medicinal substances, and precious stones from the Indian heartland were not just passing through Otrar, but were the very currency of its cosmopolitan life.

In the city of Taraz in Kazakhstan, we see an even older reflection. Being one of the most ancient continuously inhabited cities in Kazakhstan, Taraz sat at the crossroads where the foothills of the Tian Shan mountains gaze towards the broader Eurasian horizons. To read classical and medieval chronicles is to see a city that was a vivid, multicultural kaleidoscope. It was a place where merchants from the Indian plains bartered alongside traders from Persia and China. The city's wealth was built on its genius for mediation; it acted as a 'civilisational translator' between the settled farmers of the south and the mobile pastoralist tribes of the north, proving that the Kazakh heartland was the essential gear in the machine of Eurasian prosperity.

Yet, beyond the physical exchange of gold and silk, there existed a more profound reflection – the 'Commerce of Trust'. In an age without international banks or digital contracts, long-distance trade was an act of faith, requiring reliable systems of credit, mutual norms of conduct, and reputational networks that ignored political borders. Indian merchant guilds operating in Central Asia did not rely on the swords of kings, but on the strength of their diasporic ties and ethical codes. This was a world where a man's word, rooted in kinship and religious identity, was his bond. These practices enabled centuries of commercial harmony, reinforcing the idea that the bond between India and Kazakhstan was built on the most durable material of all: mutual dependence and social credibility. Through these great hubs, India and Central Asia were bound in a tapestry of exchange that integrated the material with the moral, and the merchant with the monk, creating a legacy of trust that still defines our modern partnership.

V. The Persianate Bridge and Medieval Synthesis

As we move into the medieval era, we encounter perhaps the most sophisticated intertwining of language and law – the consolidation of the Persianate cultural sphere. This was the time when Persian became far more than a regional tongue; it evolved into the primary language of administration, historiography, and high culture across the vastness of Eurasia. In this reflection, we see a world that was politically fragmented into various Sultanates and Khanates, yet remained intellectually and culturally seamless. Persian functioned as the 'connective grammar' that allowed a scholar in the Kazakh steppe to correspond effortlessly with a courtier in the Indian heartland. This was marked by the Central Asian dynasties – the Samanids, Karakhanids, and Timurids acting as the patrons of this refined world. As Turkic migrations swept across the steppe, introducing new warrior elites, these leaders did not seek to impose a nomadic isolation. Instead, they adopted the Persian language for their governance and its literature for their cultural prestige. This created a shared civilisational framework, a blueprint of 'refinement' that linked the cities of Central Asia directly with the burgeoning courts of northern India.

The Persian influence was carried south into the Indian subcontinent by Turkic-origin polities. We see Central Asian influences embedding themselves within Indian institutions, shaping the soaring arches of architecture, the meticulous records of historiography, and the rhythmic protocols of court life. It was a process of creative adaptation. Urdu, a new language, evolved from the intermixing of Sanskrit, Hindavi, Arabic and Persian. Thus, even as political borders shifted, the intellectual heartbeat of the two regions remained synchronised.

VI. Mughal Memory and Central Asian Consciousness

The establishment of the Mughal Empire in India preceded the stage of slowdown of relations. Although Mughal authority would eventually become synonymous with the Indian soil itself, its founders lived with a gaze that was perpetually fixed towards the northern horizon. This 'Central Asian Consciousness' was not a fleeting nostalgia; it was the very cornerstone of their identity. In Babur's memoirs (*Baburnama*), we find a deep reflection of this bond. Even amidst the heat of the Indian plains, Babur's prose repeatedly evokes the crisp air of his homeland. The Mughal courts patronised historians from Central Asia. For the Mughal rulers, the Central Asian region was the 'Ancestral Reference Point'. Every meticulously laid out garden, every marble dome, and every courtly ritual was a reflection of aesthetic traditions born in the Central Asian and Persianate world and local Indian traditions amalgamated into one.

Even during periods when direct political contact with the Kazakh steppe grew quiet, the region remained symbolically present in the Indian imagination. Central Asia was never forgotten in India. This persistence proves that civilisational ties are not just about trade or treaties, but about people-to-people ties and the travelling of ideas and cultures.

VII. The Colonial Interruption

The beginning of Company rule in India, followed by British colonialism between the eighteenth and nineteenth centuries, marked a rupture in the Eurasian story. As British colonial power solidified its grip on India and the Russian Empire expanded across the Central Asian plains, the historically porous corridors of culture were replaced by the jagged edges of rigid political frontiers. The strategic rivalry, or 'Great Game', in Central Asia effectively converted the Eurasian heartland into a sterile buffer zone. This geopolitical manoeuvring blocked trade, severed traditional land routes that had been India's lifeline for millennia, and marginalised patterns of interaction that had flourished for ages.

VIII. The New Eurasian Order: India's Independence and Post-Cold War Era

India attained independence from British rule in 1947. The first PM of India, Pt. Jawaharlal Nehru, and his daughter, Indira Gandhi, visited Almaty in 1955. As the Vice President of India, Dr. S. Radhakrishnan visited Kazakhstan in 1956. India became one of the first countries to recognise the independence of Kazakhstan in 1992. Since then, many Indian heads of government and diplomats have visited Kazakhstan and received their counterparts too. The current Indian PM, Hon'ble Narendra Modi, visited Kazakhstan in 2017.

IX. Contemporary Perspectives in India-Kazakhstan Ties

With historical ties dating back 2,000 years, the two Asian nations have stood the test of time. The path ahead lies in mutual cooperation and exploring contemporary areas of partnership. India is the fastest-growing economy in the world and Kazakhstan is its largest trading partner in Central Asia. As the world stands at the crossroads of turbulence and turmoil amidst growing trade wars, the two Asian nations have the opportunity to engage in dialogue, people-to-people ties, and expand economic cooperation. The India-Kazakhstan Inter-Governmental Commission (IGC) was established in 1993 as an apex bilateral institutional mechanism to foster trade, economic, scientific, technological, and cultural cooperation between the two countries. As of July 2024, bilateral trade stands at US$1 billion, with Indian exports amounting to US$580.6 million and Kazakhstan exporting US$449.2 million to India. Kazakhstan, with its rich mineral resources like uranium and India's growing need for the same to fuel its nuclear power generation plants and defence requirements, offers the perfect synergy for trade in important minerals. To promote trade and economic interest, the Federation of Indian Chambers of Commerce & Industry (FICCI) and the Chamber of International Commerce of Kazakhstan have set up a Joint Business Council (JBC).

Drawing on their cultural ties, the two countries have constantly engaged in cross-cultural activities through the Swami Vivekananda Cultural Centre in Astana, ICCR scholarships to students from Kazakhstan, and specialised capacity-building ITEC training to Kazakh citizens since 1992. In 2024,

Kazakhstan celebrated International Yoga Day to celebrate the culture of a healthy life and mind that Indian civilisation has gifted to the world. The two sides have actively engaged in defence and security dialogues and joint military exercises.

Summing up, in tracing the civilisational ties between India and Kazakhstan, the time is now to build on historic linkages and to usher in a new era marked by greater cooperation, collaboration, people-to-people ties, and economic flourishing.

References

1. Alam, M. (2004). *The languages of political Islam in India.* Permanent Black.
2. Anthony, D. W. (2007). *The horse, the wheel, and language.* Princeton University Press.
3. Babur (1922). *Baburnama* (A. Beveridge, Trans.). Luzac.
4. Beckwith, C.I. (2009). *Empires of the Silk Road.* Princeton University Press.
5. Cribb, J. (1993). 'The early Kushan kings.' *Numismatic Chronicle*, 153, 1–35.
6. Dale, S.F. (2004). *The garden of the eight paradises.* Brill.
7. Eaton, R.M. (2019). *India in the Persianate age, 1000–1765.* University of California Press.
8. Hansen, V. (2012). *The Silk Road: A new history.* Oxford University Press.
9. Hopkirk, P. (1990). *The Great Game: On secret service in High Asia.* Oxford University Press.
10. Liu, X. (2010). *The Silk Road in world history.* Oxford University Press.
11. Mukherjee, B.N. (1988). *The Kushanas.* Firma KLM.
12. Narasimhan, V.M., et al. (2019). The formation of human populations in South and Central Asia. *Science*, 365(6457), 748–753.
13. Parpola, A. (2015). *The roots of Hinduism.* Oxford University Press.
14. Reich, D. (2018). *Who we are and how we got here.* Pantheon.
15. Roy, O. (2000). *The new Central Asia.* NYU Press.
16. Sen, T. (2003). *Buddhism, diplomacy, and trade.* University of Hawai'i Press.
17. UNESCO. (1992–1996). *History of civilizations of Central Asia* (Vols. I–III). UNESCO.
18. UNESCO. (2014). *Buddhist routes of Central Asia.* UNESCO.
19. Xuanzang. (1996). *The Great Tang records on the Western Regions* (L. Rongxi, Trans.).

18

Kazakhstan-India Cooperation in the Fields of Education, Culture and Tourism

Dr. Laura Nurdavletova

The Agreement between the Government of the Republic of Kazakhstan and the Government of the Republic of India on Cooperation in the Fields of Culture, Arts, Education, Science, Mass Media, and Sports, signed in 1992, laid the legal foundation for bilateral cooperation in these areas.

Based on this Agreement, a cultural exchange programme was developed, including the signing of a memorandum on organising cultural days in both countries. A significant milestone was the celebration held in India to commemorate the 150th anniversaries of Abai Kunanbaiuly and Zhambyl Zhabayev, as well as the 100th anniversary of Mukhtar Auezov. Collections of their literary works were published in Hindi. Equally noteworthy were the commemorative events held in Kazakhstan to mark the 125th anniversary of Mahatma Gandhi, including the issuance of a special postage stamp.

In 2005-2006, Days of Kazakh Culture in India and Days of Indian Culture in Kazakhstan were successfully held, reflecting mutual interest in cultural engagement and soft diplomacy.

A pivotal moment in bilateral relations was the signing of the document titled 'India-Kazakhstan: Perspectives on Strategic Partnership' in 2009. This document served as an important step in strengthening the bilateral agenda and outlined cooperation in various spheres, including tourism, education, and the preservation of cultural heritage.

Both countries actively promote cultural exchanges, joint projects, and the organisation of festivals and exhibitions aimed at fostering deeper mutual understanding between their peoples. These initiatives also emphasise the preservation of cultural heritage and the support of creative endeavours.

Kazakhstan and India are committed to expanding educational cooperation, particularly through student and faculty exchanges, and the development of joint academic programmes, which play a crucial role in building closer ties among the younger generations of both nations.

Tourism is viewed by both parties as a vital component of cultural exchange. Consequently, Kazakhstan and India are working collaboratively to improve tourism infrastructure and to promote each other as attractive tourist destinations.

The strategic document further underscores the importance of strengthening political and economic cooperation, including mutual investments, trade relations, and collaboration within international organisations.

In summary, this foundational agreement has laid the groundwork for the continued deepening of bilateral cooperation, and both nations remain committed to advancing their partnership across cultural, educational, economic, and political domains. Bilateral agreements between India and Kazakhstan in the field of Education include several bilateral agreements that have been signed between the Republic of India and the Republic of Kazakhstan to enhance cooperation in the field of education. One of the cornerstone documents is the Agreement between the Government of the Republic of Kazakhstan and the Government of the Republic of India on Cooperation in the Fields of Culture, Arts, Education, Science, Mass Media, and Sports, signed on February 22, 1992, in New Delhi.

This agreement provides for:

- Promotion of mutual cultural exchanges;
- Facilitation of cooperation and support for the development of relationships between educational, scientific, cultural, sports, and research institutions of both countries; Admission of citizens from either country to pursue studies, conduct research, and undertake professional training at educational, cultural, scientific, and technical institutions of the other country.

In addition to this foundational agreement, further educational ties were established through the signing of a Memorandum of Understanding (MoU) in 2002 between L.N. Gumilyov Eurasian National University and Jawaharlal

Nehru University, followed in 2005 by an MoU between the Faculty of International Relations of Al-Farabi Kazakh National University and research centres at Jawaharlal Nehru University. These documents significantly contribute to strengthening educational relations by creating opportunities for student and faculty exchanges, as well as for joint academic and research initiatives.

Kazakhstan and India have been progressively developing bilateral cooperation in science, technology, education, and culture. The Embassy of India in Kazakhstan plays an active role in this process by organizing and participating in numerous events across a wide spectrum of public and academic life. The embassy functions as a dynamic and reliable bridge between the two nations.

A key initiative in this regard is the establishment of the Indian Cultural Centre (ICC) under the auspices of the Indian Embassy in Almaty. Since its inception in 1995, the ICC has aimed to foster cultural ties and mutual understanding between the peoples of India and Kazakhstan.

The Centre organises a wide array of cultural activities, including visits by Indian scholars, symposia, exhibitions, book launches, and musical instrument presentations for various public institutions. In addition, the ICC implements a scholarship programme for talented Kazakhstani youth, enabling them to pursue higher education in Indian universities and other educational institutions.

Recent Developments in Kazakhstan-India Cooperation: Education, Tourism, and Cultural Exchange

During the Shanghai Cooperation Organisation (SCO) Summit held on July 5, 2024, a bilateral meeting took place between Murata Nurtleu, Minister of Foreign Affairs of the Republic of Kazakhstan, and Subrahmanyam Jaishankar, Minister of External Affairs of the Republic of India. This meeting reaffirmed the commitment of both nations to strengthening their strategic partnership.

Kairat Torebayev, Vice Minister of Trade and Integration of Kazakhstan, emphasised that educational cooperation constitutes an integral component of the strategic relationship between Kazakhstan and India. He noted that over 600 Indian students are currently enrolled at Astana Medical University, with more than 5,000 Indian students studying across various institutions in Kazakhstan – making them the largest group of international students in the country.

Kazakhstan's Minister of Tourism, Mulubhai Hardasbhai Bera, highlighted the growing trade and tourism ties between India and Kazakhstan. The introduction of a visa-free regime for up to two weeks marks a significant step towards enhancing people-to-people exchanges and boosting tourism flows, which can in turn stimulate economic growth. Cooperation within international frameworks such as the United Nations (UN), SCO, and the Conference on Interaction and Confidence Building Measures in Asia (CICA) further reinforces bilateral relations. The 'India-Central Asia' dialogue platform also holds the potential to unlock new opportunities for multidimensional development.

Tourism and cultural exchange play a pivotal role in fostering mutual understanding between the peoples of both nations. Strategic cooperation between Kazakhstan and India in these areas continues to expand, yielding tangible benefits. Several ongoing initiatives illustrate this progress and point to even greater potential for the future.

Since 2005, the Kazakhstan-India Tourism Fair has been held annually, serving as a crucial platform for professional engagement between tour operators and for the promotion of cultural and historical heritage. This fair not only facilitates business partnerships but also strengthens interpersonal ties by raising awareness of each country's unique offerings. The growing interest in each other's tourist destinations underscores the deepening connection between the two societies.

Direct flights operated by Air Astana between Almaty and New Delhi represent a significant advancement in promoting tourism and business relations. Notably, Almaty is geographically closer to New Delhi than many cities in southern India, which enhances the convenience of travel and exchange. There are expectations that flight frequencies and routes will expand in the near future, further enhancing regional connectivity.

Cultural exchange programmes – such as Kazakhstan Cultural Days in India – hold substantial value. These events not only showcase the rich cultural heritage of Kazakhstan but also captivate diverse audiences, contributing to a deeper level of mutual understanding and appreciation between the two nations.

Cultural and Academic Exchange as Pillars of Kazakhstan-India Bilateral Relations

Performances by Kazakhstani artists and exhibitions of unique artifacts serve as powerful tools for fostering mutual understanding and enriching intercultural dialogue. These events provide audiences with new perspectives and facilitate meaningful connections between peoples.

The forthcoming Days of Indian Culture in Kazakhstan, featuring a reciprocal programme, are expected to become a major cultural milestone. This event will allow Indian performers and artists to showcase their traditions and heritage, serving as a valuable continuation of ongoing cultural exchange efforts that will undoubtedly strengthen the bonds between the two nations.

A notable contributor to the advancement of cultural ties is Kazakh violinist Marat Bisengaliev, founder of the Symphony Orchestra of India. His work has become a symbol of Kazakhstan-India cultural cooperation, with the orchestra acting as a bridge between the artistic communities of both countries. Joint tours featuring musicians from Kazakhstan and India further consolidate bilateral cultural relations. The upcoming concert in Mumbai, scheduled for February, will represent another significant milestone in this ongoing collaboration.

The film industry is also experiencing a renewed phase of development. Kazakh cinema, supported by the state and equipped with modern infrastructure through the Kazakh film studio, is attracting increasing interest from Indian producers. This burgeoning partnership is poised to open new avenues for joint film projects and broader cultural initiatives. Given its unique cinematic tradition, diverse history, and picturesque landscapes, Kazakhstan presents itself as a compelling partner for India. Co-produced films have the potential to play an influential role in deepening bilateral relations and enhancing soft power.

In the coming years, cooperation between Kazakhstan and India in these domains is expected to intensify. Tourism, culture, and cinema represent not only avenues for experience sharing, but also powerful instruments for fostering mutual understanding and promoting economic and cultural collaboration. The creation of new joint initiatives, along with the expansion of existing ones, will undoubtedly lead to more robust and productive people-to-people relations.

Academic collaboration and cultural-humanitarian cooperation are also essential vectors for deepening bilateral relations and enhancing mutual understanding. Scientific and educational partnerships contribute not only to the development of the humanities, but also support economic and technological advancement in both countries.

Regular seminars, conferences, and roundtable discussions involving Kazakh and Indian policy experts and think tanks represent an excellent mechanism for the exchange of knowledge and expert perspectives, further reinforcing the strategic dimension of bilateral engagement.

Scientific, Educational, and Tourism Cooperation between Kazakhstan and India

The discussion of pressing issues in bilateral cooperation contributes significantly to deepening understanding of the political, economic, and social contexts in both countries. Such dialogue also serves as a platform for developing strategies and policy recommendations that can inform and enhance intergovernmental relations.

Scientific collaboration is a crucial element in strengthening bilateral ties, as it facilitates the exchange of advanced knowledge and promotes joint research projects in key areas such as ecology, information technology, healthcare, and other strategic sectors.

Education represents a vital dimension of cultural and humanitarian cooperation. The establishment of the Centre for Kazakh Language and Kazakhstan Studies at Jamia Millia Islamia University in 2008 marked an important milestone in advancing educational and cultural ties between the two nations. The Centre not only supports the teaching of Kazakh language to Indian students, but also enhances their understanding of Kazakh culture, history, and traditions.

Such educational initiatives foster long-term connections between the youths of both countries and create a framework for academic exchanges, collaborative programmes, and research opportunities across various fields.

Kazakhstan and India hold significant potential for future cooperation in the areas of tourism, culture, and education. With their rich cultural heritage and strong traditions, both countries offer numerous opportunities for productive partnerships in these domains. A key instrument in this regard is the Agreement on Cooperation in the Field of Tourism, signed between the two governments on June 3, 2002, in Almaty.

Under this agreement, both parties committed to fostering conditions conducive to long-term tourism cooperation, including:

Facilitating procedures for citizens travelling for tourism purposes; cooperation between authorised bodies, namely, the Agency of the Republic of Kazakhstan for Tourism and Sports and the Ministry of Tourism of the

Republic of India; the possibility of making amendments and additions to the agreement by mutual consent of both parties.

This agreement entered into force on the date of signing and has been aimed at enhancing bilateral relations in the tourism sector. It underscores the shared commitment of Kazakhstan and India to promote mutual travel, cultural understanding, and economic growth through increased people-to-people interaction.

Tourism, Culture, and Education as Strategic Pillars of Kazakhstan-India Bilateral Cooperation

The development of tourism can serve as a vital element in strengthening bilateral relations between Kazakhstan and India. Considering the historical ties, especially those associated with ancient trade routes such as the Silk Road, there is substantial potential to enhance mutual tourist flows. Kazakhstan – with its unique natural landscapes, historic monuments, and rich cultural traditions – can attract increasing numbers of Indian tourists. Conversely, India remains a popular destination for Kazakhstani travellers, offering a wide variety of cultural and historical attractions, as well as affordable resort options.

Key Directions for Tourism Cooperation

- Enhancement of transport connectivity, including the development of direct flights between the two countries;
- Introduction of joint tourism packages, incorporating visits to historical and cultural landmarks in both nations;
- Implementation of tourist exchange programmes, particularly targeting students and youth, to facilitate cultural exchange and educational travel.

Kazakhstan and India each possess distinct and vibrant cultures, offering opportunities for mutual enrichment. Indian culture – especially Bollywood cinema, classical and contemporary music, and dance – already enjoys significant popularity in Kazakhstan. In return, Kazakh culture, with its unique artistic traditions, has the potential to engage and captivate Indian audiences.

Prospects for Cultural and Educational Cooperation

- Organisation of joint cultural events, including film, music, and dance festivals;
- Development of language learning programmes, where Kazakh and Russian may attract interest from Indian students, while Hindi and

other Indian languages could be promoted among Kazakhstani learners:

  - Recognition of the large number of Indian students currently studying in Kazakhstan, particularly in medical and technical disciplines, which opens up avenues for deeper cooperation in higher education;
- Expansion of university exchange programmes between academic institutions in both countries;
- Launch of joint research and educational projects in fields such as medicine, information technology, and engineering;
- Introduction of joint degree and certification programmes, enhancing students' employability and career prospects in both countries.

The Kazakhstan-India partnership in tourism, culture, and education holds enormous potential for future growth. Joint efforts in these spheres can lead to the emergence of new business initiatives, the exchange of expertise, and the deepening of cultural and academic ties. In turn, these developments will foster stronger bilateral relations and promote mutual understanding between the peoples of the two nations.

On February 13–14, 2023, a delegation headed by Deputy Minister of Foreign Affairs of the Republic of Kazakhstan, Kanat Tumysh, visited New Delhi to participate in the 8th round of political consultations between the ministries of Foreign Affairs of Kazakhstan and India. On the Indian side, the meeting was co-chaired by Sanjay Verma, Secretary (West) of the Ministry of External Affairs of India.

Mr. Tumysh emphasised that Kazakhstan attaches particular importance to the strengthening of comprehensive cooperation with India and views New Delhi as one of Astana's key strategic partners in Asia. In the cultural dimension, the peoples of the two countries share a long-standing history of interaction. The installation of busts of the Kazakh poet and thinker, Abai Kunanbayev, in New Delhi (June 2022) and the Indian political and social leader, Mahatma Gandhi, in Astana (October 2022) stands as a symbol of mutual respect and trust between the nations and their peoples.

The Deputy Foreign Minister of Kazakhstan congratulated the Indian side on its successful chairmanship of both the Shanghai Cooperation Organisation (SCO) and the G20, noting the high-level events held under India's leadership. Both parties agreed to intensify high-level contacts, including through participation in the SCO Summit in New Delhi in late June 2023. They positively assessed the current state and future prospects of bilateral trade and economic cooperation, expressing satisfaction with the bilateral trade turnover, which reached USD 2.5 billion by the end of 2022. The two sides concurred on the need to diversify their bilateral relations through deepened collaboration in such sectors as healthcare, pharmacology, agriculture, information technology, space, energy, and others. During the consultations, both parties exchanged views on prospects for cooperation in the areas of cybersecurity, military and military-technical collaboration, as well as counter-terrorism efforts.

The diplomats also discussed multilateral cooperation within the framework of the United Nations, the SCO, the Conference on Interaction and Confidence-Building Measures in Asia (CICA), the Eurasian Economic Union (EAEU), and the International Atomic Energy Agency (IAEA). Special attention was given to the implementation of agreements reached during the First Central Asia-India Summit (held virtually on January 27, 2022), and they expressed confidence in the successful conduct of the Fourth Meeting of Foreign Ministers within the Central Asia-India Dialogue scheduled for 2023 in New Delhi.

During his visit to New Delhi, Kanat Tumysh held a series of bilateral meetings with Indian officials, including Minister of State for External Affairs and Culture, Meenakshi Lekhi; Secretary in Ministry of Petroleum and Natural Gas, Pankaj Jain; Secretary in Ministry of External Affairs for Economic Affairs, Dammu Ravi; and Director-General of the Ministry of Foreign Affairs for Disarmament, International, and Cybersecurity Affairs, Muanpui Saiyawi.

At the conclusion of his stay in Delhi, an interactive session was held with representatives from leading Indian media outlets and expert-analytical circles. They were briefed on the main directions of Kazakh-Indian cooperation, the progress of political and economic reforms initiated by the President of Kazakhstan, Kassym-Jomart Tokayev, and the upcoming parliamentary elections scheduled for March of the current year.

On July 12, 2024, a meeting took place at the Representation of the Kazakhstan Institute for Strategic Studies under the President of the Republic of Kazakhstan in Almaty with the Consul of India in Almaty, Swapnil Kothawade.

The purpose of the visit was to engage with experts and familiarise himself with the activities of the Institute, particularly its research in the Asian region, discuss potential prospects for cooperation, as well as organise joint events and projects.

Mr. Swapnil Kothawade expressed his readiness to facilitate the establishment of contacts between research and analytical centres and experts of Kazakhstan and India, thereby promoting a deeper study of the two countries and expanding bilateral relations.

Experts at the Kazakhstan Institute for Strategic Studies underscored the importance of a closer examination of developments occurring in India, given its increasing global role and economic potential. According to forecasts by global financial conglomerates, India could rank as the third-largest economy in the world as early as 2027.

The parties exchanged information and expressed interest in participating in major expert platforms of both countries, namely, the Security and Cooperation Forum in Kazakhstan and the Raisina Dialogue in India – where global issues, geopolitics, the world economy, and regional and international challenges are discussed.

Additionally, a delegation from the Ministry of Defence of the Republic of Kazakhstan, led by the Commander of the Air Defence Forces of the Armed Forces of Kazakhstan, Major General of Aviation, Ruslan Kunurov, participated in the international aerospace exhibition 'Aero India-2025.'

Within the framework of the event, the Ministry of Defence delegation attended the official opening ceremony, familiarised themselves with the exhibits of Indian and international defence companies, and conducted bilateral negotiations with the leadership of the Indian Air Force. Furthermore, the Kazakh delegation took part in the Conference of Defence Ministers.

During the meeting with the Vice Chief of Air Staff of the Indian Air Force, Air Marshal S.P. Dharkar, the high level of cooperation between the defence ministries of Kazakhstan and India was emphasised.

Conclusion

Thus, the fields of tourism, culture, and education constitute an important component of bilateral cooperation between India and Kazakhstan. In recent years, both countries have actively developed these areas, contributing to the deepening of their mutual ties. India and Kazakhstan possess rich cultural heritage and natural resources that are attractive to tourists. An expansion of mutual tourism is anticipated, particularly in the domains of cultural and ecological tourism. Kazakhstan boasts unique natural landmarks that can attract tourists from India, while India is renowned for its history, culture, and landmarks of interest to Kazakh visitors.

Regular visits and participation in tourism exhibitions strengthen business ties between tour operators and create new opportunities to expand tourist flows.

A significant symbol of cultural cooperation has been the installation of busts of the Kazakh poet and thinker, Abai Kunanbayev, in New Delhi and of the Indian socio-political leader, Mahatma Gandhi, in Astana, underscoring cultural unity and mutual respect. Additionally, cultural festivals, exhibitions, concerts, and theatrical performances are held, fostering a deeper understanding of each country's traditions and customs.

Events aimed at preserving and promoting the cultural heritage of both countries are regularly organised, thereby strengthening humanitarian ties and advancing national cultures on the international stage.

Kazakhstan and India actively develop student and faculty exchange programmes. Indian educational institutions enjoy popularity among Kazakh students, especially in the fields of medicine, engineering, and information technology. Conversely, Indian students also have opportunities to study in Kazakhstan across various disciplines. The inclusion of Kazakh and Indian universities in joint research projects promotes the development of academic ties and the exchange of expertise across multiple fields. Both countries offer scholarships to students and researchers, opening avenues for more intensive educational exchange.

In recent years, India and Kazakhstan have made significant strides in strengthening cooperation in tourism, culture, and education. These areas not only support the development of interstate relations but also create a platform for enhanced mutual understanding between the peoples, deepening cultural bonds and academic exchange, which in turn fosters more harmonious and productive cooperation in other spheres.

References

1. Agreement between the Government of the Republic of Kazakhstan and the Government of the Republic of India on Cooperation in the Fields of Culture, Art, Education, Science, Mass Media, and Sports. New Delhi, February 22, 1992.
2. Sultanov B. 'India-Kazakhstan: Prospects for Strategic Partnership.' International Seminar, 2011.
3. Diplomatic Relations between India and Kazakhstan Mark Their 20th Anniversary. https://online.zakon.kz/Document/?doc_id=31128605&pos=4;-70#pos=4;-70
4. Heads of Foreign Ministries of Kazakhstan and India Met in Astana on the Eve of the SCO Summit, July 2, 2024. https://ru.sputnik.kz/20240702/glavy-mid-kazakhstana-i-indii-vstretilis-v-astane-nakanune-sammita-shos-45379186.html

5. Kazakhstan and India: How Strategic Partnership Is Being Strengthened, July 5, 2024. https://www.nur.kz/politics/universe/2129724-kazahstan-i-indiya-kak-proishodit-ukreplenie-strategicheskogo-partnerstva/
6. F.T. Kukejeva, & K.N. Azimkhanov. Kazakhstan and India: Prospects for Cooperation, 2016.
7. Agreement between the Government of the Republic of Kazakhstan and the Government of the Republic of India on Cooperation in the Field of Tourism. Agreement dated June 3, 2002, Almaty. Entered into force on June 3, 2002. https://adilet.zan.kz/rus/docs/P020000194_
8. Ambassador of Kazakhstan to India, Nurlan Zhalgasbayev, Delivered a Speech at the Global Business Summit in Kolkata, February 18, 2025 https://www.gov.kz/memleket/entities/mfadelhi/press/news/details/940396?lang=ru
9. Meeting with the Consul of India at the Representation of the Kazakhstan Institute for Strategic Studies in Almaty, July 12, 2024. https://kisi.kz/ru/v-predstavitelstve-kisi-v-almaty-sostoyalas-vstrecha-s-konsulom-indii/

19

Role of Civil Society and Scientific Institutions in Strengthening Indo-Kazakh Relations

Prof. Tabasum Firdous and Muhtashim Ishaq

ABSTRACT

The relations between India and Kazakhstan have largely been analysed and explored through the lens of government-to-government ties. However, a need for re-assessing these bilateral relations is pertinent in the context of how civil society organisations and largely non-government actors in general are shaping and helping bolster these ties. Along with this, some focus must also be placed on the role of scientific institutions and resultant collaborations in the process. This chapter tries to explore the civil society frameworks in both states and draws a comparative outline of the two. It further tries to bring up areas where the two can learn from and grow with each other. It also attempts to draft an outline of current as well as future prospects in bilateral civil society ties and scientific collaboration between India and Kazakhstan.

Keywords: Indo-Kazakh ties; civil society; non-governmental actors; scientific institution.

Introduction

India was one of the first countries to recognise Kazakhstan as an independent state after the Union of Soviet Socialist Republics (USSR) disintegrated in 1991. A year later, diplomatic relations began between the two countries, as India set up its embassy in the former Kazakh capital of Almaty in 1992.

Before we go into the role of civil society and scientific institutions in their bilateral ties, it is important to place Indo-Kazakh relations in a proper context. In the 21st century, bilateral relations have consistently grown and presently, Kazakhstan is India's largest trade and investment partner in all of Central Asia.

2009 marked a special year in relations, as India's Republic Day ceremony was graced by the presence of the then Kazakh President, Nursultan Nazarbayev, as the chief guest – quite a high honour for any head of state/government. In the same year, Indo-Kazakh ties were officially raised to the status of a Strategic Partnership. Then, in 2015, as PM Modi visited the Central Asian state, India gifted the prized '*Param Bilim*' computer to Kazakhstan. This was followed by the holding of the 17th SCO summit in the Kazakh capital of Astana in 2017. It was attended by PM Modi, and India was admitted as a full SCO member – another significant milestone. In 2022, the 1st India-Central Asia Summit was held virtually and it was hosted by India. This coincided with the 30th anniversary of Indo-Kazakh bilateral relations as the Kazakh President marked his presence. In 2023, PM Modi chaired the SCO Heads of State summit held in Kazakhstan, along with a bilateral meeting on the sidelines.

This is a broad outline of the inter-governmental relations between the two countries. However, the current write-up tries to explore a different aspect of bilateral ties. Here we try to understand the involvement of the non-governmental aspect of relations, along with a little focus on the niche role of scientific institutions in bilateral ties. It has been widely accepted among global scholarship that traditional institutions across both domestic and international spheres have time and again fallen short of providing "effective and legitimate responses to global issues like climate change, financial instability, pandemics..." (Marchetti, McGlinchey, 2022). As a consequence, civil society has become a necessity at both levels, bringing together various stakeholders and working towards democratic accountability. It is against this backdrop that the role of civil society and scientific institutions in helping to facilitate Indo-Kazakh relations needs exploration.

The Myriad Meanings of Civil Society

The concept of civil society in the discipline of political theory has seen a significant metamorphosis and has been explored by thinkers across all time periods, from Aristotle to Kant, to Habermas.

In classical thought, the terms 'state' and 'civil society' were considered as indistinguishable. Aristotle's concept of '*politika koinonia*' revolved around the existence of a singular citizen body that would work towards the pursuit of 'the good life.' Even in later medieval thought, for example Hobbes, such a conception continued wherein civil society was equated with the state. However, it was the Enlightenment thinkers who recorded a dramatic shift in the notion of civil society in theoretical discourses. For them, civil society formed a "defence against the unwarranted intrusion by the state on the newly realised individual rights and freedoms" (Edwards, 2004). This was organised via the medium of voluntary associations. Such a view was primarily held by thinkers like James Madison (in his *Federalist Papers*) and Alexis de Tocqueville (in his famous *Democracy in America*). Although several other interpretations of the term 'civil society' were later added on, for example, Gramsci's idea of civil society as a tool of ideological hegemony of the bourgeoisie, or the Kantian idea of civil society as the tool for cosmopolitan integration, or Habermas' idea of civil society as the device of the public sphere, it is the Neo-Tocquevillian notion of "civil society as associational life" that largely pervades modern political terminology. Thus, it is stated that it is Tocqueville's ghost that wanders through the corridors of the World Bank, not that of Habermas or Hegel (Edwards, 2004).

According to this interpretation, civil society is defined as the 'third' or 'non-profit' sector that contains all associations and networks between the family and the state in which membership and activities are voluntary. As per Michael Walzer, this is the "space of the uncoerced human association" (Walzer,1992) and includes NGOs of different kinds, political parties, religious associations, professional and business associations, self-help groups, social movements and independent media (Edwards, 2004).

Civil Society in India and Kazakhstan: A Comparative Outline

The Civil Society Arena is very vast in India, with 3.1 million registered NGOs in the country as of 2015-2016 (CBI Data). The Asian Development Bank's Civil Society Brief on India states that civil society in the country does not have one holistic definition, but is rather considered synonymous with terms like 'voluntary sector', 'NGOs (Non-Government Organisations)', 'NPOs (Non-Profit Organisations).' The Ministry of Statistics and Programme Implementation (MOSPI) uses the term 'NPIs (Non-Profit Institutions)' to describe civil society in India. The brief further elucidates that Indian laws regard civil society as the non-profit sector, based on registration categories like societies, trusts and not-for-profit companies.

Data by PRIA (Participatory Research in Asia) suggests that Civil Society Organisations (CSOs) in India have evolved to adapt with changing temporal requirements. While certain functions have remained the same, like capacity building, service delivery of basic amenities, philanthropy, advocacy for legislative changes and voicing against injustice, certain new functions have also been undertaken by India's CSOs. These include:

- Acting as think tanks to draft action plans and legislation, for example, the Right to Food Act and the Right to Information Act.
- Innovation, for example, the Karnataka Government is using the innovative models for self-help groups and watershed management developed by Mysore Resettlement and Development Agency.

Further, the nature of funding for CSOs in India is also evolving. Due to stricter regulations under the FCRA (Foreign Contributions Regulation Act) and other reasons, NGOs receiving foreign funding in India are on a decline. As of 2021, only 45.4 per cent of all registered FCRA associations were active. On the other hand, CSOs have witnessed a significant uptick in domestic funding from individual philanthropy and Corporate Social Responsibility (CSR). On the other hand, the ADB's Civil Society Brief for Kazakhstan highlights that compared to India, the country has a naturally miniscule Civil Society Arena, with 23,335 registered organisations as of April 2023. (Data from Committee for Civil Society Development (CCSD) under the Ministry of Information and Social Development, Kazakhstan). CSOs in Kazakhstan operate primarily under the 1996 Law on Public Associations as per which they are widely referred to as NCOs or Non-Commercial Organisations, and are defined as 'political parties, trade unions or other voluntary associations of citizens established on a voluntary basis to achieve common goals', like public associations, consumer cooperatives, associations of entrepreneurs, and so on.

Civil Society Organisations in India and Kazakhstan differ in two major ways. The first is funding and the second is their relationship with the government. If we look at Kazakhstan, a major shift occurred in 1990. After this date, CSO funding became almost exclusively state-sponsored funding while, as earlier, it was heavily supported by international sources. While such a funding model can lead to a steady inflow of cash, it can also erode the power of the civil society groups to hold the state apparatus accountable. As opposed to the Kazakh model, the Indian model of CSO funding is quite different. It includes diverse sources like philanthropy, CSR (corporate social responsibility), government funding, and foreign funding (now under decline). As a result of this framework, Indian CSOs enjoy relatively greater freedom and leverage.

Next, we come to the topic of relationship with the state. In India, Civil Society Organisations play a dual role. While they can cooperate with the state to aid in development processes, they also act as policy watchdogs. On the other hand, in Kazakhstan, the state is highly involved in regulating CSOs. This becomes clear when we learn that in 2015, the Kazakh Government set up the institution of the Public Council to act as a bridge between CSOs and the government. In 2022, two-thirds of the members of Kazakhstan's 274 public councils were CSO representatives.

Furthermore, Indian CSO groups highlight a strong rights-based tradition, often playing a role in major movements like right to information, education and environmental protection. Their counterparts in Kazakhstan mostly focus on areas which are aligned with government priorities, like youth and social services. Advocacy for civil liberties and human rights is relatively sparse. This might greatly be due to the backdrop against which the two civil society set-ups emerged. The Indian CSOs have a deep-rooted history in anti-colonial and pre-independence social reform causes, whereas the Kazakh CSOs are a relatively recent phenomenon, emerging only post-Soviet independence in 1991.Nevertheless, both CSO cultures can learn from each other, and grow in the following manner, strengthening Indo Kazakh relations in the process:

What can India learn from Kazakh Civil Society Organisations?

- Institutionalisation of dialogue: India has had consultative bodies like the National Advisory Council but engagement therein has been largely *adhoc*. On the other hand, Kazakhstan's Public Councils run on a different model. It includes permanent and formal structures within ministries. As a result of this, different CSOs enjoy a role in reviewing policy and legislation. As far as India is concerned, this structural revamp could aid in solving issues in governance that the Indian government has been trying to deal with through measures like allowing lateral entry in civil services.
- A centralised support mechanism: The structure of civil society in India is quite fragmented. It means that no single government body exists that purely deals with CSO development in the country. To correct this loophole, in 2021, VANI (Voluntary Action Network India) made a recommendation to the NITI Aayog. As per it, the National Institution for Transforming India (NITI) Aayog should help create a dedicated central government ministry to implement a national policy for the voluntary sector in India. This is similar to the Kazakh CCSD (Committee for Civil Society Development).

But this can lead to heavy shift of leverage in favour of state apparatus and can defeat the very purpose of a healthy Civil Society.

What can Kazakhstan learn from Indian Civil Society Organisations?

- *Importance of a critical Civil Society:* India's first lesson to Kazakhstan should be highlighting that an independent and critical civil society is immensely significant for good governance. This is shown by the success of India's rights-based movements like RTI and Right to Education.

- *Funding diversification:* Kazakhstan's heavy reliance on state funding is its greatest vulnerability. This greatly compromises its indcpendence. Similar to India, it can reform its tax codes, allowing for deductions in case of donations from individuals and small-to-medium-sized businesses to CSOs, and not just from large corporations.

However, an important caveat must be noted. This shall require a cautious and a nuanced approach from the Kazakh CSOs as it can easily trigger reactionary and pro-status quo moves from the state.

Current Role of CSOs in Indo-Kazakh Relations

Track I (government to government) diplomacy has been the most highlighted type of interaction in Indo-Kazakh relations. However, relations between these two states are also characterised by strong examples of other channels of interaction, that is, Track II, III and 1.5. Let us briefly describe what they mean. Track II diplomacy involves non-governmental actors such as academics, retired officials, and representatives of civil society across both the states. This is a part of what Rafale Marchetti labels as 'Global Civil Society'. Track III diplomacy involves people-to-people exchanges and Track 1.5 diplomacy is a hybrid approach that involves both civil society and government organisations.

The earliest iterations of the India-Central Asia Dialogue can be cited as the best example of civil society facilitating bilateral relations between India and Kazakhstan. (The fourth iteration of the Dialogue recently concluded in New Delhi in June, 2025). These earlier versions of the Dialogue involved prominent think tanks from both sides like the ICWA (Indian Council of World Affairs). Of these, the second Dialogue led to the launch of the India-Central Asia Business Council (ICABC) in New Delhi on 6 February 2020, comprising the Federation of Indian Chambers of Commerce and Industry (FICCI) and the Chamber of International Commerce of Kazakhstan, among other civil society organisations, as a strong B2B body between the nations involved.

Examples of Track 2 engagements abound, and these include: growing scope of collaborations between research institutions like the Kazakhstan Institute for Strategic Studies (KazISS) and the Institute of Global Studies; the India-Central Asia Business Forum whose latest edition was held in 2025.

Many examples of cultural exchanges and people-to-people relations between voluntary members and organisations of both nations exist, for example, the Swami Vivekananda Cultural Centre in Astana and the India-Central Asia Youth forum. Also, a hybrid mode of relations plays an important role. This involves the role of both CSOs and governmental structures, for example, student exchanges under the Indian Council for Cultural Relations (ICCR). The current version of the India-Central Asia dialogue also represents hybrid bilateral relations.

Current Role of Scientific Institutions in Indo-Kazakh Relations

One of the earliest examples of partnership on the science front was the signing of the Indo-Kazakhstan Nuclear Cooperation Agreement in 2011, covering supply of uranium by Kazakhstan to India and comprehensive cooperation in the civil nuclear programme. The agreement was later revived in 2015. However, on the solar front, while Indo-Kazakh relations were meant to be driven under the banner of the India and France co-led ISA (International Solar Alliance), Kazakhstan is not yet a full-fledged member, although upon being invited to do so, the Kazakh administration responded positively in 2018.

In the field of information technology and high-performance computing, the best instance of scientific institutions strengthening Indo-Kazakh bilateral relations is the gift of the '*Param Bilim*' supercomputer by India to Kazakhstan in 2015. Now fully functional in 2025, it was a direct collaboration involving C-DAC (India's premier R&D organisation in IT and electronics). This was not just a hardware transfer, but involved training, technical support and potentially joint research in the field.

Scope for more such collaboration is provided by the defence and space sectors. In the context of joint military bilateral exercises like KAZIND, bilateral defence cooperation to the extent of defence industrial collaboration becomes important. Further, as per the briefing of India's Ministry of Defence, Indian companies have been in talks with Kazakhstan defence industries for co-production and co-development in defence production. This is where institutions like the DRDO (Defence Research and Development Organisation) become extremely pertinent.

On the front of space cooperation, both countries are currently exploring the possibility of developing a space communication system satellite, KazSat-2R. Further the organisations incharge of both the nations' space programmes, that is, the Indian Space Research Organisation (ISRO) and the National Space Agency of Kazakhstan are looking to develop a satellite jointly and carry out a possible launch later. All these scientific institutions have the potential to become significant pivots and leverages for facilitating the already burgeoning India-Kazakhstan ties.

Way Forward

India and Kazakhstan hold significant stakes in one another, as has been displayed consistently by the leadership and civil society organisations of both the countries. Future areas of focus include hybridity of diplomacy, greater allocation of resources, power and decision-making ability to non-governmental fora, including scientific as well as socio-economic and cultural institutions. Furthermore, looking for diverse areas of collaboration beyond the current structural regime, for example, dry land farming and critical mineral research, joint satellite development for agriculture, partnership between India's globally recognised SHGs like SEWA with similar Kazakh institutions, joint film and arts festivals, and so on can be treated as a worthy roadmap for the bilateral future of these two immensely significant states.

References

1. Ministry of External Affairs Bilateral Brief on Kazakhstan. https://www.mea.gov.in/bilateral-briefs.htm
2. Stephen McGlinchey. *Foundations of International Relations*. Bloomsbury Publications, 2022, pp. 116–120.
3. Aristotle. *Aristotle's Politics*. Oxford: Clarendon Press, 1905.
4. Edwards, Michael (2014). *Civil Society*, Cambridge: Polity Press.
5. Walzer, Michael (1992). *The Idea of a Civil Society: A Path to Reconstruction.*
6. Asian Development Bank Civil Society Brief: India https://www.adb.org/sites/default/files/publication/879896/civil-society-brief-india.pdf
7. Participatory Research in Asia (PRIA). 2000. Defining the Sector in India: Voluntary, Civil or Non-profit. New Delhi.
8. Ministry of Home Affairs. FCRA Dashboard (2021).
9. Government of Kazakhstan. Ministry of Information and Social Development. Committee for Civil Society Development. Civil Society. https://www. gov.kz/memleket/entities/akk/activities/142?lang=en
10. C. Pierobon. 2016. *The Development of State-Civil Society Relations in Kazakhstan*. Eurasiatica. 6, pp. 203–226.
11. G. Makulbayeva. Forthcoming. Performance of Public Councils in Kazakhstan: Cultural Explanation. Ph.D. Thesis. Astana: Nazarbayev University.
12. VANI Annual Report, 2021-2022.
13. Stephen McGlinchey. *Foundations of International Relations*. Bloomsbury Publications, 2022, pp. 116–120.
14. https://www.mea.gov.in/press-releases.htm?dtl/39635/4th_meeting_of_the_India__Central_Asia_Dialogue
15. https://timesofindia.indiatimes.com/india/pm-modi-invites-kazakhstan-to-join-international-solar-alliance/articleshow/64528524.cms

20

Analysis of Contemporary Challenges and Threats to India

Ramanshi Dwivedi

"National security cannot be outsourced; it must be built patiently through strategic autonomy and institutional capacity."

—K. Subrahmanyam

The Shifting Paradigms of India's National Security

India's national security outlook has evolved through a long continuum of civilisational history, institutional rupture, and pragmatic strategic adaptation. As a foundational power within the South Asian subcontinent, India's approach to security has never been reducible to military capability alone; rather, it has historically been shaped by normative conceptions of order, legitimacy, and responsibility. Early Indian strategic thought, articulated most rigorously in the *Arthaśāstra*, advanced a conception of statecraft in which power and ethics were not mutually exclusive but co-constitutive. Governance was framed as a moral enterprise oriented towards stability, welfare, and the preservation of social order, while security was understood as an obligation owed to the polity rather than merely an assertion of sovereign dominance. This intellectual tradition reveals an early synthesis of realism and restraint, where prudence, coercion, and ethical responsibility were calibrated rather than absolutised. During its formative civilisational phases, India's security philosophy was thus embedded in a broader worldview that privileged social harmony, accommodation, and coexistence. Concepts such as ahimsa were not indicative of strategic passivity, but of a preference for legitimacy over coercion and persuasion over force. Political authority derived strength from its capacity to integrate diversity and generate consent, rather than from territorial expansion or sustained militarisation. The transregional spread of Buddhism across South, Central, and Southeast Asia exemplified this mode of influence: ideas, norms, and institutional practices travelled without the accompanying machinery of conquest. This pattern of non-coercive projection contributed to an early form of strategic culture in which security was pursued through cultural embedment rather than domination, embedding restraint as a durable element of Indian political thought.

The medieval and colonial epochs, however, introduced a decisive rupture in this indigenous security imagination. Successive external regimes, culminating in British colonial rule, displaced India's normative agency and subordinated its strategic priorities to imperial interests. Security ceased to be a function of societal welfare and instead became an instrument for maintaining extractive control. India's forced participation in global conflicts, particularly the two World Wars, underscored the extent to which colonial governance divorced security from popular consent and ethical accountability. Yet this period of subordination also produced a countervailing intellectual response. The anti-colonial movement reconstructed security as a moral and political project rooted in mass participation, non-violence, and legitimacy. In doing so, it reasserted peace not as the absence of power, but as a conscious strategic choice grounded in ethical resistance.

Independence in 1947 thus marked not merely a transfer of sovereignty, but the reconstitution of India's capacity to define security on its own civilisational and political terms. The post-independence Indian state inherited a complex strategic legacy: a deep normative commitment to peace and restraint coexisted with acute awareness of vulnerability, fragmentation, and external threat. This dual inheritance would go on to shape India's subsequent security doctrine, producing a posture that consistently sought to reconcile ethical self-conception with the imperatives of survival in an anarchic international system.

Post-Independence Era

The post-independence era established a democratic political order in which citizens, through periodic and inclusive elections, could shape both domestic and foreign policy trajectories. Yet the trauma of Partition introduced profound structural disruptions, producing enduring border tensions and new security fault lines across the subcontinent. Among these, the annexation of Tibet by the People's Republic of China in 1950 represented a pivotal moment in India's strategic environment. For centuries, Tibet had functioned as a neutral buffer along the Himalayas, providing India with both geographical depth and a zone of tranquillity along its northern frontier. Its absorption by the PRC eliminated this stabilising layer, transforming the Himalayan highlands from a largely passive barrier into an arena of contested sovereignty and strategic competition.

The direct proximity of two major Asian powers, India and China, along a disputed and poorly demarcated frontier fundamentally reshaped regional security calculations. The PRC's repudiation of the McMahon Line, agreed at the 1914 Shimla Conference, underscored Beijing's rejection of inherited colonial-era agreements and signalled the inception of a protracted diplomatic and military contest. India, for its part, confronted the sudden removal of a buffer that had historically enabled a degree of strategic depth, compelling a recalibration of its northern defence priorities. The Himalayan ranges, previously a domain of relative peace, now assumed critical importance in India's security calculus, necessitating a balance between territorial defence and broader diplomatic engagement. Motivated by a belief in normative internationalism and the promise of post-colonial solidarity, Prime Minister Jawaharlal Nehru approached this tectonic shift with a preference for dialogue and diplomatic engagement, seeking to reconcile India's ideals with the stark realities of a changing northern frontier. The 1954 Panchsheel Agreement was emblematic of this approach, codifying principles of peaceful coexistence and mutual respect. Yet in formalising these principles, India effectively constrained its leverage over Tibet and accepted the new status quo imposed by the PRC. While morally and ideologically consistent with India's civilisational ethos, anchored in persuasion, ethical statecraft, and non-aggression, this approach simultaneously introduced strategic vulnerabilities, exposing India directly to a rising and assertive China without the intermediation of an autonomous buffer state.

Nehru's commitment to a partnership-oriented vision of Asia, influenced by the ideals of post-colonial solidarity and anti-imperialism, reflected an emphasis on cooperation over confrontation. However, the idealism inherent in this approach carried tangible costs. By privileging diplomacy and accommodation, India's early post-independence leadership underestimated the strategic assertiveness of the PRC, inadvertently diluting attention to frontier preparedness. The disappearance of Tibet as an independent entity left India vulnerable along the northern boundary, a structural challenge that continues to influence strategic planning, force posture, and defence prioritisation in the contemporary era. The Himalayan frontier thus became a litmus test of India's capacity to reconcile its normative commitments with the imperatives of territorial integrity and enduring India's security spectrum.

Strategic Concerns of India and China

The Himalayan frontier, long a theatre of both natural grandeur and geopolitical tension, has come to embody the enduring strategic imperatives confronting India and China. India's security calculus, historically informed by centuries of civilisational experience and territorial stewardship, now contends with a direct and assertive northern neighbour whose ambitions extend across land, resources, and influence. In this evolving context, the interplay of geography, history, and ideology defines the contours of contemporary strategic concerns.

The strategic and security significance of Tibet for both India and China had long been recognised well before the mid-twentieth century. During the nineteenth and early twentieth centuries, when imperial powers engaged in what has often been termed the 'Great Game,' Tibet's position as a buffer zone played a crucial role in sustaining regional equilibrium. The logic resonates with the principles of the balance of power, which posits that intermediary territories serve as stabilising cushions between competing powers. The removal of this buffer, brought about by the annexation of Tibet by the People's Republic of China, fundamentally reconfigured the geostrategic dynamics of the Himalayan frontier, tilting the regional balance that had historically preserved peace. Tibet's strategic relevance also extends beyond its location; it is often described as the water tower of Asia. Ten of the continent's major rivers, including the Indus, Sutlej, Brahmaputra, Irrawaddy, Salween, Yellow, Yangtze, and Mekong, originate from the Tibetan Plateau and nourish large populations across China, India, Bangladesh, Nepal, Bhutan, Pakistan, Vietnam, Thailand, Myanmar, Cambodia, and Laos. Nearly two billion people depend upon these river systems for their ecological and economic sustenance. China's control over Tibet has thus given it a significant hydrological advantage. As the upper riparian power, it possesses the capability to regulate, obstruct, or divert the water flow in the event of diplomatic or strategic friction. A notable instance occurred after the Doklam crisis in 2017, when China withheld hydrological data on the Brahmaputra and Sutlej rivers for an entire year, disrupting India's water management and flood forecasting efforts.

Indian strategic discourse has historically drawn upon civilisational concepts such as *Vasudhaiva Kutumbakam* to articulate a normative grammar through which restraint, accommodation, and external engagement have been understood and justified. Rooted in Buddhist and Gandhian traditions, Indian political thought has placed nonviolence and moral restraint at the heart of both domestic and international conduct. The independence movement epitomised this ethos, as the struggle for liberation was carried out through nonviolent means, establishing peace as a moral and strategic ideal of the Indian state. China, in contrast, shaped under a markedly different historical and philosophical tradition, has inherited a worldview influenced by The Art of War, attributed to Sun Tzu. This classical treatise extols strategic deception, pragmatism, and expansion as legitimate instruments of statecraft, as interpreted by analysts, it has often been framed as prioritising positional advantage and incremental territorial consolidation. Mao Zedong's leadership imbued these ideas with revolutionary fervour, and the Communist Party's protracted Long March gave birth to a political culture that valorised endurance, struggle, and territorial consolidation. The modern PRC thus emerged through violent revolution, framing its national identity around unity, power, and geopolitical reach. Under the Communist Party's rule, expansionism has remained embedded, albeit reframed within the idiom of socialism and national rejuvenation, as a consistent aspect of Chinese foreign and security policy.

The divergence between India's civilisational ethos and China's strategic praxis is not merely historical but operational. The 1962 Sino-Indian War stands as a stark illustration of how the absence of a buffer and the assertive deployment of territorial claims can redefine regional hierarchies. India, adhering to Nehru's philosophy of moral restraint, faced strategic surprise as the People's Liberation Army leveraged both geography and rapid mobility to achieve tactical dominance. In the decades since, the LAC (Line of Actual Control) has remained a zone of persistent ambiguity, where strategic signalling, infrastructure development, and incremental territorial assertions have become the instruments of statecraft. The Galwan Valley clashes of 2020 exemplify this continuum: Chinese border intrusions, coupled with the militarisation of forward posts and road networks, underline a pattern of coercive diplomacy that challenges India's historical reliance on patience and negotiation.

India's doctrinal response, grounded in defensive realism, emphasises calibrated deterrence and the integration of civilisational ethics into modern force posture. Operations such as 'Operation Snow Leopard' in Eastern Ladakh illustrate a strategic blend of conventional readiness, high-altitude acclimatisa-tion, and psychological signalling. Beyond kinetic measures, India has also pursued asymmetric strategies: enhancing surveillance capabilities, fortifying forward infrastructure, and engaging in multilateral forums to assert the legitimacy of its territorial claims. The operational emphasis is on constraining coercion without escalating conflict, reflecting a nuanced interpretation of Clausewitzian principles adapted to a Himalayan theatre constrained by altitude, terrain, and population sensitivity. Hydro-strategic concerns further amplify the security calculus. China's upper riparian advantage, including control over thc Brahmaputra and Sutlej rivers, situates India in a position where military and ecological security are intertwined. Water diplomacy, therefore, becomes inseparable from national defence. India's downstream infrastructure, dams, flood monitoring systems, and bilateral mechanisms for data sharing, is essential not merely for agricultural and industrial continuity but for maintaining strategic leverage in the context of potential hydrological coercion. Events post-Doklam demonstrate that ecological dependencies can be exploited for both tactical and psychological advantage, and they necessitate a holistic security outlook that blends geography, hydrology, and force readiness.

The civilisational divergence informs the doctrinal dimension of strategic culture. India's normative restraint is complemented by constitutional democracy, participatory governance, and a pluralistic approach to national decision-making, ensuring that strategic choices are debated, deliberated, and socially legitimised. China's centralised authoritarianism, conversely, allows for rapid, coordinated action but often prioritises geopolitical ambition over procedural legitimacy. The asymmetry between deliberative moral restraint and centralised coercive pragmatism underpins the contemporary security tension: India must navigate the dual imperatives of maintaining principled diplomacy while preparing for contingencies driven by an expansionist and assertive neighbour. The strategic and security concerns emanating from Tibet, the LAC, and Chinese hydrological leverage thus operate at multiple layers, geographic, doctrinal, and civilisational. They demand that India continuously recalibrate its posture, blending hard power preparedness with soft power diplomacy, moral legitimacy, and normative influence. In essence, the Himalayan theatre encapsulates a collision of two worldviews: one that prizes enduring ethical engagement and territorial prudence, the other that operationalises expansion and consolidation as instruments of state legitimacy and power projection. The challenge for India, therefore, is not only territorial defence but also the preservation of a civilisational ethos that situates security within a broader ethical, historical, and strategic framework.

The Inescapable Neighbourhood: India–Pakistan Dynamics and the Architecture of Permanent Conflict

India and Pakistan represent one of the most paradoxical dyads in international politics: two states bound by an exceptionally dense civilisational, linguistic, and social inheritance, yet separated by one of the most enduring and violent strategic antagonisms of the post-colonial world. Unlike most rival states, their conflict is not the product of distant geopolitical competition but of a shared historical rupture, Partition, whose unresolved political, territorial, and psychological legacies continue to shape policy choices on both sides. Since 1947, India and Pakistan have fought three full-scale wars, one limited war, and have remained locked in a near-constant cycle of militarised crises, proxy violence, and narrative confrontation. One of the most defining features of this relationship in the contemporary era is neither conventional warfare nor territorial dispute alone, but the systematic deployment of terrorism as an instrument of statecraft by Pakistan, and India's evolving attempt to respond without destabilising the regional or global order.

At the core of this rivalry lies a pronounced asymmetry of power and purpose. India, by virtue of its demographic scale, economic trajectory, and global aspirations, has increasingly sought to situate its Pakistan policy within a wider strategic framework aimed at regional stability, strategic autonomy, and international legitimacy. Pakistan, by contrast, has historically constructed its national security doctrine around a persistent India-centric threat perception, in which hostility functions not merely as an episodic policy choice but as a foundational principle of state orientation. Within this framework, the systematic employment of cross-border terrorism has emerged as a central instrument through which Pakistan seeks to offset conventional asymmetry, sustain domestic power hierarchies, and internationalise its disputes with India. Rather than serving as an aberration, terrorism has been embedded as a structural tool of statecraft, one that enables confrontation under the nuclear threshold while preserving deniability. In this sense, durable peace does not simply threaten policy leverage; it undermines the very strategic logic through which Pakistan's security establishment maintains institutional primacy and political relevance and it destabilises Pakistan's internal civil–military equilibrium. This structural logic explains why Pakistan's formal democratic architecture has failed to constrain the security establishment. While Pakistan has held periodic elections and maintained civilian governments, real authority over foreign and security policy has remained concentrated within the military-intelligence complex, particularly the Pakistan Army and the Inter-Services

Intelligence (ISI). The use of non-state armed groups, ranging from Lashkar-e-Taiba to Jaish-e-Mohammed, has allowed Pakistan to pursue revisionist objectives under the nuclear shadow, exploiting the space between war and peace. This strategy of sub-conventional warfare has been described by scholars such as Vipin Narang and T.V. Paul as a form of "stability–instability paradox", wherein nuclear deterrence at the strategic level emboldens lower-level aggression.

For India, this has produced a uniquely complex security dilemma. Traditional deterrence models, designed for symmetrical state adversaries, offer limited utility against a neighbour that denies formal responsibility for violence while tacitly enabling it. The 2001 Parliament attack, the 2008 Mumbai attacks, the 2016 Uri assault, the 2019 Pulwama bombing, and subsequent incidents collectively illustrate a pattern rather than a sequence of isolated events. Each attack functioned not merely as an act of terror but as a strategic probe, testing India's thresholds, political resolve, and international tolerance for escalation. India's response to this challenge has undergone a gradual but significant transformation. For much of the post-independence period, India adhered to a doctrine of strategic restraint, grounded in its self-image as a civilisational state committed to moral leadership, diplomatic engagement, and conflict avoidance. They formed a foreign policy culture that prioritised normative legitimacy and long-term stability over immediate retaliation. However, as repeated provocations eroded the credibility of restraint, Indian strategic discourse began to shift from moral exceptionalism towards conditional assertiveness. This shift became visible after the Uri attack in 2016, when India publicly acknowledged conducting surgical strikes across the Line of Control. The Balakot airstrikes following Pulwama marked an even more consequential departure, signalling India's willingness to cross long-held red lines under certain conditions. These actions were not simply military responses; they were strategic communications aimed at multiple audiences. Domestically, they reassured a public increasingly intolerant of perceived passivity. Internationally, they sought to redefine India's image from a restrained victim to a responsible actor exercising proportional self-defence. Regionally, they attempted, however imperfectly, to alter Pakistan's calculus by introducing uncertainty into the escalation ladder.

Yet, crucially, India has stopped short of embracing punitive escalation as a permanent strategy. Instead, its approach reflects a calibrated effort to balance deterrence with escalation control, recognising the catastrophic risks inherent in full-scale conflict between nuclear-armed neighbours. This reflects a broader evolution in Indian strategic thought, influenced by scholars such as K. Subrahmanyam and practitioners within India's strategic community, who emphasised that credibility does not require constant retaliation, but predictable resolve under clearly articulated thresholds. Alongside kinetic responses, India has increasingly invested in non-military instruments of pressure. Diplomatic isolation of Pakistan, efforts to expose terror financing networks, and sustained engagement with mechanisms such as the Financial Action Task Force (FATF) represent attempts to shift the battlefield from contested borders to international institutions. While these measures have not dismantled Pakistan's terror infrastructure, they have raised the reputational and economic costs of continued sponsorship of militancy. More importantly, they reflect India's recognition that contemporary conflict is fought as much in legal, financial, and narrative domains as on the battlefield.

Narrative warfare has thus emerged as a critical dimension of the India–Pakistan confrontation. Pakistan has consistently sought to internationalise disputes, particularly Kashmir, by framing them within human rights and self-determination discourses, often detached from its own role in sustaining violence. India, conversely, has attempted to recast the narrative around cross-border terrorism, responsible state behaviour, and adherence to international norms. This contest is not merely about persuasion; it is about legitimacy. In an era where global power increasingly depends on perception and credibility, the ability to shape narratives has become a strategic asset. The persistence of this rivalry is further complicated by the broader regional environment, particularly the deepening strategic convergence between Pakistan and China. While India's Pakistan challenge is not reducible to Chinese influence, Beijing's diplomatic shielding of Pakistan in international forums, its economic investments through the China–Pakistan Economic Corridor, and its reluctance to unequivocally condemn terrorist actors have reinforced Pakistan's sense of strategic insulation. For India, this creates a compound security environment, wherein sub-conventional threats from the west intersect with conventional and territorial pressures from the north.

Nevertheless, it would be analytically misleading to interpret India–Pakistan relations solely through the lens of hostility. Periodic attempts at engagement, ranging from the Simla Agreement to the Lahore Declaration and backchannel dialogues, demonstrate that the possibility of détente has never been entirely foreclosed. However, these initiatives have consistently collapsed under the weight of asymmetric incentives. While India views peace as a pathway to regional integration and global engagement, Pakistan's security establishment has often perceived it as a threat to its internal coherence. In this sense, the India–Pakistan relationship exemplifies a broader challenge in international security: how to manage a neighbour whose strategic rationality is shaped less by external threats than by internal institutional imperatives. Terrorism persists not because it delivers decisive victories, but because it sustains a particular political economy of power within Pakistan. India's challenge, therefore, is not merely to respond to attacks, but to navigate a structural antagonism without allowing it to dominate its broader strategic trajectory.

India's approach reflects an attempt to reconcile two imperatives that often sit uneasily together: the need to deter aggression and the desire to remain anchored within a rules-based international order. This balancing act, between restraint and resolve, morality and realism, defines India's contemporary security posture vis-à-vis Pakistan. It is a posture shaped not by idealism alone, nor by brute force, but by a growing recognition that enduring security lies in strategic patience combined with selective assertiveness. Therefore, the India–Pakistan dyad is not merely a bilateral dispute; it is a test case for how rising powers manage asymmetric, ideologically entrenched adversaries in an era of nuclear weapons, global norms, and narrative competition. The conflict, therefore, remains unresolved not because solutions are unavailable, but because the incentives sustaining hostility remain structurally embedded on one side of the border. For India, this structurally embedded threat environment has necessitated a recalibration of doctrine rather than a wholesale abandonment of restraint. The persistence of cross-border terrorism, combined with Pakistan's reliance on deniability and nuclear overhang, has compelled India to evolve a security posture that privileges controlled escalation, strategic signalling, and credibility maintenance. This evolution is visible in India's gradual shift from passive deterrence to a framework that tolerates limited, overt responses below the threshold of full-scale war, while remaining anchored in international legality and proportionality. Rather than pursuing punitive retaliation as an end in itself, India's doctrinal adjustment reflects an attempt to restore deterrence at the sub-conventional level without destabilising the broader regional balance. The challenge, however, remains acute: India must continuously demonstrate resolve against terrorism while simultaneously avoiding the strategic traps of escalation, international opprobrium, or crisis fatigue, conditions that Pakistan's strategy implicitly seeks to induce.

India and Bangladesh: Managing Cross-Border Infiltration Amid Political Realignments

With cross-border infiltration intensifying as a critical security concern, the bilateral relationship faces strains. The political upheaval in Bangladesh since August 2024, including the rise of an interim government led by Nobel laureate Muhammad Yunus, Dhaka's foreign policy pivot towards closer relations with China and Pakistan has added new complexity to bilateral ties. This political realignment coincides with an escalation in illegal migration from Bangladesh into India, posing security and socio-economic challenges. India's Border Security Force (BSF) data reveals that over 5,000 Bangladeshi nationals were intercepted and pushed back between 2022-2025, with hotspots including West Bengal,

Mizoram, Tripura, and Meghalaya. These infiltration attempts involve human trafficking networks exploiting unfenced border stretches, causing demographic shifts that pressure public services and inflame local tensions in border districts.

India's countermeasures include enhanced fencing, technological surveillance, and strict border patrolling, alongside legal reforms aimed at detecting, detaining, and deporting infiltrators. Yet, these security imperatives coexist uneasily with the extensive socio-economic interdependence between the countries, including trade, water sharing, and cultural linkages. The imposition of trade curbs by India on critical Bangladeshi exports like garments in 2025, and tightened transit controls, are partly responses to escalating security concerns, including strategic apprehensions about Dhaka's growing external alignments that may undermine India's northeast security. While these measures have fueled some anti-India sentiment in Bangladesh, New Delhi remains committed to diplomatic engagement, promoting democratic stability and cross-border cooperation. In a region burdened by complex histories and evolving geopolitics, the challenge lies in balancing hard security measures with sustained dialogue to ensure that cross-border infiltration does not erode the foundation of one of South Asia's most important bilateral partnerships.

India and Sri Lanka: Regional Dynamics

India's relationship with Sri Lanka in 2025 reflects deepening cooperation anchored in shared cultural ties and converging regional security interests. For decades, the complex legacy of the Tamil ethnic issue, including the aftermath of the Indian Peace Keeping Force (IPKF) intervention and India's early designation of the LTTE as a terrorist organisation, shaped a cautious bilateral security outlook. Yet recent developments signal a significant shift. During Indian Prime Minister's April 2025 visit, Sri Lanka and India signed their first MoU on Defence Cooperation, a landmark accord reflecting mutual recognition of evolving regional geopolitics, particularly in the Indian Ocean littoral. This defence engagement promotes joint maritime security, intelligence sharing, and counter-terrorism efforts, vital as strategic competition intensifies with increased presence from external actors. Economically, India remains Sri Lanka's largest trading partner, while supporting Sri Lanka's economic stabilisation through IMF-backed debt restructuring and financial aid packages. Cultural diplomacy remains a pillar, exemplified by India's grant assistance for the restoration of Buddhist monasteries. Amid rising uncertainty in South Asia, this multifaceted partnership positions India and Sri Lanka as complementary anchors of stability for the Indian Ocean region.

Expanding the Security Discourse: The Rise of Non-Traditional Threats

Beyond the conventional paradigms of territorial defence and interstate rivalry, India's national security landscape is increasingly defined by non-traditional threats whose consequences extend across social, economic, and geopolitical domains. Persistent terrorism, particularly emanating from Pakistan-based groups such as Jaish-e-Mohammed, Lashkar-e-Taiba, and their affiliate networks, continues to constitute the most salient challenge to India's internal and regional security. The 2016 Pathankot airbase attack, the 2019 Pulwama suicide bombing, and repeated cross-border ceasefire violations in Jammu and Kashmir underscore that terrorism remains not merely episodic but strategically embedded in Pakistan's approach towards India. These events reveal a deliberate orchestration of violence intended to destabilise democratic governance, undermine civilian confidence, and impede economic and developmental progress. India's resolute response, combining surgical counter-terror operations, enhanced intelligence coordination, and proactive diplomacy, exemplifies a national security philosophy that treats terrorism as both a strategic and civilisational affront. Simultaneously, the acceleration of technological innovation has introduced cybersecurity and information warfare as defining dimensions of national vulnerability. State and non-state actors increasingly employ cyber intrusions, ransomware attacks, and disinformation campaigns to weaken institutional resilience and shape public perception. The 2020 cyber-attacks targeting critical infrastructure, including the Kudankulam nuclear plant and Indian financial institutions, illustrate the multifaceted nature of digital threats. India has responded through the establishment of the National Cyber Security Strategy (NCSS), the Defence Cyber Agency (DCA), and coordinated public-private cyber resilience frameworks, recognising that cybersecurity is inseparable from both operational continuity and societal trust in governance. Moreover, the proliferation of narrative warfare, encompassing strategic misinformation, radicalisation, and ideological propagation, underscores the intricate interplay between information ecosystems, national cohesion, and foreign policy objectives.

India's border security imperatives remain equally critical, encompassing both terrestrial and maritime theatres. The extensive northern frontiers with China and Pakistan necessitate constant vigilance, infrastructure modernisation, and rapid reaction capabilities. Initiatives such as the construction of all-weather roads in the Ladakh region, the strengthening of Forward Operating Bases (FOBs), and high-altitude military exercises including Operation Snow Leopard, reflect a doctrine that integrates terrain, technology, and civilisational prudence. Meanwhile, India's western border with Pakistan demands a multi-layered defence approach combining physical barriers, electronic surveillance, and intelligence-driven counter-infiltration operations. The maritime domain, spanning 7,516 kilometres of coastline, is protected through a tiered security architecture: local coastal police maintain vigilance within 12 nautical miles, the Indian Coast Guard operates across the Exclusive Economic Zone (200 nautical miles), and the Indian Navy projects power in the high seas, ensuring maritime continuity and deterrence. Coastal communities serve as integral nodes of observation, exemplifying a civil-military synergy that links local resilience to national security. Non-traditional threats also encompass the security of vital resources. Water, energy, and food security increasingly intersect with strategic calculus, particularly in light of China's upper riparian control over Himalayan rivers and the growing fragility of global supply chains. India's hydrological vulnerabilities, including dependence on the Brahmaputra, Sutlej, and Indus river systems, necessitate comprehensive water diplomacy, technological investment in dam and flood management systems, and a preparedness to pre-empt ecological coercion as a tool of hybrid warfare. Energy security, too, is interwoven with strategic autonomy: India's expanding reliance on uranium imports, critical minerals, and renewable energy infrastructure demands protection against both economic leverage and transnational sabotage.

On the diplomatic and institutional front, India has pursued a normative, outcome-oriented strategy, leveraging multilateral frameworks and bilateral engagements to counter non-traditional threats. Initiatives such as the Indo-Pacific collaboration on counter-terrorism, the SAARC and BIMSTEC security dialogues, and the Quad's security-oriented maritime cooperation exemplify India's capacity to merge principled diplomacy with operational preparedness. Domestically, programmes such as Atmanirbhar Bharat and Make in India reflect an integrated understanding of security as both material resilience and civilisational continuity, linking industrial self-reliance to broader geopolitical leverage.

India's contemporary security discourse integrates conventional military readiness with non-traditional threat management, combining civilisational ethics, technological foresight, and strategic pragmatism.

Terrorism, cyber aggression, hydrological leverage, border vulnerabilities, and resource security converge to form a complex threat matrix. India's approach, a synthesis of moral restraint, doctrinal sophistication, and operational innovation, positions it to address challenges across multiple domains while preserving its civilisational ethos. The contemporary security architecture thus reflects not merely a response to immediate threats but a long-term strategy of resilience, deterrence, and normative influence, ensuring that India remains both materially secure and strategically autonomous in an evolving global order.

Envisioning India's National Security Paradigm: Prospects & Challenges

India's national security paradigm is entering a phase that transcends conventional metrics of defence and deterrence, moving instead toward an integrated conception that fuses strategic foresight, civilisational ethos, and normative influence. In this evolving landscape, security is no longer solely a function of territorial defence or military capability; it embodies the capacity to harmonise power with principle, assert agency within a multipolar world, and project values alongside interests. This intellectual expansion positions India not merely as a regional stabiliser but as a potential architect of global governance frameworks that reconcile ethical imperatives with strategic necessity. In essence, the challenge of India's contemporary security architecture lies in synthesising the lessons of history with emerging technologies, environmental contingencies, and normative leadership in a rapidly shifting international system.

The central tenet of India's forward-looking security paradigm is strategic autonomy, conceived not as isolationism but as the deliberate cultivation of operational independence across domains. This autonomy enables India to engage selectively, align purposefully, and navigate great power rivalries without succumbing to external coercion. In practice, it demands the capacity to balance hard power capabilities, conventional, nuclear, cyber, and space-based, with soft power instruments rooted in diplomacy, normative leadership, and civilisational influence. Strategic autonomy also entails resilience in domestic governance, technological self-reliance, and societal cohesion, recognising that national security extends beyond borders and battlefields to encompass economic stability, digital integrity, and ecological sustainability. A defining feature of India's emerging security doctrine is the integration of civilisational philosophy into statecraft. The ancient conceptualisation of *Vasudhaiva Kutumbakam*, which envisions the world as an interconnected moral community, offers a lens through which foreign policy and security strategy can be calibrated. Applied practically, this ethos guides engagement in multilateral institutions, normative coalition-building, and conflict-prevention initiatives. India's security calculus increasingly incorporates ethical foresight, whereby anticipatory strategies consider not only the immediate threat environment but also the normative and moral consequences of action. This civilisational grounding differentiates India's approach from purely power-centric paradigms, enabling it to operate with both credibility and moral leverage in arenas ranging from global climate negotiations to cyber governance.

Emerging non-traditional threats shape this paradigm as critically as traditional state-centric challenges. Technological proliferation, spanning cyber intrusion, artificial intelligence, quantum computing, and space-based reconnaissance, has transformed the contours of vulnerability. India's response necessitates a dual lens: one that strengthens technical resilience through indigenous research and innovation, and another that leverages normative frameworks to establish ethical standards for emerging domains of conflict. For instance, the governance of space-based assets, cyber infrastructure, and critical digital networks is inseparable from broader strategic considerations, as disruptions in these realms can produce cascading effects on economic, social, and military stability. By embedding anticipatory technology strategies into national security planning, India positions itself to pre-empt adversarial exploitation while promoting rules-based conduct in emerging theatres of global competition. Environmental and resource security represent another dimension where India's conceptual framework intersects with practical imperatives. As climate change, water scarcity, and food insecurity intensify, national security cannot be confined to military preparedness alone. India's policy vision increasingly conceptualises resilience infrastructure, hydrological management, energy diversification, and sustainable agriculture, as integral to strategic endurance. In the geopolitical sphere, this vision extends to transboundary cooperation and contestation, requiring India to navigate upstream-downstream river dynamics, regional energy interdependencies, and climate-sensitive migratory pressures. In doing so, national security is reframed as a systemic concept, encompassing ecological stability as inseparable from geopolitical strength.

India's civilisational lens also informs its approach to normative leadership in multilateralism. Recognising that contemporary security is intertwined with legitimacy, India actively champions frameworks that balance sovereignty with collective responsibility. Its engagement in platforms such as the Quad, G20, BRICS, and ASEAN-associated dialogues illustrates a strategic preference for rules-based engagement rather than unilateral assertion. Within these forums, India leverages its moral and intellectual capital to influence norms on cybersecurity, counterterrorism, digital governance, and climate resilience. The underlying thesis is that sustainable security derives not from coercion alone but from the cultivation of cooperative systems where ethical legitimacy enhances operational leverage. Operational readiness remains an essential pillar, yet it is now complemented by a more expansive doctrine of anticipatory strategy. India's military modernisation is therefore interlinked with civilisational foresight: advanced surveillance, artificial intelligence-enabled decision systems, space-based reconnaissance, and rapid-response capabilities are conceptualised not as instruments of aggression but as enablers of deterrence and strategic signalling. This approach reflects a nuanced interpretation of classical and contemporary strategic thought, blending Clausewitzian realism with ethical restraint, and Machiavellian pragmatism with civilisational morality. In the Himalayan theatre, littoral zones, and cyber domains alike, the operational dimension is inseparable from anticipatory planning, technological sophistication, and normative influence.

The fusion of civilisational philosophy with strategic pragmatism enables India to position itself as a stabiliser amid regional turbulence. In South Asia and the Indo-Pacific, the capacity to harmonise deterrence, diplomacy, and development creates a platform from which India can both project influence and mediate conflict. This duality is central to India's role as a constructive balancer: it combines assertive presence with normative guidance, ensuring that its strategic footprint is simultaneously credible and ethically grounded. Furthermore, India's growing economic and technological clout amplifies the effectiveness of such an approach, as security is increasingly inseparable from development, connectivity, and digital sovereignty. Looking forward, the primary challenge lies in integrating multiple dimensions of national power into a coherent, intellectually rigorous security framework. India's approach must synthesise traditional statecraft, non-traditional resilience, technological foresight, and civilisational ethos into an operationally viable paradigm. This requires innovation in doctrine, adaptive governance structures, and anticipatory policymaking that can respond to hybrid threats, ranging from state-sponsored coercion to digital subversion and environmental shocks. By maintaining a principled stance while investing in hard and soft power capabilities, India is poised to transform its security strategy from reactive containment to proactive, globally resonant leadership.

India's national security vision embodies the convergence of history, ethics, and strategic foresight. It draws upon a civilisational imagination that emphasises moral legitimacy and regional stewardship while embedding these values within a practical, multidimensional security architecture. In doing so, India aspires not only to safeguard its sovereignty but also to serve as a normative exemplar: a nation capable of harmonising power with principle, deterrence with diplomacy, and resilience with ethical engagement. The Indian paradigm, thus, transcends the conventional confines of national security, signalling an enduring ambition to shape a global order that is strategically robust, morally coherent, and sustainably just, one in which India's voice, rooted in civilisational wisdom, resonates across both regional and global theatres.

References

1. Menon, S. 2016. *Choices: Inside the Making of India's Foreign Policy.* New Delhi: Brookings India.
2. Arpi, Claude. 2020. *India-Tibet Relations, 1947–1962: Part 4.* New Delhi: Vij Books India Pvt. Ltd.
3. Deepak, J. Sai. 2022. *India, Bharat and Pakistan: The Constitutional Journey of a Sandwiched Civilisation.* New Delhi: Bloomsbury India.
4. Jaishankar, S. 2023. *Why Bharat Matters.* New Delhi: Rupa Publications.
5. Krishnan, S. 2020. *"India China Tibet."* The Statesman, September 19, 6.
6. Ministry of External Affairs, Government of India. 2023. *Annual Report.* New Delhi: Ministry of External Affairs.
7. Rangarajan, L.N. 1992. *The Arthashastra.* Gurgaon: Random House India.
8. Menon, S. 2021. *India and Asian Geopolitics: The Past, Present.* New Delhi: Brookings India.
9. Rangarajan, Suresh. 2020. *"Changing Dimensions of Security: An Indian Perspective." In Palgrave Encyclopedia of Interest Group Lobbying and Public Policy.* Palgrave Macmillan.
10. Suresh, R. 2015. *The Changing Dimensions of Security: India's Security Policy Options.* New Delhi: Vij Books India Pvt. Ltd.
11. Tharoor, Shashi. 2021. *The Battle of Belonging: On Nationalism, Patriotism, and What It Means to Be Indian.* New Delhi: Aleph Book Company.
12. Viswambharan, R. 2021. *India, China, and Tibet: A Quest for Autonomy.* New York: Nova Science Publishers.

21

Forecasting the Development of Relations in the Long-Term Perspective

Dr. Syrym Parpiyev

Setting the Stage

Kazakhstan and India, despite differences in size and geography, have steadily built a strategic partnership that is poised to influence the geopolitics of Eurasia in the coming decades. This chapter seeks to forecast the long-term development of Kazakhstan-India relations by examining past and present dynamics and outlining possible future scenarios. The scope encompasses bilateral interactions as well as engagements in multilateral frameworks that shape this relationship. Methodologically, the chapter adopts a qualitative foresight approach, drawing on historical analysis, geopolitical and geoeconomic trend assessment, and scenario planning to envision how ties may evolve. The analysis is grounded in academic and policy sources, including peer-reviewed studies, think-tank reports, and official data, ensuring a rigorous and evidence-based narrative.

The chapter operates at the intersection of geopolitics and geoeconomics, recognising that strategic partnerships are driven both by security imperatives and economic interests. A geopolitical lens is used to assess how power dynamics (regional security, great-power influence, multivector diplomacy) shape Kazakhstan-India relations. Simultaneously, a geoeconomic lens examines trade, investment, energy, and connectivity initiatives that bind the two economies. The interplay of these dimensions is analysed within international relations theory, drawing on concepts of regional security complexes and strategic interdependence. Given the forward-looking aim, scenario analysis is employed: the chapter will outline multiple plausible future scenarios (such as optimistic, status quo, and pessimistic trajectories) based on key drivers such as connectivity breakthroughs, shifts in global power alignments, and domestic policy priorities.

The structure of the section is as follows. First, setting the stage defines the scope and approach, clarifying that our forecast will consider both bilateral and multilateral facets using the above analytical framework. Second, historical and contemporary dynamics reviews the evolution of Kazakhstan-India relations from the early 1990s to the present, identifying continuity and change in key sectors of cooperation (energy, defence, infrastructure, education, trade). Third, a strategic analysis delves deeper into geopolitical and geoeconomic drivers, analyzing how regional and global contexts (such as Central Asia's strategic landscape, great-power competition, economic complementarities) inform the partnership. Fourth, future scenarios are presented, depicting alternative paths that the relationship could take in the long term, given various assumptions about internal and external variables. Finally, the chapter concludes with policy recommendations, suggesting strategies for both Kazakhstan and India (and their partners) to realise a mutually beneficial long-term relationship, followed by a summary conclusion. This narrative, descriptive in tone yet analytically rigorous, aims to provide a comprehensive graduate-level examination of where Kazakhstan-India relations might be headed, and how policymakers can steer them towards a favourable outcome.

Historical and Contemporary Dynamics of Kazakhstan-India Relations

Early Relations and Strategic Partnership Formation: Diplomatic relations between India and Kazakhstan began soon after the latter gained independence in 1991, but the 1990s saw relatively limited engagement. India, while historically cognizant of Central Asia through ancient Silk Road ties, largely neglected Kazakhstan in the 1990s as it focused on domestic economic reforms and more immediate neighbours. The turn of the millennium brought about a policy shift: by the early 2000s, New Delhi had reconsidered its approach to Central Asia, recognising Kazakhstan's strategic importance as the region's largest economy and a repository of energy resources. A milestone was reached in January 2009, when Kazakhstan's President Nursultan Nazarbayev was hosted as India's Republic Day chief guest, during which the two sides signed a Declaration of Strategic Partnership and a civil nuclear cooperation pact – Kazakhstan agreed to supply uranium fuel to India's nuclear energy programme. This established a high-level political commitment and opened a new chapter in bilateral ties.

In subsequent years, both countries built upon this foundation. High-level visits became more frequent, signalling growing political will. Indian Prime Minister Manmohan Singh visited Kazakhstan in 2011, and Prime Minister Narendra Modi made a historic tour of all five Central Asian republics (including Kazakhstan) in 2015. Modi's July 2015 visit to Astana notably bolstered ties: agreements were signed across various sectors, including a major contract for Kazakhstan to supply 5,000 tons of uranium to India between 2015 and 2019, and a Memorandum of Understandings on defence cooperation. These agreements reinforced energy and defence links that remain pillars of the relationship. By 2015, Kazakhstan and India had developed a comprehensive dialogue, prompting observers to note 'considerable dynamism' in the partnership over the last decade. The planned visit of Kazakhstan's current President Kassym-Jomart Tokayev to India (which eventually took place in 2022 after a delay) was expected to open new horizons for a fully-fledged partnership.

India articulated a dedicated strategy for the region via its 'Connect Central Asia' policy, announced in 2012, which treats Central Asia as India's 'extended neighbourhood' and calls for proactive political, economic, and cultural engagement. Under this framework, Kazakhstan quickly emerged as the focal point, given its relative economic weight and compatibility with India's interests. On the Kazakh side, the relationship is pursued within Kazakhstan's signature 'multi-vector foreign policy,' which emphasises pragmatic and non-ideological partnerships across all major powers. Both nations thus approach each other with a desire for diversified relations: India seeks to reconnect with a region historically linked to it, and Kazakhstan aims to balance ties with all global and regional powers, including India.

Institutionally, a robust architecture supports bilateral cooperation. A high-level India-Kazakhstan Inter-Governmental Commission (IGC) meets regularly to coordinate across trade, economic, scientific, technological, industrial, and cultural spheres. Specialised joint working groups address sector-specific issues, ensuring continuous dialogue at the working level. A joint business council was established between the Federation of Indian Chambers of Commerce and Industry (FICCI) and Kazakhstan's Chamber of International Commerce to spur private-sector linkages. These mechanisms have provided continuity and problem-solving channels as the relationship matures.

Economic relations have grown markedly since the 2000s, albeit from a low base and still below potential. In the early 2000s, bilateral trade was negligible (for instance, around $78 million in 2003 according to historical records). Following the Strategic Partnership and India's active Central Asia outreach, trade expanded. By 2012, India-Kazakhstan trade had reached about $500 million; it then more than doubled to $1.3 billion in 2014. A downturn in global commodity prices and other factors led to a dip, with trade falling to around $618 million in 2016. However, the trend recovered in subsequent years. By 2019, bilateral trade hit $1.8 billion, and despite pandemic disruptions, it climbed to a record $2.3 billion in 2020. After a slight pullback in 2021, trade surged to an all-time high of $2.5 billion in 2022. Kazakhstan today is by far India's largest trading partner in Central Asia, accounting for over 80 per cent of India's trade with the region (and nearly 99 per cent of India's imports from Central Asia, largely due to oil).

The composition of trade reflects complementary needs. Indian exports to Kazakhstan consist chiefly of manufactured and consumer goods, notably pharmaceuticals, medical products, tea, textiles, and machinery. India's affordable pharmaceuticals have a strong market in Kazakhstan, contributing to India's image as a reliable supplier in the health sector. Kazakhstan's exports to India are dominated by natural resources – petroleum oils and minerals account for roughly 80 per cent of Kazakh exports to India. Energy thus underpins the trade relationship, aligning with India's quest for energy security and Kazakhstan's role as a hydrocarbons and minerals exporter. Additionally, Kazakhstan has been a critical source of uranium for India. Under long-term contracts (2009–2014 and 2015–2019), Kazakhstan supplied 8,000 metric tons of uranium to fuel India's nuclear power plants, making it India's largest supplier of this commodity. A new agreement for 2020–2024 was under discussion to provide 7,500+ tons. These uranium deals exemplify the strategic nature of economic ties – beyond regular commerce, they address India's critical infrastructure needs (energy) while providing Kazakhstan a steady export revenue stream in a high-tech sector.

Investment flows and commercial projects, while modest, have been growing. More than 600 entities with Indian capital operate in Kazakhstan, with around 400 registered in just the past few years. These include joint ventures or subsidiaries in pharmaceuticals, mining, banking, and information technology. For example, Indian pharmaceutical companies have established a presence to tap into Kazakhstan's healthcare market, and Indian IT services firms have explored opportunities as Kazakhstan digitalises its economy. Conversely, direct Kazakh investments in India have been limited, though Kazakhstan's sovereign wealth entities have occasionally expressed interest in India's infrastructure sector. An area of notable Indian investment was oil exploration: in 2011, India's ONGC Videsh acquired a 25 per cent stake in Kazakhstan's Satpayev offshore oil block. However, after drilling two exploratory wells with no commercial discovery, ONGC exited the project in 2018. This setback illustrated the challenges Indian companies face in Central Asia's energy sector, but it has not deterred ongoing interest – Kazakhstan continues to invite Indian investment in areas like petrochemicals and metallurgy. Both governments see potential for greater economic engagement if logistical and financial hurdles can be overcome.

Security ties have become a cornerstone of the bilateral relationship. A 2002 defence cooperation memorandum and subsequent agreements paved the way for training exchanges and defence industry collaboration. Cooperation deepened significantly after the 2015 Agreement on Defence and Military-Technical Cooperation, which provided an umbrella for broad-based military ties. Since 2016, India and Kazakhstan have held annual joint military exercises known as 'Exercise KAZIND' (previously 'Prabal Dostyk'), alternating between the two countries. The 8th KAZIND exercise in 2024 was conducted in India's Uttarakhand state, focusing on joint counter-terrorism operations in mountainous terrain. These regular drills enhance interoperability and trust between the armed forces. They are especially focused on counter-insurgency and peacekeeping skills; for instance, Kazakhstan's peacekeeping troops trained with the Indian Army before deploying alongside Indian units in the UN Interim Force in Lebanon (UNIFIL) in 2018. As of 2021, 246 Kazakh officers had undergone training in Indian military institutions under various programmes, reflecting India's role in capacity-building for Kazakhstan's defence personnel. Moreover, in recent dialogues the two sides have explored joint production of military hardware and maintenance of equipment. India, with its experience in Soviet/Russian-origin defence systems, sees an opportunity to collaborate on servicing the equipment used by Kazakhstan's military (most of which is of Russian make), an idea which led to discussions of joint ventures for spare parts.

Counter-terrorism and intelligence sharing form another vital aspect of security cooperation. Both nations face threats from terrorism and extremism in their respective regions and have cooperated under bilateral and multilateral platforms to address these issues. For example, at the India-Central Asia Dialogue forums, India and Kazakhstan (along with others) have emphasised combating radicalisation and the flow of terrorists, particularly with the looming uncertainty in Afghanistan. Kazakhstan, a secular Muslim-majority state, has been largely successful in containing extremism, and it values exchanges with India on best practices in law enforcement and de-radicalisation. The two countries also participate in regional security mechanisms, notably the Shanghai Cooperation Organisation (SCO) to coordinate on terrorism and drug trafficking. While India's security cooperation with Kazakhstan is not directed against any third country, it has the effect of diversifying Kazakhstan's security partnerships beyond its traditional ally Russia, and gives India a strategic foothold in a region where China and Pakistan are increasingly active.

People-to-people ties between India and Kazakhstan have flourished, adding resilience to the relationship. A striking phenomenon in recent years is the influx of Indian students to Kazakhstan. Over 9,400 Indian students are enrolled in Kazakhstani universities, overwhelmingly in medical programmes (Kazakhstan's medical universities offer affordable MBBS degrees popular among Indian students).These students not only receive education but also become informal ambassadors of India, fostering cultural understanding. Kazakhstani students have opportunities to study in India as well, supported by India's Indian Council for Cultural Relations (ICCR) scholarships and ITEC (Indian Technical and Economic Cooperation) training courses – more than a thousand Kazakh professionals have attended short-term courses in India under ITEC. Such educational exchanges contribute to capacity-building in Kazakhstan and create a network of Kazakh alumni with first-hand experience of India.

Cultural diplomacy has been another success. India's soft power (from Bollywood films to yoga) enjoys tremendous popularity in Kazakhstan. The Swami Vivekananda Cultural Centre in Astana has been active since 1994 in promoting Indian dance, music, and language. In Almaty, local enthusiasts have established centres for Indian classical dance and yoga, reflecting genuine grassroots interest. Reciprocally, Kazakhstan's culture is being increasingly introduced to Indians; for example, Kazakhstan gifted a statue of the poet, Abai Qunanbaiuly, for installation in Delhi in 2022. These cultural exchanges build mutual goodwill and understanding, reinforcing the notion that beyond strategic interests, there is a foundation of shared affinity. Notably, both societies value multi-ethnic and multi-religious harmony, and Kazakhstan regularly invites India to its Congress of World and Traditional Religions – a dialogue initiative for religious leaders, which India appreciates.

In the last few years, despite global upheavals, Kazakhstan-India relations have shown continuity and even new initiatives. In January 2022, India hosted (virtually) the First India-Central Asia Summit, where Prime Minister Modi and President Tokayev (along with other Central Asian leaders) discussed a roadmap for regional cooperation. Several agreements involving Kazakhstan were signed at this summit, including on connectivity and trade promotion. Kazakhstan expressed support for India's active role in Central Asian affairs, and India, in turn, backed Kazakhstan's regional initiatives (such as Kazakhstan's chairmanship of SCO in 2023 and its CICA process). Bilaterally, periodic foreign office consultations have identified emerging areas of collaboration – a February 2023 round of political consultations in New Delhi, for instance, agreed to diversify cooperation into medicine, IT, agriculture, space, and energy (renewables). This indicates a forward-looking agenda that goes beyond the traditional spheres of hydrocarbons and defence. Also noteworthy is Kazakhstan's support for some of India's global aspirations: Kazakhstan has consistently endorsed India's bid for a permanent seat at a reformed UN Security Council, aligning with the shared view that global governance structures should reflect current realities.

To sum up, the historical and contemporary trajectory of Kazakhstan-India relations reveals a steady upward curve, with deepening engagement across multiple domains. From a slow start in the 1990s, the relationship gained strategic momentum post-2009 and especially post-2015. Today, it encompasses a strategic partnership marked by growing trade, critical energy ties, robust defence cooperation, and vibrant educational and cultural exchanges. However, both governments acknowledge that full potential is yet to be realised, as various constraints (geographical distance, insufficient transport links, and limited private-sector awareness) have moderated the pace of progress. This recognition has spurred them to 'search for new mechanisms' and expand into emerging spheres like cyber, fintech, and green energy to ensure that the partnership remains dynamic. With this context in place, we now turn to a strategic analysis of the relationship's key drivers, which will inform our later discussion on future scenarios.

Strategic Analysis: Geopolitical and Geoeconomic Dimensions

Geopolitical Dimensions

Kazakhstan-India relations do not exist in a vacuum; they are profoundly influenced by the broader geopolitical landscape of Central Asia and Eurasia, as well as by geoeconomic forces linking the two countries. In this section, we analyze the strategic underpinnings of the relationship through two lenses: geopolitical dynamics, including security concerns, regional power configurations, and multilateral engagements and geoeconomic factors encompassing trade, investment, energy security, and connectivity infrastructure. This dual analysis helps explain why both countries value the relationship and how they leverage it amid external opportunities and challenges.

Regional Power Balance and Multivectorism. Central Asia's post-Soviet geopolitics has been characterised by the influence of great powers, notably Russia and China, with the USA and the EU also vying for presence. Kazakhstan, sharing long borders with both Russia and China, has skilfully pursued a 'multi-vector' policy to maintain balanced relations. India's growing engagement in Central Asia and with Kazakhstan in particular can be seen in the light of this context. In the third decade of the 21st century, Central Asia faces a complex geopolitical environment: Russia remains a dominant political-military actor, while China's economic footprint (via the Belt and Road Initiative) is expanding rapidly. India's role, albeit more limited, is increasingly that of a stabilising partner and a fellow Eurasian player that Kazakhstan and others welcome to avoid over-reliance on any single power. For Kazakhstan, courting India (alongside partners like Turkey, the EU, Japan, etc.) is part of its strategy to diversify strategic ties. For India, engagement with Kazakhstan is a way to project influence in a region where it has historical links but from which it was long absent, thereby enhancing its profile as a regional power and emerging global player. From India's perspective, stronger ties with Kazakhstan serve to counter-balance the 'China-Pakistan-Russia triangle' that has emerged in Eurasian affairs. China's BRI projects in Central Asia and Pakistan's growing links with the region (through Gwadar port and promises of transit routes) have somewhat marginalised India in Central Asia over the past decade. Indian strategists view Kazakhstan as central to reclaiming a foothold: it is the largest and most stable Central Asian state, and generally receptive to India's overtures. Notably, Kazakhstan has no direct conflicts of interest with India; on the contrary, it shares India's concerns about religious extremism and has demonstrated an independent foreign policy despite its close ties with Moscow and Beijing. Kazakhstan's emphasis on principles like 'Unity in Diversity' and respect for sovereignty resonates with India's own outlook. Thus, geopolitically, the partnership allows India and Kazakhstan to jointly advocate for a multipolar regional order where no single power dominates and sovereign decisions are respected.

Security and Afghanistan. A key shared geopolitical interest is the stability of Afghanistan and the broader region. Both India and Kazakhstan have been stakeholders in Afghanistan's peace due to concerns over terrorism, drug trafficking, and regional spillover of instability. Kazakhstan, which borders three Central Asian states adjacent to Afghanistan, views a peaceful Afghanistan as vital to Central Asian security. India as a South Asian neighbour of Afghanistan has invested in Afghanistan's development and likewise fears a resurgence of extremist groups that could target Indian interests. In various forums (like the SCO Afghanistan contact group or CICA), India and Kazakhstan have coordinated calls for an inclusive Afghan government and protection of Afghan human rights, while also preparing to mitigate any 'spill-over effect of terrorism' from Afghan soil. This common interest reinforces bilateral security cooperation. For example, intelligence-sharing on terror networks has reportedly increased. Additionally, Kazakhstan has supported India's inclusion in regional discussions on Afghanistan (India was invited as an observer in talks where typically only Central Asian and great powers participated). The two countries also agree on rejecting safe havens for terrorism across Eurasia, a thinly veiled reference to concerns about Pakistan's role in fomenting instability. In essence, geopolitical convergence on regional security, particularly regarding Afghanistan and counter-terrorism, forms an important rationale for sustained strategic dialogue between Astana and New Delhi.

Multilateral Engagements. Kazakhstan and India actively collaborate within multilateral institutions, enhancing their strategic synergy. Both are full members of the Shanghai Cooperation Organisation (SCO), with Kazakhstan being a founding member and India joining in 2017. Through SCO, they participate in joint counter-terror drills (SCO's 'Peace Mission' exercises) and discussions on regional connectivity. India's initial enthusiasm in SCO was partly to engage more deeply with Central Asia; however, SCO's effectiveness for India has been mixed, given Pakistan's presence and SCO's limited action on issues like terrorism. Nonetheless, Kazakhstan has been supportive of India's constructive role in SCO; during Kazakhstan's chairmanship of SCO (2023), it worked closely with India (which chaired the G20 in 2023) to ensure synergy in agendas. Another forum is the Conference on Interaction and Confidence-Building Measures in Asia (CICA), a Kazakh-initiated platform. India is a founding member of CICA and values it as a venue for Asian security dialogue. The fact that India consistently participates at high levels in CICA summits underscores respect for Kazakhstan's leadership in multilateral norm-building. Additionally, Kazakhstan has backed India's long-standing call for UN Security Council reform, as President Tokayev explicitly supported expanding UNSC membership and making it more representative, aligning with India's campaign for a permanent seat. This multilateral cooperation amplifies each country's voice: India gains a partner that adds Central Asian weight to its positions, and Kazakhstan gains an influential Asian ally endorsing its diplomatic initiatives.

It is also notable that Kazakhstan has positioned itself as a bridge between regions, for instance, by organising the Astana International Forum to connect voices from East and West. India's participation and attention to such Kazakh initiatives (such as sending ministers or envoys to Astana forums) reflect a strategic choice to support Kazakhstan's emerging role as a regional convenor. In sum, geopolitically, the Indo-Kazakh relationship is mutually beneficial – Kazakhstan diversifies beyond its giant neighbours by engaging India and India extends its reach into Central Asia, contributing to a more pluralistic balance of power in Eurasia

Geoeconomic Dimensions

Trade and Investment Potential vs. Constraints. As discussed, bilateral trade has grown significantly, yet experts widely agree it remains below potential. One major geo-economic constraint is the lack of direct connectivity. There is no shared border, and transport routes are circuitous. The traditionally used route for Indian goods to Kazakhstan has been via the Arabian Sea to Iran's Bandar Abbas port, then overland through Turkmenistan or via the Caspian Sea, part of the multi-country International North-South Transport Corridor (INSTC). Both countries are members of INSTC, which aims to cut transit time between India and Central Asia/Russia. However, until recently, INSTC was underutilised. The activation of new segments (such as rail links from Iran into Central Asia) is gradually making INSTC a viable option: in 2022, some pilot shipments from India to Kazakhstan via Iran were recorded. According to Kazakhstan's Ministry of Trade, transport communication remains the main constraint on bilateral trade. Goods have to traverse long distances, and political issues, notably sanctions on Iran and instability in Afghanistan, complicate transit. Recognising this, both nations are investing diplomatic capital in improving connectivity. India has developed the Chabahar Port in Iran, which is envisioned as its gateway to Central Asia (India and Kazakhstan formally cooperate under the Ashgabat Agreement on international transport and transit corridors). There is also interest in establishing direct shipping links across the Caspian: An Indian-backed proposal mooted using Iran's Caspian port (Anzali) to Aktau in Kazakhstan, allowing container trade that bypasses longer land routes. Additionally, Kazakhstan has invited India to consider investing in the Khorgos Gateway on the China-Kazakh border, a major BRI rail hub to use that route for accessing Chinese rail lines to South Asia. While unorthodox (as it would involve cooperation via China), this signals Kazakhstan's eagerness to leverage all routes to increase trade with India.

Despite connectivity hurdles, the geoeconomic logic for deeper trade/investment ties is strong. India's enormous market and growing middle class present opportunities for Kazakh exports beyond raw materials – for instance, metals, chemicals, and agricultural products. Indeed, Kazakh officials identified a basket of 80 export-ready goods worth $600 million (metallurgy, chemicals, food, etc.) that could find buyers in India. For India, Kazakhstan offers not only oil and uranium but also fertilizers (phosphates), metals like copper and zinc, and potential in rare earth elements which are crucial for high-tech industries. As global supply chains diversify away from China, India has an interest in sourcing strategic minerals from reliable partners like Kazakhstan. Both governments have set an ambitious trade target (mentioned in 2023) of reaching $5 billion in annual turnover in the medium term, which would require broadening the trade basket and reducing transport costs.

Investment is another area with room for growth. Kazakhstan's 'NurlyZhol' economic policy and drive to attract FDI can align with India's outward investment push. Sectors like energy infrastructure, mining, pharmaceuticals, and information technology are promising. For example, Indian companies could participate in Kazakhstan's oilfield services or petrochemical plant projects (beyond exploration deals which have proven challenging). In pharmaceuticals, setting up joint ventures to produce medicines in Kazakhstan (for local and regional consumption) is a win-win, given India's expertise and Kazakhstan's Eurasian Economic Union (EAEU) market access. The IT and tech sector cooperation is on the rise: in 2022, at a Central Asia-India Business Council meeting, digital technology and fintech were highlighted as new frontiers for collaboration. India's strengths in software and digital finance can complement Kazakhstan's digitisation agenda. Moreover, Kazakhstan's Astana International Financial Centre (AIFC), which aspires to be a regional fintech hub, has seen interest from Indian fintech firms and banks, indicating a geoeconomic linkage through financial services.

Energy Cooperation. Energy is arguably the linchpin of the geoeconomic relationship. Kazakhstan is rich in oil, natural gas, and coal, and is the world's largest uranium producer; India is energy-hungry, importing over 80 per cent of its oil and seeking diversified sources. While geography prevents large-scale direct oil trade (Kazakh oil mostly exports westward via pipelines to the Black Sea or eastward towards China), some arrangements have been made. One mechanism has been swaps or indirect sales: Kazakhstan's oil can reach Gujarat's refineries via traders, sometimes classified under third-country exports. In 2020, India's import of Kazakh crude was significant enough that Kazakhstan accounted for nearly 99 per cent of India's imports from Central Asia by value. To streamline this, discussions have taken place about routing more oil through a Kazakhstan–Turkmenistan–Iran corridor to India, leveraging the INSTC. Another long-term idea is a trans-Afghan pipeline: India once proposed extending the TAPI (Turkmenistan–Afghanistan–Pakistan–India) gas pipeline north to Kazakhstan's oilfields.

The uranium partnership has already been highlighted. It stands as a model of a straightforward commodity supply relationship serving strategic needs. Kazakhstan's reliable delivery of uranium has helped power India's nuclear plants, especially after India obtained a waiver from the Nuclear Suppliers Group in 2008. This will likely continue, with volumes increasing if India expands its nuclear energy capacity. Additionally, cooperation may extend to civil nuclear research and training, given both are interested in nuclear technology for peaceful uses. In 2019, the two sides agreed to explore joint research in reactor technology and applications of nuclear science in medicine and agriculture. Kazakhstan is also investing heavily in renewable energy (it hosted the Astana EXPO 2017 on Future Energy). There is scope for Indo-Kazakh collaboration in solar and wind projects, Indian companies are global players in renewables and could help Kazakhstan reach its goal of raising renewable share in its energy mix. Such collaboration would align with global sustainability trends and provide a new dimension to energy ties beyond the traditional fossil fuels.

Connectivity and Infrastructure. Beyond trade corridors, infrastructure cooperation includes telecommunications and transport projects. India has shown interest in projects like the KazSat communication satellites (built by Kazakhstan) and possibly cooperating on space applications; Kazakhstan for its part is interested in India's space capabilities for launching satellites and remote sensing (hindustantimes.com). In 2021, Kazakhstan signed onto the International Solar Alliance (ISA), an India-led initiative, reflecting another avenue of geo-economic partnership in sustainability efforts.

On the ground, Kazakhstan's strategic location makes it a potential logistics hub for Indian goods entering Eurasia. Already, dry runs have proven that sending goods from western India to Kazakhstan via the Iran-Caspian route can save time compared to the traditional sea route to Russia. If sanctions on Iran ease or workaround solutions (like currency swap mechanisms) are implemented, INSTC could see much higher traffic, integrating Kazakhstan firmly into India's trade network. The two countries have even discussed the possibility of direct flight resumption; currently there is no non-stop flight, but establishing one (such as Almaty–Delhi) would boost business travel and tourism. Air connectivity was part of the Connect Central Asia policy (India earlier ran a limited flight to Tajikistan), and Kazakhstan's growing aviation sector might revisit this with India as a priority destination.

Defence Industry and Technology. While defence ties were covered earlier in a bilateral context, in geoeconomic terms there is interest in defence industrial cooperation – an area that blends geopolitics and economics. In 2020, an online India-Kazakhstan Defence Expo discussed co-development and co-production possibilities. Kazakhstan, which has modest defence production capacity, could benefit from India's burgeoning defence manufacturing (India is developing everything from combat vehicles to missiles). One concrete step has been the memoranda between India's National Cadet Corps and Kazakh military universities to exchange know-how and eventually perhaps engage in joint R&D. Although no major joint defence product has yet emerged, this remains a long-term prospect, especially if Kazakhstan seeks to diversify arms procurement (currently dominated by Russia). India's offer to set up joint maintenance facilities for military equipment, noted by the Kazakh ambassador in 2019, is an example of practical cooperation that has economic benefits (creating jobs, building technical skills in Kazakhstan) while deepening strategic trust.

Interplay of Geopolitics and Geoeconomics. It is crucial to note that in the case of Kazakhstan-India ties, geopolitical and geoeconomic elements reinforce each other. For instance, Russia's war in Ukraine (2022) has upended some trade routes and led to Western sanctions on Russia; this geopolitical shock created opportunities for geoeconomic reorientation: Kazakhstan and India both looked more keenly at the International North-South Corridor as a route that bypasses Russia for trade. Likewise, as Kazakhstan seeks to dilute overdependence on China (a geopolitical motive) it is eager to open its markets to Indian companies and investments (a geoeconomic benefit). Through strategic partnership with India, Kazakhstan can diversify and balance Chinese and Russian influence in the region, while India gains access to Central Asia's vast consumer market and resources. Both countries also emphasise soft power and people-to-people ties as part of their strategy, understanding that cultural and educational links (soft geoeconomics, in a sense) bolster political relationships and distinguish their partnership in a crowded geopolitical arena. Thus, analysing the current state, Kazakhstan-India relations are strategically significant to both. Geopolitically, they align on fostering a multipolar Asia, combating common security threats, and engaging through multilateralism. Geoeconomically, they see each other as key to diversification: for India, Kazakhstan is a gateway to Eurasia and a source of energy; for Kazakhstan, India is a gateway to South Asia and a source of technology and investment. Despite impediments, the trajectory is upwards, and the stage is set for potentially transformative growth in ties if enabling conditions improve. To understand how this might unfold, the next section presents future scenarios that project the long-term development of Kazakhstan-India relations under different assumptions.

In sum, the geoeconomic dimension of Kazakhstan-India relations is characterised by high complementarity but also high friction from distance. They have complementary needs, resources for markets, technology for investments, which create a natural economic partnership. Trade growth and energy deals demonstrate this potential being tapped. However, unlocking the full geoeconomic partnership requires overcoming connectivity bottlenecks and competitive pressures (particularly China's dominant investment role in Central Asia, which can overshadow Indian efforts). Both governments acknowledge these challenges and have prioritised initiatives like INSTC and diversification of trade goods to realise the geoeconomic promise. As one analysis notes, "the modest level of economic and trade relations is not an accurate indicator of India's position in the region," because politically India enjoys goodwill that economic figures do not yet match. Bridging that gap is a strategic task in moving forward.

Future Scenarios for Kazakhstan-India Relations

Forecasting the long-term trajectory of Kazakhstan-India relations involves envisioning how current trends and external variables might play out. In this section, we outline three plausible scenarios for the future: (a) an Optimistic Scenario of enhanced strategic partnership; (b) a Baseline Scenario of gradual growth with some constraints; and (c) a Pessimistic Scenario of stagnation or setbacks. These scenarios are not predictions but analytical constructs that highlight opportunities and risks. They draw on the geopolitical and geoeconomic factors discussed, including energy dynamics, connectivity projects, multilateral engagements, and the influence of third-party actors.

(a) *Optimistic Scenario: 'Strategic Elevation – A Comprehensive Eurasian Partnership'*

In this scenario, Kazakhstan-India relations accelerate rapidly, achieving a level of closeness comparable to India's ties with its most important partners. Several enabling conditions drive this outcome: regional stability improves, particularly in Afghanistan; major connectivity projects are completed; and both countries prioritise bilateral cooperation in their foreign policies. By the mid-2030s, one could see the following:

Robust Trade Expansion: With the full operationalisation of the INSTC and stabilisation of Afghanistan, direct trade routes flourish. Goods move efficiently via Iran or even through a peaceful Afghanistan, slashing transit times and costs. Annual bilateral trade growth rates stay in double digits, and trade volume surpasses, say, $10 billion by 2030 (a notional figure for illustration). The trade basket diversifies substantially: along with oil and metals, Kazakhstan exports processed commodities (like petrochemicals, metals, grain) to India, and imports a greater array of Indian goods including automobiles, machinery, and services (IT, financial). Free trade arrangements might be negotiated; for example, India could sign a free trade agreement with the EAEU (of which Kazakhstan is a member), reducing tariffs and boosting commerce. Indian companies become more visible in Kazakhstan's economy, perhaps managing industrial projects or IT parks, while Kazakhstan's investment in India, though smaller, finds niches in energy infrastructure (such as Kazakh oil firm KMG partnering in Indian refinery projects).

Energy Alliance: The two countries form an energy alliance encompassing hydrocarbons, nuclear fuel, and renewables. In oil and gas, India finds innovative ways to access Kazakh hydrocarbons. One possibility could be participating in a Trans-Caspian pipeline initiative or an expanded swap deal whereby Kazakhstan's oil effectively reaches India via swaps through Russia or Azerbaijan. Additionally, if the geopolitical climate warms, the concept of an extended TAPI pipeline from Kazakhstan might be revived and gradually realised by the late 2030s, creating a physical energy corridor linking Central and South Asia. On nuclear energy, Kazakhstan continues as a leading supplier of uranium, meeting a large share of India's needs as India's nuclear power capacity multiplies. Cooperation in nuclear research also deepens – joint centres might be established for studying reactor safety or fusion research. Moreover, both nations collaborate on green energy projects: Indian firms invest in Kazakhstan's vast steppe wind farms and solar plants (Kazakhstan has huge renewable potential), and Kazakhstan benefits from technology and financing, contributing to its goal of reducing carbon intensity. Through ISA and other platforms, India and Kazakhstan champion solar energy expansion in Asia, showcasing successful joint ventures. In sum, energy interdependence becomes a cornerstone of the partnership, reducing India's dependence on Middle Eastern oil and helping Kazakhstan diversify its energy client base beyond China.

Defence and Security Partnership: The optimistic scenario sees a quantum leap in defence ties. Regular military exercises continue and expand in scope (such as including naval components through Caspian Sea cooperation or special forces drills). By 2030, a formal Defence Partnership Agreement could be signed, providing for high-level defence dialogues and intelligence sharing on a permanent basis. Kazakhstan might start procuring select military hardware from India; for example, Indian-made defence systems like communications equipment, BrahMos cruise missiles (if exportable with Russia's consent), or Dhruv helicopters could be on the table. Joint production could commence in Kazakhstan's free economic zones for certain equipment, serving Central Asian markets. The two countries could also coordinate closely in multilateral security settings; for instance, if an expanded SCO anti-terror force is ever created, Indian and Kazakh officers might take joint leadership roles. Both being committed to UN peacekeeping, they might lead joint peacekeeping operations in conflict zones, building on their UNIFIL cooperation. Essentially, Kazakhstan and India become each other's key security partners in their respective regions (Central and South Asia). Politically, this could manifest in Kazakhstan unequivocally backing India in regional disputes (for example, supporting India's stance on cross-border terrorism issues), and India likewise lending strong support to Kazakhstan's regional security initiatives.

***Connectivity and Infrastructure Integration*:** Under this rosy scenario, not only are transport corridors realised, but institutional connectivity improves. Perhaps a Kazakhstan-India direct flight is launched, greatly facilitating travel for business and tourism. Tourist flow increase as Indians discover Kazakhstan's attractions (Almaty's ski resorts, Astana's modern marvels, Silk Road heritage sites) and Kazakhs visit Indian destinations (from the Himalayas to medical tourism in Indian hospitals). Educational ties might see Indian universities opening satellite campuses in Kazakhstan or a new 'India-Central Asia University' (once proposed in 2012) coming to fruition in Central Asia, with substantial Kazakh-Indian collaboration in curriculum and research. Culturally, the optimistic future could witness even greater intermixing; for example, annual Kazakhstan-India cultural festivals, thriving film co-productions (Bollywood shooting in Kazakh locales), and increased linguistic exchange (Hindi being taught in Kazakh universities and perhaps Kazakh language courses in select Indian universities). All these foster a sense of familiarity and goodwill that underpins political trust.

Multilateral Impact: In this best-case trajectory, the bilateral relationship positively influences multilateral outcomes. With a stronger partnership, Kazakhstan and India could jointly drive new regional initiatives, possibly establishing a 'Central Asia-India Development Partnership' fund to invest in regional infrastructure, or co-chairing a new conference on connectivity. If both continue on their growth paths, by 2040 India is the world's third-largest economy and Kazakhstan a high-income economy, their cooperation might be a stabilising factor in Eurasia, offering smaller countries alternatives and promoting an inclusive regional architecture. Both might also coordinate positions on global issues like climate change, trade rules, and reform of international institutions, amplifying each other's voices.

This optimistic scenario requires sustained political will, resolution of conflicts in the wider region, and an ability to manage the reactions of other powers that might be wary of an Indian role in Central Asia. It assumes Kazakhstan and India successfully navigate pressures from Russia or China (who could see a too-strong Indo-Kazakh alignment as diluting their influence). It also assumes internal stability in both countries and their economies performing well. If those conditions hold, the momentum of the past decade could indeed carry the relationship to new heights, making it a model South-South partnership connecting two critical regions of Asia.

(b) Baseline Scenario: 'Incremental Progress – Steady but Limited Growth'

In the baseline scenario, relations continue to improve at a measured pace, essentially extending current trends into the future without dramatic breakthroughs or breakdowns. Many of the existing constraints persist, but neither country loses interest in the other. Outcomes in this scenario might include:

Moderate Economic Growth: Trade grows, but slowly and sometimes unevenly, tracking overall economic growth rather than leaping ahead. By late 2020s, bilateral trade might be in the range of $3-4 billion, climbing to perhaps $5-6 billion by late 2030s – a healthy increase from today but far below potential. Progress comes from incremental improvements: some INSTC shipments materialise regularly, shaving a bit off costs, but volumes remain limited due to lingering sanctions on Iran or occasional regional disruptions. The commodity composition of trade remains largely as is (energy still dominant on Kazakhstan's side, pharmaceuticals and light manufactures on India's side). Investment linkages see some notable projects, for instance, an Indian pharmaceutical park in Kazakhstan or a Kazakh mining company partnering with an Indian firm but these are the exception rather than the rule. Private sector enthusiasm remains tempered by the distance and unfamiliarity, and many plans discussed at official levels (for instance, joint ventures in agriculture or textiles) take long to actualise.

Selective Connectivity Improvements: In this scenario, perhaps one route becomes significantly operational, likely the maritime + rail route via Iran, but others (like the Afghan route) remain impractical due to chronic instability. The INSTC sees moderate use: some Indian exporters of tea or pharmaceuticals send goods to Kazakhstan using it, but for heavy trade the route's capacity or ease is still not world-class. No direct flight opens, but travel improves slightly via third countries (for instance, more flights from Almaty to Delhi with a stop in Dubai or Tashkent). Bureaucratic hurdles in customs and visa regimes ease somewhat (with introduction of e-visas, etc.), making business and student exchange easier, but full free movement is not achieved. Essentially, connectivity no longer severely constrains trade as before, but it remains an irritant and an extra cost that prevents explosive growth in commerce.

Continued Sectoral Cooperation: Energy cooperation continues with existing patterns – Kazakhstan reliably supplies uranium (perhaps even increasing volumes marginally as India's demand grows) and occasionally some crude oil via traders. No major pipeline or energy infrastructure is built specifically linking the two (due to geopolitical and economic viability issues), so cooperation in oil/gas remains opportunistic. In renewables, a few test projects might happen (like an Indian company building a solar plant in Kazakhstan's south), but not on a transformative scale. Defence cooperation stays strong in training and exercises, but Kazakhstan, constrained by its long-standing ties to Russian weaponry does not make big purchases from India. The defence industrial collaboration idea yields limited output; maybe an MOU or two on joint research exists, but tangible joint production is minimal. However, the annual KAZIND exercises continue without fail and possibly extend to trilateral formats (such as involving a third country observer like Uzbekistan or others in some years). Counter-terror cooperation remains important as Afghanistan's situation remains fluid – Kazakhstan and India share intelligence occasionally and coordinate in SCO's RATS (Regional Anti-Terrorist Structure) to keep pressure on groups like ISKP or other extremists.

Multilateral and Diplomatic Alignment: Kazakhstan and India maintain a friendly diplomatic alignment. India remains engaged in Central Asia through the India-Central Asia Dialogue (which by 2030 maybe reaches its eighth or ninth meeting) and annual ministerial meetings. These dialogues produce Memorandum of Understandings and statements but modest concrete outcomes, much like today, reiterating shared goals on Afghanistan, connectivity, etc., and announcing small-scale initiatives (scholarships, cultural days, etc.). In the UN and other bodies, Kazakhstan and India often support each other's candidacies and resolutions, but this is now seen as routine. Kazakhstan continues balancing major powers, so while it values India, it also remains very close to China and Russia; if push comes to shove on big geopolitical issues (like votes on Ukraine or Indo-Pacific matters), Kazakhstan hedges to not upset its bigger neighbours, and India understands that. Essentially, diplomacy stays warm and cooperative, but without a dramatic strategic shift; for example, Kazakhstan stops short of openly siding with India in any India-China disputes, just as India respects Kazakhstan's positions vis-à-vis Russia.

Social and Cultural Links: These continue to deepen organically. More students and tourists trickle each way, but not a flood. Indian universities and Kazakh universities expand partnerships (exchanges, dual degree programmes). Cultural centres remain active, and perhaps by 2030, Indian cultural festivals in Almaty or Kazakh cultural troupes in Indian metros are common annual events. Bollywood might feature a Kazakh actor or scenes shot in Kazakhstan occasionally, which creates temporary spikes of interest. The underlying people-to-people connection grows in familiarity, aided by the Internet and social media (for instance, Indian yoga influencers attract Kazakh followers, and Kazakh music finds niche audiences in India). These ties, while under the radar, ensure that the foundation of mutual goodwill stays solid, even if strategic relations are only inching forward.

Overall, the baseline scenario is essentially business-as-usual plus incremental gains. There are no big shocks; relations neither face a crisis nor a spectacular boom. Over a couple of decades, this would mean a considerably stronger relationship than in the early 2020s, but it might still feel underwhelming compared to its potential. This scenario might materialise if neither new obstacles nor catalytic developments occur; for example, if Afghanistan remains unstable (blocking one route) and US-Iran relations remain tense (constraining the other route), but simultaneously, nothing pushes India and Kazakhstan to dramatically scale up ties (for instance, India might remain preoccupied with its immediate neighbourhood and Indo-Pacific rivalry with China, while Kazakhstan might focus more on managing ties with Russia/China and internal economic reforms). The relationship improves, but in a slow, evolutionary manner.

(c) Pessimistic Scenario: 'Drift or Decoupling – Missed Opportunities'

In a pessimistic scenario, various adverse factors prevent the relationship from developing further, and it either stagnates at current levels or even deteriorates. This could happen due to external shocks or internal policy shifts. Elements of this scenario might be:

Geopolitical Frictions: A sharp deterioration in India's relations with Russia or a significant conflict between India and China could put Kazakhstan in a delicate spot. For instance, if India-China tensions escalate (over the border or influence in Asia) to a point of confrontation, Kazakhstan, a close neighbour and partner of China, might distance itself from India under pressure from Beijing. Similarly, if India were to align more overtly with Western positions that Russia perceives as hostile, Kazakhstan (owing to its security and economic dependence on Russia) might cool its enthusiasm for strategic ties with India so as not to antagonise Moscow. Essentially, Kazakhstan could deprioritise its ties with India to safeguard its core relationships with Russia/China if forced to choose. In such a case, high-level visits might become infrequent and cooperation would revert to a more symbolic nature.

Regional Instability and Isolation: If the security situation around Kazakhstan worsens, for example, if Afghanistan descends into chaos that spills over, or if a hypothetical conflict, involving Pakistan were to break out, connectivity could become even harder. A scenario often discussed in strategy circles is an Indo-Pakistan war that disrupts Central Asia's links. If Pakistan, a key transit state for any overland route, is in conflict, Central Asian trade routes might be jeopardised (such as Karachi port access or even instability reaching up through Afghanistan). Under such conditions, India's focus would shift entirely to crisis management at home, and Central Asia would receive scant attention. Kazakhstan, observing this, might double down on other partners (China's BRI routes, Russia's Eurasian integration) and the idea of substantial India-bound corridors would fade. Trade might then stagnate or even drop if global conditions worsen (say, a prolonged global recession or sanctions regimes complicating transfers of money and goods). Without connectivity improvements, businesses could conclude the costs outweigh benefits and reduce engagement. Therefore, trade could languish around the current $2–3 billion or fall if, for instance, India finds alternative suppliers for oil/uranium or Kazakhstan finds closer suppliers for pharmaceuticals.

Domestic Changes and Policy Shifts: Another driver of a pessimistic outcome could be internal politics. If either country's government becomes less interested in the partnership or faces domestic nationalist pressures that disfavour foreign engagements, momentum could be lost. For example, if Kazakhstan were to have a nationalist turn that views foreign influence sceptically, Indian businesses or cultural centres might face more barriers. Conversely, if India, consumed by a focus on the Indo-Pacific, downgrades its 'Connect Central Asia' emphasis (perhaps due to budgetary constraints or a belief that returns have been minimal), then the diplomatic energy invested in Kazakhstan would wane. In both countries, leadership plays a role – a change of leadership that does not prioritise the relationship could lead to benign neglect. Since current ties are still somewhat personality-driven (Modi and Tokayev have invested personal capital in outreach), a lack of follow-through by successors might let things drift.

Minimal Strategic Outcomes: In this pessimistic scenario, very little new is achieved beyond existing frameworks. Joint statements remain full of promises but see poor implementation. No significant new treaties or projects come to fruition. Defence cooperation might be limited to a token exercise irregularly held, or in a worst case, suspended if political trust ebbs. Energy cooperation might not extend beyond renewing the uranium contract occasionally; if global markets shift (for instance, if nuclear energy faces decline or if Kazakhstan finds higher bidders for uranium), even that could become less significant. Both countries might then view the relationship as secondary. Multilaterally, they might not coordinate much, each hedging in different directions, for instance, Kazakhstan might stick closer to China's initiatives while India deepens alignment with Quad countries (USA, Japan, etc.), leaving less common ground.

Public and Cultural Disconnect: While it is hard to imagine a reversal in people-to-people goodwill, a truly negative scenario could see less contact simply due to lack of support. If scholarships or flights are cut due to budget or sanctions issues, student flows could dry up. Without encouragement, the number of Indians studying in Kazakhstan could decline (especially if other countries like Russia or Ukraine, historically popular for Indian students, become more stable again and compete for students). Similarly, without high-level backing, cultural events might dwindle. Misunderstandings or incidents (for instance, any mistreatment of citizens in each other's country without proper diplomatic handling) could create negative perceptions. However, it must be noted that presently, there are no major societal frictions between Kazakhs and Indians; a downturn would likely be due to apathy rather than animosity.

The pessimistic scenario essentially represents missed opportunities. The relations remain correct and cordial at a formal level (there is no plausible trigger for outright hostility between Kazakhstan and India given lack of direct conflicts), but they fail to progress, making both sides fall short of benefiting from each other. This could leave Kazakhstan even more tightly bound to its immediate great-power partners, and India effectively absent from a region of growing importance. Such a scenario might unfold if, for example, external crises dominate (great-power tensions forcing everyone to take sides, or regional wars cutting off corridors) or if domestic priorities shift sharply (as if economic troubles forcing retrenchment in foreign engagements).

These scenarios highlight that the future is not pre-determined – it will depend on policy choices and external developments. The Optimistic Scenario shows the ceiling of what is possible if enabling conditions are in place and the partnership is nurtured leading to a genuine strategic alliance reshaping regional connectivity and security. The Baseline Scenario is perhaps the most likely given the inertia and known challenges – steady improvement but not a leap. The Pessimistic Scenario serves as a caution that gains of recent years could stall or reverse if not carefully tended, or if larger geopolitical storms intervene. Notably, even in the baseline or pessimistic cases, a total rupture is unlikely; more plausible is a plateauing of ties. For a forecast, one might lean towards a middle path: Kazakhstan-India relations in the long-term will likely continue strengthening, but in increments unless critical bottlenecks are removed. Key swing factors will be the success of connectivity projects like INSTC, the evolution of the Afghanistan situation, the state of global power rivalries, and each country's foreign policy focus. With prudent policies, the baseline could be tilted upward towards the optimistic side, for instance, if India proactively addresses trade logistics and Kazakhstan actively courts Indian investment, one could see more rapid gains. Ultimately, the scenarios illuminate that Kazakhstan and India have substantial strategic rationale to grow closer (as shown in sections 2 and 3), but the long-term outcome will depend on how they navigate both opportunities and obstacles. In the next section, we translate these insights into policy recommendations, suggesting how both nations (and their partners) can steer the relationship towards a more optimistic trajectory and avoid pitfalls that would lead to stagnation.

Policy Recommendations and Conclusion

Having examined the foundations, dynamics, and possible futures of Kazakhstan-India relations, this final section provides policy recommendations to help realise the partnership's full potential, followed by a concluding assessment. The recommendations are addressed to policymakers in Astana and New Delhi, as well as stakeholders in multilateral forums who can facilitate bilateral cooperation. The overarching goal is to capitalise on geostrategic and geoeconomic complementarities while mitigating challenges such as connectivity gaps and external pressures. Implementing these recommendations would increase the likelihood of moving towards the optimistic scenario outlined above, fostering a robust long-term partnership.

Invest in Connectivity and Infrastructure. Connectivity is the linchpin for all cooperation. Both governments should redouble efforts on the International North–South Transport Corridor (INSTC) and related projects. This includes completing missing rail links, improving port facilities, and streamlining customs procedures along the route. India, along with Iran and other partners, should expedite the development of Chabahar Port and its rail connection to the Caspian; this will directly benefit trade with Kazakhstan. Simultaneously, Kazakhstan can work within the Caspian Sea framework to facilitate regular ferry services between its ports (Aktau/Kuryk) and Iranian/Azerbaijani ports that connect to India-bound routes. Both countries should consider a dedicated logistics working group to monitor and troubleshoot transit trade, for example, resolving any bottlenecks in documentation and harmonising transport regulations. On the aviation front, exploring a direct flight route (perhaps Almaty-Delhi) through a mutually beneficial agreement or even charter services for pilgrims and tourists could significantly boost people exchanges. The two governments might offer initial viability gap funding or incentives to airlines to open this route. Overall, prioritising connectivity in diplomatic dialogues, making it the first agenda item in bilateral commission meetings, will signal to businesses that solutions are forthcoming, encouraging them to ramp up engagement.

Deepen Trade and Economic Integration. To boost trade beyond commodities, a trade facilitation pact could be negotiated. Simplifying visa regimes for bona fide business travellers, organising annual trade fairs (for instance, an 'India Expo' in Almaty and a 'Kazakhstan Trade Show' in Mumbai) and upgrading the joint Business Council's role to actively match make firms are practical steps. India can support capacity-building in Kazakhstan's WTO compliance and customs automation, which will smooth trade flows. Likewise, Kazakhstan can help Indian companies navigate the EAEU regulations, ensuring they make use of preferences where applicable. In the medium term, India should revisit the idea of a free trade agreement (FTA) or Comprehensive Economic Partnership with the EAEU. Kazakhstan, as a key member of this union, can advocate within the bloc for fast-tracking FTA talks with India. A well-crafted FTA that addresses tariff and non-tariff barriers could dramatically increase trade volumes and diversify traded goods. Both nations should also encourage mutual investments: for instance, Kazakhstan could be invited to invest in India's strategic oil storage or petrochemical facilities (guaranteeing a market for Kazakh oil), and India's sovereign funds or private investors could take stakes in Kazakh mining or infrastructure projects. Offering tax breaks or special economic zone benefits for such investments would incentivise participation. Additionally, establishing an India-Kazakhstan Innovation Fund for co-financing start-ups and tech collaborations (with contributions from both governments and private sectors) could energise technology and service-sector ties, areas which are currently underdeveloped in the bilateral context.

Expand Energy and Resources Cooperation. Energy is an area where policy support can yield significant gains. The two governments should renew and expand the long-term uranium supply agreement well before the current one expires, perhaps with bigger quantities or joint ventures in uranium mining in Kazakhstan. They should also institutionalise an Energy Dialogue at the ministerial level (if not already) that meets annually to cover oil, gas, nuclear, and renewable cooperation. Through that, India can express interest in any equity stakes when opportunities in Kazakh oilfields arise (Kazakhstan can reciprocate by inviting Indian firms whenever Western companies divest or new exploration blocks open, as happened with the Kashagan field earlier). On renewables, a specific initiative could be launched, for instance, 'Green Bridge between Kazakhstan and India,' aligning with Kazakhstan's Green Bridge policy and India's ISA, to finance solar/wind projects. This could involve technical training (Indian experts helping Kazakh engineers run solar plants) and possibly manufacturing (setting up a factory for solar panels or wind turbine parts in Kazakhstan with Indian collaboration). Additionally, cooperation on oil and gas transportation should continue: they could explore creative arrangements like swapping Turkmen or Russian gas for Kazakh oil to send to India via LNG. A feasibility study for a Kazakhstan-India subsea fibre optic cable through existing pipelines might also be considered to enhance digital connectivity, complementing energy corridors. While that's futuristic, it signals intent to integrate infrastructure.

Strengthen Defence and Security Collaboration. Building on trust developed in exercises, the two countries should escalate their institutional defence ties. They could form a Bilateral Security Dialogue at the level of National Security Advisors or Defence Secretaries to have candid yearly discussions on regional security and defence-industrial cooperation. India can offer increased slots for Kazakh officers in advanced training institutions (e.g., higher command courses, technical training on new defence tech). Joint military exercises could be diversified, for instance, conducting a naval tabletop exercise on Caspian security or an air force exercise focusing on humanitarian relief operations, leveraging India's airlift capabilities and Kazakhstan's strategic airfields. On counter-terrorism, both should bolster intelligence exchanges; a formal MoU on Counter-terrorism Cooperation could facilitate real-time information sharing on terror networks and trends, particularly regarding any spillover from Afghanistan or movements of extremist groups in the region. There's also room for cooperation in newer domains: cybersecurity and space security. They can launch joint training for cyber specialists (protecting critical infrastructure from cyber threats) and coordinate under the UN or SCO on norms for cyberspace. For space, since Kazakhstan has the Baikonur Cosmodrome and interest in satellites, and India has proven launch and satellite-building capabilities, a partnership where Indian rockets launch Kazakh satellites (already done in a small way) should be continued and expanded. A formal Space Cooperation Agreement could cover satellite navigation (maybe extending India's NavIC system coverage to Central Asia), remote sensing data sharing (useful for Kazakhstan's agriculture and disaster management), and training of Kazakh space scientists in India. These defence and security measures will not only enhance bilateral trust but also contribute to regional stability.

Leverage Multilateral Forums for Bilateral Gain. The two countries should use platforms like SCO, CICA, and the UN to reinforce their partnership. For example, under SCO's economic initiatives, India and Kazakhstan could co-pilot a demonstration project of trade via INSTC to showcase in SCO meetings. In CICA, they could jointly propose a new confidence-building measure focused on 'connectivity and development,' essentially bringing their bilateral agenda (corridors, development projects) to a broader Asian audience for buy-in and possibly funding support. Kazakhstan will host and attend many Central Asia-focused summits; ensuring Indian representation at high levels in those (and vice versa – Kazakhstan's active presence in the Indian Ocean or Indo-Pacific dialogues, if invited) will keep each other visible in respective strategic communities. They should also coordinate stances in bodies like the IMF, World Bank, and Asian Infrastructure Investment Bank (AIIB) on issues relevant to emerging economies. If both speak in unison on reforms of global economic governance, it amplifies the message (e.g., both advocate for greater lending for connectivity in Eurasia). Moreover, collaboration on climate change goals, perhaps a joint Kazakhstan-India initiative on arid land agriculture under the UN Climate framework, can bind them in addressing global commons. By consistently supporting each other's initiatives (Kazakhstan supporting India's International Solar Alliance, India supporting Kazakhstan's nuclear disarmament and peace dialogue efforts), they bolster each other's leadership credentials. Multilateral settings also offer a diplomatically safe space to announce bilateral projects (for instance, at a Central Asia-India Dialogue ministerial, they could announce the launch of a new Centre for IT Excellence in Kazakhstan funded by India, thereby garnering regional goodwill too).

Enhance People-to-People and Educational Links. Soft power is a force-multiplier for the strategic partnership. Both governments should continue expanding scholarships and exchanges. India might increase ICCR scholarships for Kazakh students and offer new fellowships for areas like IT, medicine, and management – fields where Indian education is strong and Kazakh human capital development is a priority. Kazakhstan can reciprocate by inviting Indian students/researchers, perhaps by setting up an 'Abai Institute' in India to teach Kazakh language and culture, fostering deeper understanding. The success of the 9,000+ Indian students in Kazakhstan suggests potential for more structured programmes, maybe a branch of an Indian university in Kazakhstan focusing on IT or engineering could be established (with host nation facilitation), or at least twinning programmes between top universities. On cultural cooperation, both countries could institutionalise annual festivals: for example, Kazakhstan-India Year of Culture on a rotating basis, where each year one country hosts a series of events (film weeks, art exhibitions, fashion shows, yoga days, and Kazakh nomadic games demonstrations, etc.). Support for translation of literature and co-production in media (films, documentaries on each other's history) can also deepen ties. A joint initiative to promote tourism such as simplified group tour visas, or combined Silk Road/South Asia tour packages might spur travel. Both being part of the ancient Silk Road heritage, they could market tours that cover Kazakhstan's historical sites and India's, appealing to global tourists interested in the Silk Road narrative. By investing in these human connections, the two countries ensure that their partnership has a strong societal foundation, making it resilient to political changes. As one analysis emphasised, leveraging soft power and people-to-people ties will yield 'significant dividends,' setting India apart from other powers in the region.

Conclusion

Kazakhstan-India relations have come a long way from the lukewarm ties of the 1990s to the strategic partnership of today. The analysis in this chapter shows that the relationship is undergirded by both geopolitical logic, a mutual interest in a stable, multipolar Asia and balancing of influence and geoeconomic logic, complementary resources and markets with significant untapped potential. While current engagement is strong in political, defence spheres, and steadily growing in economic and cultural domains, there is broad consensus that it has not yet reached its full potential. Key obstacles, chiefly connectivity issues and the inertia of distance, have thus far prevented an exponential growth in ties. However, the momentum of recent years (trade hitting new highs, expanded security cooperation, and intensified high-level dialogues) suggests that the trajectory is positive.

The future scenarios outlined ranged from an optimistic vision of deep integration to a pessimistic one of stagnation. Realistically, elements of both will interplay; some initiatives will succeed, others may face setbacks. Yet, with prudent policy actions like those recommended, the two nations could steer closer to the best-case scenario. The recommendations aim to create enabling conditions for better connectivity, economic incentives, security assurances, and societal links that make a virtuous cycle possible. For example, improved transport corridors reduce costs, which boosts trade and investment, which in turn creates constituencies in both countries that lobby for even closer ties, and so forth. Likewise, shared projects and training in defence and education build trust and mutual awareness, which helps navigate any political disagreements smoothly.

It is important to recognise external factors: the evolving great-power rivalries (USA–China; Russia–West) and regional flashpoints (Afghanistan's trajectory, Iran's sanctions status) will inevitably affect Kazakhstan-India relations. Both Astana and New Delhi have shown an aptitude for strategic autonomy and multi-alignment: Kazakhstan by balancing its neighbourhood and India by pursuing multi-aligned partnerships across blocs. This bodes well for their bilateral ties because each understands the other's need for flexibility. They have managed to grow relations without harming ties with others: for instance, India's friendship with Kazakhstan has not been aimed against Russia or China, and Kazakhstan's friendship with India has not been at the expense of Pakistan (with whom India has issues). Maintaining this approach will be crucial; as one scholar noted, Indo-Kazakh relations "do not follow a conventional pattern but exhibit dynamic development in all spheres", meaning they have carved their own space and will likely continue to do so.

In conclusion, the long-term outlook for Kazakhstan-India relations is bright but contingent. If both countries earnestly implement supportive policies and adapt to changes, the partnership is likely to flourish and become a significant factor in Eurasian affairs. A stronger Kazakhstan-India bond will not only benefit the two nations through energy security, economic growth, and enhanced security, but also contribute to the stability and prosperity of the broader region, from Central Asia to South Asia. As analysts observe, this strategic partnership has the potential to 'play a decisive role in shaping the Eurasian geopolitical arena', promoting both economic development and security across the continent. The coming decades will test the resolve of Astana and New Delhi to translate this potential into reality. With visionary leadership and sustained engagement, forecasting the future of Kazakhstan-India relations can be less an exercise in speculation and more a blueprint for a thriving inter-regional partnership rooted in shared interests and mutual respect.

References

1. Supyaldiyarov, I. (2024). 'Charting New (Old) Paths: Unravelling India-Kazakhstan Ties in Eurasian Geopolitics.' *Electronic Journal of Social and Strategic Studies*, 5(6). https://doi.org/10.47362/EJSSS.2024.5601
2. Vice-Minister of Trade and Integration of the Republic of Kazakhstan K. Torebayev, & Embassy of India. (2022). Mutual trade between Kazakhstan and India amounted to $2.0 billion. Ministry of Trade and Integration of the Republic of Kazakhstan. Retrieved April 17, 2025, from https://www.gov.kz/memleket/entities/mti/press/news/details/332623?lang=en
3. Muratbekova, A. (2021). 'Relations between Kazakhstan and India: Discussion of Key Features.' *Eurasian Research Institute Weekly Bulletin*, 26.04.2021-02.05.2021 (No. 304).
4. Saini, A. (2025). 'Decoding the rationale behind the 4th India-Central Asia Dialogue.' *The Diplomat*. Retrieved June 13, 2025, from https://thediplomat.com/2025/06/decoding-the-rationale-behind-the-4th-india-central-asia-dialogue/
5. Laskar, R. H. (2019). 'We may scale up supply of uranium to India': Kazakhstan ambassador Bulat Sarsenbayev. *Hindustan Times*. Retrieved June 13, 2025, from https://www.hindustantimes.com/india-news/kazakhstan-may-scale-up-supply-of-uranium-to-india/story-cY7NEz4HU6GulmGFlmo3KO.html
6. Muratbekova, A., 2021.
7. Ibid.
8. Supyaldiyarov, I., 2024.

9. Vice-Minister of Trade and Integration of the Republic of Kazakhstan K. Torebayev& Embassy of India, 2022.
10. Laskar, R. H., 2019.
11. Invest Kazakhstan. (2024). Kazakhstan and India to step up bilateral investment cooperation [Press release]. *Invest Kazakhstan*. Retrieved June 13, 2025, from https://invest.gov.kz/media-center/press-releases/kazakhstan-i-indiya-narashchivayut-dvustoronnee-investitsionnoe-sotrudnichestvo/
12. Kazinform News Agency. (2025, June 5). India invested over $450 mn in Kazakhstan within 20 years. Retrieved June 13, 2025, from https://qazinform.com/news/india-invested-over-450mln-in-kazakhstan-within-20-years-f0ad01
13. ET Bureau. (2011). 'ONGC Videsh Limited buys 25 % in Kazakh oil block.' *The Economic Times*. Retrieved June 13, 2025, from https://economictimes.indiatimes.com/industry/energy/oil-gas/ongc-videsh-limited-buys-25-in-kazakh-oil-block/articleshow/10334724.cms?from=mdr
14. Yermukanov, M. (2004). Kazakhstan-India relations: Partners or distant friends? The Jamestown Foundation. Archived October 18, 2008. Retrieved June 13, 2025, from https://web.archive.org/web/20081018193815/http://www.jamestown.org/edm/article.php?article_id=2368860
15. Bhaduri, A. (2025). 'There's a country India must take more seriously: Kazakhstan' [Opinion]. *NDTV*. Retrieved June 13, 2025, from https://www.ndtv.com/opinion/why-india-should-take-kazakhstan-more-seriously-8595942
16. Muratbekova, A., 2021.
17. Saini, A., 2025.
18. Muratbekova, A. (2024). Perspectives of Central Asia for Indian students. Eurasian Research Institute. Retrieved June 13, 2025, from https://www.eurasian-research.org/publication/perspectives-of-central-asia-for-indian-students/
19. Ministry of Foreign Affairs of the Republic of Kazakhstan. (2022). Bust of great Kazakh poet Abai Kunanbayuly unveiled in Indian capital. Government of the Republic of Kazakhstan. Retrieved June 13, 2025, from https://www.gov.kz/memleket/entities/mfa-delhi/press/news/details/382375?lang=en
20. The Astana Times Staff Report. (2023). Kazakhstan, India explore ways to strengthen bilateral cooperation. *The Astana Times*. Retrieved June 13, 2025, from https://astanatimes.com/2023/02/kazakhstan-india-explore-ways-to-strengthen-bilateral-cooperation/
21. Supyaldiyarov, I., 2024.
22. Bhaduri, A., 2025.
23. Pant, H. V., & Wani, A. (2022). 'OnlyIAS PSIR Bulletin: Building up connections in Central Asia [PDF]. *OnlyIAS PSIR Bulletin*. Retrieved June 13, 2025, from https://pwonlyias.com/wp-content/uploads/2022/11/OnlyIAS-PSIR-Bulletin-January-2022.pdf
24. Saini, A., 2025.
25. The Astana Times Staff Report, 2023.
26. Vice-Minister of Trade and Integration of the Republic of Kazakhstan K. Torebayev & Embassy of India, 2021.
27. The Astana Times. (2025). 'Kazakhstan, India strengthen ties via North–South Transport Corridor.' *The Astana Times*. Retrieved June 13, 2025, from https://astanatimes.com/2025/03/kazakhstan-india-strengthen-ties-via-north-south-transport-corridor/
28. Vice-Minister of Trade and Integration of the Republic of Kazakhstan K. Torebayev & Embassy of India, 2022.
29. DK News. (2023). Kazakhstan and India discussed prospects for economic cooperation [News article]. *DK News*. Retrieved June 13, 2025, from https://dknews.kz/en/articles-in-english/313418-kazakhstan-and-india-discussed-prospects-for-economic
30. Laskar, R.H., 2019.

31. The Hindu. (2012). India proposes hydrocarbon pipeline from Kazakhstan. *The Hindu*. Retrieved June 13, 2025, from https://www.thehindu.com/news/national/india-proposes-hydrocarbon-pipeline-from-kazakhstan/article4479665.ece
32. Laskar, R. H., 2019.
33. IMPRI India. (2024). Forging synergies: India's strategic engagement with Central Asia [Insight article]. *IMPRI India*. Retrieved June 13, 2025, from https://www.impriindia.com/insights/india-strategic-engagement-centrl-asia/
34. Al-Farabi Kazakh National University. (2020). Students of the military department of KazNU named after Al-Farabi visited the National Cadet Corps of the Republic of India [News release]. Al-Farabi Kazakh National University. Retrieved June 13, 2025, from https://welcome.kaznu.kz/en/10057/news/one/18924/.

Index